Anonymous

H.H. Dodd and Co.'s Indianapolis City Directory

and business mirror for 1863

Anonymous

H.H. Dodd and Co.'s Indianapolis City Directory
and business mirror for 1863

ISBN/EAN: 9783337291457

Printed in Europe, USA, Canada, Australia, Japan

Cover: Foto ©Andreas Hilbeck / pixelio.de

More available books at **www.hansebooks.com**

H. H. DODD & CO.'S

Indianapolis City Directory,

AND

BUSINESS MIRROR.

FOR 1863.

PUBLISHED ANNUALLY.

H. H. DODD & CO.

BOOK AND JOB PRINTERS, STEREOTYPERS, AND BOOK BINDERS.

1863.

C. F. SCHMIDT,

BREWER OF

LAGER - BEER

AND

BEER,

CORNER OF HIGH AND WYOMING STREETS,

INDIANAPOLIS, IND.

SUGAR GROVE

DAIRY,

RES ONE MILE NORTH-WEST OF CITY,

JOHN REILLY. - - PROPRIETOR.

PURE MILK

DELIVERED IN ANY PART OF THE CITY,

WHOLESALE AND RETAIL,

AT REASONABLE TERMS.

PREFACE.

In presenting our patrons and the public with this our second edition of the Indianapolis City Directory, the publishers desire to acknowledge their appreciation of the liberality, enterprise and public spirit of those gentlemen who have given their support to the undertaking. It is hoped the book may meet their expectations, and it is confidently believed that in fullness, accuracy of detail, and convenience of arrangement this volume far excels all its predecessor. Certain it is that no pains have been spared either in the compilation or the mechanical department to insure the highest degree of excellence and utility.

In the present fluctuating condition of our population, perfection is perhaps impossible, and for such occasional omissions or inaccuracies as may have crept in, we ask the indulgence of a generous public. To those parties who lacked the courtesy to give their names and the necessary information to our agents of course no explanation is necessary. In justice to ourselves we feel compelled to add that we have reason to believe that a few families purposely withheld the true and proper information on account of their apprehension of the approaching enrollment, (mistaking our agents for the enrolling officers,) ; but it is believed that errors and omissions from this cause are compartively few and unimportant, and are confined of course to the lowest class of our population.

To those gentlemen who have assisted us in procuring statistical and other information, and to the gentlemen of the press, we would extend many thanks. Respectfully,

H. H. DODD & CO.

Indianapolis, June 12, 1862.

CONTENS.

SMITH & TAYLOR'S

NO. 20.

TOY STORE,

East Washington St.,

INDIANAPOLIS,

INDIANA.

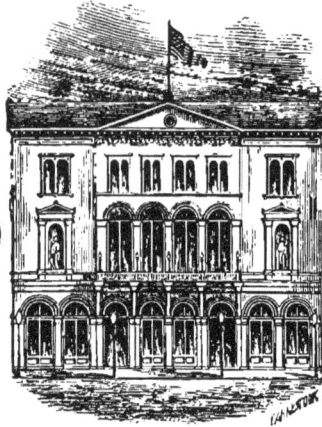

CLASSIFIED INDEX TO ADVERTISEMENTS.

NOTE.—The advertisements will be found printed on colored paper, and either facing or immediately following the page referred to.

MERCHANTS' DESPATCH,

Fast Freight Line.

AMERICAN EXPRESS COMPANY, PROPRIETORS.

A. W. MILLAR, Superintendent, Buffalo.

CAPITAL, - $1,000,000.

FROM N. YORK & BOSTON TO THE WEST & S. WEST.

Our Goods are Shipped in Chartered Cars,

ON EMIGRANT PASSENGER TRAINS.

Forward Goods at a more expeditious rate than any Line running West, except the Regular Express Company.

MARK PACKAGES

"MERCHANTS' DESPATCH"

And deliver at Depot, corner Hudson and Thomas Streets, New York, and Western Railroad Depot, Boston.

Procure Bills of Lading of

A. H. LIVINGSTON,   G. G. KIDDER,

Agent, 1½ Murray Street, near Broadway, New York.   Agent, 69 Washington St., Boston.

W. T. CLARK, Western Agent,

INDIANAPOLIS.

H. H. DODD & CO.,

BOOK-BINDERS

AND

BLANK BOOK

MANUFACTURERS,

No. 16½ East Washington Street,

INDIANAPOLIS, IND.

Book-Binding for Publishers.

H. H. DODD & CO.'S

Indianapolis City Directory,

FOR 1863.

ABBREVIATIONS.

Bds., *boards*; cor., *corner*; res., *residence*; col., *colored*; wid., *widow*; opp., *opposite*; bet., *between*; ave., *avenue*; e., w., n., s., *East, West, North, South.* The word *street* is implied.

A

Aaron Adolphus. salesman, bds. 118 n. Ala.

ABBETT LAWSON & SON, (Lawson Abbett & Chas. H.,) PHYSICIANS AND SURGEONS, 20 Vir. ave., res. same.

Abbett Chas. H., (L. Abbett & Son,) bds 20 Vir. ave.

Abrams John, clerk, res. 71 n. noble.

Abromit Adolphus, clerk Ætna Ins. Co., res. 153 s. Tenn.

Achenback Hermon, photographer, bds. 20 n. Penn.

Achenback Paul, painter, res. 223 w. Wash.

Achey Ann, bds. 57 Ky. ave.

Achey Henry, res 5 Ky. ave.

Achey John H., bds. 5 Ky. ave.

Adair Luther G., accountant, bds. 64 Mass. ave.

ADAMS EXPRESS CO., (John H. Ohr, agent,) 12 e. Wash.

ADAMS GEORGE F., WHOLESALE FURNITURE, STORE, 56 e. Wash., res. 30 n. Del.

ADAMS GEO. H., (Asher & Co., and Parsons, A. & Co.,) res 86 n Ala.

Adams H. S., res. 61 s. N. J.

Adams John W., boots and shoes, bds. 74 n. Tenn.

Adams Ruben, dep. sheriff, res. 71 s. N. J.

Adams Samuel, brickmaker, res. 91 n. Mer.

Adams Thomas E., printer, cor. South and Canal.

Adams Wesley M., carpenter, res. 184 n. Ill.

Adams Wm. L., (Hume, Lord & Co.,) res. e National road.

Adkins Martin, rail roader, res. 78 n. East.

ÆTNA BUILDING, s. Penn., bet. Wash. and Market.

ÆTNA INSURANCE CO., Wm. Henderson, agent. See card.

Affantranger Josiah, blacksmith, 139 Ind. ave., res 111 w North.

Afton Andrew, laborer, res. 3. n. New Jersey.

Augustus John, produce, res. 37 e. ash

Ahrens Rev. Wm., Ger. Meth., res parsonage, 3 Ohio.

Albersmier Henry, student at Bryant's Commercial College.

Albert Jacob, plasterer, bds. 210 n. Ala.

Albert Jerome, baker, bds. 219 n. Ala.

Albert John, saddler, res. 210 n. Ala.

Albert Lawson, blacksmith, res. 107 w. Ohio.

Albert Samuel S., salesman, 210 n. Ala.

Albor James, architect, Journal build'g.

Albrecht Geo., varnisher, res. 95 Davidson.

Albrook O. II., moulder, res. 225 s. Delaware.
Aldag August, shoemaker, 137 e. Wash., res. 40 Spring.
Aldag Charles L., Sr., res 50 n. Liberty.
Aldag Charles L., shoemaker, 137 e. Wash., res. 32 n. Liberty.
Aldag Louis, shoemaker, res. 30 n. Liberty.
Aldrich John, carpenter, res. 131 Davidson.
Alexander George, laborer, res cor South and Tenn.
Alexander George W., (col.,) barber, bds. 145 w. Wash.
Alexander James L., student Bryant's Com. College, bds. 307 Vir. ave.
Alexander John, grocer and silversmith, res. w. Indianapolis.
ALFORD, MILLS & CO., (Thomas G. Alford, Howard W. Mills, William H. Morrison, & Richard L. Talbot,) WHOLESALE GROCERS, 36 e. Wash.
Alford Thomas G., (Alford. Mills & Co.,) res. 83 n. Alabama.
Allamon Samuel, (Osgood, Smith & Co.,) res. 205 n. Ill.
Alldair James, bricklayer, res. 138 n. Ala.
Allen Rev. Archebald C., res. 38 e. N. York.
Allen Mrs. E., music instructress, res. 38 e. N. York.
Allen Emery, (col.,) teamster, res. 133 n. Ala.
Allen Henry, res. 66 w. Vermont.
Allen James, pressman in Braden's printing office, 114 w. Ohio.
Allen Mrs. Johanna, wid., res. 8 s. Penn.
Allen Joseph, (col.,) wood chopper, res. 186 w. North.
Allen Thos. C., book binder, bds. 38 e. N. York.
Allen W. A., bds. Littles Hotel.
Allen William, machinest, res. 105 e. Market.
Allbands John, laborer, res. 171 n Noble.
Allison John, brakesman, T. H. R. R., bds. National Hotel.
Alred Garrison, city sexton, res. 137 w. South.
Alred Jane, wid., res. 9 Bates.
Altland Hiram, baker, 165 n. Noble, res. same.
Altland Samuel T., carpenter, res. 122 n. East.
Altman Hermann, (Langenberg & Co.,) res. 194 w. Wash.
ALVORD, CALDWELL & ALVORD, Edmond B. Alvord, John M. Caldwell, Henry B. Alvord,) WHOLESALE GROCERS AND LIQUORS, 68 e. Wash.
Alvord Edmond S., res. 54 n. Penn.
Alvord Edmond B., (Alvord, Caldwell & Alvord,) res. 141 n. Ill.

Alvord Henry B., (Alvord, Caldwell & Alvord,) res. 54 n. Penn.
Alwands Sumuel, clerk, bds. 23 s. Del.
Ambrose Mary, superintendent St. John Sisters of Providence, cor. Georgia and Tenn.
Ames James, piano maker, res. 2 and 3 Blake building, up stairs.
AMERICAN EXPRESS CO., J. Butterfield, agent, cor. Meridian and Wash.
Ammons Thomas, plasterer, bds. 64 Mass. ave.
Amos James, spinner, res. w. National road.
Amos Mrs. Nancy, wid., res. 143 n. Noble.
Amos Thomas, res. 75 Spring.
Anderson Charles, carpenter, bds. 53 e. Market.
Anderson Cynthia, wid. res., 53 e. Market.
Anderson David, carpenter, res. 52 Ind. ave.
Anderson Geo. P., clerk, res. 88 n. N. Jersey.
Anderson Henry, bds. 53 e. Market.
Anderson C. S., clerk, bds. 42 n. Miss.
Anderson James W., mess. Am. Ex. Co., res. 111 n. East.
Anderson James, carpenter, bds. 53 e. Market.
Anderson Martin, plasterer, bds. 182 e. N. York.
Anderson Milton, brakeman, I. P. & C. R. R., bds. Wabash, near Liberty.
Anderson Nancy, (col.,) weaver, res. 63 s. Noble.
Anderson Robert J., brickmason, res. 156 n. Del.
Anderson Samuel, (col.,) woodsawyer, res. 63 s. Noble.
Anderson Susan, wid., washer, res. alley bet. Vermont and Mich., e. of N. Jersey.
Anderson Thomas, railroader, res. 84 Ind. ave.
Anderson Wm., clerk Hogshire & Co., bds. 53 e. Market.
Anderson Wm., plasterer, res. 182 e. N. York.
ANDRA JOHN, HARNESS STORE, 169 e. Wash., res. 152 e. N. York.
Andrew Henry, (col.,) cook, res. near Col. Bap. Church.
ANDREWS LYMAN N., GEN'L FREIGHT AGENT, P. & I. R. R., res. 260 n. Tenn.
Andrews Robert, rolling mill, res. s. Missouri, s. of South.
Andrews Samuel B., photographer, res cor Ohio and Ill.
Andy Jacob, blacksmith, res. 199 s. Del.
Angle Thomas, soldier, 70th reg., Ind. Vol., res. E. Wash.
Anspach Andrew, shoe and bootmaker, Ind. ave.

Anthes Jacob, res. 215 s. Penn.

Anthony David, carpenter, res. 51 n. East.

Antles Esther Ann, seamstress, res. 50 n. East.

Apple Cyrus, res. 50 Bates.

Applegate Burg, book-keeper, Schnull & Co., bds. Bates House.

Applegate Peter V., blacksmith, res. 164 s. Penn.

Appleton James R., (H. H. Dodd & Co.,) res. 100 w. Vermont.

Arbuckle Hiram, teamster, res. 8 Penn.

Archy David, (col.,) laborer, res. cor. Alabama and Ft. Wayne ave.

Armbruster Jacob, bookeeper, Meikel's brewery.

Armantrant Lavina, (wid.,) res. 129 n. Liberty.

ARMSTRONG, WM., CLERK, bds. Bates House.

Armstrong Wm., agent American Bible Society, 4 New & Talbot's block, res. 186 n. Ill.

Arnald Alferd, clerk, res. 124 s. Noble.

Arnold Peter, laborer, res. 7 n. N. Jersey.

Arter Christ., laborer, res. 144 e. Georgia.

Arter Henry, laborer, res. 144 e. Georgia.

Arthur Thomas, moulder, res. 117 s. Tenn.

ASBURY CHURCH, 106 s. N. Jersey.

Ash Frances, laborer, res. 14 e. Georgia.

Ash Isaac A., clerk, res. 119 w. Wash.

Ash Richard, laborer, res. 14 e. Georgia.

ASHER JOHN R., (Asher & Co., and Parsons, Adams & Co., res. Louisville.

ASHER & CO., (John R. Asher, and George H. Adams,) BOOK PUBLISHERS, 3 Odd Fellows' Hall, up stairs.

Ashmer James G., artist, res. 69 n. Tenn.

Askin Patrick, laborer, res. Mich., bet. East and Liberty.

Asmus Frederick, laborer, res. 72 w. Mich.

ASTON JOSEPH, CLERK JOHNSON'S LIVERY STABLE, w. Pearl, res. 9 Ky. ave.

Aston Joseph, jr., book-keeper, bds. 9 Ky. ave.

Astor Saloon, Penn., bet. Wash. and Market.

ATHON JAMES S., SECRETARY OF STATE, 11 Ky. ave., res. 82 n. N. Jersey.

ATKINS ELIAS C., SHEFFIELD SAW WORKS, 155 s. Ill., res. 141 e. South.

Atkinson Osborne, carpenter, res. 101 w. South.

Atkinson Mrs. Eliza, wid., res. 73 Merrill.

Atkinson Frank, finisher, res. 69 Meridian.

Atkinson Thomas, painter, res. 11 Mass. ave.

Aufderhaede Henry, laborer, res. 126 Davidson.

Aufderhaede Joseph, blacksmith, bds. 126 Davidson.

Aug Albert, hackman, res. 280 Indiana ave.

Augustmier Henry, laborer, res. 162 n. Noble.

Avels Mrs. Margaret, wid., res. 275 s. Delaware.

Avery John L., lumber dealer, res. 104 n. Ala.

Avery L. S., res. 10 w. Georgia.

Avil Joseph, hackman, res. 259 s. Penn.

Axe Theodore T., photographer, 8 e. Wash., bds., Oriental House.

Ayers Wm. S., carpenter, res. cor. Tenn. and First

B

Baar Gerhard L., cabinet maker, at Sloan & Burk's, res. 253 s. Del.

Babbeuseaker Gotlib, drayman, res. 108 s. Noble.

Babbitt Austin, student at Bryant's Commercial College.

Babbitt A., clerk, bds. 159 Vir. ave.

Bach Jasper, res 14 Garden.

Bachtel John S. bds. Littles Hotel.

Backesto Dr. J. P., res. 140 n. Tenn.

Backstahler Martin, confectioner, res. 50 w. South.

Bacon Daniel, proprietor Exchange Restaurant, bds. Macy House.

Bacon Mrs. Eliza, (wid.,) res. 131 n. Ala.

Bacon John, blacksmith, bds. 131 n. Ala.

Bacon Wm. M., painter, North, bet. Ala. and N. Jersey.

Bader Henry, tanner, res. 63 Bluff road.

Baggett Patrick, clerk, 74 w. Wash.

Bagget Patrick, laborer, res. 83. w. Maryland.

Baggs Frederick, book-keeper, res. 59 e. Ohio.

Baggs Samuel, book-keeper, bds 59 e. Ohio.

Baier Wm., clerk, Phœnix Saloon.

Bailey Frances J., wid. John J. Bailey, res. 71 Ind. ave.

Bailey Emanuel W. sup't gas works, res near gas works.

Bailey Julius, undertaker, res. 8 Bates.

Bailey Ranaldo A., clerk 18 w. Wash., bds. 20 n. Penn.

Bailey Robert, engineer at Insane Asylum, Mt. Jackson.

Bailey Miss Susan, bds. 207 n. Noble.

Bailiff Edmond H., laborer, res. Ash, bet Cherry and Corporation.

Bair Mrs. Lucinda, res 86 Mass. ave.

Bakeman Peter, carpenter, res. 249 s. Del.

Baker Charles, bds. Mrs. Walk, Georgia.

Baker Frederick, res. 203 n. Ill.

Baker Herominus, trunk maker, res. 3 McOuat block, Ky. ave.

Baker James M., (Baker and McIver,) res. cor. Ill. and Maryland.

Baker James E., speculator, bds. Macy House.

Baker Jesse A., salesman, 32 w. Wash., res. cor. Maryland and Ill.

Baker John W., carriage painter, bds. J. Dumfield, Vir. ave.

Baker John, harness maker, 34 w. Wash., bds, Macy House.

Baker Robert D., painter, res. 39 n. Penn.

Baker Mrs. S., milliner, 24 s. Ill.

Baker & McIver, (James M. Baker and John C. McIver,) hatters, 22 e. Wash.

Baldwick Frederick, fruit and confectioner, 30 w. Louisiana, res. s. Ill.

Baldwin J. Hermon, res. 105 n. Meridian.

Baldwin Emma R., res. 51 n. East.

Balet Louis, drayman, res. 142 e. Market.

Bali Henry, cooper, bds. 180 n. Noble.

Balke Cohas, billiard saloon, 175 c. Wash.

Ball Anthony, bakery, 128 s. Ill.

Ball Wm., carpenter, res. 83 w Md.

Ballard Austin, seal engraver, res. 5 Circle.

Ballard W. P., student at Bryant's Commercial College, bds. P. A. Brown.

Ballweg Ambrose, U. S. service, res. 57 Madison ave.

Ballweg Fred, laborer, res. 46 n. Miss.

Ballweg & Kindler, (A. Ballweg and Chas. Kindler,) gunsmiths, 17 Ky. ave.

Bals Charles, (Ruchhaupt & Balls,) res. 56 e. St. Joseph.

Bals Chas. H., rail roader, res. 91 Ind ave.

Bals Christian F., (with Ruchhaupt & Bals,) bds. Farmers Hotel.

BAMBERGER HERMAN, WHOLESALE DEALER IN HATS, CAPS, FURS, &c., 16 c. Wash. See card, opp. front cover. res 119 e. Ohio.

Bamberger Isaac, clerk, 5 Bates House, bds 119 e. Meridian.

Bamberger Solomon, clerk, H. B., bds. 119 e. Ohio.

Bames Thomas B., bds. Littles Hotel.

Banan Patrick, works Exchange stables, res. s. Meridian.

Band Riley, millwright, res. Spring, bet. N. York and Ver.

Baneuk Wm., laborer, Madison depot, res. 86 Union.

Banghart A. W., pumpmaker, res. 211 Alabama.

Banhammer Wm., plasterer, res. 169 w. Ver.

Banking Christ., painter, res., 69 Huron.

Bankley Abram, (col.,) Col. Coburn's

BANK OF THE STATE, cor. Ky. ave. and s. Ill. H. McColloch, president, J. M. Ray, cashier.

Banks Francis R., night watch, Bellefontaine machine shop, res. 66 s. Noble.

Banister Seneca, soldier, 33d Reg., res. 167 e. Ohio.

Banivert Benedick, at arsenal, res. North bet. Noble and railroad.

Barbce Robert B., res. 165 n. East.

Barbee Sampson, moulder, res. 54 e. South.

Barbour Lucien, (Barbour & Howland,) res. 107 n. Ala.

Barbour Samuel, physician, res. 126 n. West.

Barbour & Howland, (Lucian Barbour & John D. Howland,) attorneys at law, 1½ w Wash.

Bareswill Daniel, bar-keeper, cor. Wash. and Ky. ave.

Barker Mrs. Julia, wid., res. 92 n. N. Jersey.

Barker Thos. D., grocer, 190 e. Wash, res. 113 e. N. York.

Barker Wm., plasterer, res. 161 n. West.

Barmann Andrew, vinegar maker, res. Elizabeth.

Barnard J., grocer, 18 s. Meridian, res. 207 n. Ill.

Barnes Andrew, printer, Journal office, bds. 115 n. East.

Barnes Alphonso, clerk American Express office, res. 26 s. Meridian.

Barnes Ellis, city printer, Journal office, res. 115 n. East.

Barnes Henry F., physician, off. Blake's building.

Barnes Jerome B. hack driver, res. 279 s. East.

Barnes Wm., bee hive manufacturer, res. 72 s. Ill.

Barnett Thomas, clerk New York grocery. res. 12 n. East.

Barnett David W., mailing clerk, P. O., bds. 123 n. N. Jersey.

Barnicle Mrs. John, res. 23 Bates.

Barnitt Thomas, grocer, 170 e. Wash., res. 83 e. Market.

Barnitt Thomas, Jr., clerk, 19 e. Wash., res. 12 n. East.

Barnets Charles, res. 119 s. Noble.

Barnitz Charles, res. 148 n. Ill.

Barnitz Jacob W., physician and taxadimist, res. 148 n. Ill.

Barr Jacob, blind maker, res 72 n. Del.

Barr Mrs. Nancy, wid., washer, res. 129 e. N. York.

Barrett, Michael, laborer, res. 10 Ellen.

Barrit Patrick, laborer, res. 125 Benton.

Barry Edward, cabinet maker, res. 303 s. Del.

Barry Dr. E. H., secretary Grand Lodge I. O. O. F., res. cor. Tenn. and First, off. Odd Fellows' Hall.

Barry Mrs. Richard, wid., res. 306 s Del.

Barthels Ferdinand, clerk, bds. 142 e. Wash.

Bartlett John M., (U. S.,) res 260 s Del.

Bartlet Joseph, confectionery, 38 w. Louisiana.

Bartlett Joseph, eating saloon, res. 121 s. Tenn.

Barton Chas. W. blacksmith, cor. Miss. and Ind. ave., res. 290 Ind. ave.

Bary Gotliebe, laborer, res. n. Noble.

Bary John, laborer, res. 57 Huron.

Bass Lovel, (col.,) fruit dealer, cor. Bates and Benton.

Basset Horace H., with Frank Smith, res. 20 e. Ohio.

Bast John, basket maker, res. 178 e. Market.

Basten Edward, carpenter, I. & C. R. R. Co., res, near cor. Orient and East.

Bates City Mills, (C. Heckman and J. H. McArthur,) cor. Wash. and Noble.

Bates Harvey, Sr., res. 67 e. Market,

BATES HOUSE, n. w. cor. Wash. and Ill., J. L. Holten, proprietor.

Bates Harvey, Jr., bds. Bates House.

BATTY JOHN H., BUTCHER, 8 n. Penn.

Bauer Mary, wid. Geo. Bauer, res. 63 n. Ill.

Bauldin Eli, carpenter, bds. E. Knights.

Bavington Albert, plasterer, res. St. Clair, bet. Ala. and N. Jersey.

Baylor John S., hack driver, bds. 210 Ind. ave.

Baze Frederick, works Terre Haute engine house, res. 13 Peru R. R.

Beach Wm. B., clerk in Sinking Fund office, res. 102 n. West.

Beals Jerome, salesman, Boston store, bds. 106 n. Penn.

Beal John A., attorney at law, res. 82 n. East.

Beal Joshua, painter, res. 173 e. South.

Beal Samuel L., gunsmith, res. 92 w. N. York.

Beam David, (Byrket & Beam,) res. 125 s. Tenn.

Beard Amos, carpenter in plow factory, res. 67 n. Tenn.

Beard Benjamin F., carpenter, res. 58 Vermont.

Beard David, plow maker, res 58 w Ver.

Beard John, student of Bryant's Commercial College, bds. n. Penn.

Beard John, bds. California House, 139 s. Ill.

Beard Notsil, plasterer, res. 28 e. Wash.

Beard Solomon, (Binkley, Wilson & Co.,) res. 58 w. Wash.

Bearss Charles W., clerk, res. 13 Ky. ave.

Beasley John E., boot and shoe cutter, res. 105 n. Tenn.

Beasley Thomas, boot and shoemaker, bds. 105 n. Tenn.

BEATY DAVID S. PRESIDENT INDIANAPOLIS GAS AND COKE CO., res. 80 e. Mich.

Beaver Elisha, teamster, res. 32 Michigan road.

Beck Christian, gunsmith, res. 80. n. N. Jersey.

Beck Jacob, gunsmith, res. 76 e. St. Clair.

BECK EDWARD, CRYSTAL PALACE, SALOON, 44 w. Wash., res. 19 w. Maryland,

Beck James A., conductor on T. H. R. R., res. 69 w. South.

Beck Samuel, gunsmith, 80 e. Wash., res. 21 s. Delaware.

Becker Jacob, (Tapking and Becker,) res. 23 n. Liberty.

Becker John, baker, res 46 Ft. Wayne ave.

Becker & Vieweg, clothing store, 103 e. Wash.

Beckman Harman P., cabinet maker, res. 249 s. Del.

Beder Henry, currier, res. cor. Ill. and McCarthy.

Bedford Nelson F., clerk, bds. Pyle House.

Beduer Joseph, porter, 289 Mass ave.

BEEBE RODERIC, EMPIRE SALOON, 22 w. Wash.

Beeber Geo. B., carpenter, res. 50 Ind. ave.

Beese Mrs. Catherine, res. s. e. cor. Cherry and Oak.

Beever Thomas, teamster, res. 101 n Liberty.

Behrisch Bernhard, merchant, Spencer House block, bds. Spencer House.

Behrmann John, works Union Depot, res. 112 n. Noble.

Behymer Daniel, door, sash and blind manufactory, opp. Court House, res. 65 n. Penn.

Behymer Simeon, carpenter, res. 32 e. Georgia.

Beilstein Ernest, sign painter, bds. Beck's 21 s Del.

Beisner Charles, blacksmith, bds. 215 Mass. ave.

Belcher, Wm., teamster, res. Cherry, bet. Chatham and Noble.

Bell A. C., watchmaker, 37 w. Wash., bds. Bates House.

Bell Chas. G. Photographer, cor. Ill. and Wash., up stairs.

Bell John E, (col.,) res. 128 Ind. Ave.

Bell Thomas, plasterer, bds. Farmers' Hotel.

Bell Wm., wood dealer, res. 64, cor. Blackford and North.

Belles John T., book-keeper, Oriental House, res. same.

Belles Joshua, (Belles & Tarlton,) Oriental House.

BELLES & TARLTON, (Joshua Belles and John Tarlton,) PROPRIETORS ORIENTAL HOUSE, s Ill.

Bellis Samuel, (Sharp & Bellis,) res. 110 n. N. Jersey.

Bellows Elihu, blacksmith, res. 173 n. Alabama.

Belzner Michael, teamster, res. 241 s. Del.

Bender David, proprietor of National Hotel, w. Wash.

Bender Tobias, laborer, res. 131 e. Market.

BENHAM A. M. & Co., (A. M. Benham & J. McLene,) MUSIC DEALERS, cor. Ill. and Wash., under Bates House.

Benham A. Morris, (A. M. Benham & Co.,) bds. Macy House.

Benham Henry, clerk for A. M. Benham & Co., bds. Macy House.

Beninger John, works in Model mills res. Mo., bet. Market and Wash.

Beninger Phlip, laborer, res. 72 n. Noble.

Benjamin Desmond O., res. cor. Merrill and Meridian.

Bennett W. Henry, pattern maker, res. 92 n. Meridian.

Bennett James M., printer, Gazette office, res. 92 n. Meridian.·

Bennett Wm. H., res. 119 n. Penn.

Benning Achnis, U. S., res. 65 Hosbrook.·

Bennoe Charles, res. 39 Harrison.

Benson Mrs. Anne, (wid.,) Mich. road.

Benson Henry C., egg packer, 11 Vir. ave. res. 51 s. Benton.

Bentley Wm. D., cabinet maker, bds. Ray House.

Benton Harvey S., boilermaker, res. National road, e. of Pogues Run.

Benton Spencer, laborer, (col) bds alley, bet Del and Penn.

Bents Robert, Dr., 33d reg. Ind. vol., res. 47 n. Del.

Benendes Joseph, cabinet maker, bds. Chicago House, s. Ill.

Bergenr Gustave, assistant book-keeper, Indianapolis Branch Banking Co., bds. 89 w. Wash.

Beringer Joseph, turner, bds. 186 s. Ill.

Bernaurd Joseph, brickmaker, res. 52 Huron.

Berner John, drayman, res. 90 n. Davidson.

Berry Augustus E., marble cutter, bds. 18 n. Delaware.

Berry Cynthia, wid., washer, res. 77 n. Noble.

Berry Geo. W., 79th reg. Ind. vol., res. 100 e. Makret.

Berry John, teamster, res. 137 n. Miss.

Berry Mrs. Mary, wid., res. 212 e. St. Clair.

Berry Michael, stone cutter, res. 46 Spring.

Berry Wm. H., res. 212, e. St. Clair.

Berry Thomas, collector, res. n. Tenn.

Berryman John, blacksmith, res. 50 s. Noble.

Bertelsman Mrs. Lisette, seamstress, res. 108 n. Noble.

Bertling H. T., bar keeper, Union Hall.

Bessing Ben., watchman at Central Depot, res. 229 Ala.

BESSONIES REV. AUGUSTUS, PASTOR ST. JOHN'S CHURCH, res. Georgia, bet. Ill. and Tenn.

Bethel S. School Chapel, cor. Noble and South.

Bettise Wm., salesman, J. K. Sharpe, res. Mass. ave.

Beynon Thomas, wood sawyer, res 241 Mass. ave.

Bichtel John S., butcher 8 n. Penn., bds Littles Hotel.

Bick Frederick, butcher, res. cor. Bluff road and McCarty.

Bicker John, James' marble works, res. 57 St. Joseph.

Bickford Geo. W., carpenter, res. 129 Blake.

Bidleman Silas, res 34 e. Georgia.

Biedenmaster Charles A., res. 59 n. East.

Bigelow Herbert M., Dep. U. S. Marshal, bds. 100 w. Mich.

Bigelow Increase S., Dep. U. S. Marshal, res. 100 w. Mich.

Bigelow Ira P., plasterer, res. 178 e. N. York.

Billingsley ——, book-keeper, bds. 64 Mass. ave.

Billingsley David E., student in Bryant's Commercial College, bds. at Mrs. Hoyt's.

Bimmerman Frederick, wagon maker, res. 140 n. Ala.

Bingham James stone cutter, res. Mich. road.

BINGHAM JOSEPH J., (Elder, Harkness & Bingham,) EDITOR STATE SENTINEL, res. 88 w. Maryland.

BINGHAM W. P., JEWELER, 50 e. Wash., res. 53 n. Meridian. See card.

Binkley Samuel, Marion Agriculture Works, res. Norwood.

Binkley & Wilson, (S. Binkley & —— Wilson,) Marion Agriculture Works, 85 w. Wash.

Bippus John, tailor, 16 n. Penn., res. s. Ill.

Bird Abram, res. 95 n. Ill.

Birney Pat. G., shoemaker, e. Wash.

Bisbing Charles M., engineer, bds. 52 s. Del.

Bisbing Jacob J., marshal Union depot, res. 124 n. West.

Bishop John S., book-keeper, bds. Mrs. Jack, n. Penn.

Bishop Mrs. Sarah, wid., res. 193 n. N. Jersey.

Bissett Wm., clerk, 14 Bates House.

Black George H., carpenter, 121 n. Miss.

Black Wm., (col.,) cook at Ray House.

Black Wm. M., tanner, res. 251 Ind. ave.

Blaes Nicholas, saloon, 48 s. Del., res. in rear.

Blain James W., painter, res. 86 n. Miss.

Blain Thomas, works Washington Foundry, res. 95 w. N. York.

Blair James M., harnessmaker, res. 198 w. Wash.

Blair Napoleon, teamster, bds. 176 Mass. ave.

Blake Henry, soldier, 31st Ill. reg., res. 189 n. N. Jersey.

BLAKE JAMES, res. 186 n. Tenn.

Blake James R., clerk Rolling Mill Co., bds. 186 n. Tenn.

Blake John, (Blake, Helwig & Co.,) res. 134 n. West.

Blake, Helwig & Co., (John Blake, Chas. Helwig, Chas. Post & Gustavus Sherman,) plaining mill and lumber yard, cor. N. York and Canal.

BLAKE WM. M., U. S. QUARTER-MASTER'S DEPARTMENT, res. 201 n. Tenn.

Blakely James, laborer, bds. 204 w. Wash.

Blanc, Borst & Lake, (John Blanc, Fred. Borst & John Lake,) meat market, 16 n Ill., Bates House.

Blanc John, (Blanc, Borst & Lake,) res. 74 n. N. Jersey.

Bland Hiram, carpenter, res. 166 s. N. J.

Blank Anthony, clerk, 142 e. Wash.

Blauvelt John H., brakeman, bds. 61 Spring.

Bledsoe Mrs. Ellen, wid., res. 131 s. Ill.

Bless Eliazer, res. 168 n. N. Jersey.

Blettzinger Eronimus, laborer, res. w. Indianapolis.

Bligh Gottlieb, blacksmith, bds. 61 Bluff road.

BLIND ASYLUM, W. H. Churchman, Sup't, North, bet Penn. and Meridian.

Bloom Solomon, book-keeper, bds. Bates House.

Bloomer John, laborer, res. 260 s. Del.

Blue Cyrus B., carpenter, res. 153 n. East.

Bly John, clerk, res. 19 e. Market.

Bly Oliver H. P., trader, res. 32 n. East.

Blyth Wm., Engineer, res. National road, e. of Pogues Run.

Blythe Samuel, city fire department, bds. Ray House.

Boardman David, res. 125 w. N. York.

Bonz Naomi J., wid. Charles T. Boaz, res. 20 w. North.

Boaz Wm., receiver in land office, res. 261 s. Penn.

Boaz Wm., student commercial college, res. 261 s. Penn.

Boaz Wm. T., clerk, I. & C. R. R., bds. 20 w. North.

Bodman Elam, physician, res 144 n Ill.

Boeksthaler Martin, baker, res. 50 South.

Boerum Joseph S., mail agent, res. 200 n. Ill.

BOETTICHER JULIUS, EDITOR AND PROPRIETOR INDIANA VOLKS-BLATT, 130 e. Wash., res. same.

Bogart Cornelius, works in Wiggins & Chandler's foundry, res. Patterson n. North.

Boger Christ., brewerer, bds. w. National road.

Boggess Henry C., student Bryant's commercial college, bds cor Ill. and Georgia.

Bogle Ralph B., livery stable, Littles Hotel, res 18 n East.

Bohlen David A., architect, Ætna building, res out corporation, n Ill.

Bolen Michael; laborer, res. 39 Henry.

BOLLIER PAUL, MEAT MARKET, res 241 n Ill.

Bollman Frederick, bakery, 87 e Wash., res same,

Bolmann Henry, laborer, res 74 s Noble.

Bolster Fred., woodsawyer, res 89 w N. York.

Bolton Mrs. Sarah T., res. 58 s Tenn.

Bombarger David, carpenter, res 207 Ind. ave.

Bomford J. V., chief mustering and disbursing officer, head-quarters cor. Maryland and Del.

Bond Abraham, bootmaker, res 33 w N. York.

Bond Caroline, wid. Clauson Bond, res 144 n. Miss.

Bond Joel L., livery stable, res North, bet Penn. and Del.

Bond Pleasant, principal 2d ward school, Bond Wm. E., teamster, res 144 n Miss.

Bone John, railroader, res 51 Hosbrook.

Boney Joseph, U. S. service, 17 res s Ala.

Bonta Moses, bds 33 n Ala.

Borcherl Frederick, coppersmith, res 232 e. Wash.

Borehers Frederick, bds 130 Mass. ave.

Borem James, carpenter, bds e Wash.

Borgert Andrew, bds 281 s Del.

Borrows Hollis W., machinest, res 71 Bright.

Borst Frederick, (Blanc, Borst & Lake,) meat market, under Bates House. res 65 Merrill.

Bosh George, laborer, res Wabash, bet N. Jersey and East.

Bosledon Wm., (col) barber, res alley, bet Penn. and Meridian,

Bossert John, baker, 54 Bluff road, res same.

Bothwell Henry, clerk, res cor Penn. and McCarthy.

Bouvy Adren, tinner, res 264 s. Del.

Bourgon Etin, cigarmaker, bds California House, 136 s Ill.

Bourser Levi C., laborer, res 167 s Noble.

Bovard James, in Hinesley's livery stable, res 136 Ind. ave.

Bower Jacob, shoemaker, bds 25 s Meridian.

Bower Nicholas, laborer, res Bluff road, Doughertyville.

Bowler Martin, laborer, res 6 Bates,
Bowles Thomas H., (Davis & Bowles,) res
108 n Meridian.
Bowlus Geo. A., book-keeper, Wiley &
Martin, bds Mrs. Smith, 44 s Penn.
BOWEN, STEWART & CO., (Silas T.
Bowen, Chas. G. Stewart,) WHOLE-
SALE AND RETAIL BOOKS AND
STATIONERY, 18 e Wash. See card.
Bowen Silas T., (Bowen, Stewart & Co.,)
126 n. Ill.
Bowman Archibald G., brakeman, res
124 Davidson.
Bowman Wm., farmer, res w Indianap'ls
Boyd David M., trader, res 37 s Meridian.
Boyd Frank, messenger for American
Express Co., bds 49 w Georgia.
Boyd Frank A., (Boyd & Palmer,) bds
Palmer House.
Boyd James, butcher, res 118 n Ala.
Boyd James T., homœopathic physician,
res 112 n N. Jersey.
BOYD & PALMER, (F. A. Boyd & F. T.
Palmer,) DRUGGISTS, 14 w Wash.
Boyden Myron J., grocery and liquors,
res 134 w Wash.
Boyer Wm., (col) white-washer, res 53 w
Georgia.
Boyle John, shoemaker, bds Mrs. Kitely.
Boyles M. W., salesman, bds 139 n N. J.
Boyless George A., clerk at Terre Haute
depot, bds 86 w Md.
Brackebush Charles, clerk, bds 74 n Tenn.
Bracken Alexander, brickmason, res cor
Ash and corporation.
BRACKEN CPAT. JAMES R., LOCAL
EDITOR STATE SENTINEL, bds Lit-
tles Hotel.
Bracken Wm., U. S. service, res 46 Mass.
ave.
Brackin Thomas, carpenter, res St. Joseph
bet Ill. and Meridian.
Braden David, U. S. A., res 75 w New
York.
Braden James, clerk at 24 w Wash., bds
191 w Wash.
Braden Patrick, moulder, res cor Miss.
and Henry.
BRADEN WILLIAM, BLANK BOOK
AND STATIONERY, 24 w Wash., res
191 w Wash.
Bradenilt Charles, teamster, res 101 e
Market.
Brademilt Christian, laborer, res 152 Da-
vidson.
Brademire John F., teamster, Mich. bet
N. Jersey and East.
Bradly Jepha, res 69 s Benton.
Bradly Wm., contractor, res bet South
and Louisiana.
Bradley Wm., laborer, res 98 Maryland.
Brado Joseph, clerk, bds cor East and
South.
Brado Thomas, grocer, res cor East and
South.

Bradshaw John, horse dealer, res 12 e
Vermont.
Bradshaw Wm. A., assessor for internal
revenue,6th district, 14 New & Talbot's
block, res 70 n East.
Bradshaw James M., Quarter-master U.
S. A., res out-side city, n Penn.
Bradshaw J. W., (Wm. A. Bradshaw &
Son,)
Bradshaw Mrs. Margaret, wid., res 161 s
Alabama
BRADSHAW WM. A. & SON, (Wm. A.
Bradshaw & J. W. Bradshaw,) FLOUR
AND FEED STORE, 5 s Del. See card.
Bramble Zenis, engineer, I. C. R. R., res
66 Merrill.
Bramwell John M., book-keeper, Brown-
ing & Sloan, res 48 s Miss.
Branan John, P. O. clerk, bds 356 Vir.
ave.
BRANCH BANK OF THE STATE OF
INDIANA, Yohn's block. Geo. Tousey,
president, David E. Snyder, cashier.
Brandt Christ., grocer, National road, e
of Pogues Run.
Brandt Geo. I., cistern maker, 25 Bluff
road.
Brandow John, foreman I.C. R. R. machine
shop, res cor Meek and Benton.
Brannan Daniel, 79th Ind. vol., alley rear
of engine house.
Brannan John porter U. S. court house,
res 356 Vir. ave.
Branson John, cooper, bds 232 w Wash.
Branyon Daniel, rolling mill, res s Mo.,
s of South.
Brat Leopold, bakery and grocery, 46 Ft.
Wayne ave.
Bray John S., res 104 n East.
Brayboy David E., (col) barber, Yohn's
block, bds Johnson saloon.
Breckweg Theodore, cooper, res 89 Bluff
road.
Brennan John, cooper, shop Carlisle mill,
res w Wash.
Bretney W. H., telegraph operator, Belle-
fontaine R. R., bds at Littles Hotel.
Bretney Wm., res 81 s N. Jersey.
BRETT MATTHEW L., TREASURER
OF STATE, 13 Ky. ave., res cor Penn.
and Vir. ave.
Bretz Adam, grocer, cor Ill. and Louisi-
ana, res 68 s Ill.
Breuninger August, grocery, w Wash. res
same.
Brewer Cynthia R., wid. Daniel Brewer,
seamstress, res 8 w Wash.
Brewer Edward, (col) barber, 53 s Ill.,
bds Macy House.
Brewin Dillard A., in 20th Ind. battery
res extreme w end Ind. ave.
Brick Daniel, laborer, bds 16 e Georgia.
Brickett Deborah Ann, (wid. Thomas N
Brickett,) res 135 w Market.
Bricking R., drayman.

Briggs Charles H., fireman, bds 64 Mass. ave.

Briggs James, butcher, res 280 Ind. ave

Brigham Charles E., foreman Wm. Braden's office, 24 w Wash. res N. Jersey, s of South.

Bright Amos, printer, H. H. Dodd & Co., bds 45 n Penn.

Bright C. E., artist, 33 w Wash., res n Ill.

Bright Mrs. Eliza, boarding house, 45 n Penn.

Brimmerman Caston, carriage maker, res 148 n Del.

Brink Christ. A. D., clerk, bds Spencer House.

Brink Wm., tailor, res 182 e Mich.

Brinker August, grocery, res 94 w N. York.

Brinker Wm., cooper, res 163 n N. Jersey.

Brinkman Charles, (Brinkman & Ruschhaupt,) res country.

Brinkman John F., carpenter, res 191 n Noble.

BRINKMAN & RUSCHHAUPT, LIVERY STABLE, 17 s Del. See card.

Brinkman Wm., barkeeper, 83 e Wash.

Brinkmyer Fred, works 82 w Wash., res 127 Davidson.

Brinkmeyer George, liquor agent, 82 w Wash., res 129 Davidson.

Brinkmeyer John C., (J. C. Brinkmeyer & Co.,) res 152 Liberty.

Brinkmeyer & Co., (J. C. Brinkmeyer, & F. L. Kasting,) foreign and domestic liquors, 82 w Wash.

Brinning Fred., carpenter, res 295 s Del.

Bristol Anthony I., salesman, bds 87 n Penn.

Briston Samuel M., carriage maker, res 51 n Del.

Bristor Samuel M., wagon maker, 68 Ky. ave., res 51 n Del.

Bristor Wm., student at Bryant's commercial college.

Brite Thomas, works at rolling mill, bds 188 s Tenn.

Britton John G., (col) barber, res 218 e Wash.

Brittingham Hetty, tailoress, res 6 Blake building.

Broche Frederick, shoemaker, res 60 Bluff road.

Brocksmith Henry, blacksmith, res 44 Huron.

Broden James, moulder, res 118 e N. York.

Broden James, machinest, res 178 s Tenn.

Broden Michael, printer, res 127 e. New York.

· Broderick Patrick, Purdy's Commercial College.

Broderick Patrick, barkeeper, bds Macy House.

Broking Christian, drayman, res 27 Un.

Brokiuk Richard, drayman, res Yoming.

Bromheffer Henry, carpenter, res 236 Madison Av.

Bronson G. W., Principal 5th ward school, res Oak, near Church.

Bronson Robert T., carpenter, res 103 n Ala.

Brooks Helen, dressmaker, res 14 n New Jersey.

Brooks Mrs. Sidney, widow, res w Indpls.

Brothers John, blacksmith, res e. Wash.

Brothers, William H., photographer, Post office Gallery, bds Pyle House.

Brons Henry laborer, res 186 n N. J.

Brouse Alin R., student, Greencastle College.

Brouse Andrew, (Brouse Andrew & Son) res 60 e New York.

Brouse Andrew & Son, (Andrew Brouse, David W. Brouse,) 56 e New York.

Brouse Charles W., Capt. Co. K., 100th Reg. Ind. Vols.

Brouse David W., (Andrew Brouse & Son) 60 e. New York.

Brouse John A. Rev., Methodist, res 38 e Market.

Brouse Sarah, (wid. Adam Brouse), bds 34 e. Market.

Brouse Thomas W., carpenter, res 62 e New York.

Browman John, clerk A. D. Streight, bds Palmer House.

Brown Albert, laborer, Yoming.

BROWN AUSTIN H., Local State Journal. Res cor Meridian and Merrill.

Brown A., attorney, res 151 e South.

Brown A., saloon, in Little's Hotel, res same.

Brown Mrs. Catharine, washer, bds e Wash.

Brown Charles H., carpenter, res 217 Ind. Av.

Brown Emanuel, bricklayer, res w Indpls.

Brown Ernist, res 168 n Noble.

Brown George, carpenter, res 168 n Ala.

Brown George P. C., machinist, res 167 n Ala.

Brown George, laborer, (col), lives with Gen. Dumont.

Brown Hervey, conductor, Jeffersonville R. R., bds Palmer House

Brown Henry C., carpenter, res 47 n Noble.

Brown Ignatius, attorney at law, 19½ e Wash., res 151 e Wash.

Brown James porter, (A. Clem & Bro.) bds n Liberty.

Brown James, musician, 268 Madison Av.

Brown James H., clerk, (Vicker's) res 70 n Ala.

Brown James W., res 22 n Meridian.

Brown Jerry, (col) engineer at Sentinel office, res 151 n Ala.

Brown Jesse B., machinest, res 11 Henry.

Brown John, cabinet-maker, bds California House.

Brown John G., res 144 n New Jersey.
Brown John L., County Treasurer, C. H., res 67 n New Jersey.
Brown John W., sr., res 144 n New Jersey.
Brown John W., jr., baker, 150 n New Jersey, res same.
Brown John, carpenter, bds California House, 136 s Ill.
Brown John, (col) teamster, w Georgia.
Brown John, boot and shoemaker, res 80 w Vermont.
Brown John, plasterer, res 182 n Liberty.
Brown Joseph, hostler
Brown Louisa, res 223 w Wash.
Brown Maria G., plain sewing, res 71 n Missouri.
Brown Mary R., res 14 n New Jersey.
Brown Nathan B., bds 15 s Miss.
Brown Obediah S., res 269 Mass. Av.
Brown Orin H., student at Bryant's Commercial College, bds in the country.
Brown Patrick, laborer, res 176 s Ala.
Brown Philip, res 275 Mass. Av.
Brown Philip A., attorney at law, res 130 n New Jersey.
Brown Richard T., railroad agent, res 48 n East.
Brown Robert D., attorney at law, office, State House, res 15 s Miss.
Brown Miss Whitener, res 209 w Wash.
BROWN WILLIAM P., hatter shop, 20 Ky. Av.
Brown Willis, (col), res 186 w Georgia.
Browning Edmond, U. S. Register, P. O. Building, res 8 Va. Ave.
Browning George T., res 107 Ind. Ave.
Browning Robt., (Browning & Sloan) res 102 n Ill.
BROWNING & SLOAN, (Robt. Browning & Geo. W. Sloan), wholesale druggists, 22 w Wash. See card.
Broyles Rev. Moses, col., Baptist minister and school teacher, res Manerva, bet Mich. and North.
Brubaker Dr. Henry W., office, 18 s Miridian, res 24 s Miridian.
Bruer William H., res cor East and St. Clair.
Bruenning Edward, (E. & J. Bruenning,) res 6½ e Wash.
BRUENNING E. & J., (Edward & Joseph B.), photographers. 6½ e Wash.
Bruenning Joseph, (E. & J. Bruenning), res 6½ e Wash.
Brueggemann William, tailor, res 192 e Ohio.
Bruff J. W., clerk at Belf. R. R., res 217 Ala.
Brumer Frederick, foreman at C. F. Smith's brewery.
Brumer Frederick, bar keeper, res s Ill.
Brummer Carl, teacher of music, res 12 e Mich.
Brumfield J., teamster, res 136 Va. Av.

Brumfield William, teamster, bds at C. C' Reeves', e Wash.
BRUNDAGE ED. C., (M. Hunter & Co.) res 167 e Market.
Bruner Charles, shoe and boot store, 38 w Wash., res 112 s New Jersey.
Bruner Roman, blacksmith, res 14 McCarthy.
Brunner Frederick, saloon keeper, res 126 s Ill.
Bruning Frederick, drayman, res 69 Bluff road.
BRYAN JAMES W., druggist, Spencer House Block, see adv., bds at Spencer House.
BRYANT'S COMMERCIAL COLLEGE, cor Washington and Delaware. See adv.
Bryant A. C., bds Little's Hotel.
Bryant John S., res Henry, near Miss.
Bryant Joseph W. C., railroader, res 280 Mass. Ave.
BRYANT THOMAS J., President of Bryant's Commercial College, res 31 Ky. Ave.
Bryant J. G., book agent, bds s Penn.
Bryson Mrs. Julia A., (widow), res 91 Peru railroad.
Buchannan A, pedler, res 218 s Ala.
Buchannan Mrs. Catharine, (widow), res 262 e Washington.
Buchannan Cyrus F., carpenter, Mount Jackson.
Buchanan George W., carpenter, res 83 s East.
Buchanan James, printer, Journal office, bds Edwards' Hotel.
Buchanan John A., clerk Postoffice, res 26 s Miss.
Buche Frederic, shoemaker, 58 Bluff rd., res same.
Buckhart Andrew J., ice dealer, res 146 n Miss.
Buckley John, brakesman, I. & C. R. R., res Lord.
Buckley Timothy, laborer, 45 s East.
Buckner Elijah D., bds 151 n East.
Buckner James, (col), laborer, bds 183 Mass. Av.
Bucksot William, horse buyer, res 84 e Wash.
Bucter George, weaver, res cor Madison and California.
Buddenbaum Henry, carpenter, res 206 e Ohio.
Buddenbaum John, clerk, bds Mrs. Walk.
Budenc Henry, tailor, res 190 s Penn.
BUEHRIG HENRY E., proprietor of Farmer's Hotel. See card.
Buehrig Henry, saloon keeper, bds Farmer's Hotel.
Buell C. H., patent medicine manufacturer, res 105 Va. Av.
Buehrig William, barkeeper National Saloon, bds same.

Bufkin John C., attorney, 43 e Wash. res 7 e Ohio.

Bugly Parker E., fireman, I. P. & C. R. R., bds 7 Peru R. R.

Bugley Mrs. Polly A., (widow), res 7 Peru R. R.

Bugg Samuel, (col), servant Mrs. Mary J. Vance.

Buist Thos., retired, res cor Cal. and Vt.

Bullard Charles G., cabinet maker, res 145 n Ala.

Bullard Talbot, M. D., 23 s Meridian, res 87 e Ohio.

Bullard Wm. R., M. D., office, 23 s Meridian, bds 87 e Ohio.

Bullin William S., carriage trimmer, res 107 e Vt.

Bunday Major M. L., Paymaster U. S. A. 10½ e Wash.

Bumer John, gardener, (blind asylum), bds same.

Bunson Wm. wagonmaker, res 136 East.

Bunte John, house builder, res 118 n Miss.

Burbidge Thomas, baker, 11 n Penn., bds Mr. Nutts, e Md.

Burdett Frances, (wid) William Burdett, res 184 w Wash.

BURDICK WILLIAM P., wholesale jeweler, &c., 8 Yohn's block, res 10 w North.

Burgess C. Chapin, dentist, Odd Fellow's Hall, bds 86 n Ala.

Burgess Cornelius N., printer, res 129 Mass. Ave.

Burgess Henry, soldier, res 155 w Mich.

Burgess J. E., bds Little's Hotel.

Burgess Jno. W., bds Little's Hotel.

Burgess Loyd A., saddler, 20 w Wash., res 41 w St. Clair.

Burgner John, basket maker, res 17 Chatham.

Burguor Henry, works in armory, res 243 s Penn.

Burk Mrs. F., (wid) res 105 South.

Burk George, saloon keeper, Wash., res 104 s New Jersey.

Burk John, dealer in coal, res 148 n Tenn.

Burk Wm. C., (Sloan & Burk), bds 148 n Tenn.

Burkamayer Henry, laborer, res 332 Va. Ave.

Burke Christ., res 266 Madison Ave.

Burke George, proprietor Burke's saloon, 13 w Wash., res s New Jersey.

Burke Henry, stone mason, res 274 s Del.

Burke Henry, machinest, res 156 s Tenn.

Burke John, laborer, res 6 Bates.

Burket John W., carpenter, res Norwood.

Burkhart A. H., ice dealer, cor Miss. and Mich.

Burnett Jerome C., (Jordan & Burnett,) bds 22 s Meridian.

BURNHAM NORMAN G., Physician and Surgeon, res and office, 10 w Market.

Burns James, Madison R. R., bds Ray House, e Del.

Burns Mrs. Margaret A., seamstress, res 167 e Ohio.

Burns Michael, laborer, res 46 Massachusetts Ave.

Burns Patrick, works at Gas house, res 243 s Penn.

Burns Patrick, laborer, res 1 Willard.

Burns William F., rope maker, res s West.

Burns William V., in the army, res 247 Ind. Ave.

Burns John, plasterer, res 108 s Tenn.

Burrows George W., auction sale stable, 14 n Penn., res 142 Va. Ave.

Burt Alfonso S., saloon, 16 n Penn., res 56 Ind. Ave.

Burt Edward, bookbinder, res 85 n Miss.

Burt George, machinist, bds Tully House.

Burton George H., cooper, res 78 n Miss.

Burton John, bds 202 n Ill.

Burton John C., res 221 n New Jersey.

Burton Martin, (Burton & Shilling,) res 202 n Ill.

BURTON & SHILLING, (Martin Burton & R. L. Shilling), TRUNK, VALISSE, AND CARPET-BAG MANUFACTURERS, 13 s Ill. See card.

Busch Adam, carpenter, res 188 n Ill.

Busch Christian, shoe and boot maker, res 138 w Wash.

BUSCHER HENRY, BREWER, 14 s Ala., res same. See card.

Buscher Henry, saloon keeper, 51 e South, res same.

Buscher Jacob, switchman, Union depot, res 5 Water.

Buser Jacob, res 116 s Ill.

Buser Samuel, policeman, res 60 La.

Bush Jacob, res 250 e Wash.

Bush James, (col), cook in Mason's saloon, bds same.

Bush William S., bds 130 n New Jersey.

Buskel William, U. S. service, res 56 s Benton.

Busking Christ., sen., sheepshearer, res 58 Huron.

Busking Christian, paint mixer, Huron.

Bussell Erastus, M. D., res 132 n Ala.

Bussell William, clerk, coal office, 12 w Md., bds 132 n Ala.

BUSSEY JOHN, VERANDAH SALOON, AND BILLIARD ROOM, 36 w La., res 144 w Md. See adv.

Buswell William M., clerk with Perine, coal dealer, bds 152 n Tenn.

Butler William M., bricklayer, bds Washington House.

Butler Ovid D., deputy clerk, C. H., res 123 n Del.

Butler Smith, clerk, (A. Clem & Bro.) bds A. Clem.

Butsch George, grocer and liquor dealer, 173 Del., res same.

Butsch John, res 42 w South.

Butsch Joseph, ice dealer, res 84 w South.

Butsch Peter, U. S. service, res 26 Union

BUTSCH VALENTINE, (Butsch & Dickson,) res 73 w South.
BUTSCH & DICKSON, (Valentine Butsch and James Dickson,) WHOLESALE LIME, COAL AND CEMENT MERCHANTS, off e South, opp Madison and Jeff. R. R. offices. See card.
Butterfield Cyrus, city clerk, bds at Ray House, s Del.
BUTTERFIELD JAMES A., teacher of Music, P. O. box, 1222.
BUTTERFIELD JEREMIAH, agt American and U. S. Express Co's, res 103 n Tenn.
Butterfield John W., pressman, bds 44 n Penn.
Butterfield Merano, patent honey, res 183 n East.
BUTTERFIELD SEYMOUR A., Surgeon, res 162 n East.
Bydon Mrs. Ellen, dressmaker, 139 e Wash., res same.
Byfield Thomas, clerk New York Store, res 127 w New York.
Byran Norman S., (Tousey & Byran,) res 84 e Ohio.
Byrket John W., book-keeper, res Norwood, bet Tenn. and Ill.
Byrket Martin, (Byrket & Beam), res 62 s Tenn.
Byrket Socrates, printer, State Sentinel, res 81 n New Jersey.
Byrket & Beam, planing mill, (Martin Byrket, David Beam,) mill 60 s Tenn.
Byrkett Albert, works at rolling mill, res 85 w South.
Byrkit David Y., student at Bryant's Commercial College, bds s Tenn.
Byrkit Philip, carpenter, res 81 n N. J.
Bywater Edward, grocer, 226 e Wash., res same.
Bywaters Patrick, res 226 e Wash.

C

CABINET MAKERS' UNION, cor Market and Vincent. Henry Elstrad, prst. Gustavs Stark, sec'y.
Cady Abby A., (wid Charles W. Cady,) res Circle.
Cady David, salesman, (Chase & Dawes), res 71 n Ala.
Cahalane Patrick, laborer, res 82 s Noble.
Cahill John S., res Wabash, bet Liberty and Noble.
Cahill Mrs. Mary, res 239 w Wash.
Cahill Michael, laborer, res 52 n Liberty.
Cahnn Hyman, pedler, res 28 s Penn.
Cain John, res cor East and Wood.
Calaghan Michael, blacksmith, res n w cor McCarthy and Delaware.
Caldwell John M., (Alvord, Caldwell & Alvord), res 248 n Ill.
Cale David G., resident farmer, 135 n East.

Call Hugh, laborer, res cor Oak and corp line.
Call Dennis, peddler, bds 142 n Liberty.
Callaghan Mrs., (widow), washerwoman, 105 Madison.
Callaghan Stephen, salesman, New York Store, bds 20 s Miss.
Callahan John P., clerk, res 103 e South.
Callahan Michael, lab, h 27 Elsworth.
CALLINAN DANIEL J., dry goods, 28 e Wash, res Smith's block, w Ohio. See card.
Callinan Dominick W., salesman, bds at Macy House.
Callmyer Henry, shoemaker, res 155 s Alabama.
Campbell Andrew, tailor, res on West, bet Madison and Georgia.
Campbell Charles, res 2 w North.
Campbell Michael, engineer, bds at Mrs. Draper's, n Miss.
Campbell Moses, blacksmith, res w Indpls
Campbell Richard, City Hospital, res on Elizabeth, w end.
Campbell Samuel L., bookbinder, H. H. Dodd & Co., bds 2 n. North.
Campbell Thomas A., 2d Lieut. 70th Ind. Vol., res 79 n Meridian.
Campbell William H., proprietor Macy House.
Campbell Wm. L. (Campbell & Hewitt).
CAMPBELL & HEWITT, attorneys at law, 34 e Wash., (William L. Campbell, Charles Hewitt.)
Campion Daniel, carpenter, res 203 n Noble.
Cameron George, brickmaker, res 285 s East.
Cameron Mary, (widow), res 88 s East.
Cameron R. S., clerk N. Y. Store, bds at Macy House.
CAMERON WILLIAM S., printer, 8 e Pearl, res 116 n Ala. See Card.
Cannon William B., salesman, bds Baldwin House.
Cannon Wilson B., bookkeeper, bds cor St. Clair and Meridian.
Cantwell, patternmaker, Sinker & Vance, res Winston, bet Ohio and New York.
Carleton James M., groceries and provisions, 101 w Wash., res 108 Ind. Av.
Carlisle Mrs. Ann M., (widow), bds 67 n Miss.
Carlisle Daniel, freight agt Ind. Cent. R. W., res 46 w Walnut.
Carlisle Hamilton, flour packer in Model Mills, res w Market.
Carlisle John, "Model Mills," w Wash., res 204 w Wash.
Carmichael Jesse D., res 123, n Meridian.
Carnon Johnson, barkeeper, bds at Pearl St. Saloon.
Carney George, painter, bds 131 n Miss.
Carney George, carpenter, bds California House, 136 s Ill.

Carr Henry, boot and shoemaker, bds at Little's Hotel.
Carr Patrick, laborer, res 141 n Liberty.
Carr Rowland S., (Donaldson & Carr,) bds 222 North.
Carr Thomas, laborer, res s Mo. s South.
Carrico John, carpenter shop, 22 Ky. Av. res e Dougherty.
Carrington Gen. Henry B., bds at Bates House.
Carson Miss America, dressmaker, 26 and 28 w Wash., bds 164 n Tenn.
Carter Alexander, clerk, 37 s Penn., res cor Alabama and McCarthy.
Carter Alexander, carpenter, res 116 McCarthy.
Carter Caswell, carpenter, res 125 n Del.
Carter Charles E., policeman, res 91 n Illinois.
Carter David E., M. D., office, 18½ n Ill., res 79 n Ill.
Carter Enoch B., carpenter, res 14 Ind. ave.
Carter George, (Leathers & Carter,) res 113 n Ala.
Carter Henry C., carpenter, res Georgia, bet West and Canal.
Carter John, (with Frank Smith,) res 197 n East.
Carter Samuel, cooper, res w Indpls.
Carter Sanford, eng. on Jeff. R. R., res 227 s Ala.
Cartney Andrew, laborer, res Sinker.
Casanova Balthasar, Farmers' Saloon, res 214 w Wash.
Case Elam E., (Case & Marsh,) res 59 n Miridian.
Case John B., engineer, res 75 w Noble.
Case John L., engineer, res 43 e Georgia.
CASE & MARSH, (Elam E. Case and Henry B. Marsh), manufacturers of Agricultural implements, 86 w Wash.
Casey Mrs. Mary, washer, res e Market.
Casey Patrick, laborer, res 41 Hosbrook.
Casey Peter, blacksmith, bds at W. McVen, s Cal.
Cashman Michael, laborer, 129 e N. Y.
Cashon Michael, laborer, res Yoming.
Casselbaum John, grocer, 153 Mass. ave., res same.
Casselberry Miss Mary, dressmaker, res 181 Mass. ave.
Cathcart Andrew, res 162 s New Jersey.
Catlin Ebenezer, house mover, res w Market.
Catterson Abraham, Night Police, res 56 s Noble.
Catterson Cyrus W., contractor, res 176 e South.
Catterson Elizabeth, (widow), seamstress, res 127 Peru R R.
Catterson James B., Capt Co F, 79th Ind Regt., res 241 Ind. ave.
Catterson Sarah, (wid. James Catterson,) res 197 Ind. ave.

CAVIN JOHN, Mayor, office, Glenn's Block. bds Bates House.
Cavin Stephen D., carpenter, bds Siever Bruder's Hotel.
Cavinaugh Patrick, laborer, P. O., bds at Mrs. S. Kelly's.
Caylor Anthony, peddler, res 158 n Noble.
Caylor Frank, hackman, res 74 n Noble.
Caylor George, carpenter, res Ash.
Caylor Jacob, horse dealer, res e Wash.
Caylor John, hackman, res 134 n Noble.
Caylor Otho, res 125 Peru R R.
Caylor Sanford, saloon, res 220 e Wash.
Cayzer James, barkeeper Atlantic Saloon, bds Palmer House.
Ceipperle John, boot and shoemaker, res w Indpls.
Ceiter Casemere, cooper, res 27 w Noble.
Celschlager J. Benjamin, laborer, res St. Clair, bet Noble and R R.
Central Engine House, Benton, bet Wash. and Meek.
Ceicrest Henry A., collector for Journal, res 15 e Ohio.
CHADWICK LEVI W., clerk, res 59 w New York.
Chain Zenis, laborer, 15 s Ala.
Chambers Abram, eng. res 79 Mass. ave.
Champion Wm., pressman H. H. Dodd & Co., 165 s Tenn.
Chandler George, printer, res 72 w Md.
Chandler Henry C., (Chandler & Co.,) res 258 w Wash.
Chandler H. C. & Co., (Henry C. Chandler, George Merrit), Job printers and engravers, 8 e Wash.
Chandler Samuel, deputy clerk, U. S. Court, bds Pyle House.
Chandler Thomas E., (Wiggins & Chandler), res 258 w Wash.
Chandler Wm. G., pattern maker, bds 258 w Wash.
Chaple Christian, cor Ohio and Del.
Chapman Albert F., bar keeper at saloon, 32 s Ill.
Chapman C. R, lightning rod maker, res w Indpls.
Chapman Fred. B., harness maker, 34 w Wash., bds n Ill.
Chapman George H., Major 3d Cav U S A, res 37 w Ohio.
Chapman John, wagon maker, Mt. Jackson.
Chapman Joseph F., foreman A. J. Hinesley & Co., 34 w Wash., res n Ill.
CHAPMAN SAMUEL, Auctioneer, res 19 Bates. See card.
Chapman Thomas, carpenter, res James, bet St. Clair and Ind. ave.
Charles Daniel, res 11 e Mich.
Charles Moore, hostler, bds Kesler saloon n Ill.
Charles John P., R R agt, 6 New & Talbots building, res 106 n Meridian.

Charles Joseph B., bar keeper Ohio House, bds same.

CHARLES SALOON, HENRY KOLLMAN, PROPRIETOR, 73 s Ill. See card.

Charles Thomas, cab driver, res 65 s Noble.

Chase Andrew E., mail agent, L. & Chicago R. R., res 99 Vir. ave.

Chase David H., (Chase & Dawes,) res 20 n Del.

Chase James F., conductor, Bellefontaine railroad, res 237 s Del.

Chase Joseph W., conductor Bellefontaine railroad, res 223 s Del.

CHASE & DAWES, (David H. Chase, & Adelbert Dawes,) NEW YORK BOOT AND SHOE STORE, Glenns' block, e Wash.

Cheek Edmund C., res Daughertyville Bluff road.

Cherry Andrew, carpenter, bds 60 e N. York.

Cherry Mrs. Elizabeth, (wid. Thomas Cherry,) bds 34 e Market.

Chester G. W., moulder, bds Ray House, s Del.

CHICAGO HOUSE, HENRY KOLLMAN, PROPRIETOR, 73 and 75 s Ill.

Childers John, herdsman, cor Pine and Fletcher's ave.

Childers John P., pump-maker, 68 s Del., res 151 s Noble.

Childers Levina, res 19 Willard.

Chilly Horace, (deaf and dumb,) res 152 n. Penn.

Chipman Leander, res 128 n Tenn.

Chittenden Mrs. Ruth, (wid.,) res North, bet Liberty and Noble.

Chollete Jacob H., grain buyer, res 22 n Miss.

Christ Church, Episcopalian, n e cor Circle and Meridian.

Christian Church, cor N. York and Ala.

Christy Albert, grocer, 24 w Louisiana, res 55 w South.

Church Joseph A., miller, res 35 s Noble.

Church Nelson R., Marble Hall saloon, 32 s Ill.

Church Robert, clerk, New York store, bds Macy House.

Churchman Frank, clerk, Fletcher's bank, res 56 n Ala.

Churchman Mrs. Lou, dress making, 8 e Wash., res w Market.

CHURCHMAN WM. H., SUPERINTENDENT BLIND ASYLUM, res same.

CHURCHMAN W. H., PRESIDENT OF INSTITUTE FOR THE BLIND, res same.

Churchwell Robert, mail deliverer, P. O., bds Mrs. Hues.

Chwark Louis, bar tender, 80 w Wash., res 184 s Del.

City Brewery, Charles Yaiger, proprietor, 187 s Penn., res in rear.

City Council Chamber, 4 on third floor, Glenns' block.

City Police Office, 1 second floor, Glenns' block.

CLAFLIN C. C. AGENT FOR WHEELER & WILSON'S SEWING MACHINES, 19 w Wash., res 60 e Ohio.

Claery Patrick, in Bates House, res cor Mich. and Powell.

Clark Alfred L., res 79 n Meridian.

Clark Alson, painter, bds 72 s Ill.

Clark David R., (Cox & Clark,) res 72 n Ala.

Clark Edmund, agent Ind. & Ill. R. R., 24 e Wash., res 36 n Del.

CLARK F. D., PHYSICIAN, 24½ e Wash.

Clark H. C., Adams express, bds Oriental House.

Clark Hampton in engine house No. 1, res 139 w N. York.

Clark Hugh, wagon maker, res 35 St. Clair.

Clark John, works in Capital Mills, res w Market.

Clark John, teamster, res 12 Grier.

Clark J., telegraph repairer, bds Ray House, s Del.

Clark Josiah, student at Bryant's commercial college.

Clark Miss Lizzie, dress maker, bds 36 n Ill.

Clark Maria, wid. James B. Clark, dress maker, res 95 w Ver.

CLARK MIKE, SALOON KEEPER, 67 s Ill., res 12 w Georgia.

CLARK PHILO, MINERAL WATER, 109 e Wash., res Louisville, Ky.

Clark Rev. J. N., baptist, res 127 n Pennsylvania.

Clark Reuben O., carpenter, res 198 w Mich.

Clark Stephen A., carriage trimmer, res 96 n East.

CLARK WM. F., AGENT MERCHANTS DISPATCH, off. cor Vir. ave. and Ala., bds Kinder House.

Clarke Alfred D., clerk, 18 w Wash., res 67 n Miss.

Clarke Edward (M. G. Clarke & Co., publishers of The Witness,) Odd Fellows' Hall, res 151 n Penn.

Clarke John N., book-keeper, Witness, Odd Fellows' Hall, res Pratt.

Clarke Minor G., (Clarke & Co., res Chicago, Ill.

Clarke M. G. & Co., (M. G. Clarke and Edward Clarke,) publishers of The Witness, Odd Fellows' Hall.

Clarke Wm. (Clarke & Co.,) res Chicago, Ill.

Claufy Conrad, laborer, res Huron.

Clawson Alford, blacksmith, bds 58 n Ver.

Clay Hilliary, receiver at Sinking Fund, off. s Penn., res same.

Clayton Charles, laborer, res 3 Willard.

Cleaver John, brickmason, res 197 n Noble.

Clem Aaron, (A. Clem & Brother,) res cor Mass ave., and Ala.

Clem W. Frank, (A. Clem & Brother,) res 110 n Ala.

Clem A. & Brother, (Aaron Clem, and W. Frank Clem,) grocery dealers, cor Mass. ave. and n Ala.

Clemments John, carpenter, res s Ill.

Clifton Joseph B., laborer, res 174 n N. J.

Clines Elias, res s West.

Clines Isaac, teamster, res s Mo. and s of South.

Clines Peter, teamster, res s West.

Clinton Wharton R., res 29 n Noble.

Close Mrs. Elizabeth, (col) res 183 Mass. ave.

Close Wm. H., (col) barber, 49 Mass. ave. res 155½ n East.

Clump Frederick, brewer, res 135 w Md.

Coats Bayless, bds Littles Hotel.

Coburn Col. John, 33d reg. Ind. vol., res 60 e Ohio.

Coburn Mrs. Ann, res 185 n East.

Coburn Henry, (Coburn & Jones,) res 37 e Michigan.

Coburn Isaac, silver plater, res 114 n Noble.

Coburn James F., machinest, res 184 Vir. ave.

Coburn Sarah, (wid. Henry P. Coburn,) res 47 n Del.

Coburn & Jones, (Henry Coburn and Wm. H. Jones,) lumber, cor Del. and Mass. ave.

Cochran Wm. A., carpenter, res s Ill. near Pogues Run.

Cochoran Thomas, laborer, res w Indianapolis.

Coen John, boarding house, 107 s Tenn.

Coffield Joseph, laborer, bds 102 n Penn.

Coffin B. & Co., (Barnabas Coffin, W. S. T. Morton, and Stephen Coffin,) pork packers and commission merchants, 14 s Meridian.

Coffman Adam, laborer, res 17 Willard.

Coffman Jacob, carpenter, res 171 s N. Jersey.

Coffman Samuel, carpenter, res 192 n Miss.

Colahan James P., carpenter, res 2 second floor, Blake building.

Coleman Jacob, rag buyer, res 201 s Del.

Cole John, farmer, res w Indianapolis.

Cole Joseph, bricklayer, res 69 St. Mary.

Cole Theodore, works at rolling mill, bds 81 w South.

Coleman Benj. F., printer, bds Mrs. Igo, Md.

Coleman Charles, laborer, res Bluff road Doughertyville.

Coleman Henry, laborer, res 66 Ind. ave.

Coleman Wm., cigar maker, res 133 n Miss.

Colemann Herman, butcher, res 122 e Mich.

Colerick John, (Colerick & Jordan,) bds 4 e Vermont.

COLERICK & JORDAN, (John Colerick and Lewis Jordan,) ATTORNEYS AT LAW, 18 e Wash.

Colesby Henry, (col) white washer, res n Mo.

Colestock Ephriam, carpenter, res 150 n Ill.

Colestock Henry, res 22 w North.

Colestock John A., bds 22 w North.

Collins E. J., 2d Lieut., 26 reg. Ind. Vol., res 148 e N. York.

Collett Wm., student at Bryant's commercial college, bds 48 w Ver.

Colley Isaac J., detective police, 46 w Md.

Colley Sims A., attorney at law, res 161 n N. Jersey.

Collins Abner, farmer, res Mich. road.

Collins Cornelius, laborer, res 180 Ala.

Collins John, carpenter, res 37 s Ill.

Collins, Nathaniel, painter, res 204 s Del.

Colly Shallis, U. S. Arsenal, res 125 Ala.

Colman Christina, (wid) res cor McCarthy and Bluff road.

Colman Frederick, stone mason, res 64 Huron.

Comegys Levi, carpenter, res 62 n Del.

Compton Thomas W., carpenter, res 12 Ellen.

Conaty James B., bonnet bleacher, 22 s Ill., up stairs.

Condell James, blacksmith, alley, e of East.

Conklin Israel, conductor, T. H. R. R., res 98 s Penn.

Conklin Henry N., (Conklin & Cook,) bds n Tenn.

CONKLIN & COOK, (H. N. Conklin and J. V. Cook,) WHOLESALE DEALERS IN FOREIGN AND DOMESTIC LIQUORS, 140 w Wash.

Connelly George, boiler maker, res 34 e Georgia.

CONNER A. H., P. M., bds Macy House.

Conner Daniel, laborer, res 25 Peru R. R

Conner Eliza L., (wid) boarding house, 159 Vir. ave.

Connor Mrs. Mary, res Wabash, bet N. Jersey and East.

Conner Oliver I., mailing clerk, P. O., bds 85 n N. Jersey.

Conner Patrick, laborer, bds Peru track, bet Ohio and N. York.

Connett Matthew, engineer, res 168 s Ill.

Connor Michael, U. S. service, res 177 s East.

Converse Joel, soldier, 70th reg., res 157 n East.

Conray Patrick, tailor, res 9 s West.

Constant F. M., M. D., agent A. D. Streight, bds Palmer House.

Conway Isaac, baker, 11 n Penn , res 254 s Del.

Conway John, saloon, res Md., near Ala.

Cordray Noble, laborer, res 89 s Tenn.

Cook Alfred, carriage trimmer, res 16 Ala.

Cook Baldwin, (Thayer & Cook,) res 168 n Del.

Cook Frank, laborer, res 11 Ellen.

Cook Frederick, driver Adams Express Co., bds Spencer House.

Cook Frederic, laborer, res 86 s Liberty.

Cook Henry brickmason, bds 20 Chatham.

Cook Henry, car greaser, res 45 e Ga.

Cook James A., student at Bryant's commercial college, bds Mrs. Julia Cook.

Cook Jesse S , carpenter, res 195 Indiana ave.

Cook John V., (Conklin & Cook,) res n Tenn.

Cook John, machinest, bds 20 Chatham.

Cook John M., student at Bryant's commercial college, bds Mrs. Julia Cook.

Cook Julia, (wid. James Cook,) res 59 w N. York.

Cook Mrs. Mary, (wid.,) res 20 Chatham.

Cook Moses R , painter, shop cor Meridian and Md., res 75 w Md.

COOK & CO., (W. Cook and J. Cook,) DRY GOODS AND GROCERIES, 189 e Wash. See card.

Cooke Miss Jane. res 22 Ind. ave.

Cooly Charles, res 87 Davidson.

Cooley John W., carpenter, res w Indianapolis.

Coouey Dennis laborer, res 9 n East.

Coons Charles N., western meat market, res 107 w Mich.

Coous Mrs Elizabeth, res 83 Davidson.

Cooper Catherine, (wid) res 95 McCarthy.

Cooper Charles A., jewelry, 9 e Wash., res 155 Vir ave.

Cooper John, machinest, Washington foundry, res 229 s Del.

Cooper Joshua, shoemaker, res 81 n Ala.

Coover David M., clerk, 24 w Wash., bds Mrs. Carlton.

Copeland Gideon, miller, res w Indianapolis.

Copeland James, carpenter, bds 179 e Market.

Copeland Jesse, (Eden & Copeland,) res 128 e Market.

Copeland John W., milliner, res 105 s N. Jersey.

Copeland Joshua W., bonnet bleaching, 7 s Meridian. res 105 s N. Jersey.

Copeland Samuel P., bonnet presser, res 101 n Miss.

CORBALEY S. B. BOOK-KEEPER, Spiegel, Thoms & Co , res 40 e St. Clair.

Corbly Samuel book-keeper, res 168 n Del.

Cord M. W. L., bds Littles Hotel.

Cordray William, laborer, res old fair ground.

Corliss Dr. Corydon T., Homœopathist, 288 e Market, res 106 n. Penn.

Corn Martin, tanner, res 171 n New Jersey.

Cornelius C., plasterer, res 166 s Ala.

Cornelius Mrs. D., (wid.) res 237 Ala.

Cornelius Ewd., lab., res 237 Ala.

Cosler David, carpenter, res 86 Davidson.

Cosley Richard M., carpenter, res 183 n East.

COSTELLO JOHN, NEWS STAND, near Postoffice, res South, near Mud. depot.

Costello John, finisher in Dumont & Sinker's Foundry, res w Market.

Coster Henry, teamster, 128 e St. Clair.

Costigan Francis, architect, res Oriental House.

Costigan Frank, res 107 Va. ave.

Costigan Theodore I., student at law, bds Oriental House.

Costello John, machinist Sinker & Vance, res w Market.

Costello John, lab, res 33 e South.

Cotton John R., bds 161 e Market.

Cottman John A., Lieut. 19th Ind. Vol., res 159, w Vermont.

Cottrell Thomas, (Cottrell & Knight), gasfitter and coppersmith, res 102 s New Jersey.

Cottrell & Knight, (Thos. Cottrell, John Knight), coppersmiths, 94 s Del.

Coughlin William, (Merritt & Coughlen,) res 154 w New York.

Cowgill William, retired, res 186 Va. av.

Coulon Charles, junr., student Bryant's College, res Cumberland, bet Ala. and Del.

Coulon Charles, atty. at law, 97 e Wash., res Cumberland, bet Ala. and Del.

Council John F., (Hogshire & Co.), res 80 w Georgia.

Courtney William, teamster, res 23 e McCarthy.

Cousins Joseph, horse buyer, w Wash., near Canal.

Covert Isaac. silver plater, 8 w Wash., res 114 n Noble.

Covert William T., plater, res 23 Union.

Covington Susan, (wid. Wm. Covington,) res 142 w Market.

Cowgill Stephen, farmer, res 186 Va. ave.

Cox Andrew J., (Cox & Clark), res 145 n New Jersey.

Cox Bosley, lab, Mt. Jackson.

Cox David, tinner, 12 Pearl, res 43 s Meridian.

Cox Elisha, medical student. 52 s Ill.

Cox Henry, carpenter, res 124 w Wash.

Cox Jacob, artist, res 42 s Meridian.

Cox Mrs. Jane, res w Indpls.

Veranda Saloon,

No. 36 Louisiana Street,

OPPOSITE UNION DEPOT,

INDIANAPOLIS, IND.

JOHN BUSSY, PROPRIETOR.

CHOICE WINES AND LIQUORS.

Billiard Table for the Convenience of our Customers.

HOWARD & DAVIES,

PHOTOGRAPHERS,

OVER HUME & LORD'S (FORMERLY FLETCHER'S) STORE,

No. 26 and 28 West Washington Street,

INDIANAPOLIS, IND.

All kinds of Photographic Pictures executed in the best style of the Art. Twenty Dollars in Premiums were awarded them at the State Fair of 1862.

Mr. B. S. HAYES,

The well-known Artist has his Studio connected with this Gallery, and gives their work the preference, thus enabling them to finish their Colored Work promptly and satisfactorily.

Cox Jefferson R., carpenter, res 75 e Ga.

COX, LORD & PECK, Stove and machine foundry, Del., bet Cin. and Cen. depots.

Cox Morgan, clerk M. H. Good's, bds Oriental.

Cox Mrs. Sophia, (wid. Nathaniel Cox,) res 148 w Market.

Cox William C., (Tomlinson & Cox), res 40 w Ohio.

Cox & Clark, (Andrew Cox, Daniel R. Clark), Metropolitan Photograph Gallery, 43½, e Wash.

Coyner Martin, res 209 e St. Clair.

Cozin, William, (col), plasterer, res 151 w Wash.

Craft Frost, Branch Bank, bds Towsey's.

Craft John, furnace builder, bds Union House.

Craft William H., watchmaker and jeweller, Odd Fellow's Hall, res 77 n Ala.

Craglow Jacob, carpenter, res 40 St. Clair.

Craig William M., principal teacher in 8th ward school house, res 109 s Ala.

Craft Harry, watchmaker, 2 Odd Fellow's Hall, res 79 n Ala.

Craft Smith, blacksmith, res 210 Ind. ave.

Crane Dennis, porter Farmers' Hotel, res 202 s Tenn.

Craighead Mrs. Mary I., res 18 w Md.

Craighead D. D., clerk, bds 18 w Md.

Crail Silvester, soldier, res w Indpls.

Cramer Henry, butcher, res 71 St. Mary.

Cramer Samuel A., dept Sheriff, C H, bds William J. H. Robinson.

Cramer William, cabinet maker, res 178 Ala.

Crammer Philip, tailor, works 38 s Ill, bds at California House.

Crane Franklin, artist, 17 w Wash.

CRANE & SONS, Photographers and Ambrotypists, 19 w Wash, res in same building.

Crane Worth, (Crane & Sons), 17 w Wash, in Daguerreian rooms, res same.

Craney Lewis M., clerk, (Heidlinger & Co.,) bds Pyle House.

Craney Clark, clerk, Davis' hat store, bds Pyle House.

Crapo R. P., Ambrotype stock dealer, 17 w Wash, bds Pyle House.

Crawford Eli, moulder, res 250 s Del.

Crawford James, res 65 s Penn.

Crawford James P., moulder at Sinker & Vance's, bds 65 s Penn.

Crawson David, head cook Oriental house, bds same.

Craycraft Wm., student at Bryant's Commercial College, bds cor Ill and Ga.

Craft Henry, res Bluff road, Doughertyville.

Crale George, printer, Sentinel office, bds 119 w Wash.

Crappa Rowand F.,teamster, res 11 Huron.

Crink Henry, barber, res 125 s Ill.

Criyui M., merchant tailor, res 173 e O'

Crookshank Robert, carpenter, bds 117 n Missouri.

Cropper Alexander, hack driver, res 11 Huron.

Crops Moses, bricklayer, bds Un. House.

Cropsey James E., cabinet maker, res 99 w Ohio.

Crosby Albert, driver Adams' Express, res 70 w Vt.

Crosby Arthur T., driver American Express, bds 111 n East.

Crosby Elizabeth, (wid) seamstress, alley, near East.

Crossland Jacob A., wholesale dry goods, 75 and 77 w Wash, res 224 n Ill.

Crossley Thomas B., saddler, 20 w Wash, bds Patterson House.

Crotcher Simon, lab, bds 1 sq s Lawrenceburgh machine shop.

Crouch George, horse dealer, res 143 Va.

Crowley William, tongsman rolling mill, res 71 Mad ave.

Crozier George, watchman N. Y. store, res 89 n Meridian.

Crozier George, clerk N. Y. store res 89 n Meridian.

Crum John, brass foundry, res 129 Virginia ave.

Cruse John P., brick mason, cor Ill. and Maryland.

Crystal Palace Saloon, Edward Beck, proprietor, 44 w Wash.

Culley Wm. shoemaker, res 119 s Tenn.

Cullum Eberle, printer, res St. Clair.

Cullum Milton H., (Love & Cullum,) bds Macy House.

Cully Daniel B., bookkeeper, res 156 n Penn.

Cully David V., President Board School Trustees, res 13 e Ohio.

Cully Wm., bds 119 s Tenn.

Culver Elihu, res 84 n Tenn.

Cumerford Martin V. B., salesman, 40 w Wash., bds. 39 w Mich.

Cumins Lewis, barber, (col.,) res Michigan road.

Curren John, laborer, res 127 e New York.

Currens Henry, (Lines & Currens,) res 65 s Ill.

Currens Patrick, laborer, res 6 Huron.

Curry James H., barber, (col.) 50 e Wash, bds Johnson's Saloon.

Cursey Oliver, carpenter, res 303 s East.

Curtis Andrew, Justice of the Peace, office 39 e Wash., res 11 Ft. Wayne ave.

Curtis Charles, engineer Marion engine house, res 56 n Del.

Curtis Joseph, (col) cook, res 101 w North.

Curtis Truman M., engineer, res 2 Water.

Curtis Walter, driver at Marion engine house, bds 50 n Del.

Curzon Joseph, architect, (Journal Building,) res 228 n Ill.

Cussan Garret, peddler, res 153 w Mich.

2

Cusick John, grocer, res 43 s West.
Cuykendall Warren A., engineer on I. &
C. R. R., res 100 e Louisiana.

D

Daggett William, tea store, 22 s Meridian,
bds cor Penn and Md.
Dahl Henry, shoemaker, 39 w Wash., res
Montgomery.
Dailey John, railroader, res w St. Clair.
Dailey Nathaniel H., saddler, 34 w Wash.,
res Huron.
Daily Condy, huckster, res 144 n Liberty.
Daily Eugene, lab, res 217 s Del.
Daily Miss Jennie, res cor Market and
New Jersey.
Daily John, lab, bds 16 e Ga.
Daily N. H., saddler, res 42 e La.
Daily William, res 153 n Liberty.
Dain Robert C., paper hanger, res 106 n
East.
Dain Thos., night watchman at Arsenal,
res 18 Mich. road.
Dame Jason, marble shop, 67 e Wash, res
70 s East.
Dana Mrs., (wid. Amos Dana,) res 87 n
Del.
Danahan Mrs. Mary,washer, res e Market.
Danforth Albert J.,(Danforth & Simpson,)
res 112 n Penn.
Danforth & Simpson, (Albert J. Danforth,
Franklin F. Simpson,) grocers, Odd
Fellow's Hall, 3 and 5 n Penn.
Daniels Caroline T., (wid. Odid Daniels,)
res 60 n Del.
Daniels S. P., tailor, res 63 s N. Jersey.
Darnell William W., Lt. Col. 11th Regt.
Ind. Vol., res 71 n Del.
Daraugh William, tailor, res 30 s West.
Darby John, grocer, cor Md. and Meri-
dian, res 189 s Ala.
Darr George, lab, res 61 n West.
Darrow Benjamin C., (M. Hunter & Co.,)
res 146 n Ill.
Darrow George, laborer, bds 67 n East.
Darrow James, sutler post, Camp Morton,
res 67 n East.
Daugherty J. F., delivery clerk, P. O., res
61 Mass ave.
Daumont H. & Co., clock dealers, 17 n
Penn., res Ft. Wayne ave.
Daumont Peter A., clocks, watches and
jewelry, 9 s Meridian, res same.
Davelin James H., (L. & D.,) res Chicago.
Davenport Andrew, brakesman on T. & R.
R. R., res 29 Henry.
Davenport John, engineer Blake, Helwig
& Co., res 67 n West.
Davenport Joel, book keeper, bds 29
Henry.
David Mrs. Ann, seamstress, res 20 n
East.
David George, book keeper, bds 20 n East.
David Thomas, butcher, 83 South.

Davids John, (Riggs & Davids,) res 83
e South.
Davidson John, collector for Journal Co.,
res 85 Davidson.
Davis Thomas J., (Howard & Davis,) bds
Macy House.
Davis Ben., Roadmaster T. H. &. R. R. R.,
res 51 La.
Davis Bennet, laborer, bds 135 n Ala.
DAVIS CHARLES B., Insurance agent,
Odd Fellow's Hall, res 137 n Penn.
Davis Edward, constable, res 129 n Penn.
Davis Edwin A., (Davis & Bowles,) bds
Bates House.
Davis E. J, boot and shoe store, 187 c
Washington, res same.
Davis E. W., (Deitz & Davis,) bds Wash.
Hall, 78 and 80 w Wash.
Davis Flemming, boiler maker, res 124
s Noble.
Davis Frederick W., Teller in Indianapo-
lis Branch Banking Co., bds cor Meri-
dian and Ohio.
Davis George D., blacksmith, bds 179 e
Market.
Davis Harvey, clerk, (Wood & Davis,)
bds 156 e New York.
Davis Ira, res 70 n Meridian.
DAVIS ISAAC, dealer in hats, caps,
straw goods, and ladies' furs, 15 n
Penn., bds Bates House.
Davis I. S., Express messenger, bds at
Palmer House.
Davis James H., (Davis & Co.,) res Cin-
cinnati, Ohio.
Davis James, shoemaker, Orient.
Davis James, resident farmer, res 135 n
Ala.
Davis Jenny, boarding house, 66 Meek.
Davis John I., painter, bds 129 e Market.
Davis Joseph W., (Davis & Co.,) res 129
Vir. ave.
Davis Levi, (Wood & Davis,) res 156 e N.
York.
Davis Mrs. Maria, (wid) tailoress, res 79
e N. Jersey.
Davis Milton, farmer, res cor McCarthy
and Union.
Davis Milton, baker, 11 n Penn.
Davis Newton, baker, res. 17 Vir. ave.
Davis Robert R., clerk, M. H. Goode, bds
Oriental House.
Davis Rollin, hack driver, res 150 n Del-
aware.
Davis Rowen, painter, bds 129 e Mar-
ket.
Davis Smith, painter, 129 e Market.
Davis Wells, engineer, I. C. R. R., res 34
Davidson.
Davis Wesley, carriage trimmer, res
Penn., out corporation.
Davis Wm. M., (Jones, Hess & Davis,)
res 114 n Penn.
Davis Wm., soldier, 26th reg. Ind. vol.,
res 221 n Noble.

DAVIS & BOWLES, (Edwin A. Davis and Thomas H. Bowles,) ATTORNEYS AT LAW, 3 New & Talbot's block.

Davis & Co., (Joseph W. Davis and James H. Davis,) brass foundry, s Del., near railroad track.

Dawes Adelbert, (Chase & Dawes,) bds Palmer House.

Dawson Daniel, blacksmith, res 43 e McCarthy.

Dawson Rev. George, pastor Christian church, res Mich. road.

Dawson George, tinner, res 14 Mich. road.

Dawson Riley, laborer, res 72 St. Clair.

Dawson Wm., driver, Marion engine, res 50 n Del.

Day Frank, student at Bryant's commercial college.

DAY REV. HENRY, PASTOR BAPTIST CHURCH, res 60 n Penn.

Day Jerry, butcher, res cor Mass. ave. and East.

Day Joel H., carpenter, res 55 s Noble.

Day Leroy, student at Bryants commercial college.

Day Peter, laborer, res 97 McCarthy.

Day Wm. W., butcher, res 198 e St. Clair.

Dearbach C., laborer, res 129 McCarthy.

Deaver Geo. W., steward, soldier's home, res 140 n Ill.

Debbee Iria, moulder, res 144 s Ill.

Debor John, laborer, res 116 s Noble.

Deboice Albert, (col) barber, bds Johnson saloon.

Decher Conrad, blacksmith, res 146 Davidson.

Deford Melville, rail roader, bds 113 Mass. ave.

Deford Mrs. Wm. R., res 113 Mass. ave.

Deforest Daniel, laborer, res 124 e Mich.

Dehart Austin, teamster, res old fair ground.

De Hart Tallison, watchmaker, 18 e Market, bds same

Deirr Philip, laborer, res 135 n Davidson.

Deitz Peter, brewery, res Blake, n North.

Delane Peter, laborer, bds Ray House, s Del.

Delaney W., laborer, res Sinker.

Delcomp Christian, U. S. service, res 150 s N. Jersey.

Deleany Michael, laborer, res 33 e South.

Deleany Patrick, bds n West.

Delany Michael, rail roader, res 73 n Noble.

Deller Frederick, painter, res 102 n Noble.

Delzell Hugh, (Delzell & Todd,) bds Littles Hotel,

Delzell Samuel, (Delzell & Jones,) res 91 n Ala.

Delzell & Jones, (Samuel Delzell and Barton D. Jones,) real estate agents, off. 37 e Wash., up stairs.

DELZELL & TODD, (Hugh Delzell and Samuel A. Todd,) LIVERY STABLE, Md., bet Penn. and Meridian.

Demmier Christian, contractor, res 129 s Ill.

Demmy Martin, harness maker, 20 w Wash.

Demoss Leander, saddler, res 13 w St. Clair.

De Mott Wm. H., teacher deaf and dumb asylum, e Indianapolis.

Dempsey Robert, machinest, bds 229 w Wash.

Demunn George, railroader, res 12 Bates.

Deneen Miss Amanda, res 157 n Ala.

Denk Andrew, vinegar factory, res 135 Ind. ave.

Denine Wm. tailor, res 53 w South.

Denneen James M., salesman, res 157 n Ala.

Denning Henry, laborer, res 204 Ind. ave.

Dennis Charles W., clerk, Vickers, bds Mrs. Dennis, East.

Dennis Peter, watchman, arsenal, res 13 s Del.

Dennis James M., photograph painter, 83 e Wash., bds Oriental House.

Denniston Elizabeth A., (wid) dress maker, res 73 n. Mo.

Denny Andrew, city expressman, res 173 n Noble.

Denny Andrew, porter, G. F. Adams, res n Noble.

Denser Mrs. Tracy, (wid) bds 158 n N. Jersey.

Dint George, clerk, New York store, bds Macy House.

Deppe Hartwig, school teacher, German Presbyterian school, res country.

Deppel L., cabinet maker, Wyoming.

DePuy George G., salesman, 3 Odd Fellow's Hall, res 22 Md.

DePuy George, clerk, bds 26 w Md.

Derregh William, cutter, Moritz, Bro., & Co., res cor West and Md.

Derringer Simeon, plasterer, res 17 e Georgia.

Desdler Joseph, saloon, 168 e Wash., res 5 n N. Jersey.

Desheel Maston, soldier, 3d cavalry, res 159 n Noble.

Deshler John, cabinet maker, bds 21 s Meridian.

Deshong Hiram, carpenter, res 139 e Ga.

Despa Ernest, painter, [res 3 Laukabee.

Dessar David, (Dessar & Bro's,) res 135 n Ill.

Dessar Joseph B., (Dessar & Bro's,) res Maysville, Ky.

Dessar & Bro's, (Adolphus Dessar, David Dessar and Joseph B. Dessar,) wholesale and retail merchant tailors, 4 e Wash.

Dessar Adolphus, (Dessar & Bro's,) res 135 n Ill.

Devenish, Cali, gas fitter, bds Mrs Skelly, s Del.
Devennish John J., moulder, res 140 e N. York.
Devenish Samuel R., gas fitter, bds 139 c South.
Devenish Sol., tailor, res 139 South.
Devoll Mrs. Sarah, (wid) res 112 Vir. ave.
DeWatt Mathias, porter, Holland & Son, res 71 n Davidson.
DeWare James, machinest, res 172 e Ohio.
Dickens Ephriam, res cor Mich. and West.
Dickert Jacob, works in arsenal, res 128 n West.
Dicky James P., carpenter, res e Daugherty.
Dickinson James L., M. D., res last house s East.
Dickinson John C., farmer, res 109 s Ala.
Dickman Charles, tailor, bds 64 Mass. ave.
Dickman Francis, renovator, 19 s Meridian, res same.
Dickman Frederick, carpenter, res 41 n East.
Dickson Carlos, book-keeper, Hume, Lord & Co., bds 87 n Penn.
Dickson James, (Butsch & Dickson,) res Vernon, Jennings Co., Ind.
Dickson George, (col) carpenter, res 123 w Ohio.
Dickson James H., (col) barber, under Palmer House, res 123 e Ohio.
Dickson Wm. C., student at Bryant's commercial college.
Diesler John, proprietor Jefferson House, 31 e South.
Dieter Ernst, shoemaker, res 133 Peru R. R.
Dietrichs Margaret, milliner, 63 e Wash., res in rear.
Dietrichs Wm., distributing clerk, P. O., res 63 e Wash.
Dietz George, (Dietz & Davis,) bds Washington Hall, 78 and 80 w Wash.
Dietz Ferdinand, (Street & Dietz,) res Market, bet Noble and Davidson.
DIETZ & DAVIS, (George Dietz and E. W. Davis,) WASHINGTON HALL, 78 and 80 w Wash.
Dietzel Adam, city expressman, res 77 Davidson.
Dill H. Clay, clerk, res 15 e North.
Dill Ezekiel B., grocery, cor Ala. and North, res St. Joseph, bet Ala. and N. Jersey.
Dill John P., printer, res 15 e North.
Dill James, laborer, res 15 e North,
Dillon Mrs. Sarah, res Willard, near rolling mill.
Dippel Henry, carpenter, res 101 e South.
Dipple Henry, clerk, National saloon, bds same place.

Dipple John, carpenter, res 37 n Noble.
Dipple Joseph, woodsawyer, res 111 n Noble.
Dilley John, engineer, res Norwood.
Dipple Peter, city expressman, res 107 n Noble.
Ditzler Christian H., tailor, res 213 Ind. ave.
Diver Charles, laborer, res 44 Mass. ave.
Diver James, grocery, 42 Mass ave.
Dixon I. C., physician, bds Palmer House.
Dixon James W., laborer, res s Mo., s of South.
Doarr George, barkeeper, Spencer House, bds same.
Dobbins Clew, laborer, bds Washington House.
Dobson Catharine, (wid. Henry Dobson,) res 170 w Market.
Dodd Harrison H., (H. H., Dodd & Co.,) res 168 w N. York.
Dodd John, clerk, bds Ray House.
Dodd John W., res 127 n Ill.
DODD H. H. & CO., (H. H. Dodd, J. R. Appleton, C. P. Hutchins, and J. J. Parsons,) PRINTERS, BOOK BINDERS AND STEROTYPERS, 16½ e Wash.
Dodds Harry, conductor, Ind. Cen. R. R., bds Palmer House.
Dodson Joseph, soldier, 26th reg., res 192 e St. Clair.
Doeppo Louis, carpenter, res 159 n Noble.
Doer George, barkeeper, Spencer House, res 34 s Ill.
Dogget George, harness maker, res cor Huron and Noble.
Doggett Richard, boot and shoemaker, 5 Ind. ave., res cor Ver. and Tenn.
Doherty Charles, drayman, res 145 s Del.
DOHN PHILIP, FURNITURE STORE, 24 s Del., res same.
Dolis John, laborer, res 56 Hosbrook.
Dolton Thomas, saloon, res 178 s. Tenn.
Domon Emil P., grocer, 138 s Ill., bds California House, 136 s Ill.
Domon Jacob, grocer, 138 s Ill.
Donaldson Claiborne, (Donaldson & Carr,) res 222 n Ill.
DONALDSON & CARR,)Claiborne Donaldson and Rowland S. Carr,) DEALERS IN HATS, CAPS AND STRAW GOODS, 71 w Wash. See card.
Donalt Elizabeth, bds 12 Willard.
Donavan John, engineer, bds Littles Hotel.
Donavon Peter, laborer, res w Ind'apolis.
Donley Francis, laborer, res 22 Henry.
Donnan Barbary, (wid. David Donnan,) res 74 n Tenn.
Donough Daniel, clerk, I & C R R office, res 101 s N. Jersey.
Donovan Ephriam, soldier, res 184 n East
Donovan Harvey, soldier, res 184 n East.

Donovan James, laborer, res 194 w North.

Doran M. W. G., millwright, res cor Forest ave. and Pine.

Dorsch Mrs. Maria, res 21 Ky. ave.

Dorsey Nicholas J., physician, 48 n Penn., res same.

Dorsey Michael, cooper, res 11 w St. Clair.

Dorsey Thomas, laborer, res 104 n Miss.

Dottson J. H., physician, res w Ind'polis.

Doty David, (Doty & Lee.)

Doty John, teamster, res w Indianapolis.

Doty & Lee, (David Doty and Wm. Lee,) State House saloon, 95 w Wash.

Dougherty Andrew, res Bluff road, Doughertyville.

Dougherty Bernard, res Bluff road, Doughertyville.

Dougherty James, laborer, res 2 s Liberty.

Dougherty Michael, res Bluff road, Doughertyville.

Dougherty William, res Bluff road, Doughertyville.

Dougherty Zadock, physician, res Cal., bet Market and Wash.

Douglass Andrew, street paver, res Lou.

Douglass George W., bds 130 w N. York.

Douglass James G., book-binder, Journal building, bds 130 w N. York.

Douglass Maria, (wid. John Douglass,) res 130 w N. York.

Douglass Samuel M., baggage agent, Union depot, bds 130 w N. York.

Downey James E., proprietor gazette job printing office, res 38 e Market.

Downey M., marble yard, 127 e Wash., res same.

Downey Jno., stonecutter, res 11 e Georgia.

Downey Mrs. Melissa, res 43 n Penn.

Downing William, (col.) teamster, res 190 w North.

Doyel Elisha G. L., colier, res e St. Clair, bet Chatham and Noble.

Doyle George H., baker, 11 n Penn., bds Mr. Nutt's, e Maryland.

Doyle Lany, moulder Sinker & Vance, res 196 s Delaware.

Doyle Lawrence, shoemaker, res 196 s Delaware.

Doyle Stephen, railroader, res 234 Indiana ave.

Doxon Mrs. Mary M., res cor Oak and Vine.

Dræger Charles, watchmaker, res e Washington.

Drain George C., bds Little's Hotel.

Drake Edward B., (Drake & Merryman,) res 88 n Alabama.

Drake Robert H., bookbinder, bds 20 n Penn.

Drake & Merryman, (E. B. Drake and J. M. Merryman,) manufacturers of white lead and colors, 47 e South.

Draper Granville W., grocer, 32 n Ill., res 70 n Miss.

Draper Joseph F., clerk, 32 n Ill., res 31 Indiana ave.

Dreher Mathias, salesman, 70 e Wash., res 46 n Liberty.

Dresback C. H., Express agent, bds Oriental House.

Drew John A., carriagemaker, res 76 n Tenn.

DREW SAMUEL W., CARRIAGEMAKER, E. MARKET SQUARE, res 68 Mass. ave.

Driggs Nathaniel S., clerk, 22 w Wash., bds 102 n Ill.

Drinkout Wm., watchman in Terre Haute engine house, res 89 s New Jersey.

Driskell Mrs. Ellen, res Willard, near rolling mill.

Driskell Jeremiah, works at rolling mill, res Willard.

Drum George, U. S. service, res 11 s New Jersey.

Drum James, Qr. Master 9th Ind. Vol., res 144 n Penn.

Drum Robert, teamster, res 142 e New York.

Drum Wm., saloon keeper, res 238 s Ala.

Drum Wm. H., ten pin alley, 248 e Wash., res 238 s Ala.

Drumins Joseph, laborer, res 114 w Geor.

Duchene Charles, baker, 11 n Penn.

Ducker John B., 79th Reg. Ind. Vol., res rear of 184 e Wash.

Duffey John, tailor, res 30 s West.

Duffy James, laborer, res Huron.

Duffy James, laborer, 33 Ellsworth.

Duffy Michael, tailor, Keely's block, res Clinton.

Dugan Neal, laborer, bds 44 Mass. ave.

Dugan Thomas, French bootmaker, res 152 e North.

Duggins Richard, res 76 Ky. ave.

Duke Mrs. Catharine, res w Indpls.

Dukwaler Jacob, railroader, res e end Market.

Dumadah Frank, shoemaker, res 61 Bluff road.

Dummire Frederick, drayman, res 146 e Ohio.

Dumont Ebenezer, Congressman, res 60 n Alabama.

Dumont John J., res cor Louisiana and New Jersey.

Dull Charles C., carpenter, res 135 n West.

Dunbar Melzor, brickmason, res 178 s Penn.

Duncan John, brakesman, res 155 e New York.

Duncan Daniel, (Duncan & Co.,) res 104 n Meridian.

Duncan & Co., (Jacob Duncan and Daniel Duncan,) wholesale dealers in Bourbon whisky, brandy, wines and cigars, 28 s Illinois.

Duncan John S., delivery clerk, P. O., bds out city.

Duncan Robert B., attorney, 50 e Wash., res Ft. Wayne ave.

Duncan Robert P., deputy clerk, C. H., bds Robert B. Duncan.

Dunlap Mrs., (wid. Dr. Livingston Dunlap,) res 12 Virginia ave.

Dunlap James, artist, McOuat building, Kentucky ave.

Dunlap John W., M. D., bds Oriental H.

Dunlap Robert, laborer, res 86 Huron.

Dunleagh Charles, Adams' Express, res 35 s Meridian.

Dunlop John, retired, res 72 n Meridian.

DUNLOP JOHN S., INSURANCE AG'T, 7 n Meridian, res 114 n Penn.

Dunmire Anthony, drayman, res 40 Davidson.

Dunmire Christ., (Hebble & Co.,) City Hotel, res 77 and 79 s Illinois.

Dun John C., gasfitter and plumber, 24 Kentucky ave.

Dunn Edwin, clerk M. H. Good's, bds Bates House.

Dunn Jacob P., res 248 n Tenn.

Dunn Lizzie, Sisters of Mercy College, bds 45 e South.

Dunn T. J., flour peddler, res 92 n Ala.

Dunn William A., clerk, res 5 n Meridian.

Dunn Mrs. Wm. A. & Co., (Mrs. W. A. Dunn and Mrs. Sally A. France,) Milliners, 5 n Meridian.

Dumigan Sarah, (wid. Barna Dumigan,) res rear 38 n Alabama.

Dunning Robert P., paver, bds 27 Ind. ave.

Duprez Jno. Chas, student at Bryant's Commercial College, bds at Lafayette House.

Durham George W., brickmason, 142 e O.

Durie Henry, engineer, res 149 e Ohio.

Durnin W. J., clerk at Merchants' Despatch office, cor Virginia ave. and Ala.

Dury John, salesman Center Shoe Store, res 72 n East.

Dury William, U. S. Inspector, cor Louisiana and Meridian, bds Mrs. Tyler's, Virginia ave.

Dushaine Charles, confectioner, res 19 Peru railroad.

Duvall David, clerk at Roll & Smith's, res 113 n Illinois.

Duval Prior I., constable, res 260, Madison ave.

Duzan James, printer, res 132 e North.

Duzan William N., M. D., (Duzan and Parr,) res 250 n Tenn.

Dwight Giles, salesman, bds 51 e Ohio.

Dwyer Thomas, clerk Oriental Saloon, bds Pyle House.

Dye Byron E., at work's Mineral water factory, res 109 e Wash.

DYE JOHN T., ATTORNY AT LAW, Blackford's Building, cor Washington and Meridian, res 111 w South.

Dyer Miss Augusta, Music teacher Blind Asylum.

E

Eaesenmon Joseph, laborer, res Madison ave., corporation line.

Eagle John H., foreman Journal office, res 142 n Alabama.

Early Peter, works rolling mill, res s Meridian, bet McCarthy and Merrill.

Early P., U. S. service, res 178 s East.

East Street House, H. Hahn, proprietor, s East.

Eavick Catharine, (wid.) res Bluff road.

Ebert John, carpenter, shop 32 Ky ave., res 135 w South.

Eccles William, salesman, 26 and 28 w Washington, bds 71 n Tennessee.

Echols William, switchman I. P. and C. R. R., res Wabash, bet Lib. and Noble.

Eck Joseph, works at rolling mill, res 176 s Miss.

Eckhart William, clerk Moritz & Bros, bds Macy House.

Eddy Augustus, Post Chaplain, res 156 n Tennessee.

Eden Asa, brickmason, res 190 Va. ave.

Eden Carlton, (Eden & Copeland,) res 86 Ohio.

EDEN & COPELAND. (Carlton Eden and Jesse Copeland,) CARPENTERS AND JOINERS, 27 e Market.

Edgar James, res 47 n Delaware.

Edmonds Wm., (V. K. Hendricks & Co.,) res 85 n Meridian.

Edmonson Mrs. Laura A., (wid. Joseph E.,) bds 64 Mass. ave.

Edmunds William, salesman, 76 w Wash., res 85 n Meridian.

Edwards Edward, Bicking House, 53 s Illinois.

Edwards John, Messenger Telegraph Office.

Edwards Joseph F., (Ivens & Co.,) res 203 e St. Clair.

Edwards Lewis, clerk Bicking House.

Eerlking Frederic, laborer, res 73 Bluff road.

Egan Patrick, night watchman Lafayette depot, res 8 Michigan road.

Egner Franz, (Egner & Woocher,) bds Union Hall.

EGNER & WOOCHER, (Franz Egner & Ferdinand Woocher,) DRUGGISTS, 85 w Washington.

Ehrensperger Frank, porter Mayhew & Co, res Vermont, bet East and N. J.

Eiler Mrs. Margaret, (wid.) res 101 Peru railroad.

Elder Alex., clerk in P. O., res 98 n West.

Elder Eli A., chief clerk P. O., res 98 n West.

ELDER, HARKNESS & BINGHAM, (John R. Elder, John Harkness and Joseph J. Bingham,) PROPRIETORS OF INDIANA DAILY AND WEEKLY SENTINEL, 2 s Meridian.

Elder John R., (Elder, Harkness & Bingham,) res 78 n New Jersey.
Elder T. J., machinist Sinker & Vance, bds Knight's, e Georgia.
Elder William, res 118 n Alabama.
Eldridge Jacob, Real Estate agent, over City Grocery, w Washington, res 50 s Mississippi.
Elff Frank, barber, res 175 s New Jersey.
Ellenbergen Elias M., salesman, 2 Palmer House, bds Mason House.
Ellerby James, Veterinary Surgeon, office Wood & Foudray's livery stable, bds Pyle House.
Elliott Byron K., Attorney at Law, 24½ e Washington, res 16 California.
Elliott W. J., County Recorder, Court house.
ELLIOTT CALVIN A., WHOLESALE LIQUORS, 32 s Meridian, res 76 n Ill.
Elliott Jonathan, feed store, s East, res 31 n Noble.
ELLIOTT JOHN F., AGENT SINGER'S SEWING MACHINE, res 48 e Wash.
Elliott John H., barkeeper City Saloon, bds same.
Elliott Russel, bookkeeper, Boston Store, bds 126 n Pennsylvania.
Elliott Thomas B., dealer in flour and and produce, cor Ala. and R. R. track.
Elliott William J., agent Penn. Central R. R., res 89 e Ohio.
Elliott Jonathan, (Elliott & Lucky,) res 29 n Noble.
ELLIOTT & LUCKY, (Jonathan Elliott and George Lucky,) FLOUR AND FEED DEALERS, 19 s East.
Ellms Cornelius, engineer, res 119 e Ga.
Ellsworth Henry, attorney, res 88 n Meridian.
Elmer John, res 140 McCarthy.
Elmer J. W., receiving clerk T. H. R. R., res 140 McCarthy.
Elstrod Henry, machinist Cabinetmakers' Union, res 143 n Liberty.
Elvin W. G., fireman Belf. R. R., res 170 s Alabama.
Ely Alfred, carpenter, res w Indpls.
Ely Joseph W., carpenter, res n Tennessee, out corporation.
Embree Norris J., clerk Wiggins & Chandler, bds 258 w Washington.
Emerich Nicholas, student at Bryant's Commercial College, bds Indiana ave.
EMERSON BOSWELL B., CARPENTER, res 141 w Market.
Emmenegger M., proprietor Union Hall, 111, 113, 115 and 117, e Washington, res same.
Emmerich Henry, (Emmerich & Reese,) res 91 w Washington.
Emmerich & Reese, (Henry Emmerich & Henry Reese,) groceries and provisions, 91 and 93 w Washington.
Emmitt Robert, laborer, res 7 e New York.

Emmitt William, bds Pyle House.
Enger John, butcher, res 32 n Noble.
Enggoss H., clothing store and tailor shop, 188 e Washington, res same.
English John, laborer, bds 23 e Georgia.
English Joseph K., City Treasurer, office, Glenn's Block, res 113 n East.
English King, res 113 n East.
English William, laborer Sinker & Vance, bds corner Georgia and Liberty.
Ennis Louis, butcher, res 223 n Noble.
Ennis Philip, grocer, res 229 Mass. ave.
Ennis William, cabinetmaker, res 225 n Noble.
Enos Benjamin V., builder, 82 n Del.
Enwall Benjamin, barkeeper Deitz & Davis, res 123 w Meridian.
Epperts John, salesman, 48 w Wash., bds Ohio House.
Ernest Frederic, Express driver, res 23 Union.
Essike August, (A. & R. Essike,) bds at Union House, cor Illinos and South.
Essike Richard, (A. & R. Essike,) res 24 s Illinois.
Essike A. & R., (August Essike and Richard Essike,) butchers, 122 s Illinois.
Espy Mrs. Margaret F., res 85 s Tenn.
Estes John, carpenter, res cor Pratt and Mississippi.
Etehman Zedick, peddler, res 37 Spring.
Etsler Lloyd, wagonmaker, res 150 n East.
Eudaly Elisha, res 113 n Tenn.
Eudaly H., teamster, res cor Fletcher's ave. and Huron.
Eurich John, (Eurich & Schaffer,) res s Illinois.
Eurich Joseph, stone cutter.
EURICH & SCHAFFER, (John Eurich and Cornelius Schaffer,) ST. NICHOLAS SALOON, 7 n Illinois.
Evans G. F., (I. P. Evans & Co.,) bds at Macy House.
Evans I. P., (I. P. Evans & Co.,) bds at Macy House.
Evans & Co., (I. P. Evans and G. F. Evans,) Capital Flouring Mills, cor Market and Missouri.
Evans John, shoemaker, res 65 w South.
Evans Mrs. Lucinda, (wid.,) res 112 Virginia ave.
Evans Rev. Thomas, United Brethren, res 27 n Liberty.
Evans Wallace, carpenter, res National road, e Pogue's run.
Evertt Richard, works at rolling mill, res 37 s Illinois.
Evert Samuel, carpenter, res 92 w Meridian.
Ewell Peter, cigarmaker, res 68 n Noble.
EWING DAVID, M. D., (J. & D. Ewing,) bds Palmer House.
EWING JACOB, M. D., (J. & D. Ewing,) bds 44 n Pennsylvania.

EWING J. & D., (Jacob Ewing and David Ewing,) PHYSICIANS AND SURGEONS, 18 Vir. ave.

EXPRESS COMPANIES: Adams, 12 e Wash; American, s e cor Wash. and Meridian; United States, s e cor Wash. and Meridian.

F

Fack Herman F., stone cutter, res 86 w Ohio.

Fagan Geo. W., clerk, City Hotel.

Fahle Henry, works Washington foundry, res 56 e South.

Fahnestock Obed, res 42 w Maryland.

Fahnestock Dr. Samuel, physician and surgeon, res 115 n Ala.

Fahrion Christian, cabinet maker, res Mich., bet Liberty and Noble.

Fahrback Philip, plasterer, res 20 Garden.

Fahrback Philip, bricklayer, res 42 w South.

Fairback Andrew, plasterer, res 148 s N. Jersey.

Falling Frederick, clerk, res 125 South.

Fanning Fergus, laborer, res 39 w St. Clair.

Fanning Frank, laborer, res 184 Ala.

Fant Wm. O., saddler, 34 w Wash., bds 168 n N. Jersey.

Farion George, grocery, res 288 Ind. ave.

Farley Richard, laborer, res near city Hospital.

Farley Thomas, sawmaker, Sheffield works, bds Spencer House.

Farmer Jerome B., clerk, res 280 Madison ave.

Farman Frank, stone cutter, bds Beck's.

Farnsworth Charles O., salesman, bds Patterson House.

Farrell Mrs. C. J., dressmaker, 39 n Penn.

Farrell John, clerk, P. O., res Davidson, bet N. York and Ver.

Farries Mrs. Mary E., (wid) res e Market.

Farris Wm., tailor, 86 e Wash., bds Farmers Hotel.

Farry James, messenger, Adams express, res 68 w Vermont.

Fassol Eli, clerk, 48 e Wash., bds Ind. ave.

Fatout Joshua L., carpenter, res 85 Ind. ave.

Fatout Moses K., carpenter, res 85 Ind. ave.

Fatout J. L. & M. K., (Joshua L. Fatout and Moses K. Fatout,) carpenters and builders, 109 Ind. ave.

Fawcett Alpheus H., machinest, bds 258 w Wash.

Faulkner Isaac B., agent for Wm. Sheets, res 26 s Meridian.

Feager Louis, express driver, bds 26 n Del.

Feald Goodheart, saloon, e Wash., res same.

Feary Henry, printer, res 154 e North.

Feary Jeremiah E., carpenter, res 154 e North.

Featherston Wm. E., auction and commission house, 78 e Wash., res 115 Mass. ave.

Feck Fred., stone cutter, res 68 w Ohio.

Fedrick, Hide & Co., butchers, 73 e Wash.

FEG R., PROPRIETOR EXCELSIOR SALOON, 85 e Wash. See card.

Feil John, grocer, 50 Bluff road, res same.

Feild D. H., mail agent, Jeff. R. R., bds Oriental House.

Feldtbusch John, laborer, res 83 Davidson.

Feller George, watchmaker, 84 e Wash., res 172 n Tenn.

Feltmann Henry A., shoemaker, bds 330 s Del.

Fendler Nicholas, varnisher, res 7 Willard.

Fenton Frank, sawmaker, bds Ray House, s Del.

FERGUSON CHAS. A., WATCHMAKER AND JEWELER, 7 w Wash.

Ferguson Edward H., bricklayer, res 96 n Meridian.

FERGUSON KILBY, ATTORNEY AT LAW, off. 4 n Penn., res cor McCarthy and East.

FERGUSON KILBY, BANKER, 2 n Penn., res s e cor McCarthy and East.

Ferguson James E., pork packer, res 28 n Meridian.

Ferguson John A., clerk, res 25 e Georgia,

Ferguson Rezin, cutter Dessar & Bro's, res 131 n Meridian.

Ferber August, butcher, res w Indianapolis.

Ferguson Jerry, student at Purdy's commercial college.

Ferguson Wm., salesman, 26 and 28 w Wash., bds Macy House.

Ferling George, barber, res 196 Md.

Ferree Cornelia M., res 138 e Ohio.

Ferree Jerry D., printer, bds 138 e Ohio.

Ferrel Benj., laborer, bds 66 n Tenn.

Ferreton Maurice, school teacher, res 76 Bluff road.

Ferris Mrs. Mary, bds 103 w South.

Ferris Wm., tailor, bds Farmers Hotel.

Ferriton Patrick, laborer, res 35 s Liberty.

Ferry James, messenger, T. H. & R. R., res 68 w Ver.

Forsha Wm., blacksmith, res 168 s N. Jersey.

Fertig Frank, painter, res 41 w South.

Ferriten Maurice, prof. of mathematics, res 76 Bluff road.

Fetrole Alex., carpenter, res 74 s East.

Fette George, tailor, res Duncan bet Del. and Ala.

Bryant's Commercial College

INDIANAPOLIS, IND.

OPEN DAY AND NIGHT,

For the reception of Scholars in either Department,

Over the American Express Office.

The studies of this well-known School, embracing everything necessary for the Practical Accountant, Business Man, or Teacher of Penmanship, are so arranged that the student can take any number of them, omitting the balance; paying for only what he gets.

By the use of our "New Chart of Double-Entry Bookkeeping," which none but us have the right of using, and sundry other facilities, not found otherwise, we can and will make thorough Penmen in less time than we have heretofore, or than can be done in any other western school, while our charge for tuition is less than that of any other school that has ever made an Accountant, or in which the same branches are taught.

THOS. J. BRYANT, President.

WE REFER TO OUR GRADUATES & THEIR EMPLOYERS.

COURSE OF STUDIES.

BUSINESS PENMANSHIP,

For which we have been awarded the First Premium for many years at State Fairs.

Business Arithmetic, Bookkeeping by Double Entry,

Illustrated daily by Lectures and Recitations, rendering the Student familiar with its application to every kind of business.

Business Correspondence, Detection of Counterfeit Money, Ornamental Penmanship, Flourishes and Pen Drawing, embracing every kind of Pen Work taught in America, of which we have the largest and finest lot of specimens to be found.

LECTURES

Are delivered before the Students of this School on **Political Economy, Commercial Usages and Commercial Law,** fully explaining Contracts, Agency, Partnership, and all kinds of Business Papers.

GLENNS' BLOCK,

INDIANAPOLIS, IND.

See Engraving, opposite page.

This new and elegant block, erected and owned by Wm. Glenn and H. Glenn, is situated on the south side of Washington, between Meridian and Pennsylvania streets, occupying the site of the old Browning Hotel, afterwards called the Wright House. It is three and a half stories high, being 68 feet front on Washington street, and extending back to Pearl street, containing three store rooms and eight offices; the side stores are 17½ feet wide and 132 feet deep. The center store, known as the THE NEW YORK STORE, is occupied by the proprietors of the block, W. & H. Glenn, and is 32½ feet in width by 132 feet in depth. This store is the mammoth dry goods establishment of the State. The offices are occupied by the city authorities, namely : His Honor the Mayor, City Treasurer, City Clerk, Civil Engineer, Street Commissioner, Chief Fire Engineer, City Attorney, City Marshal and Police, with a chamber for the meetings of the City Council. Store south of entrance in American Alley, is occupied by the Cincinnati Gas Fitting Co. One store, (that on the east,) is occupied by Merrill & Co., dealers in law books, stationery &c. The one on the west side is occupied as a shoe store by Chase & Dawes. The appearance of this block is very attractive, chaste and elegant, without a fault, and is an ornament to our main street. It was re-built at a cost to the Messrs. Glenn of forty-five thousand dollars.

VIEW OF GLENNS' BLOCK.

WASHINGTON STREET,

BETWEEN MERIDIAN AND PENNSYLVANIA STREETS.

INDIANAPOLIS, IND.

Fetherling Samuel, laborer, res 188 Mass. ave.

Fetherling Wm., laborer, res 146 Mass. ave.

Fetty Charles, finisher in Washington foundry, res 154 Ala.

Feuti Mrs. Margaret, (wid) Wabash, e of East.

Feuiter Thomas, contractor, res 3 Bates.

Fey John, teamster, res 153 n Liberty.

Fichner Goalip, laborer, res s West.

Fiffle Abraham, butcher, bds 7 e North.

Fikes Peter, teamster, res 53 Madison ave.

Filbaum Wm., engineer, res 162 n Miss.

Fill John. grocer, 50 Bluff road.

Fillback John, laborer, res 289 s East.

Fin John, laborer, res 147 s Del.

Finister James, laborer, res 196 s Del.

Fink Mrs. Mary, res 31 e McCarthy.

Finley Henry B., wagon maker, bds California House, 186 s Ill.

Finley Sarah, (wid,) res w Market.

Finly Abraham, U. S. service, bds Mrs. Skelly, s Del.

Finlley Valentine, plasterer, res n Ala.

Finn John, cooper, res 14 Union.

Finter Fredrick, baker, 77 Ft. Wayne ave. Res same.

Fischer Charles, cooper, res 37 Spring.

Fiscus Andrew J., brickmason, res Ver. bet Liberty and Noble.

Fiscus Thomas W., brickmason, res 5 Chatham.

Fiscus William W., copper lightning rod dealer, res 155 E. New York.

Fish Elizabeth, (wid of William Fish,) dress maker, res 116 n Miss.

Fish James H., patent medicines, 18 s Ill.

Fish John L., real estate agt., res 159 n Penn.

Fish Oliva M., (Seargent & Fish,) 36 e Wash.

Fish S. William, printer, Journal office, bds Macy House.

FISHBACK JOHN, DEALER IN HIDES, OILS AND LEATHER, 30 cor Meridian and Md., res 49 s Meridian.

Fishback Mrs. Mary, (wid. Dr. Charles F.) res e New York.

Fishback William P., (Harrison & Fishback,) res 91 n Meridean.

Fisher Adam, laborer, res. 54 Bluff road.

Fisher Andrew, salesman, G. F. Adams, res 82 e Market.

Fisher Benedict, barber, cor Ill. and Louisiana, res 149 s Miss.

Fisher Charles, justice of peace, 4 You's block, res 16 w North.

Fisher Charles, tailor, res opp east end Central engine house.

Fisher Chris., hostler, Delzell & Tood, bds National saloon.

Fisher Edward, barber, res 2 s Benton.

Fisher George, shoemaker, res 79 Ft. Wayne ave.

Fisher Jesse, railroader, res 32 e Ga.

Fisher Martin, shoemaker, res 56 Bluff road.

Fisher Martin, shoemaker, res 126 s Meridian.

Fisher William, hostler, Delzell & Todd, res. cor Alabama and Washington.

Fisher William J. shoemaker, bds Pearidge House.

Fisher Wilson, laborer, res 72 w Mich.

Fisk Hiram, blacksmith, res 207 n Noble.

Fiske William, clerk at Emmerich & Reese, bds 91 w Washington.

Fisto George, auctioneer, bds 61 Mass ave.

Fitch William, cabinet-maker, res 240 w Washington.

Fitchey Michael G., carpenter, res 115 w Maryland.

Fitzgerreld John, tinner, res 327 s Del.

Fitzgerreld John, laborer, bds Peru R. R., bet Ohio and New York.

Fitzgerald William, laborer, res 208 s Delaware.

Fitz Hug Robert Porter, clerk, New York Store, bds Spencer House.

Flaig Matthew V., carpenter, bds 30 Ky. avenue.

Fleager Edward, butcher, bds 26 n Del.

Fleager George, res 26 n Delaware.

Fleitz Charles, blacksmith, res 101 Bluff road.

Fleehart E. W., carpenter, bds 72 s Ill.

Flemming David, laborer, res 100 s Noble.

Flemming Peter, drayman, res 44 Bates House.

Fleming Geo. H., clerk, post head-quarters.

Fletcher Calvin, Jr., res Plum, bet St. Clair and Cherry.

FLETCHER CALVIN, SR., (Fletcher & Sharpe,) PRESIDENT OF INDIANAPOLIS BRANCH BANKING CO., res out-side corporation, continuation of n Pennsylvania.

Fletcher David, woodhauler, res 204 s Del.

Fletcher Mrs. Elizabeth, (wid.) res 330 s Delaware.

Fletcher Ingram, Assistant Teller, Fletcher & Sharpe's bank, res. 187 n Penn.

Fletcher Horace A., bds Bates House.

Fletcher Stephen A., teller Fletcher's bank, res 187 Virginia ave.

Fletcher S. A., banker, 30 e Washington, res 88 E Ohio.

Fletcher Stoughton A., Jr., banker, res 187 Virginia ave.

Fletcher Dr. Wm. B., res 77 n Delaware.

Fletcher Zachariah, cabinet maker, res 64 w Vermont.

FLETCHER & SHARPE, INDIANAPOLIS BRANCH BANKING CO., s w cor Pennsylvania and Washington, (Calvin Fletcher, Thos. H. Sharpe.)

Flinn Byron K., porter, Munson & Johns.

Flinn Byron P., laborer, res. Wabash bet New Jersey and East.

Flinn Johannah, (wid.) res 232 Madison avenue.

Flinn Terrance, works at rolling mill, bds 188 s Tennessee.

Flint Isaac H., night watchman City Hospital.

Flowers Charles T., clerk, cor Maryland and Del., bds 113 Mass. ave.

Flowers Jemima, (wid. Aaron Flowers,) washes and sews, res 201 Ind. ave.

Flowers Samuel, carpenter, res 146 cor West and Market.

Fogle ———, cabinet maker, res. e Market.

Fogle Samuel, rag dealer, 174 e Wash.

Fogerty John, laborer, res 44 Bates.

Fogflax John, res 172 n Noble.

Foley James, waiter, Littles Hotel.

Foley Murty, laborer, res 208 s Delaware.

Foley Patrick, switchman, I. & C. R. R., res 78 e Louisiana.

Foley Patrick, laborer, res 64 Bright.

Foley Timothy, laborer, res Mich. road.

Folty Howard M., salesman, res 115 n Alabama.

Foltz Fredrick, res 113 n Alabama,

Foos Thomas J., baker, res 82 n Miss.

Foot Jeremiah, Dairyman, res 10 e Mich.

Forbes Matthew, engineer, res 67 Spring.

Ford Fletcher, brickmason, res 182 e New York.

Ford Henry, works for Murphy & Holliday, res 113 w Michigan,

Ford John, grain buyer, res 23 w Michigan.

Ford William, barber, Oriental House, bds same.

Forshee George W., blacksmith, res 93 Mass. ave.

Fonoter Alfred, machinist, res 115 e South.

Forsyth William, shipping clerk in Arsenal, res 28 Ind. ave.

Forlking Frederick, night watch, Belle Fontaine depot, res. 253 s Penn.

Foster Benj. F., pastor 1st Universalist church, res 148 n Ill.

Foster George T., miller, res 95 w Market.

Foster Wm., clerk, Empire saloon, res same.

Foster Wm. J., carpenter, res 116 n East.

Foster Capt. Thomas F., U. S. subsistence depot, w Md.

Foster Wm. R., steward, deaf and dumb asylum, res same.

Foudry John E., (Wood & Foudry,) res 109 n N. Jersey.

Foust Eliza J., (wid. Daniel Foust,) res 85 n Ill.

Fowler James P., feed store, s East, res 260 e Wash.

Fox Joseph, barkeeper, Union Hall.

Fox Solomon, salesman at Myer's clothing store.

Foy Owen, engineer, res 54 s Benton.

Frailey Joseph baggage master, Ind. Cent. R. R., res 131 Ala.

Francis Wm., baggage master, res 100 Bates.

Franco Alexander, bds 5 n Meridian.

Frank Henry, (Spiegel, Thoms & Co.,) res 180 e Ver.

Frank James, teacher in German Catholic school, res Wash., bet Liberty and Noble.

Frank J. J., laborer, res 109 South.

Frank Samuel, salesman, 2 Bates House. bds Macy House.

Frank Anthony, works at Union depot, res 60 Union.

FRANKEM ISAAC L., WHOLESALE DEALER IN STOVES, 49 and 51 e Wash., res 155 n Ill.

Frankem Jonathan, tin and stove ware, Vir. ave., res 155 n Ill.

Frankem Jonathan, sen. clerk, res 155 n Ill.

Frankinstien Frank, barber, under Mason House, res s Del.

Frankinstien George, barber.

Franklin Wm., (col) barber, Yohn's block, res 126 w Ohio.

Fraunsman Adam, salesman, bds 124 e Market.

Franz Peter, pump maker, res 122 n Noble.

Frary John C., printer, bds n Penn., at Mr. Jackson's.

Fraur Adolph, turner, res cor Liberty and Vermont.

Frauer Emanuel, German drug store, 185 e Wash., res same.

Frauer Gustave, turner, cor Wash., and East.

Frazee Samuel E., cashier, P. O., res 104 n Ill.

Frazier Frank, pumpmaker, res 53 s Benton.

Frazier John H., carpenter and joiner, res 22 Laukabee.

Frazer Wm., bridge builder, res 114 n Mo.

Frech Henry, laborer, res w Indianapolis.

Frederick Godferry, works rolling mill,

Frederick John, works 82 w Wash., res Davidson.

Fredwill John, currier, res 46 n Noble.

Freeman Nelson B., salesman, res 102 e N. York.

Freese Charles, (Freese and Kropf,) bds Union Hall.

FREESE & KROPF, (Charles Freese and Gustave Kropf,) HARDWARE AND CUTLERY, 11 w Wash.

French C. J., watchmaker, 37 w Wash., res country.

French John M., clerk, Adams express Co., bds Spencer House.

French Wm. M., teacher, deaf and dumb asylum, res same.

Frenzel John P., proprietor Kansas saloon, 85 s Ill., res same.

Freshour Casper, stone mason, res 146 s N. Jersey.

Fretz Daniel, miller, Ætna mills, bds 250 w Wash.

Freysleben Gustave, Capt. Co. A., 44th Ill. vol., res 147 n Liberty.

Frick Henry, works 6 Bates House, res w Indianapolis.

Frick Philip, tinner, res 144 e Market.

Fricke Rev. Charles, Ger. Luth., res 13 n East.

Fricke John, 1st clerk Farmers Hotel bds same.

Friday Michael, varnisher, res 167 e Mich.

Friedgan Cornelius, shoe and boot maker, 206 e Wash., res 113 e Market.

Frink E. O., dentist, 4 Yohn's block, bds 218 n Penn.

Frink S. C., dentist, 4 Yohn's block, res 118 n Penn.

Frisby Hamlin F., machinest, res 46 s Noble.

Frisbie Hopkins H., book-keeper, 20 s Meridian, bds 112 n Miss.

Fritz Joseph, tanner, res 12 w McCarthy.

Froesderf Frederick, works in slaughter house, res Patterson.

Fromholt Peter, coppersmith, res 89 Bluff road.

Frommire Henry, clerk in china store, res 76 n Miss.

Frost Charles, (Frost & Shane,) cor Georgia and Ill.

Frost Nicholas, laborer, res s Ill., near Pogues run.

FROST JAMES M., PATENT MEDICINE DEPOT, 95 e Wash., res 150 n Penn.

Frost & Shane, (Charles Frost and James Shane,) show tent, cor Georgia and Ill.

Frour Albert, cabinet maker, res 25 n Ala.

Fry Albert, (col) hostler, res 76 on alley, bet Mich. and Ver.

Fry Wm. H., Jun., (Pomroy, Fry & Co.,) bds Bates House.

Fry Miss Rebecca, boarding house, 122 n Ill.

Frybarger Frank A., clerk, Adams express, bds S. Beck's.

Frybarger Maj. W. W., 1st Ind. artillery, bds Palmer House.

Fugate James L., clerk, J. H. Vajen, res 37 n N. Jersey.

Fuller Ralph, (col) cook, Pearl saloon, res same.

Fullerton Joseph E., res 117 w Md.

Fullmer Charles, engineer, bds 45 Lou.

Fullwider John, laborer, bds 228 n Ala.

Fulton Felix M., cabinet maker, res 120 n N. Jersey.

Fulton James, brakeman, Central R. R.' res 34 e Lou.

Fulton John, millwright, res 190 e Wash., up stairs.

Fuqua Elizabeth D., (wid. Andy W. Fuqua,) res 194 w Wash., up stairs.

Furguson John A., salesman, W. J. Holliday & Co.

Furguson Leander A., clerk, bds 21 Ind. ave.

Fussle Edward, clerk, blind asylum.

G

Gabe Wm. A., printer, rooms over 9 w Wash.

Gabert Frederick, laborer, res 96 Union.

Gable Lewis, U. S. service, res Hosbrook.

Gahm John, grocery, res 151 Ind. ave.

Games Franklin, clerk, Week's grocery, res n Tenn.

Gaivet Samuel, huckster, res 80 Buchanan.

Gale John, laborer, res 43 e Md..

Galigan Mary, (wid. Michael Galigan,)

Galivan Mrs. Honora, (wid) res 77 e Market.

Gall Dr. A. D., brigade surgeon, U. S. A., res 36 n N. Jersey.

Gall John, finisher, res 38 s Ill.

Gallagher Frank, porter, Adams express, res near rolling mill.

Gallagher Francis, laborer, res 44 Mass. ave.

Gallatin Albert, (col) white washer, res 136 n Missouri.

Galloway Harvey, hostler, Hinesly's stable, bds E. Knight's.

Galligan Patrick, works at rolling mill, bds Willard, near rolling mill.

Gallivin Michael, watchman, res 25 Henry.

Galloway John, bar tender, Magnolia saloon, res 36 n Ill.

Gallup Edward P., (W. P. & E. P. Gallup,) bds Bates House.

Gallup Wm. P., (W. P. & E. P. Gallup,) bds Bates Housse.

W. P. & E. P. Gallup, (Wm. P. Gallup & Edward P. Gallup,) commission merchants, 74 w Wash.

Galvin A., bds Littles Hotel.

Gardner Conrad, (Gardner & Harbert,) res 155 n Miss.

Gardner Winter, carpenter, res cor James and Ind. ave.

Gardner & Harbert, (Conrad Gardner & Enoch Harbert,) meat market, 5 n Ill.

Garengen Landien, cabinet maker, res 81 n Davidson.

Garety Michael, at Adams express office, res 24 s Ala.

Garland Edward, clerk, bds 99 s N. J.

Garland Edward, res 118, cor East and Ver.

Garlick Henry M., clerk, American express office, res s Tenn., bet Md. and Georgia.

Garner Charles L., student at Bryant's commercial college, bds country.

Garner L. W., watchmaker, Harry Craft's bds Oriental House.

Garner Horatio S., (Pink,) printer, H. H. Dodd & Co., bds Macy House.

Garrell Mrs. Isabella J., (wid) res 78 Mass. ave.

Garrett Joseph, Phœnix bell and brass foundry, Union R. R. track e Union depot.

Garver Mathias, ice dealer, bds 84 w South.

Gaskill David, res 36 Cal.

Gass Andy, butcher, 21 n Noble, res 60 St. Joseph.

Gaston Edward, carriage maker, 37 Ky. ave.

Gaston Hiram, carriage maker, 27 Ky. ave.

Gaston Dr. John M., 28 e Market, res 77 N. Jersey.

Gates Charles, barkeeper, res 126 s Ill.

Gates John J., (Gates, Lemon & Smith,) res 85 e Market.

GATES, LEMON & SMITH, (John J. Gates, —— Lemon & —— Smith,) WAGON MAKERS AND BLACK-SMITHS, 14 s N. Jersey.

Gath Peter, grocery and feed store, res 237 n N. Jersey.

Gatling Richard J., M. D., res 44 s Md.

Gaughin Wm., laborer, bds 25 Henry.

Gavin Lawrence, laborer, res 213 Ala.

Gay Alfred, canal agent, res 20 n West.

Gebert Mary, (wid) res 41 Union.

Gebhart Anthony, works 5 n Ill., bds n Miss.

Geehen Thomas, laborer, res 71 Madison.

Giesekink Christ., carpenter, res 40 Davidson.

Geier David, tailor, (Morritz Bro. & Co.,) res Bluff road.

Geiger Robert, clerk Bellef. R. R., bds at Kinder House.

Geimmerdinger Jacob, laborer, res National road, e Pogue's run.

Geisel Henry, blacksmith, res 215 Massachusetts ave.

Geisel John, blacksmith, res 121 Davidson.

Geisendorff Christian E., (G. W. Geisendorff & Co.,) res n West.

Geisendorff G. W. & Co., (Geo. W. Geisendorff and Christian E. Geisendorff,) Hoosier Woollen Factory, 268 w Washington.

Gelzenbuchter Per., clerk German Dry Goods Store, res 169 Bellef. R. R.

Geoben Hillery, soldier, bds 64 Massachusetts ave.

George Mrs. Aun, (wid,) res e New York, bet Liberty and Noble.

George A. R., clerk, 144 w Washington, res 48 cor West and St. Clair.

George Isaac, hub turner, res 19 Blake building, up stairs.

George James, grocer, 143 w Washington.

George Otis, carpenter at Theater.

George Robert, res 48 Michigan road.

Gerard Elias, railroader, res 99 Meek.

Gerardy Nicholas, tailor, res 92 Davidson.

Gerin Francis, blacksmith, res 11 s Penn.

Gerstner Augustus J., merchant tailor and clothier, 158 Wash., res 137, up stairs.

Ghest Henry, laborer, res 74 St. Joseph.

Gibbons Joseph, laborer, bds 204 w Wash.

Gibbs Henry, (col.,) barber, 1 n Illinois, res 68 Blackford.

Gibbs Reuben, (col.,) barber, 1 n Illinois, res 68 Blackford.

Gibson John, conductor Terre Haute and Richmond R. R., bds Palmer House.

GIBSON WM. T., SECRETARY INDIAN-APOLIS FIRE INSURANCE CO., Odd Fellow's Hall, res 149 n Illinois.

Giekeler Christ., laborer, res 75 Fort Wayne ave.

Giensbru Frederic, works Union depot, res 318 Virginia ave.

Giesel Christ., carpenter, res cor Michigan and Davidson.

Giffin John A., shoemaker, res 53 Mad.

Gilbert Mrs., (wid,) 128 e St. Clair.

Gillespie Wm. J., salesman, 30 w Washington, bds 44 n Delaware.

Gillett Horace S., teacher, Deaf and Dumb Assylum, Pennsylvania.

Gillett Samuel T. Rev., (Methodist,) res 2 Circle.

Gilmore Daniel, bricklayer, res 260 Virginia ave.

Gimball Michael, salesman, res 140 e Market.

Gimbel Jacob, laborer, res 11 n Liberty.

GIMBEL MARTIN, CABINETMAKER, 147 e Washington, res 106 Davidson.

Gis Joseph, clerk Central House, bds same.

Glaser Julius, (Glaser & Bros.,) res 15 n East.

Glaser & Brothers, (Julius Glaser, Samuel Glaser, Lewis Glaser and Max Glaser,) Merchant Tailors and Clothiers, 2 Bates House.

Glass Henry, teamster, res w Indpls.

Glasscock Wm., carpenter, res Douglass.

Glazier Mrs. Catharine, (wid.,) res 114 s New Jersey.

Glazier Charles, flour, grain, &c., 16 s Meridian, res 100 Virginia ave.

Glazier Daniel, City Fire Department, res 109 s New Jersey.

Glazier Frank, engineer 5th Ward Fire Engine, res 192 s California.

Glen Mrs. Amanda, (wid.,) res 38 s Alabama.

Glenn's Block, w Wash., bet Meridian and Penn.

GLENN W. & H., (William Glenn and Hugh Glenn,) NEW YORK DRY GOODS STORE, e Wash.

Glenn Wm., (W, & H. Glenn,) res 73 n Meridian.

Glenn Hugh, (W. & H. Glenn,) res New York City.

Glenn William, (col.,) barber, 17 w Wash., res 130 Ind. ave.

Gleason John, watchman and messenger Sinking Fund, bds Ad. Libel.

Glessing Thomas B., artist, res 62 n Tenn.

Glosner Joseph, flower pot maker, res Bluff road, Dougherty ville.

Glover Joseph W., plasterer, 34 n Penn., res 98 n Meridian.

Goddard Samuel, stonecutter, res 18 s West.

Goddard & Jennings, (Samuel Goddard and Thomas W. Jennings,) stone and marble cutters, cor Tenn. and Market.

Goe Lemuel T., saddler, 20 w Wash.

Goebel John G., cabinetmaker, res 119 Bluff road.

Goepper Andrew, butcher, res 152 w Michigan.

GOEPPER FREDERIC, MERCHANT TAILOR AND CLOTHIER, 15 e Wash. res 61 n Ill. See card.

Goetz Charles, barkeeper, Astor Saloon, res s Illinois.

Gogen Michael, laborer, bds Ray House, e Delaware.

Gogen William, boilermaker, res cor Ala. and Maryland.

Gogin James, printer, res cor Maryland and Alabama.

Goings Simeon, (col.,) whitewasher, res cor Ohio and West.

Goken William, laborer, res 138 East.

Galaspy Mrs. Jane, (wid. James Galaspy,) res 44 n Delaware.

Gold Adam, Grocery and Liquor Store, res w National road.

Gold J. S., clerk Fred. Rusch.

Gold Samuel N., student at Bryant's Commercial College, bds on w Wash., near the bridge.

Golden Dennis, laborer, res 202 Vir. ave.

Golding James, blacksmith, n w cor Michigan and Ind. ave.

Golding Thomas, teamster, res Douglass, Wiley's Div., n of North.

Goldsberry Bayless S., (Goldsberry & Bro,) 182 e Wash., bds 43 n Penn.

Goldsberry George, bds 43 n Penn.

Goldsberry Livingston D., (Goldsberry & Bro,) 182 e Wash., res 53 e Maryland.

Goldsberry Samuel S., Jeweler, bds W. P. Bingham.

Goldsberry & Bro., (Livingston D. Goldsberry and Bayless S. Goldsberry,) stoves and tinware, 182 e Wash.

Goldsberry Wm., 3d Indiana Cavalry.

Goldstone Max, hoop and skirt manufacturer, 95 e Wash., bds South, Madison bakery.

Goll John, finisher, res 38 s Illinois.

Gollagher Joseph, works Gas house, bds Cincinnati House.

Golzenbeichter John, woodsawer, res 169 Railroad.

GOOD MICHAEL H., DEALER IN FANCY AND STAPLE DRY GOODS, 5 e Washington, bds Bates House.

Goodheart Benjamin F., Grocer and Commission Merchant, res 92 New Jersey.

Goodman Anthony, Tailor, 16 n Penn., res 56 e Market.

Goodman George K., Varnisher, res w Market.

Goodnoe Calvin N., works 84 w Wash., res n Tenn.

Goodperle Peter, works Speigal, Thoms & Co., res 112 n Noble.

Goodwin Angelon Q, clerk Christian Record, bds out corporation.

Goodwin Elijah, editor and publisher Christian Record, (Journal Building,) res out corporation.

Goodwin Thomas A., Soldiers' agent, res e National road.

Gootweller Joseph, laborer, res 230 Virginia ave.

Gordon Charles L., carpenter, res s Missouri s South.

Gordon George, farmer, res 57 Ind. ave.

GORDON GEORGE E., ATTORNEY AT LAW, Odd Fellow's Hall, res 92 n Penn.

Gordon James, teamster, res 69 Ind. ave.

Gordon Terressa, (wid. Benj. Gordon,) res 69 Ind. ave.

Gorham George L., bricklayer, res 169 n Mississippi.

Gorham Wm. H., railroader, res 179 n Mississippi.

Gorrell Willis A., bookkeeper, 83 e Wash., bds 78 Mass. ave.

Gosnell Greenbery, stove moulder, res 12 Henry.

Gosney George S., Teller, Merchant's Bank, res 91 Ind. ave.

Gosney John, U. S. service, res 237 Ala.

Goss Andrew, butcher, res 60 St. Joseph.

Goss Henry, laborer, res 64 St. Joseph.

Goth Valentine, cooper, res 77 Spring.

Gott John, Tailor, res 150 n Liberty.

Gott Lewis N., drayman, res 72 n Miss.

Gott Thomas, constable, res 147 s Tenn.

Gottenberry James, laborer, 246 Va. ave.

Gottwald Theodore, harness maker, res 190 s Pennsylvania.

Gouesse Francis, assistant pastor St. Johns Church, res Georgia bet Tenn. and Ill.

Goulding John, laborer, bds on Willard near rolling mill.

Gowen Canada, cooper, res w end North.

Grader Herman, bakery and confectioner, res 39 n East.

Graff Joseph, gardner, Charles Mayer, bds same.

Graham John J., (Vanhorton & Graham,) res 145 Virginia ave.

Graham Samuel, railroader, res 207 n Tenn.

Graham W. A., shingle maker, res 140 s East.

Graham William, res 24 Huron.

Graham William S., delivery agent American Express, 45 s Meridian.

Graming Joseph, blacksmith, bds Conley's Washington.

Gramling John A., cooper, res 79 n Noble.

Gramling John, (J. & P. Gramling,) res 116 n Noble.

GRAMLING J. & P., (John Gramling, Peter Gramling,) MERCHANT TAILORS AND CLOTHIERS, 41 e Wash.

Gramling Peter, (J. & P. Gramling,) res 113 n Noble.

Grand George, blacksmith, res 67 Bluff road.

Grandstaff Henry, laborer, res Bluff road, Doughertyville.

Grancy John, laborer, res 192 s Tenn.

Graning John, shoemaker, bds 51 s Ill.

Grant William, engineer, res 149 s Miss.

Grauy Thomas, laborer, res cor Ohio and Peru R. R.

Gratzer John, tailor, 36 n Penn., res out corporation.

Graven Thomas, works in arsenal, res 11 Ellsworth.

Graves Lewis W., Farmer, res. 75 n Meridian.

Gray Miss Allis, teacher, 6th ward school house, res 64 e South.

Gray John, laborer, res bet Md. and Georgia on West.

Gray John W., shoemaker, res 81 w South.

Gray Jonathan, brickmason, res Wabash, bet New Jersey and East.

Gray Joseph, H., horse dealer, res 11 s Penn., up stairs.

Gray Robert, works I. & C. R. R. shop, res 18 Lord.

Gray Thomas, saddler, 17th Reg., res 11 Peru R. R.

Gray Thomas, baker, 64 e South.

Gray William, Sen., baker, 64 e South.

Gray William Jr., baker, 64 e South.

Graydon Alexander, Sr., res 184 e Ohio.

Graydon William M., general freight agent I. P. & C. R. R., res cor Merrill and New Jersey.

Grayson John W., printer.

Grayson Andrew J., printer, Journal office, bds Edwards Hotel.

Green ——, painter, res. 136 s Alabama.

Green E. S., with Parsons, Adams & Co., bds 22 s Meridian.

Green George, grocer, res 13 Willard.

Green James, cooper, bds Ohio House.

Green John, laborer, res 35 Huron.

Green Michael, laborer, res 241 s Penn.

Green Thomas, contractor, 15 s Alabama.

Green Miss Mollie, res 13 n New Jersey.

Green James, quarter-master's department, res 93 n Meridian.

Green Norvell S., clerk, 18 w Washington, res 93 n Meridian.

Greenert Henry, tailor, res 85 s West.

Greenfield Robert, miller, res 229 w. Wash.

Greenleaf Edwin, foreman, Sinker & Vance, res out city limits.

Greenwoldt Albert, clerk, 56 s East.

Greenwald Henry, cabinet maker, 79 Davidson.

Greenwallet John, laborer, 298 s East.

Greenright William, pump maker, res 26 Huron.

Green James, cabinet maker, res s Miss., near rolling mill.

Greer William H., carpenter and joiner, shop 68 s Del., res on Green.

Gregg Dennis, res 19 w St. Clair.

Gregg James, wagon maker, res 36 n Ill.

Gregory David, fur trader, res 103 s Penn.

Grein Henry, baker, bds 214 e Wash.

Grein John, baker, 214 e Wash., res same.

Greisel Michael, laborer, res 91 Ft. Wayne avenue.

Greisheimer Moritz, salesman, Simon & Dernham, 1 west Wash., bds Bates House.

Greuzard L. S., sign and ornamental painter, 136 e Wash.

Gridley Fayette R., res 39 n California.

Grieb Gotlieb, stonemason, res 149 n Liberty.

Griese Frank, cabinet maker, res 3 e Mccarthy.

Grieshaper Sebastian, boiler maker, res 231 Alabama.

Griff John, boiler maker, Sinker & Vance.

Griffenstein William, butcher, res 7 North.

Griffin Dennis, laborer, res s Missouri, s of South.

Griffin Emeline, (col. wid.,) 143 e Wash.

Griffin James F., gas fitter, bds Mr. Skelly, s Del.

Griffin James, messenger, State House, res 300 s Del.

Griffin James, laborer, res 1 Water.

Griffin Martin, laborer, res 42 Bates.

Griffin Michael, drayman, res 67 Bright.

Griffin Patrick, laborer, bds on William, near rolling mill.

Griffin Patrick, laborer, res 316 s Del.

Griffin Timothy, U. S. service, res 316 s Delaware.

Griffith Bartholomew, I. & C. depot, res 153 w Mich.

Griffith Geo. W., plasterer, res 155 n Alabama.

Griffith Humphrey, retired watchmaker, res 52 n Ill.

Griffith Josiah, res 32 s Miss.

Griffith Samuel, foreman I. & C. car shop, res 263 s East.

Griffith Samuel I., 18th U. S. Inf., res Alvord's block.

Grigsby James, laborer, res Mich. road.

Griner, John, shoemaker, res 73 e Wash.

Grinsteinner George, undertaker, res 114 e Market.

Griswold Joseph, cabinet maker, G. F. Adams, res 8 n Penn.

Grobe Charles, (Grobe & Hider,) res cor Wash. and Ala.

Grobe & Hider, (Charles Grobe and Augustus Hider,) carriage makers, Doughertyville, Bluff road.

GROFF DANIEL B., FRUIT AND CONFECTIONERY DEALER, 51 s Ill., res same.

Groff Joseph, works rolling mill, bds Washington House.

Grooms Moses, printer, bds 119 w Wash.

Grooms A. C., book-keeper, Journal office, res 87 Ind. ave.

Grosch John, ale peddler, res 113 n Noble.

Groscher Charles, tailor, res 131 n Noble.

Grosvenor Julius res A., Miss., bet La. and South.

Grout John, laborer, res s Mo., near rolling mill.

Grout Joseph B., shoe store, 5 w Wash., res 83 n Ill.

Grove Benjamin, laborer, res e Wash.

Grubbs Daniel W., (Martindale & Grubbs,) bds Bates House.

Grube Isaac, student at Bryants commercial college.

Grube Jacob, carpenter, res 26 s Ill., s of Pogues run.

Grunart Herman, shoemaker, 51 w Wash., res w South.

Grundy Charles, clerk, N. Y. store, bds Macy House.

Grusely ——, 82 Pratt.

Guanter C., bakery, 181 e Wash., res same.

Guddy John, res s Mo., s of South.

Guewockowa Fritz, barkeeper, 85 e Wash.

Guezet Alexander, historical painter, res 159 s Del.

Gulliver Wm., (col) barber, cor Wash. and Ky. ave., res 63 Ky. ave.

Gundelfinger Benj., salesman, 2 Bates House, bds Union Hall.

Gundelfinger Samuel, clerk, bds Union Hall.

Gunn Michael, Lewis & Develin's Museum, s Ill.

Gustin Lewis Q., brakeman, Central R. R., res 17 w Georgia.

Gustin Levi, eye and ear doctor, res 101 s Tenn.

Guth Edward, finisher, res 32 s Ill.

Gutnicht John painter, res 105 Ft. Wayne ave.

Gutnicht Milton, gardener, 113 Ft. Wayne ave.

Guthridge Charles, clerk, bds 26 w Md.

Guthridge John W., agent Penn. Cent. R. R., res 49 e Md.

Gutig Henry, barber, under Odd Fellows' Hall, res 116 e Market.

H

Habeney Henry, laborer, res 103 w N. York.

Hacket Wm., laborer, res 22 s Liberty.

Hackleberg Charles, tailor, res 33 s Meridian.

Hackleberg Samuel, at Myer's clothing store, res s Meridian.

Hackney Mrs. Josephine, res s Tenn., near Pogue's run.

Hadley Wm., res 151 n Del.

HAERLE WM., FANCY DRY GOODS, 36 w Wash., bds Palmer House.

Hagar Edward C., book-keeper, Fletcher's bank, res 21 s Del.

Hagerhorst Mrs. Christina, res 156 s Tenn.

Hagerhorst Christian F., clerk, 34 n Ill., res 160 n Tenn.

Haggerty Patrick, teamster, res s Tenn., near Pogues run.

Hahn Charles, bds n Ala., bet Market and Ohio.

Hahn Henry, proprietor East Street House., bet Pogues run and Georgia.

Hahn Louis, meat market, w Wash., res 120 n Miss.

Hahn H. & Co., confectioners, Talbot & New's building, n Penn.

Haisch John, printer, bds 130 e Wash.

Halbrook Thomas E., res 77 n Ala.

Hale Henry J., machinest, Washington foundry, res 151 n Ill.

Halford Elijah W., printer, bds 114 e Ver.

Halford Mrs. Maria, (wid) res 114 e Ver.

Hall Charles W., res 170 n Ill.

Hall Erl, carpenter, res cor Pine and Fletcher's ave.

Hall Eli, merchant tailor, res 148 n Penn.

Hall Leonard A., heater at rolling mill, res cor Tenn. and Garden.

Hall Marcus, U. S. service, res cor Huron and Noble.

Hall Reginald H., (Rand & Hall,) res 47 n Meridian.

Hall Thomas O., cabinet maker, bds 121 n East.

Hall Wm. M., student at Bryant's commercial college.

Hall Wm., book binder, bds 121 n East.

Hall Wm., machinest, res 99 Bates.

Hallam Thomas, res s Ill., near Pogues run.

Haller Leon, clerk, bds Union Hall.

Haller Wm., cabinet maker, res 150 n Noble.

Hallihan Jeremiah, wood sawyer, res Elizabeth.

Hallweg Lewis, salesman, bds 44 s Penn.

Hully Theodore, shoemaker, 87 w Wash., res 41 w Georgia.

Halmann John, laborer, res 121 Bluff road.

Halmann Wm., laborer, res 121 Bluff road.

Halpin M. H., printer, Journal office, bds Kinder House.

Halsted Abraham C., stone cutter, res 3 Stephen.

Halter Casper, works in arsenal, res Wyoming.

Halter Wm., shoemaker, Mt. Jackson.

Hambergh John F., tailor, bds 63 w N. York.

Hamer Francis G., student at law, with Perrin & Manlove, bds Farmers Hotel.

Hamiell Philip, works at rolling mill, bds 188 s Tenn.

Hamilton Eliza, (wid. John W. Hamilton,) bds near old post office.

Hamilton Francis W., dep. auditor C. H., res 48 Cal.

Hamilton Mrs. Jane, res 44 s Noble.

HAMILTON JOHN W., COUNTY LIBRARIAN, C. H., res e National road.

HAMILTON J. D., PROP'R PATTERSON HOUSE, n. Ala., bet. Ohio and Market.

Hamilton Mrs. Sarah, res Mich. road.

Hamilton Wm. H., book-binder, Wm. Sheets, bds Pyle House.

Hamlin Carlin, (Hamlin & Protzman,) bds Pyle House.

HAMLIN L H., REAL ESTATE AGENT, 16½ e Wash.

HAMLIN & PROTZMAN, ATTORNEYS AT LAW, (Carlin Hamlin, Ferdinand Protzman) 16½ e Wash.

Hammel Daniel, expressman, res Patterson n of North.

Hamel Geo., cigar maker, bds 151 n. East.

Hammond Mrs. Kate, res 336 s Del.

Hammons Thomas, (col.) barber, bds 127 n East.

Hampton James, engraver, bds Ray House, s Delaware.

Hance Joseph, salesman, res 13 Henry.

Hand Hiram, printer, bds 237 Ind. ave.

Hand Mary A., dress maker, 11 n Meridian.

Hand Thomas P, res 11 n Meridian.

Hankin H. C., bds Little's Hotel.

Hanlin J. Ross, clerk, Bates House.

Hanlin Mrs. Catharine, res 57 Ky. ave.

Hanna Mrs., (wid.) res 112 McCarthy.

Hanna Ann, (wid. Thomas Hanna,) res e New York.

Hanna John L., Capt. Co. H., 79th Reg., res 191 e St. Clair.

Hanna Valentine C., Maj. U. S. A., res 35 n Meridian.

Hannah John, U. S. District Attorney, off. P. O. building, 2d floor, res Greencastle.

Hannah John W., student at Bryant's Com. Col., bds n Penn.

Hannah Samuel, Sec'y and Treas., Ind. Central R. R. office, res 26 Meridian.

Hannegan Michael, machinist, Sinker & Vance, res 51 n Del.

Hannegan Salem H., bds Mrs. Morrison, n Penn.

Hanning John G., (Ramsay & Hanning,) res 130 n Del.

Hannahan Frank, laborer, res 194 s Tenn.

Hannahan Patrick, saloon keeper, res 184 s Tenn.

Hanson Charles, res cor South and Tenn.

Hanway Samuel, mail agent, Jeff. & I.R. R., res 75 n New Jersey.

Happe George, Lafayette House, e end of Union Depot.

Harahan Cathrine, res 196 s Tenn.

Harbert Enoch, (Gardner & Harbert,) res w St. Clair.

Harbine Mrs. Elizabeth N., res cor Md. and Meridian, up stairs.

Harbison Alex. L., engineer, Journal off. bds 70 w Vermont.

Harbison Robert, driver Adams Express, res 70 w Vermont.

Harbison Sarah, (wid. Robert Harbison,) res 70 w Vermont.

Harcourt Theodore, cabinet maker, res Blackford's building.

Hardesty Jackson, engineer, Jeff. R. R., res 164 Alabama.

Hardin Ezra C., carpenter, res 87 e Market.

Hardin Richard E., carpenter, res 87 e Market.

Harding Martha A., res 106 n Penn.

Hardwick John, carpenter, res 309 s East.

Hardwick Lucius, U. S. service, res 258 s Delaware.

Hardy Robert B., salesman, 26 and 28 w Wash, bds Macy House.

Harieger Michael, machinist, res 51 St. Joseph.

Harkness John, (Elder, Harkness & Bingham,) res 77 n Penn.

Harley Moses F., hack driver, res 81 Bluff road.

Harlin Geo W., turner, res 78 n Tenn.

Harlin James, tinner, res 78 n Tenn.

Harlin James W., student, Bryant's Com. College, bds n Tenn.

Harman Gustave, cabinet maker, res 79 Davidson.

Harman John, cabinet maker, res Winston, bet Ohio and New York.

HENRY BUSCHER,

BREWER

No. 14 South Alabama Street,

INDIANAPOLIS, IND.

Keeps constantly on hand a full Stock of all kinds of Ale and Beer.

WILLIAM H. TAYLOR,

MANUFACTURER OF

Tin, Sheet Iron and Copper,

Also, Jobbing, Tin Guttering and Roofing,

Particular attention paid to all kinds of JOB WORK. All Work
WARRANTED.

Shop 268 East Washington Street, Indianapolis, Ind.

C. J. MEYER,

Wholesale and Retail Manufacturer of

CHAIRS & FURNITURE,

Warerooms 171 E. Washington St., two doors E. of Little's Block,

INDIANAPOLIS, IND.

☞ALL ORDERS PROMPTLY ATTENDED TO.☜

RAY HOUSE,

Two squares S. E. of Union Depot, cor. Delaware & South Sts.,

INDIANAPOLIS, IND.

RAY & LAMBERT, - - PROPRIETORS.

AS GOOD FARE AND CHEAPER BILLS,

Than any Public House in the City, and Meals always ready in time for Railroad
Trains. Large and well supplied Stables, Sheds, and Yard for Live Stock, and

STOCK RECEIVED AND FORWARDED

With promptness, on any of the Railroads.

HAR 33 HAT

Harman Patrick, works at Glazier's feed store, res 108 Davidson.
Harman Valentine, res w Indianapolis.
Harmanink Mrs. Christene, (wid.) res 13 Peru R. R.
Harmenning Christian, grocer and liquor dealer, 205 s delaware, res same.
Harnes Solomon, res in rear 23 e McCarthy.
Harper Henry, res 92 Bluff road.
Harper Jeff, carpenter, res 132 w New York.
Harper J. L., book keeper, (Mayhew & Co.,) bds 94 n Ill.
Harper John W., carpenter, bds 34 Ky. ave.
Harper Winfield, press boy, res 92 Bluff road.
Harriman J. H., (Minnie & Harriman,) Palmer House.
Harriman Joseph H., M. D., Alopathic, res 134 w Wash.
Harrington Dennis, Terre Haute freight house, res 260 s Del.
Harrington Patrick, saloon, res 127 w South.
Harrington Patrick, grocer and saloon, 58 e South, res same.
Harris Charles E.,carpenter, res 66 North.
Harris George, U. S. service, res 29 e Meek.
Harris Harvey, farmer, Mt. Jackscn.
Harris Henry, (col.) whitewasher, res 143 e Wash.
Harris Henry, laborer, cor Ill. and Md., up stairs.
Harris Isaac, miller, Patterson's mill, res 169 w Vermont.
Harris Irwin, bds 51 n Penn.
Harris Joseph, dye house, cleaning and repairing establishment, 38 s Ill., res 32 s Ill.
Harris Mumford, (col.) works for J. M., Frost, res 66 Powell.
Harris Obediah, farmer, Mount Jackson.
Harrison Alfred, (A & J. C. S. Harrison,) res 61 n Meridian.
HARRISON A. & J. C. S., BANKERS, 15 e Wash.
Harrison Benjamin, (Harrison & Fishback,) Col. 70th Reg. Ind. vols, res 127 n Alabama,
Harrison James, cooper, res 293 Mad. ave.
Harrison James H., Suttler 39th Ind. Regt, res 115 n Ill.
Harrison John C. S., (A. & J. C. S. Harrison,) res 63 n Meridian.
Harrison William M., book keeper, bds 63 w N. York.
Harrison & Fishback, (Benj. Harrison, W. P. Fishback,) attorneys, 62 e Wash.
Harrison Jacob, livery, 112 e Market.
Harrman Lawrence, wood sawyer, 65 s Delaware.
Harry Joseph, res 169 n Noble.

Hart Abraham, pedler, res 197 n Ill.
Hart Michael, laborer, res 5 Buchanan.
Hart Thomas J., carpenter, res. 8 w Garden.
Hart James C., carpenter, res 189 n New Jersey.
Hartawig Henry, drayman, res 123 Davidson.
Harten Fred., (Harten & Co.,) res cor Ill., on Bluff road.
Harten Henry, (Harten & Co.,) res cor Ill., on Bluff road.
Harter John A., tinner, res New Jeasey, bet Wash. and Market.
HARTH M., PROPRIETOR OF SPENCER HOUSE, cor Ill. and Louisiana.
Harting William, drayman, res 94 Union.
Harting & Harting, brewers, (Henry Harting, Fredrick Harting,) bet Ill. and Bluff road.
Hartbrod Charles, cooper, bds w North.
Hartman Charles, cook at Bates House, res 63 n New Jersey.
Hartman Christian, laborer, res 139 e Ohio.
Hartman Henry, laborer, res 215 n New Jersey.
Hartman Matthew, plasterer, res 108 n Alabama.
Hartman Oswald, shoemaker, bds 34 s Ill.
Hartman William, wagon maker, bds Christ Yeager, e Wash.
Hartwell Ephraim, clerk Palmer House.
Hartwig John, shoemaker, 176 e Wash., bds same.
Harvey Alden C., res 22 s Meridian.
Harvey Alonzo D., 1st Lt. 15th Bat., bds n Tenn.
Harvey Eli, bds 23 Henry.
Harvey Jonathan S., res 54 s Meridian.
Harwood Ervin M., boot tree maker, res 11 s Madison ave.
Hascall William, student, P. G. C. Hunt.
Haskell James A., Student, Bryants' Com. College, bds w Md.
Haskell Thurloon, carpenter, res 82 w Maryland.
Hasler Emanuel A., salesman in German dry goods store, res 166 n Tenn.
Hasmin Henry, res 21 w South.
Hass David, laborer, res 350 Virgina ave.
Hasselman Lewis, (Hasselman & Vinton,) res 38 s Meridian.
Hasselman & Vinton, Washington Foundry, (Lewis Hassleman, Almus E. Vinton,) s Meridian, near Union Depot.
Hassett David, works at rolling mill, bds on William near rolling mill.
Hassion John, hostler, res 20 n Penn.
Hasson Charles, res 117 n Meridian.
Hasson James, res 127 n New Jersey.
Hastings Edward L., printer, 67 n Del.
Hasty John, showman, res 74 n Ill.
Hatch Joseph, carpenter, res 51 e McCarthy.

(3)   Every Florence Machine has the reversible feed.

Haten & Co., Brewers, cor Ill and Bluff road, (Henry S. Harten, Fred Harten.)
Hattan Thomas, cigar manufacturer, bds 72 s Ill.
Hattendorf, saloon, 186 e Wash., res Liberty, bet N. York and Vermont.
Hatz & Co., (George Hatz, William Pope.) merchant tailors, 69 s Ill.
Hauch ——, res 208 n Alabama.
Hauck John, works in arsenal, res 215 s Penn.
Haneison William, clerk, Charles Mayer, bds Union Hall.
Hauf Henry, laborer, 51 n N. Jersey.
Haufler John, gardner at Harrison's, res 22 w Mich.
HAUG MICHAEL, GROCER AND SALOON, 60 e South, res same.
Haugh Benjamin F., foreman, Williamson & Haugh, res 164 n Penn.
Haugh Emanuel, (Williamson & Haugh,) wrought and cast iron railing shop, res 116 e Vermont.
Haughey Theo. P., 12 New & Talbott's block, res 100 n Penn, Collector U. S. Revenue 6th district Ind.
Hauk Thomas A., carpenter, bds 27 s Del.
Hause Andrew, painter, bds 64 Mass ave.
Hauser Martin, barkeep Spencer House.
Hawes George W., State Gazetteer, off. 13 old Sentinel building, res cor Georgia and Meridian.
HAWES & REDFIELD, (G. W. Hawes, and David A. Redfield,) PUBLISHERS NORTH-WESTERN SHIP'RS GUIDE, AND CLASSIFIED BUSINESS DIRECTORY, 18 e Wash., rooms 12 and 13, up stairs.
Hanley James G., bds Little's Hotel.
HAWTHORN CHARLES E., CHINA AND QUEENSWARE, 83 e Wash. res 53 n Delaware.
HAY LAWRENCE G., principal Hays' academy for boys, res 180 n Tenn.
Hay William, Quarter-master's department, bds 8 Virginia ave.
Hayden Hal. J., student at Bryant's Com. Col., bds at J. J. Hayden's.
Hayden John J, insurance and general collecting agent, res 58 n Ill., cor Meridian and Wash.
Hayden Nehemiah R., clerk in Sinking Fund office, res 62 n Missouri.
Hayden Garnet, harness maker, res 198 w Wash
Hayne Philip, res 39 w Mich.
Haynes Henry M., wholesale confectioner, 40 w Wash., res 39 w Mich.
Haynes Lewis, agent Fairbanks' scales, 74 w Wash., bds Bates House.
Haynes Wm. H., printer, H. H. Dodd & Co's book and job office, bds 44 s Penn.
Hays Abraham, (Hays, Kahon & Co.,) res 24 n Miss.

Hays B. S., portrait painter, res 20 w St Clair.
Hays Charles, Government teamster, bds. 176 Mass ave.
Hays E. M., (Hays, Kahn & Co.,) clothing store, res 10 n Miss.
Hays Isaac C., res s Ill., near Pogues run.
Hays James M., clerk at Little's Hotel.
Hays, Kahn & Co., (Emanuel Hays, Abraham Hays, Henry Rosenthal, Morris Kahn,) clothing store, 9 Bates House block.
Hayslip Joseph, res 221 s East.
Haywood Alfred, carpenter, 129 e Wash.
Hayward Catharine, washerwoman, res w Indianapolis.
Hazzard Charles K., medical student, bds 44 n Penn.
Heaf August, 10 s Penn, res same.
Healy Mrs. Ann, (wid.) dress maker, 13 n Alabama.
Healy Bernard, wagon maker, bds 50 Bluff road.
Healy Jeremiah, laborer, res Coburn.
Healy Lawrence, laborer, res e Wash.
Healy Moses, works at post office, res Clinton Keely's block.
Healy Oliver, engineer, no 142 e Daugherty.
Heany Barney, laborer, res Plum near Oak.
Heavilon Joseph, student at Bryant's Com. Col., bds 48 w Vermont.
Hebble John W., (Hebble & Co.,) City Hotel, res 77 and 79 s Ill.
HEBBLE J. W. & CO., (John W. Hebble, Christ. Dunmire,) PROPRIETORS CITY HOTEL, 77 and 79 s Ill.
Hebner Jacob, cooper, res 9 Elsworth.
Heckards Mrs. Maggie, (wid.) seamstress, 131 e N. York.
Heckman Christopher, (Heckman & McArthur,) flour and feed store, 266 e Wash., res same.
HECKMAN & McARTHUR, BATES CITY MILLS, e Wash.
HECKMAN REV. GEO. C., PASTOR THIRD PRESBYTERIAN CHURCH, res 134 n Tenn.
Heddle Joseph, porter at Mason House, res 123 w Md.
Heddrick Peter, machinist, res 66 n Noble.
Hefler Christian, teamster, res 1 Water.
Heiber Theodore L., clerk, bds Macy House.
Heider Julius, carpenter, res 160 E Wash., third story.
HEIDLINGER JOHN A., WHOLESALE MANUFACTURER AND DEALER IN CIGARS, TOBACCO, SNUFF, &c., 3 Palmer House, and 10 Bates House, res cor Wash and Del.
Heimer Andrew, watchman, I. C. R. R., res 34 s Noble.
Heiser Henry, plasterer, res 177 R. R.

Isaac Davis, dealer in Hats, Caps, Straw Goods and Furs.

Heiser John, laborer, res Mich., bet Noble and R. R.

Heiss Levi, Indiana grocery, res 37 Ind. ave.

Heitkam Charles, cabinet maker, res 184 s Delaware.

HEITKAM G H., MERCHANT TAILOR, 17 n Ill., res 25 n Liberty.

Heitkam John, varnisher, res cor Winston and Bellefontaine R. R.

Heizer Mrs. Elizabeth, (wid.) res 243 n New Jersey.

Heizman Mathius, saw filer, 33 s Penn., bds at Walks.

Helainburg Anna, res 127 n Del.

Helli Lewis, house and sign painter, res 36 w Louisiana, shop same.

Helm Adam, carpenter, res 62 n Noble.

Helm Henry, stone mason, res e Pogues run, on s side.

Helm John, grocery and feed store, 104 Davidson, res same.

Helmsetter John, tailor, res 59 n Miss.

Helpin William, printer, bds Mrs. Kinders.

Helwig Charles, carpenter and joiner res 113 e Ohio.

Henderson Duncan, salesman of sewing machines &c., 84 w Wash., res 52 Bates.

HENDERSON WILLIAM, ATTORNEY AT LAW, Ætna Building, res n Meridian.

Henderson William, peg and last factory, res 288 Madison ave.

- Henderson William W., plasterer, res 147 e New York.

Hendricks Charles, res cor N. Y. and Peru R. R.

Hendricks Isaac C., Captain in 33d Ind. Vol., res 52 e Market.

Hendricks Thomas A., (Hendricks & Hord,) bds Bates House.

Hendricks Victor K., (V. K. Hendricks & Co.,) bds Mrs. Chapman's, 37 w Ohio.

Hendricks William, U. S. A., res 85 n Miss.

HENDRICKS & HORD, (Thomas A. Hendricks and Oscar B. Hord.) ATTORNEYS AT LAW, Ætna Building.

Hendricks V. K. & Co., (Victor K. Hendricks, William O. Stone and Timothy S. Stone,) wholesale dealers in boots and shoes, 76 w Washington.

Hendrickson Andrew, laborer, res 234 w Washington.

Hennesey Patrick, laborer, 263 s Del.

Hennesey Daniel, works in Lafayette depot, res 65 Bright.

Hennesey John, dining room, Bates House.

Henning Fred. A., (Henning and Stelzell,) res 63 n Ill.

HENNING & STELZELL, (Fred. A. Henning and John Stelzell,) PROPRIETORS BATES HOUSE HAIR DRESSING SALOON, 12 n Illinois.

HENNINGER EDWARD, (Wild & Henninger,) 71 s Ill., res rear of store.

Henniger Gustavus, (Henniger & Co.,) res cor Louisiana and Illinois.

Henniger Charles, (Henniger & Co.,) res cor Louisiana and Illinois.

Henniger & Co., (Charles Henniger and Gustavus Henniger,) Tobacconists, 87 s Illinois.

Henry James F., compositor, bds City Hotel.

Henry John, laborer, res 61 St. Joseph.

Henry Joseph, carpenter, res 227 s Penn.

Henry Lawrence, laborer, res 182 East.

Henry William, engineer, res West, bet Maryland and Georgia.

Heoffner Henry, student Purdy's Commercial College, bds 40 Penn.

Herbert George, Principal St. Mary's school, res 14 n Meridian.

Hereth George, carpenter, res 117 w East.

HERETH JOHN C., HARNESS AND HARDWARE STORE, 89 e Wash.

Hereth Louis, res 181 e Vermont.

Hereth Peter, carpenter, res cor Vermont and Spring.

Herrod Edward, watchmaker H. Craft.

Herron Fred, watchman at McLene's, bds 8 Va. ave.

Hespett Charles, baker, bds 4 s Meridian.

Hess Mrs. Emeline, res 68 Merrill.

Hess Fred., woodsawer, res 66 w Ohio.

Hess James W., (Jones, Hess & Davis,) res 11 Ind. ave.

Hesse Henry, painter and varnisher, res 68 e Merrill

Hessberry Christ., laborer, res 108 s Noble.

Hessling Bernherd, tailor, res 141 e Market.

Hester H., Adams' Express, bds Oriental House.

Hester James M., Messenger Adams' Express Co., bds Palmer House.

Hetherington Benjamin, machinist, res 91 Bates.

Hetselgesser Samuel, flour dealer, res 148 s Illinois.

Hettle Joseph, porter, Mason House.

Heun Charles, planer, res 216 n Davidson.

Henschew John, carpenter, res 170 Virginia ave.

Hewes Rev. Charles W., Princial Indiana Female Institute, cor North and Pennsylvania.

Hewitt Charles, Attorney at Law, 84 e Wash., bds Mrs. Cook's, w New York.

Hickey John, laborer, bds Willard, near rolling mill.

Hider Augustus, (Grofe & Hider,) res Market, bet Noble and East.

Hider Charles, salesman Jones, Hess & Davis, bds 17 Ind. ave.

Hieninger Richard, editor Free Press, res 51 Huron.

Hiess August, carpenter, res Patterson, n North.

Hiess Sebastian, woodsawer, res 271 n Illinois.

Higgins William B., silver plater, 8 w Wash., res 161 n New Jersey.

Higgins William W., 16½ s Illinois.

Highstreet John, U. S. service, res 107 South.

Hight Ferd, actor at Metropolitan Theater, res 29 n Liberty.

Hight George, cooper, 58 s East.

Hild August, laborer, res 156 Davidson.

Hildebrand Henry, carpenter, res 130 Massachusetts ave.

Hilderbrant J. S., clerk I. H. Vagen, res 7 Madison ave.

Hiles Isaac, carpenter, res 36 Ind. ave.

Hilgemeier Christian, street sprinkler, res 23 Wyoming.

Hilgemier Herman, shoemaker, 2 n Noble.

Hilgenberg Christ., farmer, res 124 n Miss., up stairs.

Hill Charles, (col.,) works at Johnston's stable, res outside corporation, in Pee Dee.

Hill G. W., sawmill, res 68 s East.

Hill James Rev., (Methodist,) res 118 n West.

Hill James, laborer, res 170 w Market.

Hill James B., mailing clerk P. O.

Hill John F., nurseryman, res 38 n Ala.

Hill Lucian, agent Bellef. R. R., res 49 w Maryland.

Hill Nelson, (col.,) laborer, res cor East and St. Clair.

Hill Wm. B., student at Bryant's Commercial College.

Hill William H., printer, bds 115 n East.

Hillgamayer Christ., street sprinkler, res Wyoming.

Hillis David, student with John T. Dye, bds 137 n New Jersey.

Hilman Charles, carpenter, res 9 Water.

Hilman Wm., blacksmith, res 310 Virginia ave.

Hilmire Frederick, switchman Peru depot, res 11 Water.

Hilt Frank L., blacksmith, res 99 w Md.

Himbaugh Kate, (wid.,) res 44 s East.

Hime John, speculator, res cor National and Michigan roads.

Himmerling George, brickmaker, res 65 Hossbrook.

Hind Ed., dealer in groceries and liquors, 155 e Washington.

Hinde Patrick J., grocer, 155 e Washington, res 37 n East.

Hinderer John G., woodsawer, res 226 n New Jersey.

Hindman Mrs. Sarah, (wid.,) res s Penn.

Hinds Jesse, brickmason, res 74 n East.

Hine Charles, planer Speigel, Thoms & Co., res 154 Davidson.

Hines Edward, teacher of Music, bds 71 Indiana ave.

Hinesey John, laborer, res 49 s New Jersey.

Hinesley Andrew J., (A. J. Hinesley & Co.,) res 119 Mass. ave.

A. J. Hinesley & Co., (Andrew J. Hinesley and James Hufford,) saddle and harnessmakers, 34 w Wash.

HINESLEY WILLIAM, LIVERY AND SALE STABLE, Pearl, in rear of the Palmer House, res 73 w New York. See card.

Hinkly D. J., bds Oriental House.

Hinkley Oliver W., bookkeeper Asher & Co., bds 86 n Alabama.

Hinsdale Miss Emma, (Quimby & Hinsdale,) 18 s Illinois.

Hinton William, res 263 Mass. ave.

Hippard Samuel, salesman, 48 w Wash., res cor Meridian and Washington.

Hire Frank, laborer, res 35 s Liberty.

Hirsh Levi, salesman, Moritz, Bro. & Co., bds Farmers Hotel.

Hiss Henry, clerk, George Krug, bds cor Georgia and Liberty.

Hitchcock Alexander, trader, res 119 n Ala.

Hitchcock Sidney, 5th Ind. cavalry, res 149 e Ohio.

Hitchens John, blacksmith, res 157 Mass. ave.

Hite Mrs Elizabeth, (wid) res 146 e Wood.

Hitz Louis, plow grinder, res e Washington.

Hobart Lucretia, teacher, 6th ward school, bds 109 Ala.

Hobbs Abner, land agent, res 232 w Wash.

Hodgson Isaac, architect, 4 Vohn's block, res 135 n Meridian.

Hoefgan John, toll gate keeper, on Bluff road, Doughertyville, res same.

HOEFGEN SAMUEL B., ATTORNEY AT LAW, 15½ e Wash.

Hofamars Lewis, shoemaker, 48 Mass. ave.

Heper George, shoemaker, res 185 w Wash.

Hofferberth Wm., laborer, res 69 Bright.

Hoffman Theodore, salesman, 26 and 28 w Wash.

Hoffman Valentine, laborer, res 68 s Noble.

Hoffmayer Henry, tailor, res Liberty, bet Ver. and N. York.

Hoffmeyer Frederick, laborer, res 71 n East.

Hoffmeyer Henry, tailor, res Liberty, bet N. York and Ver.

Hofminn Michael blacksmith, res 63 Union.

Hofmeister Christian, eating saloon, 75 e Wash., bds 82 n Noble.

Fine Silk Hats, at Davis', 15 Pennsylvania St.

Hofmeister & Hofmeister, (Nicholas Hofmeister & Christian Hofmeister,) grocers, 82 n Noble.
Hofmeister Nicholas, (H. & H.,) grocer, 82 n Noble, res same.
Hogan John, laborer, res Mich. road.
Hogel S. M., carriage maker, res 205 Ala.
Hogstine Christ., works pork house, res 50 Union.
Hogshire Samuel H., (Hogshire & Co.,) res 80 w Georgia.
Hogshire Wm. R., (Hogshire & Co.,) bds 80 w Georgia.
HOGSHIRE W. R. & CO.,) Samuel H. Hogshire & Wm. R. Hogshire,) WHOLESALE AND RETAIL GROCERS, AND DEALERS IN ALL KINDS OF PRODUCE, 25 w Wash.
Hohl Christ. C., grocery and saloon, 77 e Wash., res same.
Hoit Mrs. Harriet, (wid. Bennagah Hoit,) res 64 Mass. ave.
Holbrook Clay, book-keeper, 18 w Wash., res 77 n Ala.
Holbrook Henry C., clerk, bds 77 n Ala.
Holcomb Rev. Theodore, Episcopal, res 13 Circle.
Holdykon Charles, bds California House, 136 s Ill.
Holdzkom Charles, whip maker, bds California House.
Holla Henry, laborer, bds 109 n Penn.
Holladay Elias G., attorney at law, off. Littles Hotel.
Holladay & Neff, (E. G. Holladay & Wm. Neff,) real estate and soldiers' claims agents, 157 e Wash.
Holland Charles W., res 173 n Miss.
Holland Frank R., salesman, Holland & Son, bds 8 e Mich.
Holland George B., book-keeper, 9 w Wash, res n Penn.
Holland John, carpenter, res 217 s Delaware.
Holland John H., student at Bryant's commercial college, bds John W. Holland.
Holland John W., (Holland & Son,) res 58 n Penn.
Holland Theodore, (Holland & Son,) res 8 e Mich.
HOLLAND & SON, (Theodore Holland & John Holland,) WHOLESALE GROCERS, 72 e Wash.
Hollar Rheinhardt, bricklayer, res 31 Vir. ave.
Hollaran John, laborer, res 177 s East.
Holler George, plasterer, res Loukebee, bet East and Liberty.
Holler Philip, engineer, res 117 n Noble.
Holler Philip, stone mason, res 218 n Noble.
Holliday Cortez H., clerk, bds 117 e Ohio.
Holliday Rev. F. C., res 117 e Ohio.
Holliday Gideon, laborer, res 42 Pratt.

Holliday Rev. Wm. A., Presbyterian, res 102 n Ala.
Holliday Wm. J., (Murphy, Kenneday & Co.,) res 145 n Penn.
Holliday W. J. & Co., (Wm. J. Holliday & John W. Murphy,) wholesale dealers in iron, steel, &c., 34 e Wash.
Holloway Wm. R., Governor's private secretary, bds Palmer House.
Holmes Charles, clerk, bds 42 n Miss.
Holmes Henry, plasterer, res 3d house s of Maryland on Cal.
Holmes James S., teamster, res cor Ash and corporation.
Holmes Jonathan, res 141 n Meridian.
HOLMES C. L., CITY GROCERY, WHOLESALE AND RETAIL, bds 42 Miss.
Holmes Michael, hostler, Hinesly's stable, bds E. Knight's.
Holmes Wm., clerk, res 61 e Market.
Holt Mrs. Louisa, (wid) res 87 n East.
Holt S. A, bds Littles Hotel.
Holton Charles A., bds 111 w South.
HOLTON J. L., PROPRIETOR BATES HOUSE, res same.
Homan Mrs. Mary E., res 14 s West.
Homburg Dr. K., off. 26½ w Wash.
Homburg Wm. C., student, 26½ w Wash.
Homburg Wm. F., student in Bryant's commercial college.
Homen Jeremiah, hatter, res 17 Vir. ave.
Hook Menah, washer, res 65 n Noble.
Hooker E. M. B., 20th Ind. regiment.
Hooker Henry, T. H. R. R., res 145 e South.
Hooper Chas. A., jeweler, res 155 Vir. ave.
Hooper Walter, blacksmith, res 112 n East.
Hoover Perry, grocer, Mt. Jackson.
Hopkins Chas. G., student at Bryant's commercial college, bds Isaac H. Hopkins, 60 s Ill.
Hopkins Isaac H., traveling agent, New York Central R R., res 60 s Ill.
Hopkins James H., book binder, 24 w Wash., bds 20 Cal.
Hord Oscar B., Attorney General, res 160 w N. York.
Horn Henry J., at city grocery, 31 w Wash., res 4 n Miss.
Hosbrook Daniel B., res 108 n Miss.
Hoshour Samuel K., professor of languages, N. W. C. University, res n N. Jersey, bet Market and Ohio.
Hoskin Mrs. Julia, (wid) res 96 McCartny.
Hoskins Robert, forage master 11th reg., res 160 e Ohio.
Hoss Prof. G. W., N. W. C. U., res same.
Hossfeld Charles, book-keeper, 256 e Wash., bds same.
Hossfeld Lewis, clerk, Charles Mayer, bds Excelsior saloon.

The Florence Sewing Machine Co. court investigation.

Hotz George, (Hotz & Co.,) tailor, bds Farmers Hotel.

Houesiam I. T., steward, Palmer House.

Houpt Robert, dry. goods, 5 Chatham, res same.

How Michael, works Bellefontaine shop, bds Cincinnati House.

Howard Alex. C., agent for Daily Gazette, res 175 n N. Jersey.

Howard Edward, M. D., (Howard & Son,) res 52 s Ill.

Howard Henry, res 194 e St. Clair.

Howard L. Bradford, (Howard & Davies,) bds 83 n Ill.

Howard Martha S.. (wid) res 45 s Mer.

Howard Michael, laborer, res in rear of 45 s East.

Howard Margaret, (wid) res 45 s East.

Howard Wm., (Howard & Son,) res 52 s Ill.

Howard Wm. C., laborer, bds 186 Mass. ave.

HOWARD & DAVIES, (L. Bradford Howard & Thomas J. Davies,) PHOTO-GRAPHERS, 26 and 28 w Wash., over Hume, Lord & Co's store.

Howard & Son, (Edward Howard and Wm. Howard,) cancer doctors, off. 62 s Ill.

Howell Mrs. Margaret, (wid) washer, res 194 e Wash.

Howland John D.. (Barbour & Howland,) law office, 2 Wash., 2d floor, res cor Tenn. and Vt.

Howlett Thomas, laborer, res 167 e Ohio.

Hoyle Samuel M., carriage maker, bds 205 s Ala.

Hubbard Garrison, teamster, res 18 Elm.

Hubbard Wm., laborer, res s Ill.

Hubbard W. S., res 9 Circle.

Hudnut Theodore, homony manufacturer, mill Penn., bet Maryland and South, res Alvord's block.

Hueston George W., laborer, res 300 Vir. ave.

Huey Milton, (Rhodes & Huey,) res 84 w Georgia.

Huffer James M., saddler, 20 w Wash., res 89 e Market.

Huffman Casper, blacksmith, res 224 n Ala.

Huffman Henry, tanner, res 224 n Ala.

Huffman Theodore, clerk, res 56 e Market.

Hufford David, carpenter, res 131 w N. York.

Hufford James, (A. J. Hinesley & Co.,) res 89 e Market.

Hugg Joseph, works rolling mill, res e Wash.

Hugg Martin, Capital saloon, 14 e Wash., res 45 n N. Jersey.

Hughes Mrs. Eliza, res 229 s Penn.

Hughes Samuel, conductor, I. C. R. R., bds Palmer House.

Hughey Wm., res 86 e La.

Hughs Mrs. Mary, (wid) res 133 n Liberty.

Hugo Henry A., plasterer, res 249 s East.

Hulahan Patrick, works rolling mill, bds Willard, near rolling mill.

Huling John P., house painter, res South, bet Penn. and Meridian.

Hull Absalom D., cigarmaker, res 52 n East.

Hulser John, laborer, res Bluff road, Doughertyville,

Hume Isaac N., salesman, 26 and 28 w Wash., res 75 n Miss.

Hume James M., (Hume, Lord & Co.,) res 77 n Miss.

Hume, Lord & Co., (James M. Hume, Edgar Lord & W. L. Adams,) dry goods, 28 w Wash.

Hume Madison, missionary baptist, and pastor Northfield church, res 75 n Miss.

Humphrey C. T., watchmaker, 37 w Wash , bds in country.

Humphrey James, cooper, res St. Clair.

Humphrey Samuel C., cooper, 211 Ind. ave.

Humphrey John, cooper, res 188 Ind. ave.

Hunt Aaron L., auctioneer, res cor East and St. Clair.

Hunt Andrew M., surgeon, 33d reg. Ind. vol.

Hunt Albert, engineer, res 180 Penn.

Hunt Arnestress, laborer, res w Ind'pls.

Hunt Charles C., cigars, &c., 61 e Wash., res in rear.

Hunt David B., clerk, U. S., mustering office, bds 78 Mass. ave.

Hunt Jesse, 2d Lieut., Co. I., 63d reg't, res 65 n West.

Hunt Julia, (wid. David P. Hunt,) plain sewing, res 6 Circle.

Hunt P. G. C., dentist, 32 e Market, res same.

Hunt Thomas E., stove dealer, res 156 n Penn.

Hunt Walter W., sells spectacles, 78 e Wash.

HUNTER M. & CO., (Moses Hunter, Benj. C. Darrow & Ed. C. Brundage,) BOOTS AND SHOES, 19 e Wash.

Hunter Moses, (M. Hunter & Co ,) bds cor Market and Penn.

Hunter Ralph, machinest, res 72 s East.

Hurd Daniel B., boarding house, 117 n Missouri.

Hurd Eugene, expressman, res 162 Ind. ave.

Hurle Abraham, marble polisher, bds Cunningham's.

Hurley Patrick, hackman, res 73 Bright.

Hurrle Ignatius tailor, res 23 n Noble.

Hurst Herman, tailor, res 233 s Penn.

Hurstman Henry, teamster, res 15 Harrison.

All kinds of soft Hats at No. 15, Pennsylvania St.

Hurslinger Leonard, blacksmith, res e Wash.

Husted Hiram, currier, res 15 w McCarthy.

Husten Malvina, seamstress, Wright's Hall, e Wash.

Huston Ephas B., salesman, 51 e Ohio.

Hut George, laborer, res s West:

Hutchins Emma, (wid. John Hutchins,) dressmaker, res 116 n Miss.

Hutchins Henry H., book-keeper, res 148 Vir. ave.

Hutchinson Chas. P., (H. H. Dodd & Co.,) bds 45 n Penn.

Hutchison John, machinest, res cor McCarthy and Grier.

Hutton Thomas, boarding house, 48 n Tenn.

Hæzele John, clerk, Louis Lang, bds same.

Hyatt Cecelia, res 21 Ky. ave.

Hyatt John, barkeeper, Pearl saloon, res same.

Hyatt James, school teacher, Mt. Jackson.

Hyde Arthur, cabinet maker, res cor Liberty and Ohio.

HYDE ABNER R., PROPRIETOR LITTLES HOTEL, cor New Jersey and Wash.

Hyde Rev. Nathaniel A., pastor Congregational Church, bds 87 n Penn.

Hyman Robbison, baker, res 165 s Del.

I

Inhley Jacob, laborer, bds California House, 186 s Ill.

Ideer Clinton, machinest, res 113 w South.

Igoe Martin, quartermaster 35th reg., res 17 e Loukebee.

Igau John W., in Government employ, 22 w Maryland.

ILG GEORGE, PROPRIETOR UNION HOUSE, cor Illinois and South. See card.

Iliff Charles E., salesman, Baker & McIver, bds 37 n Ala.

Iliff James, salesman, Baker & McIver, bds 37 n Ala.

Iliff Richard W., res 37 n Ala.

ILLINIOS AND INDIANA CENTRAL RAILWAY OFFICE, 24½ e Wash., Edmund Clark, agent.

Ince Joseph, soldier, res 176 Massachusetts ave.

Indicut John, (col) white washer, res 86 alley, bet Mich and Ver.

Indicut Isom, (col) in saloon, res 134 n Missouri

Indiana Central Railway engine house, bet Noble and Benton.

INDIANA CENTRAL RAILWAY OFFICES, cor Vir. ave and Del.

INDIANAPOLIS DAILY GAZETTE, s Meridian, daily and weekly, Jordan & Burnett, proprietors.

INDIANA FREE PRESS, 83 e Wash., R. Heninger, proprietor; German weekly.

INDIANAPOLIS GAS WORKS, Penn. bet South and Pogue's run.

INDIANA SCHOOL JOURNAL, monthly publication off., Journal building, cor Circle and Meridian.

INDIANA STATE SENTINAL, Meridian, bet Wash. and Pearl, Elder, Harkness & Bingham, proprietors, daily and weekly.

INDIANA U. S. ARSENAL, Market, bet Tenn. and Miss.

INDIANA VOLKSBLATT, 132 e Wash., Julius Bœtticher, proprietor, German weekly.

INDIANAPOLIS BAPTIST FEMALE INSTITUTE, cor Penn. and North, Rev. C. W. Hewes, principal.

INDIANAPOLIS BRANCH BANKING CO., s w cor Wash. and Penn., Calvin Fletcher, president; T. H. Sharpe, cashier.

INDIANAPOLIS GAS LIGHT AND COKE CO., D. S. Beaty, president; Samuel Vanlaningham, secretary, off. in Ray's building.

INDIANAPOLIS JOURNAL CO., Journal building, cor Circle and Meridian, daily and weekly, J. M. Tilford, president.

INDIANAPOLIS McLEAN FEMALE INSTITUTE, cor Meridian and N. York, Rev. C. Sturdevant, principal.

INDIANAPOLIS, PITTSBURG & CLEVELAND RAILROAD LINE, part of Bellefontaine line, off. cor Meridian and Lou.

INDIANAPOLIS ROLLING MILL CO., J. M. Lord, president and superintendent; A. Jones, treasurer; C. B. Parkman, secretary; John Thomas, manager; Tenn., three squares s of Terre Haute depot.

INDIANAPOLIS & CHICAGO AIR LINE, via Kokomo and C. & C. air line, off. at Peru & Indianapolis R. R. office

INDIANAPOLIS & CINCINNATI RAIL ROAD, offices cor Del. and Lou.

INDIANAPOLIS AND CINCINNATI FREIGHT DEPOT, s Del., bet Maryland and South.

INDIANAPOLIS & PERU R. R., Freight Office, cor N. Jersey and Union track, General Ticket Office, cor Wash. and Del., D. Macy, sup't, V. T. Malott, ticket agent.

Ingerman Wm., laborer, res w Indianapolis.

Ingersol Frank, city fire department, bds Ray House, s Del.

Military Hats and Caps, at Davis' hat store.

Ingham James, stone cutter, res 16 s West.

Ingle Jacob, coal hauler, res 35 Spring.

Ingle John, carpenter, res 90 Bates.

Inglekink Wm., switchman, res 99 Peru railroad.

INSURANCE COMPANYS — Charter Oak Fire, Columbia Fire, Manhattan Fire, Niagara Fire, Phœnix Fire, Rising Sun Fire, Manhattan Life; C. B. Davis, agent.

Ætna, (Hartford,) Wm. Henderson, ag't. Artic, N. T., Home; Martindale & Grubbs, agents.

Continental Fire, Security Fire, Market Fire, Lorillard Fire, Springfield Fire, New England Fire, N. Y. Mutual Life; John S. Dunlop, agent.

Liverpool & London Fire, Metropolitan Fire; John S. Spann, agent.

Phœenix (Hartford) Fire, Hartford Fire, City (Hartford) Fire, Ætna Life, New England Mutual Life, Home (N. Y.) Life; J. J. Hayden, agent.

Indianapolis Fire Insurance Co., home office Odd Fellows' Hall.

Irick Adam, laborer, res alley, bet East, and Liberty.

Irick Morris, bds 156 N. Jersey.

Irick Wm. C., brickmason, res 173 n N. Jersey.

Irick Wm. H., brickmason, res 156 n N. Jersey.

Ireland Wm. H., carpenter, res 130 n N. Jersey.

Iresly John, engineer, res 75 s East.

Irons Mrs. Catherine, res 119 w Md.

Irons Harry T., messenger telegraph office.

Irving Cornelius, brickmaker, res. Grove.

Irvin Thomas, laborer, res 39 Henry.

Irwin James, Government hostler, bds 11 s Penn.

Irwin Joseph, (Irwin & Patterson,) res 23 w Ohio.

Irwin & Patterson, (Joseph Irwin, Robt. M. Patterson,) livery stable, 24 s Penn.

Isgregg James A., carpenter, 13 Ky. ave.

Iske Christ., laborer, res 344 Va. ave.

Ittenbach Frank, (Ittenbach & Co.,) res 180 s Del.

Ittenbach Gerhard, (Ittenbach & Co.,) res 180 s Del.

Ivens Henry, (Ivens & Co.,) res Philadelphia.

IVENS & CO., CLOAKS AND MANTILLAS, old P. O. building, s Meridian.

J

Jack Henry W., bds 44 n Penn.

Jack Matthew, propritor Jack boarding house, 44 n Penn.

Jackson Allen S., tinner.

Jackson Alonzo, bds 2 s Tenn.

Jackson Mrs. Ann, res 59 Ky. ave.

Jackson Bird, (col.) laborer, res 143 n Alabama.

Jackson Ellel, tinsmith, cor Elm and Forest ave.

Jackson Henry, blacksmith, Marsh and Case, cor Tenn and Wash., res 2 Tenn.

Jackson John T., law student, Hendricks & Hord, bds cor Ala. and Mass. ave.

Jackson Marshal, blacksmith, Marsh & Case, cor Tenn. and Wash., bds 2 s Tenn.

Jackson Oscar, hostler, bds Pea Ridge House.

Jackson Thomas B., clerk in fruit house, bds 116 Ohio.

Jackson William, roofing, res 26 n Liberty.

Jackson William N., ticket agent, Union Depot, bds 22 s Meridian.

Jacobs Elizabeth, (wid) res 165 e Wash.

Jacobs Milton, laborer, bds 59 Md.

Jacobs Captain Valentine, res 58 e Md.

James W. John, soldier, res w Indian'plis.

James Joseph, laborer, res w Indianap'lis.

James Seth, stone cutter, res 3 Stephen.

James Thomas C., harness maker, 34 w Wash., bds 24 n Penn.

James Thomas S., (H. W. James & Co.,) bds Bates House.

James Wilson W., (James & Co.,) res 163 n Tenn.

JAMES W. W. & CO., (Wilson W. James, Thomas S. James,) MARBLE WORKS, 58 s Meridian, near Union Depot. (See card.)

Jameson Alex. C., U. S. A., bds 79 w South.

Jameson John H. Chaplain 79th Reg. Ind. vols, res 97 w South.

Jameson Patrick H., M. D., (Jameson & Funkhouser,) res 51 cor Ohio and Ala.

Jameson & Funkhouser, M. D., (Patrick Henry Jameson, David Funkhouser,) off. 5 s Meridian.

Jasper Frederick, grocer and liquor dealer, 281 s Del.

Jeck Fredrick, carpenter, res 215 s Del.

Jefferson Robert, (col.) carpenter, res Manerva, bet Mich. and and North.

JEFFERSONVILLE R. R. OFFICE, 43 e South.

Jamison John, harness maker, res 29 Union.

Jenison Alexander F., watch maker, Talbott & Co., res 9 w Ohio.

Jenison George M., Talbott & Co., res 9 w Ohio.

Jenkens A. W., grocery dealer, 120 n Penn, res same.

Jenkins John, salesman Jenkins' grocery, res 126 e Market.

Jenkins John M., Watchman at Gov. stables, res 215 Mass. ave.

Jennings George, breakman, I. P. & C. R. R., res Wabash, bet Liberty and Noble.

The Florence Machine will sew over the heaviest seams.

H. S. ROCKEY,

Wholesale and Retail Dealer in

Coal & Carbon Oils,

COAL OIL LAMPS

Of every variety, from the Cheapest to the most Magnificent

HALL, CHURCH, & PARLOR CHANDELIERS.

ALSO,

Coal Oil, Lard Oil, and Candle Lanterns

Of all the different kinds, **Chimnies, Wicks, Brushes and Globes** of every variety, **Shades, Brackets, Hangers, &c.** Cans from one quart to forty gallons. Every variety of

Lubricating Oils, Benzole and Naptha, for Painters.

ALL KINDS OF REPAIRING NEATLY DONE.

No. 7 South Meridian St., Indianapolis, Indiana.

GEORGE W. PITTS,

Wholesale and Retail Dealer in

ICE,

Office and Res. 78 Indiana Ave.,

INDIANAPOLIS, IND.

D. J. CALLINAN,

DEALER IN

STAPLE AND FANCY

DRY GOODS!

CLOAKS, SHAWLS.

EMBROIDERIES, LACE GOODS,

Ribbons, Straw Goods, Hosiery, &c., &c.,

28 East Washington St., North side,

INDIANAPOLIS, IND.

L. B. WILLIAMSON.   E. HAUGH.

WILLIAMSON & HAUGH,

Manufacturers of Wrought and Cast Iron

RAILING, VERANDAS, BANK VAULTS,

IRON DOORS, SHUTTERS, BOLTS, &c.,

Also Plain and Ornamental Iron Stairs, and general House Smithing,

Delaware St., bet. Washington and Market, West of Court House,

INDIANAPOLIS, INDIANA.

B. R McCORD.   WM. M. WHEATLEY.

McCORD & WHEATLEY,

Dealers in all kinds of

LUMBER, LATH & SHINGLES

Yard No. 119 South Delaware Street,

South of the Indianapolis and Cincinnati Rail Road Depot,

INDIANAPOLIS, IND.

☞Cash paid for Lumber, Lath and Shingles. Cash orders filled promptly.☜

Jennings Patrick, teacher, res cor Mich. and Davidson.

Jennings Thomas W., (Goddard & Jennings,) res 24 n Penn.

Jennings William, tinner, res 86 e Michigan.

Jermain John, laborer, res Wyoming.

Joachimi Augustus, candle maker, res cor Miss and Md.

Johnson Peter, shoemaker, bds California House, 136 s Ill.

John Charles, res 199 e Wash.

John Mary, Sister Providence, res cor Georgia and Tenn.

Johnson Alexander T., carpenter, res 44 Mich. road.

Johnson Alexander W., carpenter, res 57 w South.

Johnson Benjamin F., Lieut. in 17th Ind. Bat., res 240 n Ill.

Johnson B. F., clerk, Palmer House, res same.

Johnson C. A., Star Gallery, 83 w Wash. bds Bates House.

Johnson Charles R., Burke's saloon, 13 w Wash., res same.

Johnson Charles R., res 172 Blake.

Johnson Charles, clerk, 5 Bates House, res 50 s Ill.

Johnson David, (col.) Royal Arch saloon, res same.

Johnson Edmund C ,farmer, res Meridian, bet McCarthy and Merril.

Johnson Elizabeth, seamstress, Clinton, bet Ohio and N. York.

Johnson F. W., surveyor, Johnson House, Mt. Jackson.

Johnson Henry, (col.) barber, bds 127 n East.

Johnson Hubbard, salesman, bds 121 e Ohio.

Johnson Isaac B.,student at Bryant's Com. Col., bds in the country.

Johnson Isaac E., attorney at Law, off. 4 Blake's row, res 58 n Miss.

Johnson George, blacksmith, res 74 e Louisiana.

Johnson George H , salesman, 12 w Wash. res s end Alabama.

Johnson James, carpenter, res 44 Mich. road.

Johnson James B., carpenter, res 98 s Md.

Johnson James, harness maker, res 8 Bluff road.

Johnson James A., grocer and harness maker, 88 Bluff road, res same.

Johnson John, res 74 Bluff road.

Johnson John, cutter, O. McGinnis, res Walnut, bet Ill. and Tenn.

JOHNSON JOHN B., GROCERY AND PROVISION SNORE, 144 w. Wash., res 101 w Maryland.

Johnson John S., teamster, res s Meridian, bet McCarthy and Merril.

Johnson John, laborer, Nicholas McCarty res same.

Johnson Louis, works at arsenal, res 32 Spring.

Johnson Marquis De La Fayette, city policeman.

Johnson Mrs. Mary, res 101 n Noble.

Johnson Peter, shoemaker, bds California House, s Ill.

Johnson Philip A., carpenter, res 155 n East.

Johnson Robert, contractor, res North, bet Minerva and Blake.

Johnson Samuel L., (Pindy,) printer, H. H. Dodd & Co.

Johnson Thomas, builder, bds 17 Mass. ave.

Johnson Thomas, U. S. service, res n Louisiana.

Johnsohn T. D., clerk New York Store, res 17 Mass. ave.

Johnson Thompson, wheat warehouse, res 241 Alabama.

Johnson William, grocery, 167 s Tenn.

Johnson William, laborer, res 160 Blake, Johnson William J., hackman, res 110 Blake.

Johnson William S., baker, bds Mrs. Reed's, n Penn.

Johnson William W., printer, res 112 e Vermont.

Johnston Mrs. Fidelia, seamstress, res 184 n East.

Johnston John F., dentist, 11 w Md., off. same.

Johnston John, works rolling mill, bds 231 s East.

Johnston Olvier W., res 172 e South.

Johnston, Samuel A., book keeper, Munson & Johnston, bds 86 e Vt.

Johnston William A., student, Bryant's College, bds 309 Va. ave.

Johnston William J., (Munson & Johnston,) res 86 e Vermont.

Johnston William W., (Murphy, Kennedy & Co.,) res 160 s N. Jersey.

Jolly James, watchman, I. & C. R. R. shop, res 11 Lord.

Jolly John, works I. & C. R. R. shop, res 11 Lord.

Jolly William E., painter, res 11 Virginia ave.

Jones Aquilla, Sr., (Jones, Vinnedge & Co.,) res 79 n Penn.

Jones Aquilla, Jr., (Jones, Vinnedge & Co.,) bds Bates House.

Jones Barton D., (Delzell & Jones,) res 91 n Ala.

Jones Casper M., cutter, res 137 South.

Jones Edward D., Engineer, res Bellefontaine R. R., near corporation.

Jones Frank, (col.) barber shop, 53 s Del., bds. Pyle House.

Jones George E., machinist, res Wright's Hall, e Wash.

The Florence has the most practical hemmer in use.

Jones Henry W., student at Bryant's Com. Col., bds with P. A. Brown.

Jones Josiah, (col.) hostler, bds 91 n Tenn.

Jones Jesse, 31 w Wash., res 106 n Ill.

Jones John P., Clerk Supreme Court, res 88 n Tenn.

Jones John W., clerk Jones, Vinnedge & Co., bds 79 n Penn.

Jones John W., T. & R. R. R. depot, res 75 w south.

Jones Lewis H., harness maker, 34 w Wash., res cor Ill. and McCarty.

Jones Luther, farmer, res, w Indianpolis.

Jones Mary A., (wid.) res 154 w. Vt.

Jones Nathan R., conductor, T. H. & R. R. R., res 49 w Georgia.

Jones Nathan, moulder, res 127 s Ill.

Jones Robert, cabinet maker, bds at Knight.

Jones Robert A., carpenter, res 169 n Noble.

Jones Reuben, brakesman on I. & C. R. R., bds at C. C. Reeves, e Wash.

Jones Spicer, Sutler 47th Regt., res 206 n Illinois.

Jones William H., (Coburn & Jones,) res 169 n Ill.

Jones Wm. M., clerk Bates House.

Jones William T., carpenter, res 9 South.

Jones William W., (Jones, Hess & Davis,) res. 53 Ind. ave.

JONES, HESS & DAVIS, (W. W. Jones, J. W. Hess, W. M. Davis,) DRY GOODS, 3 Odd Fellow's Hall, w Wash.

Jordan Gilmore, Commissary U. S. A., res 104 n Tenn.

Jordan J. H., (Jordan & Burnett,) bds Patterson House.

Jordan Joseph, teamster, res 138 Bluff road.

Jordan Lewis, (Colerick & Jordan,) res 60 n Meridian.

Jordan Samuel J., tailor, res 157 s Miss.

Jordan Thomas, (Jorden & Spotts,) bds Palmer House.

JORDAN & BURNET, (J. H. Jordan, J. C. Burnet,) EDITORS OF INDIANAPOLIS DAILY GAZETTE, 14 and 16 s Meridian, up stairs.

Jorden & Spotts, (Thos. Jorden, William Spotts,) commission merchants and grain dealers, cor Peru and Union R. R. track.

Jose Albert, frame maker, 13 n Penn., bds Union Hall.

Jose Nicholas, furniture, &c., s Penn., near Wash.

Joseph J. G., salesman, 2 Palmer House, bds Macy House.

Joseph George W., mailing clerk P. O., bds 164 w N. York.

Joseph Richard C., res 164 w N. York, up stairs.

Joyce Edmund, laborer, res 245 s Penn.

Joytel Charles, clerk Lafayette House, bds same.

Judge James, laborer, res Wyoming.

Judson Charles E., res 97 n Ill.

Jutt Frederick, works woolen factory, res cor of California and Md.

K

Kafady Joseph, stone cutter, res 5 e South.

Kahle Samuel, cabinet maker, res Orient.

Kahn A., (A. Kahn & Co.,) bds Palmer House.

Kahn Jacob, (A. Kahn & Co.,) res 20 s Mississippi.

Kahn Morris, (Hays, Kahn & Co.,) bds 24 n Miss.

Kahn A. & Co., (A Kahn, Jacob Kahn,) clothing, 2 Palmer House.

Kahn John, laborer, res s Missouri, near Michigan.

Knidder John B., tanner and currier, res 91 e Market.

Kalle Philip, porter, Bates House, res 65 St. Marys.

Kalles9h Martin, moulder, res Madison ave., corp. line.

Kallicher John, laborer, res 118 Union.

Kamp August, carpenter, res 18 Ky ave.

Kane Robert S., machinist, bds California House, 136 s Ill.

Kantman Joseph, salesman, Jones, Hess & Davis, bds Union Hall.

Kappel John, teacher, German Lutheran Church. res 188 e Ohio.

Kappes Henry, (Seidensticker & Kappes,) res 62 North.

Karanutz John, shoemaker, Jones, Vinnedge & Co.. bds Charles Aldag.

Karcoff Charles, laborer, res 119 South.

Kareger Henry, laborer, res 101 s Ala. rolling mill.

Kares Joseph, carpenter, res 58 n Davidson.

Karitzer Henry, teamster, res 262 Mad. ave.

Karle Christ, boot and shoe maker, 73 e Wash., res 72 s Del.

Karle John J., boot and shoe maker, 33 e South, res same.

Karney John, gas fitter, res 131 Ala.

Kartepeter William, tailor, res 161 n Ala.

Katzenstein Julius, (Katzenstein & Wachtel,) bds Oriental House.

Katzenstein & Wachtel, (Julius Katzenstein, Moses Wachtel,) Peoples' Store, merchant tailors and clothiers, 3 Bates House.

Kaufman Aaron, tobacconist, 143 n Penn.

Kaufman Gerge A., collar maker, 66 s Del., res same.

Kaufman Solomon, tobacco and cigars, 81 e Wash., bds 143 n Penn.

KAUG MICHAEL,———

Isaac Davis, fashionable hatter, No. 15 Pennsylvania St.

Kaupke Fred., porter, Murphy, Kennedy & Co., bds 20 n Penn.

Kay Joseph, wagon maker, 205 w Wash., res 136 w Vermont.

Keahoe Michael, porter, Mason House.

Keane Mrs. Anna, (Lynch & Keane,) res 43 n Tenn.

Keane Daniel, grocer, res 12 Mich. road.

Kearney George, painter, 113 n Miss.

Kearney John, foreman Gas Co., res 131 s Ala.

Kearney William, porter, Farmers' Hotel. bds same.

Keating Jeffery, laborer, res 314 s Del.

Keating Joseph J., res 54 Ind. ave.

Keating Lucy E., prof. of languages, res 20 Elm.

Keeler William H., res 44 Spring.

Keeley Henry S., printer, H. H. Dodd & Co., res 159 e Ohio.

Keely Daniel brickmason, res 105 n Noble.

Keely Isaac, bricklayer, bds 105 n Noble.

Keely Elmer, (wid.) Keely's block, Clinton.

Keely George L., printer, bds 105 n Noble.

Keely Isaac I., physician and surgeon, res 62 e Mich.

Keely Henry, carpenter, bds 62 e Mich.

Keely John, brickmason, res 48 n East.

Keely Joseph, carpenter, res Mich., bet Ala. and N. Jersey.

Keely Oliver S., brickmason, res 159 e Ohio.

Keely Samuel, brickmason, res 177 n noble.

Keely Wm., Sr., carpenter, res 62 e Mich.

Keely Wm. H., grocery, cor Market and Noble, res 163 e Ohio.

Keen Earnest, tailor, bds Farmers Hotel.

Keen Hiram, W., (Tarlton & Keen,) bds 122 n Ill

Keeman Margaret, (wid) res 61 s Noble.

Keesee George, U. S. service, res 105 Madison Ave.

Keesee Wm. N., grocer, res 144 Blake.

Keeser J., cooper, res 58 s East.

Kefner August, shoemaker, res 89 w Market.

Kehoe Thomas, laborer, res 133 e N. York.

Keiser Alfred, druggist, res 99 s. N. Jersey.

Kelchor John, contractor, res 28 Forest ave.

Kelmantin James, plasterer, bds Washington House.

Kelleher James, shoemaker, res 9 n N. Jersey.

Keller Daniel, stone cutter, res 14 s West.

Keller Frederick, blacksmith, res 38 s Noble.

Keller Frederick H., local editor Free Press, res 172 n N. Jersey.

Keller Wm., laborer, res 105 South.

Keller Y., engineer, Bellefontaine R. R., res 84 s East.

Kelley James, huckster, res 66 Bluff road.

Kelley John, foreman, rolling mill, bds 81 w South.

Kelley Mrs. Mary, res 227 w Wash.

Kellis Wm. M., student at Bryant's commercial college.

Kellogg Amos, engineer, Ind. Cent. R. R., res 36 Davidson.

Kellogg, Charles, U. S. service, res 169 s Del.

Kellogg Henry S., clerk, bds 87 n Meridian.

Kellogg Newton, edge tool maker, res s e cor Market and West.

Kellogg, Mrs. H. S., res 87 n Meridian.

Kelly Cornelius, carriage painter, bds 52 s Del.

Kelly Hugh, res 184 e Wash., in rear.

Kelly James, trader, res 66 Bluff road.

Kelly John, laborer, bds 210 Vir. ave.

Kelly John B., painter, res 2 e Ray.

Kelly Thomas, currier, res 11 e McCarthy.

Kemker Charles, grocer, cor Meridian and McCarthy.

Kemkle Henry, porter, bds 35 s Union.

Kemkle John, wood sawyer, res 30 Union Hall.

Kemmer Oliver, shoemaker, 39 w Wash., bds Mrs. Simpson's, Ind. ave.

Kemper John M., carpenter, res 122 s N. Jersey.

Kemper L. J., teamster, res 122 s N. Jersey.

Kendall John, bds 36 n Noble.

Kendrick Oscar H., Justice of Peace. res 128 Davidson.

Kendrick Wm. H., electric physician, off. 33, res 35 n East.

Kene Peter, moulder, Root's foundry, res Grove.

Kenly John, laborer, res 3 Elm.

Kennedy Daniel, blacksmith, Sinker & Vance, res cor s Del. & McCarty.

Kennedy James, laborer, res 113 South.

Kennedy James, blacksmith, res cor South and Benton.

Kennedy Johanna, (wid) res 320 s Del.

Kennedy John, street contractor, res 256 Ind. ave.

Kennedy Michael, tailor, res alley, n of 156 w Wash.

Kennedy Michael, works at Mason House, bds 113 South.

Kenedy Patrick, soldier, 8th Ill. reg., res 63 Spring.

Kennedy Frank R., (Murphy, Kennedy & Co,) res 83 e N. York.

Kennedy Thomas, laborer, res 113 South.

Kennedy Wm. A., clerk, Murphy, Kennedy & Co., bds 83 e N. York.

Kenney Thomas H., tailor, res 34 s West.

Kennodle Harvey G., student at Purdy's commercial college.
Kennington Robert, laborer, res 45 e Georgia.
Kentman Mathias, well digger, res 182 Mass. ave.
Kenton John, machinest, res 127 s East.
Kentzel Joseph, printer, bds 111 n Ill.
Kenzel George, driver of hook and ladder wagon, res 15 n N. Jersey.
Keppel Henry, works at rolling mill, res 153 s Miss.
Keppel Martin, barkeeper, res 151 s Tenn.
Keppel Josiah, res 61 w Lou.
Keppel Martin, clerk, res 151 s Tenn.
Kepper Jacob, machinest, res 155 s Miss.
Kerby Nathan, engineer, res 25 e Ga.
Kerby James, painter, res 12 Huron.
Kerby Mrs. Susanah, (wid) res 15 Centre.
Kerin James, soldier, res Douglass, Wiley's div., n North.
Kerkhaf, Frederick, laborer, res 117 Union.
Kerland Pat., bds Mason House.
Kern Casper, cabinet maker, res 172 e Mich.
Kern Jacob, student at Bryants commercial college.
Kern Jacob, clerk, 26 and 28 w Wash., bds 76 e Wash.
Kern John, tailor, 15 Railroad.
Kern Joseph, brewer, C. F. Smith's brewery.
Kernel Joseph, works Washington foundry, res Bluff road, Doughertyville.
Kerper Charles, saddler, res 21 Ind. ave.
Kerper Daniel, currier, res 95 Vir. ave.
Kerty Joseph, brewer, Wyoming.
Kespare Peter, moulder, res cor Grove and Hosbrook.
Kessinger Matthew, shoemaker, bds 188 s Del.
Kest Charley, laborer, res alley, bet East and Liberty, n of Mich.
Kestner Fred., currier, res 131 e Market.
Ketcham Lewis, attorney, Blackford's building, res 97 Merrill.
Kettenbach Edward, clerk, bds 214 n Noble.
Kettenbach, Henry, Sr., grocer, Mass. ave., bet Liberty and Noble, res 214 n Noble.
Kettenbach Henry, Jr., clerk, bds 214 n Noble.
Keudemire Charles, carpenter, res 142 n East.
Kevier Mayer, blacksmith, 306 Vir. ave., res 308 Vir. ave.
Kevill Robert L., tinner, res 64 e Lou
Keyes Wm., res 12 Ind. ave.
Kidder James B., currier, res 91 e Market.
Kiefer Charles, Indianapolis bakery, res 246 w Wash.

Kiel Conrad, pump maker, res 216 e Wash.
Kiger Harrison F., attorney at law, 15 P. O., 2d floor, bds 268 n Ill.
Kiger Rev. John, res 268 n Ill.
Killinger John, cabinet maker, res 146 e Market.
Kinder Maria W., Kinder House, 79½ e Wash.
King Cornelius, dealer in lumber, cor St. Clair, and Ala.
King David, carpenter, res 157 n Miss.
King Edward, Sec'y Belf. R. R. line, res 97 n Meridian.
KING FRANCIS, GRAND SECRETARY MASONIC LODGE, res 72 n Tenn., off. Masonic building.
King Frederick C., carpenter, res 332 Va. ave.
King George, fireman on P. & I. R. R., bds 16 N. Jersey.
King Jacob, pattern maker, bds 258 w Wash.
King James H., clerk, O. B. Stout & Bros., bds 5 e N. York.
King James, shoemaker, 37 Ind. ave, res 5 e N. York.
King William B., clerk, Buckeye saloon, bds same.
Kingham Joseph, broom maker, res 72 St. Joseph.
Kingsburry John E., watch maker, res 181 Mass. ave.
Kingsley Adrial S., res Duncan.
Kinnan Mrs. Catharine, (wid.) res 227 Ala.
Kinney Charles, carpenter, res n Wiggins & Chandler's foundry.
Kirby ——, carpenter, Gov. stable, bds 176 Mass. ave.
Kirby Dennis, wagon maker, res w Market.
Kirke Daniel, turner, res 101 e Market.
Kirk Mrs. Elizabeth, milliner, 39 n Penn. res same.
Kirk Kilpatrick, blacksmith, res n end blake.
Kirk Nathaniel, res 39 n Penn.
Kirkwood George, fireman, res 93 Bates.
Kirkwood John, fireman, res cor Noble and Lawrenceburg R. R.
Kirlin James, (Kirlin & Staton.) res cor Ill. and First.
Kirlin & Staton, (James Kirlin, Joseph A. Staton,) dry goods and groceries, 27 n Ill.
Kissel Fred., painter, res 55 n Liberty.
Kissell Jacob, eating saloon, 11 n Ill., res same.
Kistner Adam, proprietor California House, 136 s Ill.
Kistner Henry, shoemaker, 80 w Market.
Kistner John G., boot and shoemaker, 51 s Ill. res in rear.

Leghorn Hats at Davis' new hat store.

FARMERS' HOTEL,

One Square North of Union Depot,

INDIANAPOLIS, IND.

H. E. BUEHRIG, - - PROPRIETOR.

BOARD, ONE DOLLAR PER DAY.

LOUIS LANG'S

RESTAURANT!

AND SALOON,

No. 17 East Washington Street

INDIANAPOLIS, IND.

CHOICE WINES, LIQUORS AND CIGARS,

ALWAYS ON HAND.

OYSTERS AND GAME IN THEIR SEASON.

F. GŒPPER'S

CLOTHING,

And Merchant Tailoring Establishment,

No. 15 East Washington Street,

ONE DOOR EAST OF HARRISON'S BANK,

INDIANAPOLIS, IND.

☞Keeps constantly on hand a well assorted stock of Ready-made Clothing and Furnishing Goods, which he sells at the lowest prices.

PALMER HOUSE

SALOON!

Newly fitted up under the management of

O'LEARY & RIEMLON.

CHOICE WINES.

LIQUORS AND CIGARS,

CONSTANTLY ON HAND.

OYSTERS AND GAME IN THEIR SEASON.

JOHN A. HEIDLINGER,

Manufacturer and Wholesale Dealer in

CIGARS,

And direct Importer of the Choicest Brands of

HAVANA CIGARS,

AND

COMMISSION MERCHANT,

No. 3 PALMER HOUSE, and No. 10 BATES HOUSE,

INDIANAPOLIS, IND.

INDIANAPOLIS

SILK & FUR HAT

MANUFACTORY,

NO. 20 KENTUCKY AVENUE, NEXT TO THE STATE

TREASURY BUILDING.

☞Hats made to order, and guaranteed to fit the most difficult shaped heads.

W. P. BROWN.

KICHEN JOHN M., M. D., s w cor Wash. and Meridian, res 69 n Penn.

Kizer Kate, (wid.) res 50 Mass ave.

Klam Frederick, policeman, res 63 Union.

Klamroth Edmond, student at Bryant's Com. College.

Klana Phillipina, (wid.) res 59 Union.

Klanner Henry, colporter, 188 e Wash., up stairs.

Klausner Henry, clerk, bds 82 n Noble.

Klaab Michael, laborer, res Bluff road, Doughertyville.

Klein Andrew, engineer, P. & I. R. R., res 96 e Louisiana.

Klein Eamel, M. D., res 109 e New York.

Klein Frank, boot and shoe maker, bds Lafayette House.

Klein Nicholas, shoemaker, Mass. ave., bet Liberty and Noble, res bet Wood and St. Clair.

Kleinschmidt Christian, street sprinkler, res 120 e Market.

Kliber Louis J., confectionery store, 115 e Wash., res same.

Kline Geo., machinist, Sinker & Vance, bds 191 s N. Jersey.

Kline, R. H., M. D., bds Palmer House.

Kling Jacob, carpenter, res 100 Bates.

Klinginsmith Jacob, broker, res 79 w Maryland.

Klinginsmith Israel, broker, res 97 w Maryland.

Kinginsmith and Bro., (Isaac Klinginsmith, Jacob Klinginsmith,) brokers, 6 Blake block, 2d floor.

Klix Hugh, Astor saloon, 9 n Penn., res same.

KLOTZ EMIL, NEW YORK BAZAAR, 87 e Wash., res 56 w Vermont.

Klotz Frank (Zimmer & Co.,) 128 e Wash., res same.

Klusman Lewis, 3d Ind. Cav'y. res 63 St. Marys.

Knabner Edward, carpenter, res 61 n West.

Knapton James, carver, res 56 n Noble.

Knapton Thomas, clerk, bds 56 n Noble.

Knaus Charles, clerk, Chicago House.

Knauss Xaver, laborer, res e Wash.

Knif John, carpenter, res 160 n Liberty.

KNIGHT ELIJAH, BOARDING HOUSE, Georgia, bet Ill. and Meridian.

Knight John, (Cottrell & Knight,) res 72 e Louisiana.

Knippenberg Jacob, salesman, Jones, Hess & Davis, res 62 North.

Knodel Mrs. Dorathy, (wid.) res 200 Mass. ave.

KNODLE ADAM, BOOT AND SHOE MANUFACTURER, 32 e Wash., res 8 Ind ave.

Knodle Gerge, with A. Knodle, boot and shoe dealer.

Knolton Silas, res 65 St. Joseph.

Knotts Nim K., sign and ornamental painter, old Capitol House, res 96 e Market.

Knowlton George F., druggist, Stewart & Morgan, bds Macy House.

Knox Frank, (col.) barber, res Ind. ave.

Knox James, (col,) res. Ind. ave., w of Canal.

Koch George, shoemaker, bds 51 s Ill.

Koch Henry, retired, res cor Fletcher ave. and Pine.

Koch Henry H, grocer, 198 Mass. ave., res same.

Koch Thomas, laborer, res 31 Meek.

Koehne Charles, saddler, res 123 n East.

Koeniger George, grocery, res s Meridian, bet McCarthy and Merrill.

Koestle Jacob, watchman at arsenal, res. 155 n Noble.

Koffman Moritz, butcher, res 119 n East.

Kolb Catharine, (wid.) grocer, 69 s Ill., res same.

Kolb Frederick, groceries and liquors, 166 e Wash., res same.

Kolb William, boarding house keeper, 30 Ky. ave.

Kollish Martin, butcher, res s Madison R. R.

KOLLMAN HENRY, PROP'R CHICAGO HOUSE, 71 s Ill.

Koontz Edward, machinist, bds 107 s Tenn.

Korn Martin, tanner and currier, res 171 N. Jersey.

Koster Charles, works in arsenal, res Blake, bet N. York and Vt.

Kottmeir William, (Thonssen & Lahey,) 67 w Wash., bds Bates House.

Kown Mrs. Hulda, (wid.) res 141 e North.

Kown William, teamster, res 66 n East.

Krappe Henry, Gardner, res National road, e of Pogues run.

Krauss Jacob, (Umversall & Krauss,) res 58 n East.

Krauss Jacob, bar keeper, Apollo Garden, bds cor of Tenn. and Ky. ave.

Krause Rhinholdt, tailor, res 107 e Ohio.

Krause William (Krause & Wittenberg,) res 75 n Ala., bet Market and Ohio.

KRAUSE & WITTENBERG, (William Krause, Charles Wittenberg,) DRY GOODS STORE, 43 and 45 e Wash.

Kraut Christ, shoemaker, 60 e South.

Krauth Caroline, (wid.) res 65 n Tenn.

Krauth Ernest W., clerk, 14 w Wash., res 65 n Tenn.

Kreglo David, res 132 n West.

Kretch Mat., 2d clerk Farmers' Hotel.

Kretsch Peter, cigar maker, 93 s Ill., res same.

Kriegar Henry, currier, res 101 s Ala.

Krome August, teacher in German, Luth. Church, bds 188 e Ohio.

Kropf Gustave, (Frese & Kropf,) bds Union Hall.

KRUG GEORGE, GROCER, cor Georgia and Liberty, res same.

Kruger Charles, clerk, 8 w Wash, bds 115 e Market.

Kruger Joseph, cistern builder, 115 e Market.

Krupp Peter, collar maker, res 255 s Penn.

Kurtz Jacob, teamster, res 70 Bluff road.

Kulhman Christian, laborer, bds 145 n Liberty.

Kuhlmann Ernest H. L., grocery store, 137 w Wash.

Kuhn William, baker, res n w cor East and N. York.

Kunker Charles, miller, res 36 Union.

Kurse Christian, carpenter, res 9 e McCarthy.

Kurtz Jacob, teamster, res 70 Bluff road.

L

Laaz Henry, blacksmith, bds s Meridian.

Laham Frederick, shoemaker, Jones, Vinnedge & Co., res corporation line, e Wash.

Laird John P., carpenter, res 38 s Noble.

Laird Wm. H., book-keeper, Hasselman & Vinton, res n Ill., out corporation.

Lake John, laborer, res Bluff road, Doughertyville.

Lake Joseph, railroader, res 85 Ind. ave.

Lake Joseph, carpenter, bds 85 Ind. ave.

Lake Mrs. Martha, dress maker, 38 n Penn., bds Mr. Jack's.

Lamb Peter, laborer, res 15 Willard.

Lamb Yancy, laborer, res 146 cor West and Market.

Lame John, conductor, Jeffersonville R. R., bds 129 w Maryland.

Lamott Charles, tinner, 163 Vir. ave.

Lamott Joseph, tinsmith, res 163 Vir. ave.

Lancaster Henry H., salesman, Glenns' dry goods store, bds 20 s Miss.

Landers Mrs. A. C., (wid) res 104 Vir. ave.

Landers John, (col) wood sawyer, res 178 w North.

Landis Jacob, (Landis & Mills,) bds Macy House.

LANDIS MILTON M., FREIGHT AGENT, T. H. & R. R. R., res 86 w Maryland.

Landis & Mills, (Jacob Landis & Layton Mills,) livery stable, 18 e Md.

Lane Miss Arabella, cloak maker, 26 and 28 w Wash., bds 141 w Market.

Lane Eda, (col., wid.,) washer, res cor East and St. Clair.

Lane Nathaniel, (col) hostler, bds Pee Dee.

Lane Uriah, laborer, res 170 n N. Jersey.

Lang David, carpenter, res 35 w ⅜ New York.

Lang Louis, restaurant, 13 e Wash., res same.

Langdein Joseph, grocer and dealer in fancy goods, 160 e Wash., res same.

Langenbergh Henry H., (Langenbergh & Co.,) res 194 w Wash.,

Langles Joshua M. W., res 26 e Market.

Langsenkemp Wm., coppersmith, res 132 s Del.

Lanchet Peter, brickmaker, res 2 s Benton.

Large Michael, teamster, res 252 Ind ave.

Larned Miss Sarah J., literary teacher, blind asylum.

Larnley George, laborer, res 77 n East.

Larue John, railroader, res 14 Mich. road.

Lashhom Martha, (wid) tailoress, res 71 n Mo.

Latham Wm. H., teacher, deaf and dumb asylum, res 93 e Ohio.

Latz Jacob, laborer, res cor Bluff road and McCarthy.

Lauer Charles, East Empire Saloon, 162 e Wash., res n East.

Laupheimer August, barkeeper, M. Hugg, res 93 St. Joseph.

Laurel John, works at rolling mill, bds 81 w South.

Lauria Francis A., (col) barber, bds Macy House.

Laurie Wm., clerk, N. Y. store, res e Ohio.

Laux Josephine, (wid) res Wash., bet Liberty and Noble.

Lavane S., sutler, 46th Ind. reg., res 22 s Miss.

Law Caroline, (wid. John Law,) seamstress, res 201 Ind. ave.

Lawbecker Joseph, bds 167 s Tenn.

Lawless Michael, grocer, 86 s Noble, res same.

Lawler Wm., porter, Bates House, res 184 East.

Lawney Dennis, laborer, res 35 Huron.

Lawrence Alexander, clerk, N. Y. store, bds Littles Hotel.

Laws Duland, laborer, res 17 n Harris.

Lawson Elijah, res cor Mich. and Tenn.

Lawson Joseph, gentleman of leisure, res n w cor Miss. and Market.

Layer Peter, plasterer, res cor Ala., and Ft. Wayne ave.

Layton T. M., shoemaker, 39 w Wash., res 71 w N. York.

Leach David J., laborer, res 161 s Tennessee.

Leary Patrick C., clerk, 8 w Wash.

Leathers George C., clerk, Adams' Express, bds 101 w N. York.

Leathers G. C., clerk, American Express res 80 s East.

Leathers Wm. W., (Leathers & Carter,) res 139 n N. Jersey.

New goods received daily at No. 15, Pennsylvania St.

Leathers & Carter, (Wm. W. Leathers & Geo. Carter,) attorneys at law, 86 e Wash.

Leatz Jacob, baggageman, Union Depot, bds California House, 136 s Ill.

LeBarre Lewis, moulder, res 17 w McCarthy.

Leddy Thomas, brickmaker, res 83 Huron.

Ledley John, Exchange Saloon, 24 w Lou., res cor Georgia and Miss.

Ledwith Thomas, carpenter, res 308 s Del.

Lee Benjamin M. D., clerk, M. H. Good, bds E. Knight's.

Lee Edward S., physician, res 17 Ind. ave.

Lee E. T., hackman, res 22 n N. Jersey.

Lee Henry H., China tea and drug store, 14 Bates House, res n Ill.

Lee Mandeville G., editor Herald and Era, res 111 n Ill.

Leeman Mrs., dressmaker, res 34 e Ohio.

Lehemyer Henry, carpenter, res 59 St. Joseph.

Lehr Ferdinand A., res 98 n East.

Lehr Henry, carpenter, res 165 e N. York.

Lehr Philip, carpenter, res 165 e N. York.

Lehraman John C. A., clerk, city treasurer's office, res Ver., bet N. Jersey and East.

Leiber Hiram, gilt frames, &c., Ætna building, res 123 n Liberty.

Deiez Anthony, clerk, 160 e Wash., res cor alley, e of No. 1 engine house.

Leinninger Michael, (Leinninger & Ferling,) res 102 e Ver.

Leinninger & Ferling, (Michael Leinninger & George Ferling,) barbers and leechers, cor Wash. and Mer.

Leiping Frederick, laborer, n N. Jersey, n of St. Clair.

Leiseman Wm., laborer, 151 n Liberty.

Lemme Wm., res 50 Bluff road.

Lemmon Wm. H., brickmason, res 173 e Ohio.

Lemoene Louis, laborer, res 160 n Noble.

Lemon Edward, blacksmith, res 309 Vir. ave.

Lendormie Mrs. Disorie, res 91 Peru railroad.

Lendormie Joseph, soldier, 70th reg., res 91 Peru railroad.

Lenix Edward, tailor, res 69 s Penn.

Lement Ferdinand T., embroidery and stamping, 16½ s Ill.

Lentz, Christ., laborer, res 115 Ft. Wayne ave.

Lentz Gotlieb, porter, 11 n Penn.

Lentz Gotlieb, laborer, res 103 Peru railroad.

Lentz Godly, works Hawthorn's store, res Bellefontaine railroad.

Lentz Wm., bds 23 Railroad.

Leonard Abigail, (wid. James Leonard,) res 116 n Ill.

Leonard Michael, res 33 e South.

Leppert Henry, res 97 Peru Railroad.

Leppert Nicholas, blacksmith, res one square s of Lawrenceburgh machine shop.

LESH AARON B., (L. & A B. Lesh,) bds 61 Mass. ave.

LESH L. & A. B., (Lewis Lesh & Aaron B. Lesh,) GENERAL PRODUCE AND COMMISSION BUSINESS, 29 s Meridian.

LESH LEWIS, (L. & A. B. Lesh,) res n California.

Lesh Robert M., clerk, German dry goods store, bds Macy House.

Letty John, saloon, res Sinker.

Levett Wm., carpenter, res 190 n Ill.

Levy Mary, (wid.) res 74 w Vermont.

Lenallen Francis, (wid.) res 78 e Wash.

Lenerd John G., clerk, Court House saloon, bds same.

Lewarre Lewis, moulder, res 17 w McCarthy.

Lewis Andrew J., blacksmith, res 53 n Noble.

Lewis A. T., ag't Great Western Dispatch, 38 Virginia ave.

Lewis Hiram, teamster, res. 281 s East.

Lewis John, (col.) organ-grinder in animal show, bds Patterson House.

Lewis John, (col) cook Mason House.

Lewis John, (Lewis & Davlin,) res Cincinnati.

Lewis Joseph A., attorney at law, s w cor Wash. and Meridian.

Lewis Thomas, clerk, 84 w. Wash., bds Pyle House.

Lewis W. W., bds Little's Hotel

Lewis & Davlin, (John Lewis, James H. Davlin,) Museum, 68 s Ill.

Lex Jacob, pressman, State Sentinel, res. Vt., bet Noble and Davis.

Lex Lewis, bds Vt., bet Noble and R. R.

Lex Mrs. ——, (wid.) res Vt., bet Noble and R. R.

Lickert Annie E., (wid.) res 238 Mad. ave.

Lieber Halmon, picture and frame store, 13 n Penn., res 123 w Liberty.

Leebing Frederick, varnisher, res cor Elm and Forest ave.

Liebrich Louis, porter, Browning & Sloan's res 172 w North.

Lietz Theobold, artist, res 131 w Vt.

Linch Mrs. Catharine R., res s Tenn., near Pogues run.

Lindley Lemuel G., conductor I. P. & C. R. R., res Wabash, bet Liberty and Noble.

Lindley Henry J., book keeper, McKernan & Pierce, 31 w Wash., res 23 Ind. ave.

Lindsay Henry, clerk, 28 s Ill., res 11 w Georgia.

Line Isaac, (Line & Currens,) res 64 s Ill.

Line & Currens, (Isaac Line, Henry Currens,) eating house, 65 s Ill.
Lineth, Frederick, blacksmith, res. 13 Water.
Lines John, laborer, bds Peru R. R., bet Ohio and N. York.
LINGENFELTER WM. H, BOARDING HOUSE, 19 Circle.
Lininger Michael, res 102 e Vt.
Linn Alexander, colar maker, res alley, n State House.
Linn Jane, (wid.,) res 91 Union.
Linnahan John, laborer, res 40 s Ill.
Linsday Mary, dress maker, 8 e Wash., bds n East.
Lintner Daniel H., res 10 Mich. road.
Lintner John, brewer, res 231 s East.
Lintner John, res 30 Mich.
LINTZ ANTHONY, WHOLESALE AND RETAIL MANUFACTURER BOOTS AND SHOES, 39 w Wash., res 17 s Miss.
Lintz John K., salesman, boot and shoe store, 39 w Wash., bds 17 s Miss.
Lipp Henry, soldier 19th Reg., res 178 e Ohio.
Lippus William, stone cutter, res 174 n east.
Liscomb Edward A., grain dealer, res 48 n Tenn.
Liskmann August, laborer, 338 Va. ave.
Little Welbur F., clerk N. York grocery, res 30 n Ala.
Little Wilham F., brass moulder, res in Fletcher's addition.
LITTLE HOTEL, A. R. HYDE, proprietor, cor Wash. and N. Jersey.
Lock Erie, Pay-master U. S. army, res 40 Calafornia.
Locke Josiah (Locke & Munson,) 163 n Penn.
LOCKE & MUNSON, COPPER LIGHTNING RODS, Blackford's building.
Lockwood Isaac, laborer, Keely's block, Clinton.
Lockwood Henry, cooper, res w Market.
Lockwood John N., cooper, res Cal., bet Market and Wash.
Logan Andrew, carpenter, res 278 Mad. ave.
Logan Bernard, grocery keeper, 129 w South.
Logan Michael, laborer, res 76 s Noble.
Logan Patrick, laborer, res 179 s New Jersey.
Logan Thomas, carpenter, res Sinker.
LOHMAN CHARLES, GROCER, 317 cor Cedar and Va., res same.
Lonergan John, grocer and produce dealer, cor Pine and Noble, res same.
Lonergan Maurice, boiler maker, bds 84 Va. ave.
Long Edward F., book-keeper in Lord's dry goods store, bds Macy House.
Long Frederick, laborer, res 143 e Ga.

Long Rev. George, Presbyterian minister, res 33 n N. Jersey.
Long Gustavus, laborer, res 216 w Wash., up stairs.
Long James, salesman, M. H. Goods, bds Palmer House.
Long Joseph, shoemaker, res cor Penn. and St. Clair.
Long Matthew, undertaker, 28 s Meridian, res in same building.
Longenecker Samuel, grocer and liquor dealer, res w Indp'lis.
Longsdorff Catharine, (wid.) res 11 Circle.
Longsdorff William, res 11 Circle.
Looker Fidelia, (wid.) boarding house 140 n Miss.
Loomis Garrett J., watch maker, 7 w Wash., bds at Macy House.
Loomis William H., nurseryman, off. 14 e Market, res 137 Vn. ave.
Lord Edgar N., (Hume, Lord & Co.,) res 12 w North.
Lord John M., Pres. rolling mill Co., res 100 n Penn.
Losy John, cooper, res 149 s Va. ave.
Loucks Calvin R., painter, bds 179 e Market.
Loucks Cornelius, res 46 s Benton.
Loucks James, city sealer, res 194 n New Jersey.
Loucks Mary, (wid.) res 33 Union.
Loucks Michael, works in foundry, res 333 s East.
Loucks William W., carpenter, res 123 n Ala.
London Andrew, res 57 n Ill.
Louder Mrs. Sarah, (wid.) res 87 n Meridian.
Louman James, clerk, A. Clem & Bro., bds 58 e St. Clair.
Love John, res 49 n Tenn.
Love Samuel, watchman at I. & C. depot, res 93 Ala.
Love William, (Love & Cullum,) res cor Arcade and Wash.
Love & Cullum, (William Love, Milton H. Cullum,) real estate agents, 1 New and Talbot's building.
Low Charles carpenter, res 148 e North.
Low John. carpenter, res 152 n Del.
Low Mrs. Margaret, res 227 w Wash.
Low Nahem, Sr., carpenter, res 148 e North.
Low Nahem, Jr., paper folder, bds 148 e North.
Lowden James, coal agent, res 140 Va. avenue.
Lowe George, carriage manufacturer, 99 e Wash., res 113 n Penn.
Lowe Captain William B., recruiting 11th U. S. infantry, 56 e Wash.
Lowrnan Nancy, (wid.) res 53 St. Clair.
Lowry John, Miller, res 247 w Wash.

Panama Hats at Davis', 15 Pennsylvania St.

Lowry George E., 13th Reg. Ind. vols.
Lowry Wiley M., druggist, 49 Mass. ave, res 53 Mass ave.
Loyd Allen, (Thomas A. Loyd & Co.,) nursery, res Gov. Noble's old homestead.
Loyd Thomas A., (Thomas A. Loyd & Co.,) bds Gov. Noble's old homestead.
LOYD THOMAS A. & CO., HARDWARE, &c., 12 w Wash.
Lubking Charles, shoemaker, res 54 n Noble.
Lucus Frank, res 98 s Md.
Lucas James, painter and whitewasher, res 149 n Alabama.
Luckey Christ, res National road, e Pogues run.
Luckey George, (Elliott & Luckey,) bds Little's Hotel.
Ludington Moses, res 143 n New Jersey.
Ludlow J., tailor, 86 e Wash.
Ludlow Joseph E., painter, res 230 n Ill.
Ludlow Stephen W., student at Bryant's Com. Col., bds at Judge Majors
Ludwig Harman, soldier 20th bat., res. 49 n Noble.
Ludlow Silas, agent, res 147 n Del.
Lukens Richard L., agricultural agent, res 76 s East.
Lundy Ira C., gunsmith, bds 8 Willard.
Lupton William C., Jr., Quarter-master U. S. A., res 160 n Penn.
Lutman Samuel, baggage-master Ind. C. R. R., res 60 n Noble.
Lynch J., laborer, res 112 s East.
Lynch James J., (Lynch & Keane,) res 100 n East.
Lych John, works in arsenal, res 127 n Miss.
Lynch Mrs. Mary, seamstress, res 33 e South.
Lynch Patrick, engineer, Sinker & Vance, res Bates, near I & C. shop.
Lynch & Keane, James A. Lynch, and Mrs. Anna Keane,) wholesale and retail dry goods, 33 w Wash.
Lynn William H., mailing clerk P. O., bds Macy House.
Lynn Winfield, clerk, 22 w Wash., bds 102 n Ill.
Lynn Robert, U. S. service, res 204 s Delaware.
Lyons George, works pork house, res 286 Mad. ave.
Lyons John, laborer, res 123 w South.
Lyons Mrs. Mary S., res s Mo., near rolling mill.
Lyons William, laborer, res 161 s Del.

M

Mabb L. H., bar keeper, Atlantic saloon, bds Palmer House.
McAnaly Terance, laborer, res 83 Huron.
McAnulta Peter A., conductor T. H. & R. R., res 39 n Mich.

MacArthur John B., (Heckman & McArthur,) res 158 n West.
McBAKER THOMAS, PEARL SALOON, 16 cor alley and e Pearl, res 68 e Mich.
McBayles Rober, laborer, res Cal., bet Market and Wash.
McBride Michael, pedler, res 142 n Liberty.
McCabe John, baggage-master at I. & C. depot, bds at Union House.
McCabe Matthew, finisher, res 5 Forest ave.
McCabe Peter, hostler, bds 20 n Penn.
McCallian John, machinist, res 284 Mad. ave.
McCann Dr. Sam'l D., Eclectic, 29 n East.
McCarron George, tailor, 158 n Del., res same.
Macarthy Mrs. A., res 132 s Ala.
McCarthy Eugene, machinist, bds 107 s. Tenn.
McCarthy ———, res 147 e Ohio.
McCarthy Simon, res 9 s Miss.
McCarthy Timothy, laborer, res Wyoming.
McCarty Eugene, moulder, Sinker & Vance, bds John Coen, Miss.
McCarty Mrs. Margaret, res 60 s Penn.
McCARTY NICHOLAS, REAL ESTATE AGENT, s w cor Meridian and Wash., bds 60 s Penn.
McCarty William, moulder, res 68 n Davidson.
McCauley Jacob, in the army at Gallatin, Ten., res 150 n Miss.
McChesney Edward, salesman, 30 w Wash., bds 132 n Ill.
McChesney George G., mailing clerk, P. O., bds 61 n Penn.
McChesney Jacob B., res 132 n Ill.
McChesney Jeremiah, res 61 n Penn.
McChesney William L., clerk U. S. pay department, bds 132 n Ill.
McClamrock Nancy, (wid.) res 90 Ind. ave.
McCleave Robert, machinist, res 108 McCarthy.
McCloskey John, carpenter, res 89 Mass. ave.
McCloud Mahaley, (col.,) res 91 s Tenn.
McClure, Mrs. ———, (wid. Benj. McClure,) res 140 w Market.
McClure Maj. Daniel, Pay-master U. S. A., 6 e Wash., bds Bates House.
McClure George H., carpenter.
McClure Patrick, teamster, res 93 Bluff road.
McClusky John W., brickmoulder, res 168 s Ill.
McColley William, Gov. teamster, bds 176 Mass ave.
McCommican Abe, farmer, res w Indianapolis.
McConnell Stephen, blacksmith, res 210 s. Tenn.

McCord B. R., (McCord & Wheatley,) res out of city.
McCORD & WHEATLEY, (B. R. McCord, Wm. M. Wheatley,) LUMBER YARD, 119 s Del.
McCormack Amos D., cutter at J. Staub's, 2 Odd Fellow's Hall, res 229 n Tennessee.
McCormack Ira, cutter Fred. Tapkins', res 63 w N. York.
McCormick Alexander, in U. S. A., res 14 w North.
McCormick Charles, moulder, res 252 s Del.
McCormick Jedediah, carpenter, res 204 n Miss.
McCormick John, farmer, res w Indianapolis.
McCormick Stephen, railroader, res 122 s Noble.
McCool William, Hub maker, res 239 s Delaware.
McCowin James H., harness maker, res 89 Mass. ave.
McCoy Elizabeth, (wid.) boarding house, 73 s Noble.
McCOY REV. JAMES, res 46 s Penn.
McCoy Robert B., (McCoy & Andrews.)
McCoy, Thomas, (col.,) barber, res 115 w Wash.
McCoy William, baggage-master, res 18 Madison ave.
McCoy William, conductor, T. & R. R. R., bds 107 s Tenn.
McCoy William W., farmer, res 132 e North.
McCoy & Andrews, photographers, 25 and 26 New & Talbot's block.
McCready James, assistant book-keeper Branch Bank, res Yohn's Block.
McCready, Nathaniel, artist, bds 202 n Illinois.
McCue Lewis, laborer, res s Missouri, near rolling mill.
McCune Thomas J., engineer I. & C. R. R., 137 e Georgia.
McCurn M., laborer, res 178 s East.
McCutchens J., bds Ray House, e Del.
McCutchen William W., clerk New York Store, bds Esq. Scudder's, Market.
McDermot, James, foundryman, res 81 w Md.
McDermott P., boiler maker, Sinker & Vance, res 81 w Md.
McDevitt John, proprietor Exchange billiard room.
McDevitt Mary, (wid) res 76 Bluff road.
McDonald Alice, res 99 w Market.
McDonald C. E., lock maker, bds 85 n Penn.
McDonald David, (McDonald & Porter,) res 85 n Penn.
McDonald Duer B., carpenter, res Ver.
McDonald Joseph E., (McDonald & Roache,) res 93 n Penn.

McDONALD & PORTER, (David McDonald & Albert G. Porter,) ATTORNEYS AT LAW, Yohn's block, cor Wash. and Mer.
McDONALD & ROACHE, (Joseph E. McDonald & Addison L. Roache,) ATTORNEYS AT LAW, Ætna building, n Penn.
McDonall Patrick, works at rolling mill, res 10 Willard.
McDonough John, issuing clerk for Government, bds Vir. ave.
McDougal John, brickmaker, res 51 s East.
McDougal Wm., brakesman, Terre Haute R. R., res 70 s Noble.
McDurmot John W., salesman, Boston store, res St. Joseph, bet Penn. and Meridian.
McElligoth John, clerk, bds Ray House.
McElwee John, carpenter, res 154 n Mississippi.
McEWEN JAMES R., (Maischoss & McEwen,) bds Andrew Flowers, near Michael's brewery.
McGaffe James, (col) whitewasher, bds 116 w Georgia.
McGaw John, stencil cutter, res 114 n Miss.
McGee David, blacksmith, res w Indianapolis.
McGee Thomas J., bds 155 Mass. ave.
McGee Wm., railroad engineer, res 86 Union.
McGehee James T., student at Bryant's commercial college.
McGiffin Samuel, sup't work shop, blind asylum.
McGinnis Geo. F., Brig. Gen. U. S. A., res n Meridian.
McGinnis John, grocery and feed store, 230 e Wash., res same.
McGinnis N., tailor, res 162 w Wash., up stairs.
McGinnis Owen, wholesale and retail clothier, and merchant tailor, 39 e Wash., res 26 Vir. ave.
McGinnis Patrick, tailor, works 38 s Ill.
McGinty Martin, laborer, res West, bet Maryland and Georgia.
McGlaughlen Timothy, works at rolling mill, bds Willard, near rolling mill.
McGlenn, Michael, drayman, res 90, cor Powell and North.
McGrath Daniel, laborer, res 19 e Ga.
McGraw H. I., shoemaker, works A. Lintz, 39 w Wash., bds Mrs. Ketely, Montgomery.
McGuire James E., clerk, Wiley & Martin, bds 20 n Penn.
Mach James D., law student, McDonald & Roache, bds National saloon, s Meridian.
McHenry Jesse, attorney at law, 18 e Wash.

Davis' hats and caps always give satisfaction.

McIntire John, paper manufacturer, res 20 n Miss.

McIntire Lucius, works rolling mill, res 14 Henry.

McIntire Thomas, sup't deaf and dumb asylum, e National road.

McIver John, (Baker & McIver,) res 25 s Ill.

Mack Henry, clerk, N. Y. store, res 14 e Ohio. ,

Mack Patrick, works Cincinnati R. R., bds Cincinnati House.

McKann Patrick, fireman, Terre Haute R. R., res 182 s Del.

Mackay David, bonnet bleacher and presser, res near rolling mill.

McKapuy John, coal carter, res 157 w Md.

McKeehan Benj., section boss, Madison R. R., res 71 Merrill.

McKelney Joseph S , carpenter, Copeland & Eaton, 27 e Market, res 19 Ky. ave.

McKelvey Mrs. Harriett, plain sewing, res 253 Ind. ave.

McKelvey Robert, eating house, 32 w Lou., res same.

McKenna James, clerk, Thompson's bakery, res 69 s N. Jersey.

McKenna John, Machinest, res 69 s N. Jersey.

McKemi, Henry, mailing clerk, P. O., res 136 St. Clair.

McKenna John, laborer, bds alley, bet Georgia and Lou.

McKenney Wm., laborer, res 88 s East.

Mackentire Charles, laborer, res w Indianapolis.

McKERNAN DAVID S., ATTORNEY AT LAW, 8 w Wash., res 10 Circle.

McKERNAN JAMES H., (McKernan & Pierce,) 39 w Wash., res 10 n w side Circle.

McKernan Michael, laborer, res Fletcher's addition.

McKERNAN & PIERCE, (J. H. McKernan & W. J. Pierce,) DEALERS IN REAL ESTATE, 39½ w Wash.

McKey Albert, carpenter, res cor Huron and Noble.

McKibbon, Joshua R., carpenter, res 226 Mass. ave.

McKinnie Henry, clerk in P. O., res 136 e St. Clair.

McKinley James, res 148 e N. York.

McKinney John C., school teacher, res 72 n Ill.

McLane Albert, painter and glazer, res 8 w North.

McLane Moses, drayman, res Mich. road.

McLaughlin James, peddler, res 234 w Wash.

McLaughlin John A., gunsmith, res 232 s Ala.

McLaughlin Timothy, works rolling mill, res Willard.

McLene Jeremiah, (McLene & MacIntire,) bds Bates House.

McLENE & CO., (Jeremiah McLene, and John MacIntire,) PAPER MILL, s side of Wash., on bank of river.

McLENE J., JEWELER, under Bates House.

McMahan Boon, student at Bryant's commercial college, bds in country.

McMahan Patrick, hostler, Wood & Foudry's.

McManmon Andy, grocer, 153 e Wash.

McMannanay James, brick layer, res 26 Henry.

McMillen Milcon, machinest, Washington foundry, bds Farmers Hotel.

McMillin Samuel, real estate agent, 19 w Wash., up stairs, res 38 e Ver.

McMullen Arthur, bds 204 w Wash.

McMurrey Robert, cigarmaker, res 101 w N. York.

McNabb Stephen, brickmaker, res 143 s Miss.

McNeely Elisha, cooper shop, above Lafayette depot, res 136 n Ill.

McNeely John, carpenter, res 151 n Miss.

McNeily John B., clerk, 5 Bates House, bds cor Miss. and Mich.

McNutt Orrin, clerk, res 104 McCarthy.

McOuat Andrew, laborer, res cor Patterson and Elizabeth.

McOuat Andrew W., (R. L, & A. W. McOuat,) res 15 Laukerbee.

McOuat George, bds n e cor N. York and East.

McOuat Mrs. J. S., (wid) res n e cor N. York and East.

McOuat Robert L., (R. L. & A. W. McOuat,) res 22 w New York, cor Illinois.

McOuat R. L. & A. W., stoves and tinware dealers, 69 w Wash.

McPherson Samuel, clerk, 22 w Wash., bds Macy House.

McPowell James, (col) barber, Yohn's block, bds Pyle House.

McRoberts Henry, carpenter, res 42 Spring.

McShane Owen, res 111 w Mich.

McSherry Daniel E., drill manufacturer, res 111 Vir. ave.

McTaggert Israel, (McTaggert & Dunn,) res 90 e Market.

McVea David, blacksmith, 283 w Wash., res Cal.

McVicker Achor W., cutter 3 Bates House, res 20 N. Jersey.

McWorkman Henry, mailing clerk, P. O., bds Littles Hotel.

MACY DAVID, SUPERINTENDENT PERU & INDIANAPOLIS R. R., res 78 n Del.

MACY HOUSE, WM. H. CAMPBELL, PROPRIETOR, cor Ill. and Market.

Ladies should examine the Florence.

Madagan Patrick, boss Bellefontaine R. R., bds 3 Bates.

Madison & Indianapolis R. R. office, 45 e South.

Maear Abers, engine wiper, res 56 Union.

Maeyer Wm., blacksmith, res 47 e Ga.

Magee Eder, boiler maker, Sinker & Vance.

Magley Jacob, Blake's planing Mill, res 60 n Del.

Maguire Douglass, (Maguire, Jones & Co.,) res 38 e Ohio.

Maguire Henry P., (Weaver & Maguire,) bds 41 e Mich.

MAGUIRE, JONES & CO.) (Douglas Maguire, Aquilla Jones, John A. Vinnedge,) WHOLESALE GROCERS, 7 and 8 Bates House, w Wash.

Mahan Dennis laborer, bds Peru R. R., bet Ohio and N. York.

Mahan Francis N., proprietor Oriental saloon, bds Oriental House.

Mahan William & Co., (Rule & Mahan,) bds Linsey's Ga.

Mahoney John, teamster, res 122 Blake.

Mahoney James, laborer, John McGinnis, Wash.

Mahoney Patrick, laborer, res 215 s Del.

Mahoney John T., wig maker, 20 n Ill.

Maier John, cabinet maker, 295 s Del.

Maier William, discharged soldier, res 214 w Wash.

Maillard Felix, carpenter, res 242 e Wash.

Mains S., grocer, 88 Va. ave., cor East.

Mains Samuel, res 59 n Penn.

Maischoss P., (Maischoss & McEwen,) bds Coen's, near Terre Haute depot.

MAISCHOSS & McEWEN, (Peter Maischoss, James R. McEwen,) CAPITAL CITY FILE WORKS.

Maker Thomas J., soldier, res 124 n Mich.

Major Samuel, attorney, res w Indianapolis.

Major Stephen, attorney, 19½ w Wash., res out city.

MAJOR & BROWN, (W. S. Major, P. A. Brown,) ATTORNEYS AT LAW, Blackford s building.

Major Stephen F., student at Bryant's Com. College, bds Judge Majors.

Maker J. R., clerk in Grout's shoe store, Wash., bds 104 Va. ave.

Maklin Matthew, bar tender, 11 n Ill., bds same.

Malinder J. W., Methodist preacher, res 173 s New Jersey.

Mallanny Edward, laborer, res cor Noble and Huron.

Mallon Miss Mary A., salesman at Bee Hive.

Malone A., carpenter, res 107 Va. ave.

Malone Patrick, laborer, bds 46 Mass. ave.

Maloney John, shoe maker, res 169 s Miss.

Maloy Roger, laborer, bds 46 Mass. ave.

Malott V. T., Sec'y and Gen'l Ticket Ag't P. & I. R. R., bds 78 n Del.

Mane John, soldier, res 2d house on Cal., s of Md.

Maney David, laborer, res cor Elizabeth

Manfield Julius, tailor, res 15 Chatham.

Manheimer David, clothing store, 55 w Wash., res 30 s Miss.

Manheimer Henry, clerk, 55 w Wash., res 28 n Miss.

Manlove William R., bds 130 n New Jersey.

Mann Alfred J., carpenter, res Davidson, bet N. York and Vermont.

Mann Daniel, soldier 79th Reg., res 179 Peru R. R.

Mann James, boarding house, res 95 s East.

Mann John, teamster, res Ash, bet Cherry and corporation.

Mann Mrs. Margaret, intelligence office, off. 37 n Penn.

Mann Miss Maria, dress maker, bds 36 n Ill.

Mann Samuel, traveling agent, res 270 Ind ave.

Mann William, shoe and boot maker, 38 w Wash., res 164 e Mich.

Mannfield George, cutter, res 146 n East.

Manny John, moulder, res 231 s Penn.

Manning E. C., boot and shoe store, 27 s Ill., res same.

Manning Joseph S., marble cutter, Jason Dame, bds Bates House.

Manning Thomas, res 38 w Ohio.

Mansfield Thomas, blacksmith, res 99 w Md.

Mansur Frank, bds 8 e Ver.

Mansur Isaiah, off. 14 s Meridian, res cor Vermont and Meridian.

Mansur Jeremiah, retired, res 8 Vt.

Mansur William, off. 14 s Meridian, res N. York, bet Penn & Meridian.

Many Adolph J., soldier, 78th Reg., bds 67 n Noble.

Many Carmile, carpenter, res 36 Spring.

Many Charles, carpenter, res 137 Peru R. R.

Many Charles, soldier 79th Reg., bds 67 n Noble.

Many Gerard, prof. of French, Indianapolis Female Institute, res 67 n Noble.

Many John B., carpenter, 34 Spring, res 67 n Noble.

Marbach Henry, bar keeper, Pea Ridge House.

March Harmen, (Ocurist,) res 114 n Meridian.

Marchant Charles, clerk, res cor Market and Cal.

Marchant Isaac, book keeper Ohio Woolen Factory, res cor Market and Cal.

Boys hats in great variety at Davis'.

Marcus Elias, carpenter, res 59 w Ga.
Marcus Joseph, clerk, bds 9 Ky. ave.
Markert George, shoemaker, res 144 e Ohio.
Markhams Thomas, blacksmith, res 26 Mass. ave.
Marlow Jackson, painter, res 65 w South.
Marmont Hugo, saloon, res 136 w Wash.
Marquart Jacob, U. S. service, res 258 s Del.
Marquis Joseph, city express wagon, res 113 McCarthy.
Marsee Joseph, (Marsee & Son,)res 147 e South.
MARSEE & SON, SAW MILLS, s N. Jersey, near Wash.
Marsh Lewis, tailor, res 149 e Market.
Marsh Henry B., res 12 w New York.
Marshall Ben. F., laborer, res 8 Chatham.
Marshall Charles M., cloak and dress maker, 12 s Ill.
Marshall Edward, Gov. teamster, Mich. road.
Marshall Frank B., (Ronstead & Marshall,) bds Palmer House.
Marshall John W., laborer, res 6 Chatham.
Marshall Levi, carpenter, 77 s N. Jersey.
Martin Dennis, clerk, M. H. Good, bds Oriental.
Martin Eli, breaksman on Terre Haute R. R., bds National Hotel, w Wash.
Martin James, tailor, bds Farmer's Hotel.
Martin John, works at rolling mill, res s Tenn., near Pogues run.
Martin John bricklayer, res 2d house from cor Orient and Michigan road.
Martin Luther R. (Wiley & Martin,) bds Bates House.
Martin Michael, 58 East.
Martin Rudolph, railroader, res 8 Wash.
Martin Robert, moulder, in Root's foundry, res 103 s N. Jersey.
Martin Robert, shoemaker, res 228 s Del.
Martin Sears, works Terre Haute depot, res 207 s Del.
Martin Wm., saloon, res 95 n Miss.
Martin Wm., tailor, 8 s Penn., up stairs, res 237 Ind. ave.
Martindale Mrs., res 110 n Penn.
Martindale Elijah B., (Martindale & Grubbs,) res n Meridian.
Martindale Samuel P., res cor Cherry and Ash.
MARTINDALE & GRUBBS, (Elijah B. Martindale & Daniel W. Grubbs,) ATTORNEYS AT LAW, 4 New & Talbot's block.
Martz Miss Clara, dressmaker, bds 39 n Ala.
Martz Henry, millwright, res 99 n Noble.
Martz Sarah, res 39 n Ala.
Masier Preston, teamster, res Elm, Fletcher's addition.

MASON HOUSE, MASON & CO., PROPRIETORS, Louisiana, opp Union depot.
MASON BENJ., PROPRIETOR MASON HOUSE, opp. Union Depot.
Mason Benj., express messenger, Bellefontaine R. R., bds Palmer House.
Mason Hampton, (col) saloon keeper, res 141 w Wash.
Mason Madison, (col) eating saloon, near Union depot, res 107 w North.
Mason Tyler A., clerk, Mason House.
Mason Wm., carpenter, bds California House, 136 s Ill.
MASONIC HALL, s e cor Wash. and Tenn.
Mass Lewis, machinest, res 139 s Tenn.
Mass Solomen, (col) hostler, bds Pee Dee.
Masters Philo, laborer, res 33 s Liberty.
Muthe Mrs. Margaret, dressmaker, 124 e Market.
Mathe Wm., clerk, bds 124 e Market.
Mathe John, engineer, I. & C. R. R.
Mathias David, boarding house keeper, res 188 s Tenn.
Mathews Allen, clerk, Beck's restaurant, bds same.
Mathews Clemens, bartender, Wright's Hall, e Wash.
Mathews F., engineer, I. C. R. R., bds Ray House, s Del.
Mathews Granville, cooper, res 137 n Noble.
Mathew Jacob R., carpenter, res 84 n Meridian.
Mathews J. Francisco, jobbing clerk, Journal office, bds 84 n Mer.
Mathews John, bartender, 44 w Wash.
Matlock James M., book-keeper, res 35 n Ala.
Matlock M. J., book-keeper, A. Wallace, 38 Vir. ave.
Matthes Clemens, barkeeper, 163 e Wash.
Matthews J. W., clerk, N. Y. store, res e Ohio.
Mattler Annie M., proprietress Washington House, 83 s Meridian.
Mattler Stephen, saloon, 2 s Del., res 174 e Ohio.
Mattler & Weaner, (Stephen Mattler & John Weaner,) U. S. saloon, 2 s Del.
Mattler Stephen, U. S. saloon, res 104 e Ohio.
Mattler Louis P., (Weinberger & Matler,) res cor South and Canal.
Mattox Solomon, teamster, res w Indianapolis.
Mauer John P., works in pork house, res Elizabeth.
Mauldin, Adams & Co., (John W. Adams and James Mauldin,) shoe store, 53 w Wash.
May Andrew, cooper, res 81 s East.
May Edwin, architect, res 75 n Penn.

Sharp & Bellis, general agents for the Florence Sewing Machine Co

May Edwin, cooper shop, 58 s East.
May John, drayman, res 119 McCarthy.
May Robert, rag and paper dealer, res 116 w N. York.
Mayer Charles, fancy goods, toys and notions, 29 w Wash., res 175 n Ill.
Mayer John F., umbrella and parasol manufacturer, 65 e Wash., res 63 St. Joseph.
Mayer Xevier, blacksmith shop, 306 Vir. ave., res next to shop.
Mayhew Enoch C., (Mayhew & Co.,) bds S. F. Smith, 42 s Meridian.
Mayhew James N., with L. D. Moses, bds Macy House.
Mayhew Oscar F., res 30 Circle.
Mayhew Parish L., book-keeper, Hunter, Darrow & Brundage, bds 102 e N. York.
Mayhew E. C. & Co., (Enoch C. Mayhew & James M. Ray,) manufacturers and wholesale dealers in boots and shoes, 8 Roberts' block, opp. Union Depot.
Mays Jacob, laborer, res 188 n Ill., up stairs.
Maxfield Geo., res 176 n Tenn.
Maxwell John, book-keeper, res n Meridian.
Maxwell Samuel D., res 156 e Ohio.
Mead James, carpenter, res cor Pine and Fletcher's ave.
Means Alferd, (col) cook, s w cor Wash., and Meridian.
Mears George W., physician, res 47 n Meridian.
Meck Lloyd, engineer, res 173 e South.
Medwick John, shoemaker, res 59 n Miss.
Meed Edwin, bookseller, res 305 s East.
Meek Alonzo, engineer, res 24 Huron.
Meek Edwin S., egg packer, 11 Vir. ave., bds 110 n Penn.
Meek James F., salesman, bee hive store, res 154 n Del.
Meek R., superintendent I. & C. R. R., res 108 s Ala.
Meeker James J., carriage maker, res 90 Ind. ave.
Meflin, Knox & Mitcham, (James H. Meflin, Francis Knox & Nathaniel Mitcham,) (col) barbers.
Megrew Willis H., soldier, 11th reg., res 181 e Ohio.
Megudy Moses, (col) wood sawyer, res bet Del. and Penn.
Meikel Catherine, (wid. Philip Meikel,) res 65 n Miss.
Meikel Charles P., printer, State Sentinel, res 68 n Miss.
Meikel John P., brewery, w Md., res 135 w Md.
Meikel Martin, bds 65 n Miss.
Meinhardt Philip, laborer, res e Wash.
Meirer Lewis, student at Bryant's commercial college.

Melfin James H., (col) res 137 West Alley.
Melville Robert B., cutter, Glaser & Bro., 2 Bates House, res 70 n Tenn.
Mendenhall John L., clerk, 13 n Penn., bds Wilson, n Penn.
Mendenhall Nathan M., traveling agent, Florence sewing machine, bds 25 n Penn.
Mengis Frank, tobacconist, 125 e Wash.
Menk Philip, laborer, res 16 Willard.
Menly Mrs. Elizabeth, seamstress, res 69 n Noble.
Menix Jeremiah, laborer, bds Washington House.
Meredith Samuel C., mail agent, res 52 Blackford.
Meredith Wm. M., Capt. Co. E., 70th Ind. reg., res N. Jersey, bet Mich. and North.
Merrill Cuyler J., res 117 n Ala.
Merrill George, (Chandler & Co.,) res n West.
Merrill John F., eclectic physician, 156 w Wash., res 134 w N. York.
Merrill Samuel, U. S. service, res 107 Ala.
Merrill Samuel, (Merrill & Co.,) res 207 s Ala.
Merrill & Co., (Samuel Merrill & Charles W. Moores,) booksellers, Glenns' block, e Wash.
Merriman Willis H., assistant surgeon, city hospital.
Merritt George, (Merritt & Coughlin,) res 102 n West.
Merrett Joseph J., boss weaver, Hoosier woolen factory, res 126 w N. York.
Merritt & Coughlin, (George Merritt, William Coughlin,) Ohio Premium Woolen Factory, s side Wash., on bank of river.
Merryman John M., (Drake & Merryman,) res cor Georgia and Benton.
Merryman Mrs. Anna, (wid.) res 131 n Ala.
Metzger A., real estate agent, res 139 n Penn.
Metzger Jacob, Sutler 54th Ind. vols., res 55 e Md.
METROPOLITAN HALL, cor Tenn. and Wash.
Meyer Adolph, blacksmith, bds 1 Tennessee.
Meyer Christ., carpenter, bds 49 Davidson.
Meyor Christian, frame maker, res 125 n Liberty.
MEYER GEORGE F., WHOLESALE AND RETAIL TOBACCONIST, 35 w Wash., res 56 w Vt.
Meyer Henry, blacksmith, res near rolling mill.
Meyer Jacob C., carpenter, res 181 Ind. ave.

Large assortment of straw goods, at Davis'.

Meyer J. C., furniture store, 171 e Wash., res same.
Meyer John, student at Bryant's Com. Col.
Meyers John H., city expressman, res 202 Massachusetts ave.
Meyer Ludwig, drayman, res 49 David-son.
Meyer William, bar tender, 44 w Wash.
Meyerhoof Henry, laborer, res 158 Ala.
Michael John, teamster, res 59 Union.
Michael Philip, cabinet maker, Davidson, bet Michigan and North.
Mick James F., salesman, res 154 n Del.
Mickles Willard, salesman, res 37 St. Clair.
Middaugh Mrs. Elizabeth, w Indianapolis.
Middlemas David C., grocery and liquor store, res 200 w Wash.
Miekel Elizabeth, (wid.) res 246 Madison ave.
Mier Charles, blacksmith, res Noble, bet Market and Ohio.
Mierstedt Augustus, paper maker, res 112 w Vermont.
Migga Michael, laborer, Wyoming.
Miksler Henry, carpenter, res 104 s Benton.
Milch Morris, in arsenal, res 69 n Miss.
Miles Abraham, laborer, Mt. Jackson.
MILITARY HALL, 24½ e Wash.
Miller Mrs. Anna, (wid.) res 11 Madison ave.
Miller Anthony, carpenter, res 109 e Vt.
Miller Anthony, drayman, res 162 s Tenn.
Miller A. R., watch maker, res 155 e South.
Miller August, school teacher, res 110 e Ohio.
Miller Emily, (wid.) res 155 w Vt.
Miller Charles G., saloon, cor Wash. and East, res same.
Miller Charles M., brickmason, res 159 n Noble.
Miller Christian, carpenter, res 301 s East.
Miller Christian F., carpenter, res 125 Davidson.
Miller Edwards, U. S. A., res 135 e Ohio.
Miller G. W., physician, res 158 n Ill.
Miller G. W., U. S. service, res w Indianapolis.
Miller George, blacksmith, res e end Market.
Miller Henry, res 118 n Missouri.
Miller Henry, brickmason, res 168 e Mich.
Miller Henry W., carpenter, res 131 n Noble.
Miller Henry, stair builder, res 154 n East.
Miller Isaac, shoemaker, works for A. Lintz, 39 w Wash., bds Mrs. Kitely.
Miller Jacob, clerk, bds 98 Md.

Miller Jacob, cigar maker, 10 Bates House, bds cor Mich and Del.
Miller James B., painter at I. & C. R. R. shop, res 54 n East.
Miller John, machinist, Sinker & Vance, bds 27 s Del.
Miller John A. D., stair builder, res 196 n East.
Miller Joel F., bds 165 w Vermont.
Miller Laneheart, tailor, res Pratt.
Miller Lewis, works in Frank. Wright's brewery, bds w National road.
Miller Margaret, (wid.) res 50 s East.
Miller Philip, carpenter, bds 64 Mass. ave.
Miller R., Musician, res 159 s Ala.
Miller Simon, ap. printer, bds out corp.
Miller Thomas, tailor, works at 134 e Wash., up stairs.
Miller Valentine, tanner, res 125 Bluff road.
Miller William, ticket agent, Union depot, bds 21 Ind. ave.
Miller William, laborer, res bet West and Cal., w Md.
Miller William, plasterer, res 83 n New Jersey.
Milligan Samuel B., student at Bryant's Com. Col.
Millinder William B., painter, 82 e Wash.
Mills Caswell S., salesman, Tousey & Byram, res 179 e N. York.
Mills Howard W., (Alford, Mills & Co.,) res 115 e Ohio.
Mills Layton, (Landis & Mills, res 134 Mass. ave.
Milnea David, mailing clerk Journal off., res 60 e N. York.
Milner Davis, laborer, res 160 e N. York.
Milner John, attorney at law, 84 e Washington.
Milton Hiram T., in the army, res 254 Ind. ave.
Minger Christian, laborer, res 144 s Ill.
Minick David C., res 39 Cal.
Minick Hiram, clerk in animal show, res 259 s Penn.
Mink Benjamin stove dealer, res 262 e Wash.
Minic D. C., (Minnie & Harriman,)Palmer House.
MINNIC & HARRIMAN, (D. C. Minnic, J. H. Harriman,) PROPR'S PALMER HOUSE.
Mires John, tinner, Wyoming.
Mitcham Nathaniel, (Mitcham & Knox,) (col.) 137 w alley, w canal.
Mitchie J. C., jeweler, bds Patterson House.
Mitchel Bussel, (col.) barber, 49 Mass. ave., bds cor Mo. and Ind. ave.
Mitchell Jacob, with Glaser & Bros., res 59 Mass. ave.
Mitchell James, cabinet maker, works 28 s Meridian, bds opp.

The Florence will sew all kinds of thread.

Mitchell Lewis, (col.,)boot black,bds Johnson's saloon.

Mitchell Robert S., brick moulder, res Mich. road.

Mitchell William M., carriage maker, res 121 n N. Jersey.

Mittey Christian, W., saddler, res 159 e N. York.

Mittey Christian W., shoe maker, res 159 e N. York.

Mittey William, bar keeper, State House Saloon, res 46 Mass. ave.

Mix Samuel N., clerk, 202 e Wash., bds at Little's Hotel.

Mock Martin, tailor, 2 Odd Fellow's Hall, res s e cor Noble and Ohio.

Mode Michael, shoemaker, res 73 e Washington.

Moesch Thaddeus, baker and confectioner, 73 e Wash., res same.

Moffit Oliver J., student at Bryant's Com. Col.

Moffitt Mrs. Sarah, (wid.) res 165 s New Jersey.

Moffitt John, in the army, res s N. Jersey.

Moffitt John, Jr., printer, 24 w Wash., res N Jersey, s South.

Moffitt Oliver J., printer, 8 e. Wash.

Moffitt William, clerk, 22 w Wash., bds 21 s Del.

Mahoney James, gas fitter, 36 s Ala.

Moling Singleton B., carpenter, res 84 n Tenn.

Mollay James, clerk, N. Y. store, res 41 w Market.

Molton Cutler, foundryman, bds 222 w Washington.

Molton Rodman, jr., res 44 Pratt.

Monnahen John, lab., bds P. Hanahan, near rolling mill.

Monninger C., billiard saloon, 121 e Washington, res same.

Monninger Daniel, saloon, res 231 n Tennessee.

Monninger Jacob, mail carrier, res 60 n Davidson.

Monroe Jackson, (col.,) bds Jos. Spray, s Pennsylvania.

Montague Wm., wagon maker, 12 n Ala., res 59 s N. Jersey.

Monteeth John, carpenter, 81 South.

Montgomery Andrew, shoemaker, res 112 n Meridian.

Montgomery William, cooper, res w Indianapolis.

Moody Lorenzo D., student at Bryant's Commercial College, bds 48 w Vermont.

Moon Miss Sally, cloak and dress maker, 26 and 28 w Wash., bds Macy House.

Moor Thomas, sexton Robert's chapel, res 144 e Wood.

Mooney James E., (Mooney & Co.,) bds 20 s Delaware.

MOONEY & CO., WHOLESALE DEALERS IN LEATHER, (Jas. E. Mooney and Alger S. Mount,) cor Meridian and Louisiana.

Mooore ——, plasterer, bds 64 Mass. ave.

Moore Chauncey G., bds 100 n Penn.

Moores Charles W., (Merill & Co.,) res 83 Merrill.

Moore George W., breakman, res 61 Spring.

Moore Mrs. Hattie, literary teacher, Blind Assylum.

Moore Henry H., physician, res 164 e Ohio.

Moore Harvey, salesman, fancy bazaar, bds n Pennsylvania.

Moore John L., book keeper, 170 n Pennsylvania.

Moore Mrs. J. M., (wid. Jos. M. Moore,) res 9 e Mich.

Moore Joseph A., book keeper, Indianapolis Branch Banking Co., res 9 e Mich.

Moore Richard, tailor, res 43 s West.

Moore Samuel R., works 84 w Wash., bds Pyle House.

Moore Thomas, janitor Robert's Chapel, res 144 Walnut.

Moore Wm., hostler, exchange stables, 25 n Ill, res Ohio House.

Moorhead Robert I., exchange stables, 25 n Ill., bds Bates House.

Moorman John J., shoemaker, n w cor East and Ohio.

Mooser Max, minister, res 191 s Del.

Moran John, laborer, 42 s Liberty.

Moras Joseph, grocer and rag dealer, cor Wilkison and Ill., res same.

Moran Patrick, lab., res 192 s East.

More Capt. L. L., bds Little's Hotel.

More P. J., brakeman, T. H. R. R., res 22 s Ala.

Morehouse William M., clerk, Grovenor & Turner, res 121 n Alabama.

Morgan Daniel, Madison R. R., res 104 McCarthy.

Morgan David, works at rolling mill, res s Mich., s of South.

Morgan David C., works at rolling mill, res Missouri near South.

Morgan Dennis, sen., 188 e Washington, up stairs.

Morgan Dennis, jr., egg packer, 188 e Washington.

Morgan John, works at rolling mill, res 166 s Tennessee.

Morgan Lawrence, 58 s East.

Morgan Pauline, (wid.,) res 21 e McCarthy.

Morgan Samuel C., with O. McGinnis, res 15 w Ohio.

Morgan Stephen W., (Stewart & Morgan,) res s side Blind Asylum.

Morgan Thomas W., grocery, 162 e Ohio, res same.

Morgan Wm. F., student at Bryant's Commercial College, bds s West.

Morgenvick Valentine, grocer, 9 Chatham, res same.

Moriarty Dauiel, lab., res 174 s Del., in rear.

Moriarty John, lab., res 199 e Ohio.

Moriarty Maurice, lab., res 210 s Del.

Moriarty Capt. Thos. J., bds Little's Hotel.

Moriraty Patrick, lab., Peiu R. R., bet Market and Ohio.

Moriarty & Co., (Thos. Moriarty and Jas. Dean,) dry goods.

MORITZ BRO. & CO., (M. Moritz, Solomon Moritz and A. Nathan,) MERCHANT TAILORS AND CLOTHIERS, 2 e Washington.

Moritz Mayer, (Moritz, Bro. & Co.,) 6th, Cincinnati, Ohio.

Moritz Solomon, (Moritz, Bro. & Co.,) bds Bates House.

Morley Edward, U. S. service, bds 66 s Noble.

Morly Patrick, teamster, res 100 s Noble.

Morrell Wm. S., book publisher, office old post office, s Meridian.

Morris Alex., painter and paper hanger, res 38 w Market.

Morris Artaineous, carpenter, res 80 e Vermont.

Morris George, sign painter, 38 w Market.

Morris Harmony, teamster, res 248 Ind. ave.

Morris James W., student at Bryant's Commercial College, bds s Meridian.

Morris John, shoemaker, Knodle's shoe shop.

Morris John, shoemaker, res s Noble.

Morris John, agt, Cincinnati depot, res 50 s Meridian.

MORRIS JOS. C., PHOTOGRAPHER, 35 e Washington, bds 38 w Market.

Morris Sanford, clerk, res 89 n New Jersey.

Morris F., clerk in Co. Court, res Delaware.

Morris S. V., in County Clerk's office, res Delaware.

Morris Wm., engineer, at Guisendorff's, res n Missouri, bet Market and Ohio.

Morrison ——, works at arsenal, res 109 Virginia ave.

Morrison James, attorney at law, 24½ e Washington, res out corporation.

Morrison James A., bds 96 n East.

Morrison James B., dep'y Sec'y of State, 11 Kentucky ave., res 70 n Illinois.

Morrison James, teamster, res 19 Union.

Morrison Lewis, book keeper, Alford Mills & Co., bds Judge Morrison's.

Morrison Michael, teamster, res No. 19 Union.

Morrison Mrs. N., (wid Alex. F. Morrison,) res 82 n Pennsylvania.

Morrison Squire, soldier in 63d reg't, res 162 Indiana ave.

Morrison Wm. H., sen., (Alford, Mills & Co.,) res Circle.

Morrison Wm. H., jr., bds Mrs. Chapman's, Market.

Morrow Francis, jr., grocery and liquor store, res 142 w Washington.

Morrow Thomas, works in Central depot, res w Market.

Morse Albert C., engineer, res 90 n Alabama.

MORTON OLIVER P., GOV. OF THE STATE OF INDIANA, res 26 w Market.

Morton Robert, lab, res Grove.

Morton Thomas, U. S. service, res 91 Virginia ave.

Mosbaugh George J., student at Bryant's Commercial College, bds Indiana ave.

Mosbaugh John H., student at Bryant's Com. College. bds Ind. ave.

Mosel Henry, works pork house, res 25 alley, bet Georgia and Pogues run.

Moseley Burton, moulder, res 63 w Louisiana.

Moser Frederick, teamster, bds 47 n Delaware.

MOSES L. W., OPTICIAN, 30 e Washington, res 13 w Market.

Moss Andrew, engineer, res 128 e Georgia.

Mossler Aaron, clerk, with Goldstone, bds Pennsylvania, opp post office.

Mossler Leberman I., auction and commission merchant, 10 w Washington, res 121 w Washington.

Mossler Solomon, book keeper, 10 w Washington, res 24 n Pennsylvania.

Mott Elijah T., manufacturer Excelsior sewing machine, bds 73 s Noble.

Mott Henry, works at arsenal, res cor Winston and New York.

Mottery Frederick, bakery, 11 n Pennsylvania, res 67 s Illinois.

Moulton Charles W., engineer, res 24 Michigan road.

Mount Alger S., (Mooney & Co.,) res 50 s Illinois.

Mount Henry, conductor Jeff. R. R., bds Ray House, Delaware.

Mount Humphrey, carpenter, res 46 s Benton.

Mount Sidney A., leather store, res 50 s Illinois.

Moynahan Andrew, works gas house, res 241 s Pennsylvania.

Muhlenbeck Augustus, miller, res bet Washington and Market, Ala. and N. Jersey.

Muir James, wholesale dealer in tobacco, teas, &c., res 33 w Market.

Muir Wm., gardner, Mt. Jackson.

Mulcahy Mrs. Margaret, (wid.,) res cor South and Benton.

The large sales of the Florence machine prove its great popularity.

Mull Jacob H., carriage maker, res 233 n Illinois.

Mullen Mrs. Ann, (wid.,) res 196 s East.

Mullany Patrick, clerk, C. A. Elliott, bds 53 s Mississippi.

Muller Henry, grocer, 142 n Noble, res same.

Muler John, importor and wholesale dealer in wines, cigars, &c., 256 e Washington, res same.

Mullenay Mrs. Mary, res 53 s Miss.

Munger Christ, telegraph repairer, s Ill., below depot.

Munhall Cornelius M., clerk, bds 121 n East.

Munhawl Harmon, salesman, fancy bazaar, bds 121 n East.

Munroe John, carpenter, res 142 McCarthy.

Munsell Ezra, carriage maker, bds 175 e Ohio.

Munsell Henry, carriage maker, res 175 e Ohio.

Mensell Henry, jr., station engineer, bds 175 e Ohio.

Munsell Newton, breakman, bds 175 e Ohio.

Munson Charles H., (Munson & Johnson,) res n Ala.

Munson David, (Locke & Munson,) res 88 e Market.

Munson Lewis, res 120 n Ala.

Munson Wm. L., grocery and feed, 21 n Ala., bds 120 n Ala.

MUNSON & JOHNSTON, (Charles H. Munson, Wm. J. Johnston, Saml. Johnston, and David Munson,) STOVE AND TIN WARE DEALERS, 62 e Wash.

Munts Thomas, plaster, res 169 n Noble.

Murdock John J., soldier, 79th reg't, res 24 n Liberty.

Murdock Joseph, stove moulder, res s Ill., near McCarthy.

Murphy Francis, watchman Terre Haute freight depot.

Murphy Henry, waiter Palmer House, res 176 s Ala.

Murphy James, res Elizabeth.

Murphy Jesse T., city policeman, res 193 e St. Clair.

Murphy John railroader, in rear 61 Madison.

Murphy John V., carpenter, bds Ohio House.

Murphy John W., (Murphy, Kennedy & Co.,) res 33 e Ohio.

MURPHY, KENNEDY & CO., (John W. Murphy, R. Frank Kennedy, W. W. Johnston and W. J. Holliday,) WHOLESALE DRY GOODS, 42 and 43 e Washington.

Murphy Lawrence J., tailor, 86 e Wash., bds 20 n Penn.

Murphy Michael, works in Little's Hotel, res Blackford.

Murphy Michael, lab., res 105 Madison ave.

Murphy Milton, engineer, alley n of Washington and e of N. J.

Murphy Nathan L., carpenter, res North, bet Liberty and Noble.

Murphy Timothy, shoemaker, e Wash.

Murphy Tobias M., travelling agt. P. & I. R. R., res 43 e Georgia.

Mursina Frank, discharged soldier, res 84 n Miss.

Murtaugh John, carpenter, res 17 Willard.

Muser George, butcher, res 167 s Del.

Musgrave Massas, soldier, res 2d house s of Madison.

Mussman Dietrich, clerk, bds Delaware, s of McCarthy.

Musmaire Richard, wood chopper, res 336 s Delaware.

Muzzy Bennett, soldier, res 150 n Miss.

Myear Wm., drayman, 90 Union.

Myer Fred, carpenter, bds 186 n Noble.

Myer Fred, works in north western meat market, bds 107 w Mich.

Myer Nicholas, shoemaker, works with Anthony Lintz, 39 w Wash., res 111 New York.

Myer Herrick, huckster, res 154 w Noble.

Myre John, umbrella maker, res 63 St. Joseph.

Myer John, carpenter, res 295 s Del.

Myer Michael, res Bluff road, Doughertyville.

Myer Moses, dealer in men's and boy's clothing, 4 w Washington, res 116 e Ohio.

Myer Philip, shoemaker, res 102 Davidson.

Myers Leonard, works U. S. arsenal, res 154 n N. J.

Myers Martin, umbrella maker and fancy turning work, 11 s Alabama.

Myers Charles, agt. for Lewis & Davlin's Museum, bds s Ill., opp Musuem.

MYERS JESSE D., FLOUR, FEED AND COMMISSION MERCHANT, 18 cor Pearl and s Meridian, res 148 n Ill.

Myers John A., tinner, res Wyman.

Myers Joseph, carpenter, res s Tenn., near Pogues run.

Myers L. F., res 164 N. J.

Myers Myer, salesman, J Kahn's, bds 100 n Ill.

Myers Peter, lab., res 266 s Delaware.

Myers William, shoemaker, res 108 n Noble.

Myers Xaver, moulder, res 254 s Del.

Myers Wm., lab., 27 w Washington.

N

Nalin Joshua D., resident farmer, res 149 n East.

Nann Wm., shoemaker, res 164 e Mich.

Nathan Abraham, (Moritz, Bro. & Co.,) res Cincinnati, O.

Neall Jonathan R., egg dealer, 188 e Wash., res 30 n East.

NEEL CHARLES, PROPRIETOR DAR-MISTADEN HAF SALOON, cor Wash. and Benton, res same.

Neep Conrad, gas fitter, bds Gas Street House.

Neff Jacob D., carriage maker, bds Patterson House.

Neff Wm., (Holliday & Neff,) res 14 w St. Clair.

Neff Wm. & Co., wholesale dealers in flour, grain, provisions and feed, 157 e Wash.

Neffle Frederick, res s West.

Neiger Fred., wagon maker, cor Mass. ave. and Noble, res 202 Mass. ave.

Neighbors Robert, drayman, res 33 Union.

Neighbors Charles, express wagon, res 23 Henry.

Neigle Daniel, laborer, res 23 Harrison.

Neiman Christian, carpenter, res 122 Davidson.

Neiman John S., porter, Ohio House, bds 31 w Market.

Neiman Laha, (wid. Martin Neiman,) proprietress Ohio House, 31 w Market.

Nell John B., teacher, res 33 n Noble.

Nelson Edward F., engineer, res cor Noble and Benton.

Nelson Henry H., sheriff supreme court, off. State House, res 73 n Miss.

Nelson Horatio L., watchmaker, W. H. Talbott & Co., bds Mrs. Smith's, 44 s Penn.

Nelson Sandy, (col) res 78 n Missouri.

Nelson Thomas, clerk, Lynch & Keane's, bds Mass. ave.

Nesbit John R., map maker, res 189 s Ala.

Nestler Frederick, cabinet maker, res e Wash., corporation line.

Neutgens J. J., salesman, 26 and 28 w Wash., bds s East.

New John B., Christian minister, res 56 n Ill.

New John C., (New & Talbot's building,) res 102 n Penn.

New & Talbot's Block, Penn., bet Wash. and Market.

Newcomb Horatio C., (Newcomb & Tarkington,) lawyer, res 58 n Ala.

Newcomb Richard H., clerk, Hogshire & Co., res 144 New York.

NEWCOMB & TARKINGTON, (H. C. Newbomb and J. S. Tarkington,) ATTORNEYS AT LAW, 24½ e Wash.

Newcomer Frisby S., physician, off. 6 Blake's building, res 161 n Ill.

Newell James, telegraph operator, bds Macy House.

Newell Lyne S., music teacher, blind asylum, res same.

Newet John, works Hinesly's livery stable, bds Knight's.

NEWMAN JOHN, PRES'T IND. CENT. R. W., res cor Mich. and Penn.

Newman Peter, laborer, res s Ill., near Pogue's Run.

Newman Tobias, salesman, 9 Bates House, bds 16 n Miss.

Newton Norman, door tender for live animal show, Varnes House.

Ney Charles, laborer, res grove.

Niccum Joel, machinest, res 114 e Ga.

Nicholis Adison, druggist, res 151 Vir. ave.

Nichols Miss Georgie, teacher, Indianapolis Female Institute, res same.

Nichols Thomas M., dentist, off. 18 s Meridian, res same.

Nicholson David, stone cutter, res 58 Madison ave.

Nicholson David, stone cutter, res 159 n N. Jersey.

Nicholson Geo. A., res 147 n Tenn.

Nicholson Wm., works I. & C. R. R., shop, res 9 Lord.

Nicholison Wm., stone cutter, res 141 w South.

Nickum John R., (Nickum & Parrott,) res 66 n east.

NICKUM & PARROTT, (John R. Nickum and Horace Parrott,) BAKERS AND CONFECTIONERY, 11 n Penn.

Nicol D., machinest, Sinker & Vance, res 183 e N. York.

Nicolai Charles, saddler and harness maker, 268 e Wash., res same.

Nicolai Julius, res 89 w Wash.

Niemeyer Henry, clerk, cor Georgia and Noble, bds same.

Niemeyer Wm., grocery and provision store, cor Georgia and Noble.

Nienaber Harmann, laborer, res 13 Centre.

Niger Lepold, porter, blind asylum.

Night J. Franklin, bds 88 n Ala.

Nill Wm. O., merchant, res 26 n Penn.

Ninch Terrace, res 244 e Wash., up stairs.

Nixon Rev. J. Howard, Presbyterian, res opp. Baptist Seminary.

Nobbe Henry, printer, Dodd & Co., res 278 s Del.

Noble Winston P., res Market, e Davidson.

NOBLE WM. H. L., GENERAL TICKET AGENT, I. & C. R. R., res s Del.

Noe Albert M., machinest, res 38 s Liberty.

Noel Edward, clerk, 3 n Ill., bds w Georgia.

Noel Vanse S., grain dealer, res 10 w Georgia.

Nofsinger Wm. R., res e Indianapolis.

Nolan Solomon C., cabinet maker, res 141 n East.

No machine gives so good satisfaction as the Florence.

Nolan Thomas, hackman, res 95 s Tenn.
Nolen John H., res 177 e South.
Nolen Oliver, carpenter, res 12 Bates.
Nolin Cornelius, cabinet maker, res 149 n East.
Noltner Agidius, sale agent, Seidensticker, res 93 s Meridian.
Nooe D., trader, res 73 s N. Jersey.
Nookes David, soldier, Co. H., 13th reg., Ind. vol., res 165 n Liberty,.
Nooman Michael, blacksmith, bds 52 s Del.
Northam Wm., carpenter, res 6 Willard,
Northway George M., plasterer, res 94 n N. Jersey.
Northway John, plasterer, 146 e North.
Norton James, hostler, Wilkinson, bds E. Knight's.
Norton John H., painter, bds Becking House.
Norwood Mrs. Margaret, res 72 s Meridian.
Norwood, Frank E., tinner, res 26 n Ill.
Norwood Geo., bds 95 n Ill.
Noy Marshal, carpenter, res 38 s Liberty.
Null Sarah, (wid. John Null,) dressmaker, res 108 w Ver.
Null Thomas, book binder, 24 w Wash., bds 108 W. Ver.
Nutts Jacob, baker, res e Md.
Nye Michael, (Nye & Oton,) 65 w Wash.
Nye & Oton, saloon keepers, 65 w Wash.

O

O'Brian Jeremiah, tinner, res Wiman.
O'Brian Jeremiah, tinsmith, res 200 s Del.
O'Brien John, laborer, res 217 Bates.
O'Brien John, laborer, res 176 Ala.
O'Brien Lawrence, works Hoosier woolen factory.
O'Brien Thomas, laborer, res 60 n Tenn.
O'Brien Timothy, lost baggage agent, I. C. R. R., res 200 s Del.
O'Callaghen Michael, laborer, res 28 e Ga.
O'Connell James, laborer, res 23 e Ga.
O'Connell Murty, laborer, res 206 s Del.
O'Connor Maurice, laborer, res in alley, bet East and Noble.
O'Connor Michael, contractor, res cor Meek and Noble.
O'Connor Thomas, R. R. engineer, res 164 s Penn.
O'Connor Thomas, railroader, res 210 s Del.
O'Courtnay Patrick, laborer, res near Lawrenceburg high bridge.
O'Daily Michael, retired merchant, res s Del.
O'Donald John, laborer, res Plum, near Oak.
Odd Fellow's Hall, cor Penn. and Wash.

O'Driscoll D. C., printer, bds. Mrs. Reid's.
O'Driscoll John, sterotyper, H. H. Dodd & Co., bds cor Market and Tenn.
Ody Mrs. Jane, (wid.) Mt. Jackson.
OEHLER ANDREW, WATCH MAKER AND JEWELER, 2 s Del., res same. See card.
Oehler David, bar keeper, bds 38 Bluff road.
Oehler Roman, watch maker, shop Pea Ridge House, bds same.
Off Jacob, sawyer, bds 103 Peru R. R.
Off John, sawyer, bds 103 Peru R. R.
Off Philip, gardener, Mt. Jackson.
Offutt Thomas H., salesman, res 35 s Noble.
O'Flaherty Mrs. Sarah M., tailoress, res 39 e Wash., 3d floor, up stairs.
O'Flaherty Thomas, works Schofield & Co.'s vinegar factory, bds at Lawrenceburg high bridge.
Ogden Charles, carpenter, bds 107 s Tenn.
Oglesby John H., river pilot, res 91 n Tenn.
Oglesby Wm. F., clerk, T. H. depot.
O'Hara Timothy, clerk at Callinan's dry goods store, bds Little's Hotel.
Ohara Timothy J., salesman, bds Little's Hotel.
O'Hara John, shoemaker, res in rear of 65 s Penn.
O'Hare Nathen, tailor, res 127 w South.
Ohaver James J., engineer at Hoosier Woolen Factory, res 109 Blake.
Ohio House, w Market, bet Ill. and Tenn. Mrs. Neiman, prop'r.
O'Horon Antony, laborer, res s West.
Ohr Aaron D., clerk Union Depot, res 41 w Mich.
Ohr Henry, cashier Adam's Express Co., res 48 n Del.
OHR JOHN H., AG'T ADAMS EXPRESS CO., 12 e Wash., res 91 e Ohio.
O'Keane Dennis, blacksmith, res 88 s Benton.
O'Key Edward, stone mason, res 167 n New Jersey.
O'Key Joseph B., trader, res 144 n East.
O'Key Phillip, carpenter, res n New Jersey, bet St. Clair and Ft. Wayne ave.
O'Leary Edward, hod carrier, res Grove.
O'Leary James, laborer, res 46 Bates.
O'Leary Jeremiah, (O'Leary & Renchan,) res cor Ill. and South.
O'Leary Michael, res 200 s Del.
O'LEARY & RENCHAN, (Jeremiah O'Leary, James Renchan,) PALMER HOUSE SALOON.
O'Lerfielt Dominic, carpenter, res 326 s Del.
Olerfielt Isodre, works Central depot, res 306 s Del.
Olin Chauncy, res 61 w N. York.
O'Mara Richard, laborer, res 111 Blake.
O'Neal John, laborer, res 77 e Market.

Beautiful styles of children's caps, at Davis'.

THE HOOSIER STATE
STOVE FOUNDRY!
AND MACHINE WORKS,

SOUTH DELAWARE STREET,

Bet. Indianapolis and Cincinnati and Indiana Central Freight Depots.

COX, LORD & PECK,

MANUFACTURERS AND DEALERS IN

Stoves and Iron Castings,

Of all descriptions. Orders respectfully solicited.

CHARLES COX.   F. B. LORD.   T. S. PECK.

C. SPIEGEL.   F. THOMS.   H. FRANK.   A. SPIEGEL.

SPIEGEL, THOMS & CO.,

Manufacturers, Wholesale & Retail Dealers in all kinds of

FURNITURE

AND

CHAIRS,

Warerooms, No. 73 West Washington Street,

INDIANAPOLIS, IND.

O'Neal Mrs. S., (wid.) res 97 Va. ave.
O'Neil Edmund, tailor, res 39 e Wash.
O'Neil Michael, cutter, res 143 s Tenn.
O'Neil Patrick, laborer, res 14 e Va.
O'Neil Roger, laborer, 15 s Ala.
O'Neil Roger, hostler, res 6 Pearl.
O'Neil Timothy, laborer, res north of Central depot.
O'Riely Timothy, laborer, res s Tenn., near Pogues run.
ORIENTAL HOUSE, Bellis & Tarleton, proprietors, s Ill.
Orlopp Richard, speculator, res 117 e Market.
Orndoff David H., clerk Adams Express Co., res e Mich.
Orndorff Henry Clay, clerk, 8 w Wash., bds 63 e Mich.
Ornsby George, foreman Gov. commissary depot, res 47 e McCarthy.
Orrick William, laborer, res w Indianapolis.
Osborn William, carpenter, bds National Hotel.
Osborn Elizabeth,(wid.) res 99 Ind. ave.
Osborn Miss Jennie, res cor New Jersey and St. Clair.
Osbourne Samuel, Deputy Clerk Supreme Court, res 236 n Ill.
Osgood Charles J., student at Bryant's Commercial Col., bds at J. R. Osgood's, s Meridian.
Osgood John B., house and sign painter, 16 e Market.
Osgood Judson R., res 52 s Meridian.
Osgood, Smith & Co., (Judson R. Osgood, Samuel Smith, Samuel Allamon,) last, hub and spoke factory, s Ill.
O'Shea, Jeremiah P., laborer, bds at random.
Osten John, res 25 e Market.
Ostermeyre Andrew, laborer, res 15 Centre.
Ostermeyer, Christian, drayman, res 137 e Ohio.
Ostermeyer Fred, (Ostermeyer & Prange,) dry goods and groceries, 25 e Wash., res e Plank road.
Ostermeyer Mrs. Jane M., res 53 s Meridian.
Ostermeyer Lewis Sr., res 125 n Liberty.
Ostermeyer & Prange, (Fred. Ostermeyer, Charles Prange,) dry goods and groceries, 25 e Wash.
O'Sullivan Ortho, laborer, res 170 s Del.
O'Sullivan Daniel, laborer, res 320 s Del.
O'Sullivan Dennis, plasterer, res 51 e McCarthy.
O'Sullivan John, laborer, res 5 e Bates.
O'Sullivan Patrick, laborer, res 35 Huron.
O'Sullivan Timothy, plasterer, res 51 e McCarthy.
Oswald Gottfried, laborer, res 165 R. R.
Otis William H., res 42 s Penn.

Ott Michael, works at rolling mill, res 77 Bluff road.
Otte William, carpenter, res 155 e Ohio.
Otten Detrick, cigar store, 159 e Wash., res 41 Spring.
Ottman Daniel, dyer, bds Jefferson House.
Otto Carle, physician and surgeon, res n Noble, bet Wash. and Market.
Otto Charles, plough grinder, res Georgia, bet Noble and East.
Otzel Adam shoemaker, 26 w Maryland.
Overfelt Philip, carriage smith, bds 326 s Ala.
Overmayer, Amos C., salesman, Fancy Bazaar, bds Palmer House
Owen John, plasterer, res w Market.
Owens Mrs. Mary, (wid.) res e La.
Owings N., res 87 South.
Owings John, P. O. clerk, res 87 South.
Owings Lydia A., res Wabash, bet Liberty and Noble.
Owings Nathaniel J., clerk in P. O., bds 87 e South.
Owsley William, carpenter, res Douglas, bet N. York and Vermont.
Oyler William, policeman, res alley, bet N. Jersey and Wash.

P

Padlow James C., blacksmith, res e Market.
Pahler Christian, laborer, res 214 Vir. ave.
Pahler Wm., laborer, res 314 Vir. ave.
Paine Daniel L., (Paine & Downey,) res 82 n Tenn.
Paine & Downey, (Daniel L. Paine, & A. C. Downey,) job printers, e Pearl.
Painter John, hack driver, res 227 n Tenn.
Palest Henry, tailor, bds California House, 136 s Ill.
Palmer Ben. G., painter and paper hanger, res n Liberty.
Palmer Charles C., bds 37 w Md.
Palmer D. C., cabinet maker, res 277 Vir. ave.
Palmer Ed. L., book binder, 24 w Wash., res 40 s Ill.
Palmer Fenner S., (Boyd & Palmer,) res 87 n Penn.
Palmer George W., book-keeper, Jones, Vinnedge, & Co., bds 44 s Penn.
PALMER HOUSE, MINNIC & HARRIMAN, PROPRIETORS, s e cor Wash. and Ill.
Palmer James, (col) barber, 143 s Tenn.
Palmer Nathan B., res 37 w Md.
Palmer T. G., deputy Auditor of State, 7 McOuat's block, res 90 n Ill.
Parisette Joseph, confectioner, res 79 w South.
Parker Edgar, guns, pistols and gun materials, 25 s Ill., res up stairs.

The Florence runs steady.

Parker George, Capt. Co. G., 79th reg., res Mass. ave., near corporation.

Parker George, moulder, res 9 Henry.

Parker Jackson, (col) teaming, res 13 n Harris.

Parker North, student at Bryant's commercial college.

Parker Alexander, clerk, N. Y. store, bds Macy House.

Parker Mrs. Catherine, (wid) res 72 n East.

PARKER REGINALD R., HOSIERY, NOTIONS, &c., 30 w Wash.

Parker Wilson, bricklayer, res 103 s Tenn.

Parker Hiram, (col) cook, res 76 s Benton.

Parkhill H. H., artist, 17 Wash., bds Pyle House.

Parkman C. B., secretary rolling mill Co., bds 30 s Tenn.

Parkman Charles, physician, bds 30 s Tenn.

Parks Miss Lizzie, res 32 Davidson.

Parks P. S., secretary for Major McClure, bds Pyle House.

Parmelee Geo. H., telegraph operator, res 38 Pratt.

Parmelee Mrs. Hannah, (wid. Lenard Parmelee,) res 38 Pratt

Parmelee Wm. H., agent Lafayette R. R. freight office, res 71 w N. York.

Parmer John J., Quartermaster, U. S., res 149 n Penn.

Parr Wm. P., (Duzan & Parr,) bds Kinder House.

Parrott Horace, (Nickum & Parrott,) res 141 n Del.

Parry Hager, blacksmith, res Henry, bet Miss. and Carroll.

Parsons John J., (H. H. Dodd & Co., and Parsons, Adams & Co.,) res 97 n Tennessee.

PARSONS, ADAMS & CO., (J. J. Parsons, G H. Adams, and J. R. Asher,) SCHOOL BOOK PUBLISHERS, Odd Fellows' Hall.

Parth Geo., laborer, res 198 Vir. ave.

Parvin Theophilus, M. D., off. 67, res 75 n Ala.

Pasco J., boiler maker, res 126 e Georgia.

Pasquier John B., carpenter, res cor Mich. and Davidson.

Patrick Washington Kennedy, res 4 s Benton.

Patterson Augustus, res 190 n Ill.

Patterson Augustus E., book-keeper, Murphy, Kennedy & Co., bds Palmer House.

Patterson Coleman B., foreman, Patterson & Co., bds Coen House.

Patterson Edward W., (Patterson & Co.,) res 91 West.

Patterbann Frederick I., cabinet maker, bds Christ. Yager.

PATTERSON HOUSE, JOHN D. HAMILTON, PROPRIETOR, n Ala., bet Wash. and Ala.

Patterson James M., livery stable, 34 e Md., bds Smith's, w Ohio.

Paterson James N., bds Littles Hotel.

Patterson John, fence builder, res 195 e St. Clair.

Patterson John, carpenter, res 30 s Ill.

Patterson John H., printer, Journal office, bds Macy House.

Patterson John P., salesman, Holland & Son, res 85 n N. Jersey.

Patterson John T., tailor, res 85 s N. Jersey.

Patterson Joseph D., (Patterson & Co.,) bds Patterson House.

Patterson Mrs Kate, (wid) res 104 Mass. ave.

Patterson Miss Lucy, dressmaker, 26 and 28 w Wash , bds s N. Jersey.

Patterson Robert, carpenter, res 239 Mass. ave.

Patterson Robert M., (Irwin & Patterson,) res Ohio, bet Tenn. and Ill.

Patterson Roll, (Patterson & Co.,) bds 91 West.

Patterson Samuel D., operator, I. & C. R. R., res Mich. road.

Patterson, Wm., attorney, res 152 e Ohio.

Patterson Wm. A., (Patterson & Co.,) bds Morrison's, n Penn.

Patterson & Co., (Edward W. Patterson, Wm. A., Patterson, and Joseph D. Patterson,) pork packers, off. New & Talbot's building.

Pattison Elijah C., trader, bds 40 n East.

Pattison Isaac, res 46 n East.

Paul Bernard, shoemaker, bds 52 e South.

Paul George Henry, shoemaker, shop 53 e South, res 52 e South.

Pawley John, carpenter, res 197 n Noble.

Paxton Mrs. Elizabeth, (wid) res 3 Circle.

Payton Wm., (col) currier at Fishback's, res 139 n West.

Pea Ridge House, 14 s Penn.

Peacock Wm., engineer, res National road, e Pogues run.

Peak Andrew, cooper, res w Ind'polis.

Peak David, carpenter, bds National Hotel w Wash.

Pearsall Peter R., professor of music, res 26 s Tenn.

Pearsall Wm., butcher, L. Hahn, bds 26 s Tenn.

Pearsen Jonas, machinest, res 127 Mass. ave.

PEARL ST., SALOON, T. McBAKER, PROPRIETOR, w Pearl.

Pearson Levi W., bricklayer, res 112 n Ala.

Peck Edwin J., president Terre Haute R. R., bds 39 w Md.

Pee Geo. W., salesman, 75 w Wash., bds 87 n Meridian.

Davis' new hat store, No. 15 Pennsylvania St.

Pedicord Mrs. Lydia, boarding house, 179 e Market.

Pedlow Robert, moulder, res 250 s Del., in alley,

Pedrick Mrs. dressmaker, 18 n Ill.

Pedrick Noah, teamster, res 235 Ind. ave.

Peerman Cass, hostler, bds E. Knight's.

Peetters John P., traveling agent, res 85 n New Jersey,

Pellet Wm., conductor gravel train, Bellefontaine R. R., res 21 e Georgia.

Peltre Leon, stone cutter, res Osbrook.

Pendergast Enos, carpenter, Mt. Jackson.

Pendergast John G., carpenter, bds 74 n Tenn.

Penn G. W., book-keeper, Sinker & Vance, bds 44 s Penn.

Pennel Harlow E., carriage painter, res 165 n Liberty.

Pennewill Daniel H., Sergeant Major, recruiting, 11th reg., U. S., Infantry, bds 16 n Penn.

Pentecost Mrs. Emma, boarding house, 20 s Miss.

Pentecost Mahlon B., fruit can dealer, 188 e Wash., res 114 n Ala.

Penticost Hugh, compositor Cameron's job office, bds 20 s Miss.

Pepbels Mrs. Nancy, res 123 n Ala.

Perdue Milton W., res 184 n Noble.

Perdy William, Principal of Perdy's Com. Col., Ætna building, bds Palmer House.

PERINE PETER R., AGENT FOR PITSBURG AND WESTERN COAL, off. 12 w Maryland, res 175 n Ala.

Perkins James A., laborer, res 42 Bates.

Perkins J. A., Gen'l Ticket Agt., Ind. C. R. R., bds Palmer House.

Perkins Samuel E., Judge Supreme Court, res 152 w N. York.

Perkins C. G., res 132 n Ill.

Perrin Gerge K., (Perrin & Manlove,) res 25 e Mich.

Perrin & Manlove, (George K. Perrin, Wm. R. Manlove,) attorneys at law, 45 e Wash.

Perrine Charles O., book publisher, 6 Odd Fellow's Hall, bds 78 s East.

Perrine George K., lawyer, res 35 e Mich.

Perrine John R., painter, U. S. service, bds Uncle Sam.

Perrott Samuel, grocery, res 193 Ind. ave.

Perry John C., salesman, res 219 n New Jersey.

Perry Matthew, moulder, Sinker & Vance, bds s Del.

Persel Charles F., carpenter, bds 78 s Penn.

Persell Peter, tinner, bds Persell, s Penn.

Peter Joseph, laborer, res 239 Mass. ave.

Peters Susan J., (wid.) res 137 Blake.

Petit Simon, laborer, Mt Jackson.

Petrie John, saloon, 222 e Wash., res same.

Petteford John, (col.) barber, Yohn's block res bet Tenn. and Miss.

Petty Julius, farmer, res 266 Ind. ave.

Pfaffin Paul, clerk, res cor North and Ind. ave.

Pfaffin Theodore, grocery, res n w cor North and Ind. ave.

Pflager Jacob, tailor, res 62 n Davidson.

Phalin Martin, currier, Yandes & Co., bds 20 n Penn.

Phelan Johanna, (wid.) res 192 s Del.

Phelps A. E., saddler, 20 w Wash., res N. Jersey, bet Wash. and Market.

Phelps Simon B., engineer Jeff. R. R., res 100 e Louisiana.

Phelps Sewell, baker, res 183 e Vt.

Phelps William, clerk and telegraph op., Madison R. R. off., 138 e McCarthy.

Philips Hugh, blacksmith, res 121 McCarthy.

Philips Jacob, laborer, res 76 s Noble.

Philips Thomas H., res 133 n West.

Phipps Henry, laborer, res 186 Massachusetts ave.

Phipps Isaac N., real estate agent, 363 Wash., res out corp.

Phipps John M., machinist, res 120 s Noble.

Phipps Joseph B., assistant book keeper, 22 w Wash.

Phipps Leonidas M., township Assessor, off. New & Talbot's block.

Pickering Charles, Ag't 33d Ind. vols. res 52 e Market.

Pickett Henry, (col.) hostler, bds any where and everywhere.

Piel William F., general store, 240 e Wash., res same.

Pieler Christian, works Louis Lang's saloon, res in country.

Pierce Samuel J., printer, H. H. Dodd & Co., bds 20 Penn.

Pierce Winslow S., McKernan & Pierce, 31 w Wash., res cor N. York and West.

Pierson Stephen D., cutter, res 109 e Ohio.

Pigg Francis, painter, res 15 Harris.

Pigg Sarah, (wid.) res 40 e Louisiana.

Pilger Joseph, carpenter, res 154 e New York.

Pissemier John, works rolling mill, res 25 s East, in alley.

PITTS GEORGE W., ICE DEALER, res 78 Ind. ave.

Pitzer Wm. H., student at Bryant's Com. Col., bds at Thos E. Holbrook's.

Plant John, clerk, Hawthorns, res 193 e Wash.

Pleasant Christian, res 206 n Ala.

Plogstarth Victor, stonemason, res 164 n Liberty.

Plumb H. H., salesman, Fancy Bazaar, bds 61 e Market.

Plummer Mrs. Mary E., (wid.) re w Indianapolis.

The Florence is more durable than any sewing machine in market.

Plummer William, clerk in Caylor saloon, res 220 e Wash.

Pomeroy John A., (Pomeroy, Fry & Co.,) bds Bates House.

POMEROY, FRY & CO., (J. A. Pomeroy, W. H. Fry, Jr., W. B. Thurston,) COMMISSION MERCHANTS AND WHOLESALE DEALERS IN IRON,NAILS,&c., 117 w Wash. See card.

Pond Fred S., turner, res 172 e Ohio.

Pool A. J., engineer I. P. & C. R. R., res 24 n New Jersey.

Pope Edgar B., salesman, Chase & Dawes, bds Oriental.

Pope Henry res 133 w Vt.

Pope William, (Hatz & Co.,) tailor, bds. California House.

Porter Albert G., (McDonald & Porter,) res 109 n Del.

Porter John, carpenter, res 1st house w canal, Wash.

Porter John S., carpenter, bds California House.

Porter Nathaniel F., res 152 w Ga.

Porter Omer T., salesman, bds 31 Ellsworth.

Post Charles,(Blake, Helming, & Co.,) res 164 w N. York.

Post Office, cor Penn. and Market, A. H. Conner, P. M.

Posterior John, laboror, res cor Meridian and South.

Pottage Benjamin, wholesale and retail dealer in hardware &c., 76 w Wash., res 91 w Market.

Potter George W., (col.,) barber, res 218 e Wash.

Potter Mrs. James, bds 55 n Noble.

Pouder Charles, tailor, res 59 n Miss.

Pouder Milton, res 60 n East.

Pouer Henry, moulder, res 186 s Penn.

Powell William, (col.) barber, Yohn's block, bds 126 w Ohio.

Powell David, butcher, corner Vt. and Mass. ave., res 77 Mass ave.

Powell Job, works rolling mill, res w Merrill.

Powell Patrick, laborer, res bet North and Elizabeth.

Power Jacob B., res 31 n East.

Powers John, laborer, res 33 s Liberty.

Powers Matthew, laborer, res 62 Ind. ave.

Powers Patrick, boiler maker, Sinker & Vance, res 209 s Penn.

Powers Steven, porter, U. S. court-rooms.

Powers William, Capt. 88th Ind. vols., bds Farmers' Hotel.

Powley Henry, carpenter, res 88 n Davidson.

Poyntz John C., clerk New York Store, res 46 w Market.

Prail Frederick, brickmason, res 173 e Ohio.

Prange Frederick, watchman at Peru depot, res Davidson, bet N. York and Vt.

Pratt William B., ag't P. & I. R. R., res 183 e Market.

Pratz John, blacksmith, res 133 Tenn.

Preis John, shoemaker, res 71 n East.

Pressel Augustus, carpenter, res cor Cherry and Oak.

Pressel Mrs. Charlotte, res Plum, out corporation.

Pressel Mrs. Mary, seamstress, res 120 e Mich.

Pressel William, carpenter, res 70 e La.

Preston Joseph, plumber, bds Washington House.

Price Mrs. E. J., Matron Blind Asylum.

Price J., pattern maker, bds Ray House.

Price John, shoemaker, 116 Va. ave.

Prince John D., clerk, Alford, Mills & Co., res 35 n Noble.

Prink Fred, works Spugel, Thomas & Co., res 184 e Vt.

Prinuel Henry, blacksmith, Sinker & Vance, res 65 Mad. ave.

Pritchard Mrs. Elizabeth, res 3d house on California, s of Md.

Prasse Henry, grocer, 322 Va. ave., res same.

Prosser Mrs. Anna, 2 Blake building, up stairs.

Prosser John, tailor, 17 n Ill., res same.

Protzman Ferdinand, (Hamlin & Protzman,) res 18 s Ill.

Protzman John H., 16½ s Ill.

Prouser John, tailor, bds 64 Mass. ave.

Prunk Daniel H., assistant surgeon U. S. A., res 21 w Mich.

Prust Daniel, shoemaker, works for A. Lintz, 30 w Wash., bds Mrs. Kitely, Montgomery.

Pugh James, soldier, res w Indianapolis.

Pugh Philip, (col.) laborer 143 Wash.

Purcell William, discharged soldier, res 36 California.

Purnell John, cabinet maker, res cor Md. and Meridian, up stairs.

Purviance J. H., Mes. American Express Co., bds Mason House.

Pursey Jonathan, shoemaker, res 78 s Penn.

Pyle John, Pyle House, cor Md. and Ill.

Pyle John E., book keeper, Jameson & Funkhouser, res 125 Mass. ave.

Q

Quaker Church, cor Del. and St. Clair.

Quciper Julius, harness maker, 34 w Wash., res 275 Va. ave.

Quigley Patrick, shoemaker, res s Ill., near Pogues run.

Quimby Harriet N., milliner, 20 s Ill.

Quimby Carlos W., attorney at law, off. 37 e Wash., res 25 s Ill.

Quinn John, hostler, res 28 s Penn.

Quinn William, railroader, res 164 s Penn.

Childrens caps, new styles, at No. 15 Pennsylvania St.

PURE SODA WATER.

W. B. VICKERS,

ODD FELLOWS HALL,

Cor. Washington & Pennsylvania Sts.,

INDIANAPOLIS, IND.

W. S. MAJOR.   P. A. BROWN.

MAJOR & BROWN,

ATTORNEYS AND COUNSELORS AT LAW,

Office in Blackford's Building,

Corner Washington & Meridian Sts.,

INDIANAPOLIS, IND.

GEO. F. MEYER,

Manufacturer and Dealer in all kinds of

CIGARS, SNUFF,

Chewing & Smoking

TOBACCO,

No. 35 West Washington Street,

INDIANAPOLIS, IND.

All goods warranted of the best quality. Orders solicited and promptly attended to.

Quinnius Harmon, Pastor of the Evangelical Zions Church, res 16 w Ohio.

Quisson Julius, saddler, res 275 Va. ave.

R

Raake Thomas, stewart Spencer House, res 58 Louisiana.

Rabbe Henry G., clerk with Weinberger & Muller, res n w cor South and Canal.

Raderstorf John, clerk Washington House, bds same.

Rafer Charles, laborer, res 79 Merrill.

Rafert Anthony, carpenter, res cor Ala. and Walnut.

Rafert Christopher, carpenter, bds 193 n Ill.

Rafert Edward, carpenter, res Pratt, bet Ill. and Meridian.

Rafert Frederick F., carpenter, res Pratt, bet Meridian and Ill.

Rafert Henry, res 193 n Ill.

Ragan Edmond, laborer, res 168 s Tennessee.

Ragan J. U., bds 94 n Ill.

Raible Charles, carpenter, res e Wash.

Raible Lewis, cabinet maker, res 28 s Meridian, up stairs.

Rail John, laborer, res 22 Henry.

Raisner, William, railroader, res 37 Union.

Raisner Mrs. Ellen, res 160 s Tenn.

Ramy James E., harness maker, 321 Va. ave.

Ramsay Barton, (col.) lives on continuation West, outside corp.

Ramsay James, Madison R. R., bds Ray House.

Ramsay James A., clerk Harrison's bank, res 21 w Md.

Ramsay John F. furniture store, 21 s Ill., res 21 w Md.

Ramsey Miss Lizzie, (col.) washer, res 147 n Ala.

Ramsey Thomas, police, res 41 St. Clair.

Ramsey Walter, (Ramsey & Hanning,) res 130 n Del.

Ramsey & Hanning, (Walter Ramsey, John G. Hanning,) gas fitters, rear Glenn's block.

RAMSEY'S BLOCK, s Ill., cor Md.

Rananan Joseph, res 240 Ind. ave.

Rand Frederick, (Rand & Hall,) res 162 n Ill.

RAND & HALL, (Frederick Rand, Reginald H. Hall,) ATTORNEYS AT LAW, 24½ e Wash.

Randall Hiram P., retired farmer, res St. Joseph, bet Penn. and Meridian.

Randell John, printer, res old P. O., up stairs.

Randolph Lot., farmer, res w Indianapolis.

Randolph Nelson, miller, res 155 n New Jersey.

Ranstead Wm H., (Ranstead & Marshall,) bds Palmer House.

RANSTEAD & MARSHALL,(Wm.H.Ranstead,Frank B. Marshall,)WAR CLAIM AGENTS, 24 Talbot's block, bds Palmer House.

Rapp Fred J., plow manufacturer, 154 e Wash., res 195 e Market.

RASCHIG CHARLES M., TOBACCO AND CIGARS, 11 e Wash., res 11 e Vt.

Raschig Capt. Edward, Post Adjutant, bds Bates House.

Rasennen William F., railroader, res 177 e Ohio.

Raskop George, pyrotechnist, res 76 n Ill.

Rastzel Christ., Washington foundry, res 130 s Del.

Raszel Mitchel D., painter, res 29 Union.

Ratti Francis, res 92 St. Joseph.

Ratti Francis A., printer, res 92 St. Joseph.

Ratti Joseph, printer, W. S. Cameron, bds 92 St. Joseph.

Rauser George, baker, bds 4 s Meridian.

Ray Andrew, carpenter, res 82 s East.

Ray Charles A., Judge of Court of Common Pleas, res 89 n Ill.

Ray David res 133 n Penn.

RAY HOUSE, Ray & Lambert, prop'rs, 65 South.

Ray Jacob, carpenter, res 11 Hellen.

RAY JAMES M., CASHIER BANK OF THE STATE, res 21 n Meridian.

Ray James N., res 86 Mass. ave.

Ray John H., book keeper, res 135 e N. Y.

Ray M. M., (Ray & Wollen,) bds Bates House.

RAY & LAMBERT, (J. Ray, Wm. Lambert,) PROPRIETORS RAY HOUSE, 119 s Del. See card.

RAY & WOLLEN, (M. M. Ray, T. W. Wollen,) ATTORNEYS AT LAW, New & Talbott's building, Penn.

Raymond Samuel, blacksmith, res 148 n Miss.

Rayer Charles, cabinet maker, res 40 n Noble.

Rea John H., Clerk U. S. Court, res 56 n Meridian.

Reading Thomas F., carriage trimmer, bds Patterson House.

Readman Thomas, merchant, res 36 Pratt.

Reagan David J., clerk, res 123 Mass. ave.

Reagger Joseph, carpenter, res 68 Bluff road.

Ream Miss Laura, 12 Va. ave., with Mrs. Dunlap.

Reemas Victor, gardner, res cor Huron and Noble.

Reaume John A., student at Bryant's Com. Col., bds at City Hospital.

Reanes Thomas, works at the gas works, res 154 s Ill.

Reber Gottferry, stone cutter, res 190 s Del.

Rech Henry, bar keeper, Florence's saloon.

Rech Mathias, watch maker and jeweler, 80 w Wash., res same.

Reck George L., carriage painter, bds 64 Mass. ave.

Recker Godfred, Sr., 152 s N. Jersey.

Recker Godfrey, clerk, Lieber, 18 n Penn., res 152 s N. Jersey.

Recker Hubert, carpenter, res e end Market.

Rector Henry, saw mill, s Penn.. res near rolling mill.

Redding Alex. D., plasterer, res 13 Loukerbee.

Redfield David A., (Hawes & Redfield,) res 43 w Mich.

Redforan James, laborer, res Grove.

Redford J. E., salesman, City Grocery, res 7 w Market.

Redman Denis, watchman Union depot, res 125 w South.

Redmeyer Charles, carpenter, bds Pennsylvania House.

Redmund Andrew, gate keeper White river bridge.

Redmond Harriette, (wid.) plain sewing, res Elizabeth.

Redmond Mrs. Margaret, res 159 w Md.

Redmond Robert, policeman, res 150 w Wash., up stairs.

Redmond Samuel, clerk, bds 134 w Wash.

Redmond William, switchman on I. & C. T. R. R., bds 159 w Md.

Redstone Albert A.,(Redstone & Bros.,) 20 n Meridian.

Redstone John H., (Redstone, Bros. & Co.,) res 20 n Meridian.

Redstone, Bros. & Co., (Albert Redstone, John H. Redstone, Jas. M. Ray,) machine works, s Del., opp. Cin. freight depot.

Reed B. F., Quarter-master U. S. A., res 62 e North.

Reed Thad T., bds 62 e North.

Reed Erastus, engraver, Talbott's jewelry store, res 106 n Penn.

Reed George, teamster, bds 245 w Wash.

Reed George, machinist, res 46 s Noble.

Reed Jacob, cooper, res 164 n Tenn.

Reed John F., millinery goods, s Ill., bds C. C. Reeves, e Wash.

Reed Joseph C., pastor Strange Chapel, res 107 n Tenn.

Reed Madison, salesman, Simon & Dernham, 1 w Wash., bds Bates House.

Reed Mrs. Martha J., bds C. C. Reeves, e Wash.

Reed Peter F., portrait painter, res 93 w South.

Reed Mrs. Sarah A., boarding house, 20 n Penn.

Reeder Benj. F., miller, bds Union Hotel.

Reeder Edward, meat market, 32 n Ill, bds Macy House.

Reeder Ephriam C., huckster, res Mich. road.

Reidemann Henry, laborer, res 15 w St. Clair.

Reese Charles, Sen., res 104 n Noble,

Reese Charles, Jr., clerk, 104 n Noble, bds same.

Reese Henry, (Emrich & Reese,) res 91 w Wash.

Rees Henry M. D., res 102 n East.

Reeves Cary C., works planing mill, res e Wash., bet Cady and corporation line.

Reeves Jesse, fireman, I. P. & C. R. R., bds C. C. Reeves, e Wash.

Reeves J. S., publishing agent, A. D. Streight, bds Palmer House.

Reeves Joshua, tinner, bds 21 Michigan.

Reeves Lewis, bds National Hotel, w Wash.

Reeves Wm. M., U. S. service, res 57 s N. Jersey.

Refert Wm., drayman, res 242 Madison ave.

Reger Chas. W., cabinet maker, res 38 Davidson.

Rehling Charles, boots and shoes, 176 e Wash., res same.

Rehling Wm., shoe store, 186 s Del., res same.

Reichwein Philip, superintendent Capitol saloon, bds same.

Reichwine John, laborer, res 98 n Davidson.

Reick August, dealer in groceries and liquors, 118 N. Jersey, res same.

Reid Earl, clerk, Jones, Vinnedge & Co., bds Oriental House.

Reid Julia A., (wid) tailoress, res 53 Vir. ave.

Reidy Charles F., architect, res Wilmington.

Reihnhamer Wm., cooper, res n N. Jersey n of St. Clair.

REILLY JOHN, SUGAR GROVE DAIRY, n of city. See card.

Reinacher Jacob, laborer, res 158 n N. Jersey.

Reinert Gottlieb, in Western meat market, bds 107 w Mich.

Reinfels Henry, teamster, res 20 Union.

Reinhardt Joseph, locksmith and bell hanger, shop and res 49 s Ill.

Reinhardt Lindnsing, shoemaker, 48 Mass. ave., res same.

Reinkin Albert, Sen., plasterer, res 204 n N. Jersey.

Reinkin Albert, Jr., plasterer, bds 204 n N. Jersey.

Reinkin Henry, cigar maker, 93 Ft. Wayne ave., res same.

Reifner Albert, currier, Yandes & Co., res Wiley's addition.

Reisner Anthony, drayman, res 15 e McCarthy.

Reister John, cooper, res 238 Mass. ave.

Reitz Francis A., clerk, German dry goods store, bds Sam. Beck's.
Reivel David, laborer, res 128 w Md.
Remington Jacob C., sawyer, res 143 e N. York.
Rennahun James, porter, Bates House, res 123 w Md.
Renard Engine, saloon, 278 e Wash., bds 151 e N. York.
Renard John B., stonemason, res 151 e N. York.
Renner Christ., blacksmith, res 61 Bluff road.
Renoldo John W., shingle maker, res 50 s Benton.
RENSHAN JAMES, (O'Leary & Renshan,) res next house to canal, Md.
Rentsch Harmon, clerk, res 217 n N. Jersey.
Rentz Edward, groceries and provisions, 126 s Ill.
Resner Christ., carpenter, res cor Wash. and Benton.
Resner Henry, boot and shoemaker, shop 309 res same.
Ress Valentine, cabinet maker, res Davidson, bet Mich. and North.
Retter Henry, stone cutter, bds Washington House.
Revels John F., (col) wagon maker, 139 Ind. ave., bds 119 n West.
Revel Wm., engineer, res 25 e Georgia.
Revels Willis R., (col) physician, res 119 n West.
Rexford Eugene M., tinshop and stencil cutting, 12 Pearl, res 133 n Meridian.
Reymond Samuel, blacksmith, 6 e Md., res 148 n Miss.
Reynolds Charles, bds 89 n Noble.
Reynolds Chesley, teamster, res Ash, bet St. Clair and Cherry.
Reynolds Clark, fireman, bds 107 s Tenn.
Reynolds Franklin, checkman T. H. & R. freight depot, res cor South and Miss.
Reynolds John, (Sulgrove, Reynolds & Co.,) res 30 w Ohio.
Reynolds John, speculater, res 44 w Ohio.
Reynolds Levi, patent right dealer, res 16 Loukabec.
Reynolds Mrs Mary, (wid) res 123 n N, Jersey.
Reynolds Nelson, bds 89 n N. Jersey.
Reynolds Mrs. Sarah, (wid) res 170 n Liberty.
Reynolds Thomas, teamster, res 89 n Noble.
Reynolds Wm., freight agent, T. H. & R. depot, bds 107 s Tenn.
Rexford Eugene, tinner, res 103 n Meridian.
Rhea John, carriage smith, bds Bicking House.
Rhener Anthony, tailor, res 2 s Liberty.
Rhinehardt Valentine, works at armory, res 59 Madison ave.

Rhoads Charles, watchman of fire alarm tower, res 131 w N. York.
Rhoads George, (col) hostler, res 143 e N. York.
Rhoda Anthony, laborer, res 148 n Noble.
Rhodes Charles, (Rhodes & Huey,) res 129 w N. York.
Rhodes James, (col) bell ringer, res 136 Georgia.
Rhodes James, (col) works for Government, res 130 Georgia.
Rhodes John W., physician, res 145 n West.
Rhodes Mountain, in the army, res 133 Blake.
Rhodes & Huey, (Charles Rhodes and Milton Huey,) watchmen, central fire alarm tower.
Rhodius George, National saloon and restaurant, 27 s Meridian, res same.
Rhondivalt Henry, laborer, res 283 s Del.
Ribbart Joseph, driver for city brewery, res in rear of city brewery.
Rice James, laborer, res 61 n West.
Rice Gustave, salesman, 6 Bates House, bds Bates House.
Rice Patrick, laborer, res 61 n West.
Rice Solomon, (Rice & Bamberger,) bds Bates House.
Rice & Bamberger, (Solomon Rice & Herman Bamberger,) clothing and gents' furnishing goods, 6 Bates House.
Richard John, carpenter, res Chestnut, bet N. Jersey and East.
Richards Richard, messenger, telegraph office, res n Mo.
Richardson David F., professor in Bryant's commercial college, bds Mrs. Reed's, n Penn.
Richardson Warren, compiler of directories, res 149 s Tenn.
Richey D. W. A., bds Littles Hotel.
Richey John, Jack of all trades, res 74 n Missouri.
Richey Julius, tinner, res 256 s Del.
Richison Mrs. Tempy, (wid) res w Indianapolis.
RICHMANN CHARLES, WAGON MAKER, 211 e Wash., res 12 Fletcher's ave.
Richman John, laborer, res 272 s Ala.
Richmond Joseph, express messenger, on T. H. & St. L. R. R, res 86 s East.
Richtenhein Zachariah, res 161 w Ver.
Richter Florence, saloon, 13 n Ill., bds on Georgia.
Richter Frederick, (Richter & Roggs,) merchant tailor.
Richter G. A., shoemaker, 161 e Wash., res same.
Richter Herman, carpenter, res 81 Davidson.
Richter Henry, laborer, res 175 s Mississippi.

No dresses ruined with oil in using the Florence.

Richter Wm., grocer, 34 Vir. ave., res same.

Richter & Roggs, (F. Richter & Rudolph Roggs,) merchant tailors, 144 e Wash.

Rickard Thomas, carpenter and joiner shop, 81 s Del, res 138 e North.

Rickards Wm. C., carpenter, bds 138 e Market.

RICKER ROBERT E., SUPERINTENDENT T. H. & R. R. R., res 93 n Tenn.

Ricketts Wm., book binder, Dodd & Co., bos E. Knights.

Riddle Geo. W., U. S. service, res w Indianapolis.

Ridgeway Wm., wagon maker, bds s Tenn., near Pogues Run.

Riecker Arnold, carpenter, res 66 Ind. ave.

Riely Edward, works gas factory, res s West.

Riemenscheider Herman, grocer, 47 s N. Jersey.

Ries Christopher, grocer, cor N. York and Noble, res same.

Ries John, works at arsenal, bds Union House, cor Ill. and South.

Riester Fred., painter, res 125, Peru R. R.

Riffel John. tailor, res w Indianapolis.

Riffel Rissel John, tailor, 192 n Penn.

Riggs & Davids, (Simpson Riggs & John Davids,) butchers, 6 s Meridian.

Riggs Simpson, (Riggs & Davids,) res 83 e South.

Rihl Chas. H., brickmason, res 38 Cal.

Riley B. F., clerk, res 92 w N. York.

Riley Calahan, laborer, bds near rolling mill.

Riley H. W., bds Littles Hotel.

Riley James, works in Palmer House, res Minerva, bet Mich. and North.

Rilzinger Frank, clerk, Fletcher's bank, 124 e Ohio.

Rilzinger, J. B., teller, Fletcher's bank, res 123 e Ohio.

Rinehart, Samuel, laborer, res 45 Lou.

Ringer Mrs. Mary, res 121 n East.

Ringer Wm., tinner, res 121 n East.

Rinkle David, barber shop, 62 e South, res in rear.

Rinson Gash, (col) barber shop, Spencer House, res Pec Dee.

Risner Albert, tanner and finisher, Yandes, res 200 w North.

RISTINE JOSEPH, AUDITOR OF STATE, 70 Ky. ave., McOuat's block, res 94 n West.

Rittenhouse Geo. L., family groceries, 88 e Wash., res 139 Vir. ave.

Rittenhouse Wm., (Wright & Co.,) res n Ill.

Ritter Peter, (Seybold & Ritter,) res cor South and Canal.

Ritzinger Augustus W., clerk in gas office, bds 124 e Ohio.

Ritzinger Frank, clerk, bds 124 e Ohio.

Ritzinger Frederick, secretary of German Insurance Co., res 124 e Ohio.

Ritzinger John B., clerk, bds 124 e Ohio.

Rively John, tailor, 16 n Penn., res 173 s Del.

Roach Charles, conductor, I. & C. R. R., res 10 Bates.

Roach James, laborer, res w India'polis.

Roach J. P., blacksmith, bds Littles Hotel.

Roach Michael, musician, res 98 e Md.

Roach Patrick J., carriage smith, bds Littles Hotel.

Roache Addison L., (McDonald & Roache,) res 97 n Penn.

Roback Eli, book binder, Dodd & Co., bds Sarah Roback's.

Roback Henry, laborer, res w Market.

Roback Sarah, (wid. Geo. Roback,) res Walnut, bet Mich. and Ill.

Robenies Frank, shoemaker, res 137 n Noble.

Roberts Catherine, (wid. Daniel Roberts,) res cor Market and Ala.

Roberts Dwight, grocery, 48 w Wash., res 83 n Del.

Roberts James R., (col) second cook, Macy House.

Roberts O. Joel, U. S. service, Mt. Jackson.

Roberts John, machinest, res 63 s N. Jersey.

Roberts Joseph T., attorney at law, bds National Hotel, w Wash.

Roberts Thomas L., machinest, res 261 Vir. ave.

Roberts Turner, (col) methodist minister, res 54 Blackford.

Robins James, bricklayer, res s Ill.

Robinson Alonzo C., grocers and produce, res 180 n Ill.

ROBINSON CHARLES B., ASSISTANT SUPERINTENDENT PERU R. R., res 249 Ala.

Robinson Edwin, blacksmith, rear Ætna building.

Robinson Edward J., res 149 n Del.

Robinson Mrs. Elizabeth, (wid) res w Indianapolis.

Robinson F. T., painter, res Duncan.

Robinson G., house painter, res 19 s Ala.

Robinson Lass, (col) barber, Spencer House block.

Robinson H. E., clerk, Adams' Express, bds Bates House.

Robinson James B., assistent packer, U. S. service, bds Littles Hotel,

Robinson John, piano maker, res cor Market and Ala.

Robinson John P., laborer, res w Indianapolis.

Robinson Mathew B., in quartermaster's department, res 93 e Market.

Robinson Robert W., carpenter, res 68 n Missouri.

No discount on the hats and caps sold by Davis.

Robinson Wm. J. H., county sheriff, court house, res court house square.
Robison Charlotte F., (wid. Wm. Robison.)
Robison Wm., plasterer, res 225 Ala.
ROCKY HENRY S., LAMPS AND COAL OIL, 13 s Meridian, res 61 n N. Jersey. See card.
Rockwell Charles B., sutler, 11th Ind. reg., res 66 n Del.
ROCKWELL RUFUS C., AGENT MADISON & INDIANAPOLIS R. R.
Rockwood Wm. O., treasurer, I & C. R. R., res 30 s Tenn.
Roderus Andrew, barber shop, 62 e South, bds same.
Rodewald Henry, laborer, res 45 Union.
Rodgers Ben. F., brickmaker, res 128 e St. Clair.
Rodgers James W., brickmaker, res 66 Harrison.
Rodifer Mrs. Sarah, seamstress, res 44 n Noble.
Roe Mrs. Elizabeth, res w Indianapolis.
Roesner Haman, hub turner at Osgood's, res Liberty, bet Ver. and Mich.
Roeth John, tailor, 2 Bates House, bds 15 w Georgia.
Rofert Charles, carpenter, res 119 n Meridian.
Rofert Henry, carpenter, res 126 Blake.
Roffert William. laborer, res 153 e Market.
Rofit Antony, carpenter, res n Alabama.
Rogers Chas., clerk, N. Y. Store, bds Mason House.
Rogers John, shoemaker, 39 w Wash. res near Rolling Mill.
Rogers Harvy, res 159 n Noble.
Roggs Rudolph, (Richter & Roggs,) res 144 e Wash.
Rohan Martin, laborer res 20 Micky.
Rohlfing Christian, laborer, res 150 n Noble.
Roland John, laborer, res w Market.
Roll Isaac H., (Roll & Smith,) res 133 n Ill.
Roll Joseph, res 145 n N. Jersey.
Roll Wm. H., (Roll & Smith,) bds 33 n Illinois.
Roll & Smith, (Isaac H. Roll, W. H. Roll, Wm. Smith,) dealers in carpets, oil cloths, wall paper and shades, 16 s Ill.
Rolling Mill, s Tenn., office, 8 Blake's Row.
Romerill Chas. E., plasterer, res 148 n East.
Roncy Pat., laborer, res 195 e Ohio.
Rooks Joseph, stone cutter, bds O. House.
Rooker Alfred J., painter, res 194 Indiana ave.
Rooker C. F., bds Little's Hotel.
Rooker Geo. L. D., painter, res 106 Indiana ave.
Rooker Samuel, painter, bds 160 n West.
Roos Emanuel, butcher, res Bluff Road.

Root Deloss, (Deloss Root & Co.,) res 38 n Meridian.
ROOT DELOSS & CO., (Deloss Root, Jerome B. Root,) STOVE AND IRON DEALERS, 66 e Wash.
Root Jerome B. (Root & Co.) res 18 s Miss. South.
Rose David G., U. S. Marshal, 6 P. O. Building 2d floor, bds Bates House.
Rose Franklin, clerk, I. C. R. R., res 23 Bates.
Rosebrock Fred., grocer, 283 s Delaware.
Rosebrock Herman H., grocer and feed Store, 168 Vir. ave. res same.
Rosembaum Christ., porter, Talbott & Co., bds 24 e Wash.
Rosenberg Samuel, works in arsenal, res 125 n Noble.
Roseugarten Henry, druggist, 172 e Washington, res 110 e Market.
Rosengarten Louis, rag dealer, res 150 Railroad.
Rosenthal Adolph, whosesalde dealer in wines, liquors, cigars, &c., 38 Louisiana.
Rosenthal Henry, (Hays, Kohn & Co.,) res 16 n Miss.
Resenthal Samuel, clerk, res s e cor Ill. and South.
Ross Bascomb, messenger, American Express Co., bds Mason House.
Ross James, laborer, res Clinton, Keelys Block.
Ross James, carriage painter, res bet East and N. Jersey.
Ross James J., clerk. 19 e Wash., bds 174 n Tenn.
ROSS JOHNSON H., AGENT FOR PITTSBUGH AND WESTERN COAL, office, 19 e Wash., res n Tenn. See card.
Ross Norman M., clerk, Indian department, Washington City, D. C., res 56 s Meridian.
Ross Robert, pump maker, res 82 St. Joseph.
Ross Wm. C., clerk, German Dry Goods Store, bds Union Hall.
Rosskey Fred., dry goods and groceries, 35 cor McCarthy and Madison ave. res same.
Rossman Charles, saloon keeper, 119 e Wash., res same.
Roth Mathew, architect student, bds D. A. Bohlen.
Roth Sebastian, works Wrights & Millards Brewery, bds w National Road.
Rothrock Valentine, res 55 n Meridian.
Rouse Jackson H., railroader, res 23 Indiana ave.
Row John, teamster, res 192 n Noble.
Rowe Geo., millwright, res w Indp'ls.
Rowe John W., saloon, under Little's Hotel, res cor East and Vermont.
Rowe Samuel J., clerk, J. H. Vagen, bds Circle.
Rowlen Michael, laborer, res 89 s Tenn.

Every family should have a Florence.

Rozier Aaron, works plaining mill, res Blackford, bet N. York and Vermont.

Rube John, woollen factory, res Cal., s of Maryland.

Rubush Alexander, teamster, res 131 n Liberty.

Rubush Fletcher, carpenter, res 59 n Noble.

Rubush Jacob, brick mason, res 62 n East.

Ruckle N. D., merchant tailor, 36 n Penn., res Second.

Ruckle Nicholas R., Capt. Co. E. 11th Ind. Regt.

Rugg Samuel L., Supt. Pub. Instruction, bds Dr. Gatling.

Rule James, U. S. service, res w Indp'ls.

Rule Robert, (R. & Mahan,) bds Linsey Georgia.

Rule & Mahan, (Rule Robert, Wm. Mahan,) City Saloon, 55 s Ill.

Ruman Augustus, U. S. service, res 131 e Wash.

Rumell John, works Rolling Mill, res 43 s Ill.

Runge Christ., butcher, bds Seifert, Madison depot.

RUNNION WM., PHOTOGRAPH ARTIST, PHŒNIX GALLERY, 32½ e Wash., bds Mrs. Morrison. See card.

Ruoff Chas., salesman, 32 w Wash., bds 101 n Meridian.

Rupp F. W., merchant tailor and ready made clothing establishment, 105 e Wash., res same.

Rusch Fred. P., produce, 83 w Wash., bds. 35 N. Jersey.

Rusche Peter, stone cutter, res Yoming.

Ruschhaupt Fred., (Ruschhaupt & Bals,) res 61 n N Jersey.

Ruschaupt August, teamster, res 168 e Michigan.

Ruschhaupt Wm., (Brinkman & R.,) res 100 e Ohio.

Ruschhaupt & Bals, (Fred. Ruschhaupt, Chas. Bals,) liquor dealers, 82 e Wash.

Rusell James, contractor, res 192 w Maryland.

Rush Mrs. (wid.) res 250 e Wash.

Rusner Fred., farmer, res 119 n New Jersey.

Russe Conrad, stone mason, res 3d house e Pogues run on Wash.

Russel Alexander, res cor Meridian and Merrill.

Russell David, moulder, Sinker & Vance, res 70 s Delaware.

Russel James M., clerk, P. O., res cor Meridian and Merrill.

Russel John, deputy marshal, res 284 s Delaware.

Russelle Laven, engineer Jefferson R. R., res 111 McCarthy.

Russell Samuel, laborer, Central Depot, res 21 Peru R. R.

Rust Ernest, carpenter, res Wash. bet Liberty and Noble.

Ruswinkel Fred., cigar maker, res bet East and Chatham, n of St. Clair.

Ruswinkel Geo., cigar maker, 10 Bates House, res 123 n East.

Rugette Arthur, res 244 e Wash.

Ryan Ellen B., res 51 s Miss.

Ryan James B., with C. A. Elliotte, res 100 n Miss.

Ryan John, works Gas House, res 198 s Delaware.

Ryan John, Plasterer, res 150 e North.

Ryan John, laborer, 35 Benton.

Ryan John A., brick mason, res 136 e St. Clair.

Ryan John B., (Ryan & Spurgin,) res 277 s East.

Ryan Mrs. Margaret, (wid.) res 16 East.

Ryan Michael, laborer, res 137 Peru R. R

Ryan Mrs. Nora B., res 51 s Miss.

Ryan Patrick, laborer, res 110 East.

Ryan Richard J., City Attorney, bds 53 s Miss.

Ryan Thomas F., wholesale grocer, 73 s Meridian, bds Bates House.

Ryan & Spurgin, (John B. Ryan, Joseph M. Spurgin,) house and sign painters, 48 w Wash., up stairs.

Ryder Phillip, photograph operator, Runnion's gallery, bds Macy House.

Ryer George, saddler, res 16 s Ala.

S

Sage Charles, teamster, res 231 w Wash.

Sage John, laborer, res 25 Henry.

St. John James, wood hauler, res 93 Bluff road.

Saire Phillip, carriage smith, res bet N. Jersey and East.

Sally Thomas, tailor, res w South.

Sample James C, carpenter, res Cherry, bet Chatham & Noble.

Sample Samuel C., res 192 e St. Clair.

St. Marys Sister of Providence school, cor Georgia and Tenn.

Sanburn Elijah, works at Geisendorff's factory, bds 229 w Wash.

Sanburn Joseph, carriage painter, res 53 s Penn.

Sanders John, carpenter, res 148 n Liberty.

Sanders William H., (col.) barber, bds Johnson's saloon.

Sanger Philip, tailor, cleaner and repairer, res 162 w Wash.

Santo Edward, clerk, Verandah saloon, res same.

Saum J. M., brickmason, 50 s East.

Sapp Wm. B., clerk, Palmer House, res same.

Sargent Andrew J., (Sargent & Fish,) bds 86 e Wash.

Sargent Francis L., blacksmith, res 29 s Liberty.

Sargent & Fish, (Andrew J. Sargent, Oliver M. Fish,) photograph artists, 86 e Wash.

Saunders Frederick, blacksmith, res 99 Bluff road.

Saunderson William, clerk Bellefontaine R. R. office, bds Kinder House.

Sawnerrs A., clerk Adams Express, bds 8 Va. ave.

Sawyer John S., wholesale and retail grocer, 9 w Wash., res 23 s Del.

Saylar Jackson, works at rolling mill, res 173 s Miss.

Sayles Horatio, blacksmith, res Mich. road.

Scarry House, 20 n Penn.

Scarry John, cattle trader, res 115 s New Jersey.

Scay Abraham, soldier, res 60 Ind. ave.

Schaaf Abel, laborer, res 49 n Noble.

Schacko Charles, machinist, Sinker & Vance, bds California House.

Schad Gotlieb, wagon maker, res 52 n Davidson.

Schad Mathias, tailor, res Vermont, bet Liberty & Noble.

Schaefer Philip, teamster, res 65 Hosbrook.

Schafer Cornelius F., (Eurich & Schafer,) res w Ga.

Schaffner Charles J., laborer, res 219 n Noble.

Schaub Henry, (Henry Schaub & Co.,) res 129 Noble.

Schaub Henry, Jr., (Henry Schaub & Co.,) res 135 Noble.

Schaub Henry & Co., (Henry Schaub, Henry Schaub, Jr.,) saloon keepers, 6 w Wash.

Schaub Peter, expressman, res 123 n Noble.

SCHEER FREDERICK, PROPRIETOR STATION HOUSE, s w cor Union depot.

Scheigert Frederick E., clerk, P. O., res cor Tenn. and Ky. ave.

Scheilmire Louis, druggist, res 97 Ft. Wayne ave.

Schellsmidt Adolph, musician, res 53 n New Jersey.

Schellsmidt Ferdinand, shoemaker, res 110 e Ohio.

Schellmyre Christian, butcher, bds 179 e Market.

Scher Philip, blacksmith, res alley, bet N. Jersey and East, n of N. York.

Schier John, laborer, res 213 n Noble.

Schildmier Frederick, tailor, res e of Pogues run on National road.

Schilling ———, cabinet maker, res Mich. and Davidson.

Schillmier Fred., laborer, res Peru R. R., near city limits.

Schindler Robert, M. D., res 158 e Wash., up stairs.

Schindler Robert, salesman, 61 and 63 w Wash., res 158 e Wash., up stairs.

Schirling Nicholas, baker, res 158 n Liberty.

Schirley Mrs. Emeline, (wid.) res 108 e South.

Schlans Frederick, watchman, T. H. & R. R. res 78 Union.

Schlater William H., Maj. 97th Ind. vols. detailed by War Depm't on duty with Gov. Morton, bds Palmer House.

Schliebetz Frederick W., watch maker, bds 172 n Tennessee.

Schlosser Martin H., works rolling mill, res 231 s East.

SCHMIDT C. F., LAGER BEER MANUFACTURER, cor High and Wyoming, res same.

SCHMIDT ROBERT, TANNER, res 47 s New Jersey. See card.

Schmick Charles, boot and shoe maker, res 124 n Miss.

Schmircker Louis, cabinet maker, bds 123 n Noble.

Schnull A., (Schnull & Bro.,) res Ala., bet Market and Ohio.

Schnull A. & H., grocers, &c., 81 e Wash.

Schnull Henry, (A. & H. Schnull,) res Alabama, bet Market and Ohio.

Schobach Henry, clerk, Kansas saloon, bds same.

Schofield Thomas B., vinegar manufacturer, 22 South, res 16½ s Ill.

Schofield T. B. & Co., (Thomas B. Schofield, Edward Drake,) vinegar manufacturers, 49 e South.

Schonacker Mrs ———, res 95 n Tennessee.

Schonacker Miss M., ornamental hair braiding, bds 95 n Tenn.

Schonaker Hubert J., prof. of music, bds 95 n Tenn.

Schopp Elizabeth, (wid.) res 26 Union.

Schoppenhorst Wm., grocer and produce dealer, 101 e Wash, res same.

Schott Charles, butcher, res 115 Union.

Schott Joseph, grocer and liquor dealer, 117 e Wash., res same.

Schovey Frederick, blacksmith, res 2 Water.

Schmaker Martin, shoemaker, 49 n New Jersey.

Schrader Anthony, laborer, res 144 n Liberty.

Schrader Charles, laborer, Washington Foundry, res 75 Merrill.

Schrader Christian, drayman, res 130 n Noble.

Schrader Fred., cooper, res 192 n Noble.

Schrader Henry, druggist, Browning & Sloan, bds 70 n Miss.

Schrader John, machinist, res 148 e Market.

Schrader Frederick, boot'and shoemaker, 38 w Wash., bds rear 70 n Miss.
Schrader John A., res rear of 70 n Miss.
Schrager Christopher, laborer, 92 McCarthy.
Schramm John C. A., clerk, res 105 e Vt.
Schreck Mrs. Mary, (wid.) seamstress, res 143 n Noble.
Schromaer Charles, drayman, res 87 Bluff road.
Schuer John, laborer, res National road, e Pogues run.
Schuller Geo., clerk New York Store, res 20-s Miss.
Schulmyer Jacob, bds 163 n N. Jersey.
Schnesaler Conrad, laborer, res 152 n N. Jersey.
Schuessler Elizabeth, shop tender for Mrs. Dietricks, bds same.
Schuimsley John, baker, 11 n Penn., res s Del.
Schumburg, William, shoemaker, 11 n N. Jersey, res alley in rear.
Schurmann, Gustavus, (Blake, Helwig & Co.,) 29 n Meridian.
Schurr Leonard, clock maker, res 64 n Davidson.
Schuster Joseph, tailor, R. R., bet Market and Ohio.
Schuyler Frank. J., foreman Daily Sentinel office.
Schwan Geo., brewer, C. F. Smith's brewery.
Schwank Lewis, bar keeper, res 182 s Del.
Schwear Charles, res 25 Chatham.
Schwear Christ H., (Schwear & Spear,) e Wash., res same.
Schwear & Spier, (Christ H. Schwear, Frederick Spier,) grocers, e Wash
SCHWEINSBERG WM., MEAT MARKET, 243 s Del. See card.
Schwomsyer Christ., street sprinkler, res 164 e Mich.
Schwomier Henry, cooper, res 180 n Noble.
Schwomier William, oooper, res 178 n Noble.
Scott Adam, (Nicholson & Co.,) res 46 n East.
Scott Almon, teamster, res 69 Spring.
SCOTT AMOS, HORSE-POWER WOOD-SAWYER, res 87 Davidson.
Scott George W., painter, res 175 e Ohio.
Scott John, clerk N. Y. store, res 156 n West.
Scott Walter R., clerk, military headquarters, bds 61 Mass. ave.
Scribner B. George, cronk beer maker, res w Indianapolis.
Scudder Caleb, boarding house, res 46 w Market.
Scudder Edward D., runs saw mill, res w Market.
Scudder Mrs. Ellen, (wid.,) res Wabash, bet N. J. & East.

Scudder Michael R., constable, res 181 Mass. ave.
Scudder William, carpenter, w N. York.
Schuler George, butcher, res 269 s Penn.
Seaman George, finisher in I. & C. R. R. shop, res 100 s Noble.
Seargant A. W., carpenter, res 160 n Penn.
Sears Andrew, works Terre Haute depot, res 207 s Penn.
Sears Martin, works Terre Haute depot, res 207 s Penn.
Sears Thomas, res 80 Meek.
Seay Jeremiah, bar keeper, Bear's Head saloon, w Wash.
Secrest John, works at rolling mill, res 176 s Miss.
Secrist Chas., brick mason, res 205 Ala.
Seeger William, works in north-western meat market, bds 107 w Mich.
Seele Henry, laborer, res 174 n Liberty.
Seeling Anton, Fort Donelson saloon, 3 s Del., res in rear.
Sefert A., butcher, res 167 s Del.
SEGRIST REV. SIMON, PASTOR OF ST. MARY'S GERMAN CATHOLIC CHURCH, res 46 s Del.
Seibert Samuel, blacksmith, 252 e Wash , res 3 w Liberty.
Seidensticker Adolph, (S. & Kappes,) res 41 n Noble.
SEIDENSTICKER & KAPPES, (Adolph Seidensticker & H. Kappes,) REAL ESTATE AGENTS, 150 e Wash.
Seilhamer William, laborer, res w Indianapolis.
Selder John B., carpenter, bds Lingenfelter's.
Seley William, brick layer, bds 123 s Ill.
Selking William, baker, 58 s Meridian, res same.
Sell Mrs. Barbara, boarding house, 108 w South.
Senior Mrs. Parthenia, (wid.,) washer, res 90 Mass. ave.
SENOUR JAMES F., WHOLESALE AND RETAIL DRUGGIST, 5 Bates House, res 208 n Ill.
Sergent Ezra, foreman at Bellefontaine R. R. shop, res 19 n East.
Serger Augustus, salesman for Moritz, Bro. & Co., bds Bates House.
Serring John, laborer, res 16 Willard.
Server Mrs. Caroline, (wid.,) res 110 n Penn.
Servita John, works at Root's foundry, bds 88 e Market.
Seventh Ward District School, 78 Virg. ave.
Severia Henry, grocery and feed store, 247 n N. J., res. same.
Sewell Joseph, bird cage maker, res 15 Elm.
Seyhold Mrs. Alice, (widow,) res 121 e Ohio.

Turbans for the little fellows, at 15 Pennsylvania St.

Seybold James H., (Seybold & Ritter,) res 151 e Ohio.
SEYBOLD & RITTER, (James H. Seybold and Peter Ritter,) MARBLE WORKS, 40 e Market.
Sexton Martin, laborer, 42 s Liberty.
Seymour A., wood carver, res 56 s East.
Shaaf Valentine, carpenter res 190 e Market.
Shackleton Joseph, pattern maker, res 31 s Liberty.
Shade George, baker, res 32 Spring.
Shade R. W., clerk, N. Y. store, res 127 w N. Y.
Shaefer Rev. Absalom B., minister Evangelical Asssociation, res rear of church.
Shafer Henry, U. S. service, res Bluff road, Doughertyville.
Shafer Simon, wood sawyer, res 67 Alley in rear of 70 n Miss.
Shaffer Adolphus C., boot and shoe maker, 5 Ind. ave., bds cor. Vt. and Tenn.
Shaffer Jacob, hostler Exchange Stables, bds Ohio House.
Shakel Christ., laborer, res 230 s Ala.
Shaler Henry, laborer, res 139 Ala.
Shane George, laborer, res 64 Bluff road.
SHANE JAMES, (Frost & Shane,) res 61 Ky. ave.
Shaneberger David H., clerk, Adams Express, bds 91 e Ohio.
Share Geo. K., (Geo. K. Share & Co.,) res cor Mass. and N. J.
Share Geo. K. & Co., carriage hardware, trimmings, &c., 72 w Wash.
Sharp A. W., cigar store, 12 n Penn., res 151 n East.
Sharp George W., salesman, bds Little's Hotel.
Sharp John G., book keeper, res 151 n East.
Sharp John S., book keeper, res 151 n East.
Sharp Joseph K., leather and shoe findings, 90 e Wash., res Mich. road.
Sharp Stephen, engineer at Capital Mills, res 108 West.
Sharp William H., (Sharp & Bellis,) res 102½ n Meridian.
SHARP & BELLIS, (William H. Sharp and Samuel Bellis,) GENERAL AG'TS FLORENCE SEWING MACHINES, 17 n Penn.
Sharpe Abraham, in Branch Bank, res 168 n Penn.
Sharpe Ebenezer, clerk, Fletcher & Sharpe's Bank, res 150 n Penn.
Sharpe Thomas H., (Fletcher & Sharpe,) res 95 n Penn.
Sharpless Purnell, book keeper, res 102 n Meridian.
Shaub George, shoemaker, res 125 n Noble.
Shaub Henry, Central saloon, res 135 n Noble.

Shaub Jacob, shoemaker, res 77 n East.
Shaub John, laborer, res 129 n Noble.
Shauchnacy Thomas, works at gas house, res 63 Madison ave.
Shaughnacy James, saddle maker, 61 Madison ave.
Shaw Augustus D., railroader, res 77 n Noble.
Shaw John P., res 78 Madison ave.
Shaw Victor, plasterer, res Mich., bet Liberty and Noble.
Shawn Sheagel, laborer, bds Michael Howard's, 45 s East.
Shawver Alexander, carpenter, res 21 Chatham.
Shawver C. J., saddler, 20 w Wash., res James, bet St. Clair and Ind. ave.
Shay James, laborer, res s Miss., near rolling mill.
Shay John, laborer, res 14 East.
Shay Tim., laborer, res 194 e Ohio.
Shea Cornelius, laborer, res 105 w N. Y.
Shea Daniel, laborer, bds 6 Bates.
Shea Daniel, brakesman, Peru R. R., res 23 East.
Shea James R., laborer, bds 140 e Market.
Shea John, hostler, bds Ohio House.
Shea Mary, (wid) res 192 s Del.
Shea Michael, laborer, res 140 e Market.
Shea Thomas, laborer, res Plum, near Cherry.
Sheahan Patrick, railroader, res 55 e South.
Shealen Patrick, laborer, res 288 Vir. ave.
Shean Daniel, laborer, res s West.
Shearer Frederick, teamster, res 133 Bluff road.
Shearer George, engineer, I. & C, R. R., res 123 s East.
Shearer Mrs. Mary, seamstress, res Blackford, bet Ver. and Michigan.
Shearly Fred., saddler, res 174 e Ohio.
Sheef Wm., works on Jeffersonville R. R., bds Ray House, s Del.
Shechan Mrs. Mary, (wid) res 192 s Delaware.
Sheehan Timothy, laborer, res 44 s Benton.
Sheets Wm., book binder, 79 w Wash., res 25 n Penn.
Shellenberger John, pattern maker, res 142 n N. Jersey.
Shellmyre Frederick, laborer, res 55 St. Mary's.
Shelt Wm., salesman, Dessar & Bro's, bds Palmer House.
Shepherd Jackson, bds 7 Ky. ave.
Shepard Thomas L., carpenter, res 107 Blake.
Sherer John, carpenter, res Elizabeth.
Sherburne Wm., engineer, res cor South and Miss.
Sherman Paul, harness maker, res 44 Ind. ave.

The Florence has no wire springs or gearing to get out of order.

Sherman Shedeur B., paper maker, bds 146, cor West and Market.

Sherwood J. W., blacksmith, Sinker & Vance, bds California House.

Sherwood Susan C., res 135 w Market.

Shilling Charles, laborer, res 10 Lord.

Shilling Henry, laborer, res 300 Vir. ave.

Shilling Richard L., (Burton & Shilling,) res 46 w Md.

Shine John, laborer, res 110 s Noble.

Shine Maurice, laborer, res 84 Viriana ave.

Shinn Charley, shoemaker, Knodle's.

Shipley David B., U. S. A., res 89 n Ill.

Shipley Ferdinand, carpenter, res 224 n Ala.

Shipley Mrs. Mary, dressmaker, res Ohio, bet Meridian and Ill.

Shlotzkouer Valentine, cabinet maker, res 75 Davidson.

Shmidt Mrs. Christina, (wid) grocer, National road, e Pogues Run.

Shoultzs John, laborer, res 141 e Ga.

Shoecraft Alviran, (col) barber, bds 127 n East.

Shoecraft Silas, (col) barber, 8 and 9 New & Talbot's block, res 127 n East.

Shoemaker Frederick, cabinet maker, res 150 w Wash.

Shoemaker Henry, laborer, res 58 n Noble.

Shoemaker Mrs. Marion, (wid) res 15 w Md.

Shoennaman Wm., laborer, res 78 Bluff road.

Shoettle Christian, barkeeper, bds 136 w Wash.

Shoppner John, carpenter, res 101 w South.

Shokey Middleton, student at Bryant's commercial college, bds in country.

Sholes Lyman, works at American Express, res 99 w N. York,

Sholes L., clerk, Adam's Express, res 101 w N. York.

Sholte Herman, laborer, res Grove.

Sholtz John, blacksmith, bds 20 Chatham.

Sholtz Louis, tailor, res 128 n Ala.

Shompine Mrs. Clemens, dressmaker, 46 w Md.

Short John, butcher, res w Indianapolis.

Shortridge A. C., prof. in N. W. C. U., and Bryant's commercial college.

Shortridge Ambrose F., collecting agent, res 118 n Ill.

Shotz John, brewer, bds 135 w Md.

Shoub Peter, city expressman, res 123 n Noble.

Shaughnessey John O., head porter, Excelsior restaurant, bds St. Nicholas restaurant.

Shoultz Louis, merchant tailor, 19 n Penn., res 123 n Ala.

Shoup John, laborer, bds 129 n Noble.

Shouse Greenbury, carpenter, res w Indianapolis.

Shovey Frederick, blacksmith, res Water.

Showe Frederick, car cleaner, res 291 Vir. ave.

Shriner William, tanner, res 78 Madison ave.

Shulymire Lewis, salesman, Stewart & Morgan, res 97 Ft. Wayne ave.

Sibert David, res 75 e Market.

Sibert H., blacksmith, 43 Vir. ave.

Siebert Peter, soldier, res 123 n East.

Siedle Engelbert, manufacturer of musical instruments, res 203 n Noble.

Siefert Lewis butcher shop, 75 e Wash., res s Del.

Siemon Christ., laborer, res 151 n Noble.

Sies Ruggles, painter, res s West.

Silvester David, farmer, res w Indianapolis.

Simcox. John W., harness maker, res 58 Mass. ave.

Simelink William, carpenter, res 157 e Ohio.

Simmerman George, drayman, res 151 n Liberty.

Simmons Henry, grocery, res 36 Ind. ave.

Simmons John H., optician, 25 s Ill., res in rear.

Simon Fred, grocer, 104 n Noble, res same.

Simon Henry W., carpenter, res 38 St. Clair.

Simon Jacob, carpenter, res Noble, bet Wash. and Market.

Simon Louis & Bro., stair builders and turners, Georgia, bet Penn. and Meridian.

Simon Peter, currier, res 141 e Market.

Simon & Dernham, (Benjamin Simon, & Max Dernham,) wholesale and retail clothiers, 1 w Wash.

Simpson Franklin F., (Danforth & Simpson,) res 117 n Penn.

Simpson James, (mute) works in arsenal, bds Ohio House.

Simpson John, laborer, res w Indianapolis.

Simpson Lavina, (wid. Oliver Simpson,) keeps boarding house, 27 Ind. ave.

Simpson Mathew, (M. & R. Simpson,) res 128 s Del.

SIMPSON M. & R., (Mathew Simpson & Richard Simpson,) GROCERS, s w cor Del. and South.

Simpson N., flour, feed and grocery store, res 137 n Del.

Simpson Richard, (M. & R. Simpson,) bds Mason House.

Sin Mrs. Barne, (wid) res 332 s Del.

SINGER I. M. & CO., SEWING MACHINES, 48 e Wash

Sinker Edward T., (Sinker & Vance) res 101 Virg. ave.

SINKER & VANCE, (Edward T. Sinker and S muel C. Vance,) WESTERN MACHINE WORKS, STEAM ENGINE AND BOILER MAKERS, s Penn., near Union track.

Sipp Charles A., machinist, res 43 n N. J.

Siple Orlando, student at Bryant's Com. College.

Sire Frederick, gardener, res w Indianapolis.

Sisco Henry, conductor wood train, I., P. & C. R. R., bds 179 e Market.

Sister Ambrose, superioress of St. John's Female Academy, cor Geo. and Tenn.

Skelly Therasa, boarding house, 52 s Del.

Skillen James, (Robert G. and James Skillen,) res 24 n West.

Skillen Robert G., (R. G. and J. Skillen,) res 248 w Wash.

Skillen Robert G. & James, Ætna Mills, 250 w Wash.

Skinner Wm. H., engineer, 35 s Noble.

Slatter Chas., carpenter, res 161 n Miss.

Slaughter Milton, carpenter, res Mich. road.

Slavin Hughey, drayman, res 157 s Tenn.

SLOANE EDWARD W., SUP'T AMERICAN EXPRESS, res 61 w N. Y.

Sloan Geo W., (Browning & Sloan,) bds 83 s Tenn.

Sloan John, (Sloan & Burke,) res 83 s Tenn.

Sloan & Burke, (John Sloan and W. C. Burke,) furniture man'fs, 197 s Penn.

Sloss George, (col.,) laborer, res 190 n West.

Small David, carpenter, res 159 n Ala.

Small Eli B., laborer, bds Bond's.

Small James, clerk N. Y. store, res 20 s Miss.

Small Rev. Gilbert, United Presbyterian, res 40 n Del.

Small R. A., foreman blacksmith Cin. R. R. shop, res Mich. road.

Small William, carpenter and millwright, res 127 e North.

Smallholz Casper, clerk at C. F. Smith's brewery, bds same place.

Smallwood John, laborer, res 82 n Noble.

Smelser Samuel W., physician, res 36 St. Clair.

Smidth A. W., teacher in Zion church, 13 n Ala.

Smith Adolph, painter, res 70 s Del.

Smith Mrs. Amelia, (wid. Wm. F. Smith,) res 82 n Tenn.

Smith Andrew, engineer, res 54 Bates.

Smith E. Athlick, musician 19th Reg'lrs, U. S A., res 50 w Vt.

Smith Caleb B., judge U. S. court, res cor N. Y. and Cal.

Smith C. F., brewer, res 131 McCarthy.

Smith Christian, (Ittenback & Co.,) res 180 s Del.

Smith Mrs. Ellen, (wid.,) res 107 s Ala.

Smith E. Henry, bread peddler, 11 n Penn., res s Ill.

Smith Frank, clerk N. Y. grocery, bds 21 w Mich.

SMITH FRANK, REAL ESTATE AG'T, 50 e Wash, res 58 s Tenn.

Smith Frederick, (Smith & Taylor,) bds 30 n Penn.

Smith Frederick, grocery and liquor store, res 126 n Miss.

Smith George, cash boy Fancy Bazaar, bds 84 n N. J.

Smith George, butcher, res 70 n Noble.

Smith George, painter, res 70 s Del.

Smith George, laborer, res 95 Peru R. R.

Smith G. W. B., printer, Sentinel office, res 12 n N. J.

Smith Geo. T., student at Bryant's Com. College, bds Rev. John C. Smith's.

Smith George T., salesman at Werden & Co.'s, bds 115 n N. J.

Smith Henry, res 196 n Ill.

Smith Henry C., laborer, bds 91 n Noble.

Smith Horace W., farmer, bds 158 w N.Y.

Smith Hugh H., shoemaker, res cor Ala. and Market.

Smith, Ittenbach & Co., (Gerhard Ittenbach, Christian Smith and Frank Hittenback,) stone cutters.

Smith Jacob, artist, res 46 s East.

Smith Jacob, book binder, 24 w Wash., bds James.

Smith James, bds Cal. House, 139 s Ill.

Smith James, res 135 n Liberty.

Smith James, res 91 n Noble.

Smith James, carpenter, bds 141 w Market.

Smith James H,, clerk at Merrill & Co.'s, bds Macy House.

Smith James R., last maker, res 116 s N. J.

Smith James W., student at Bryant's Com. Col.

Smith James W., teacher, bds e end Market.

Smith J. C., conductor on I. & C. R. R., res 161 Virg. ave.

Smith John, miller in Model Mills, res 242 w Wash.

Smith John, shoemaker, res 9 e North.

Smith John, laborer, res Spring, bet N. Y. and Vt.

Smith John C., carpenter, res James, bet St. Clair and Ind. ave.

Smith John G., blacksmith, 36 Ky. ave, res 84 n N. J.

Smith John M., attorney at law, cor Ill. and Md., up stairs.

Smith Joseph, tailor, at John Stienman's, bds National saloon.

Smith Joseph, book keeper, 55 w South.

Smith Joseph, machinist, res 42 Elm.

Smith Josiah, res 153 w Vt.

Smith Julius H. C., book binder, 24 w Wash., res 191 w Wash.

Motions all positive in the Florence.

Smith L., laborer, res 13 w McCarthy.

Smith Laypoole, turner, bds California House, 136 s Ill.

Smith Lawrence, porter Bellefontaine R. R., res 31 Davidson.

Smith Leonard, brewer, res 13 w McCarthy.

Smith Mrs. M. C., boarding house, 44 s Penn.

Smith Manning T., huckster, res 21 Elsworth.

Smith Mrs. Margaret, (wid.,) res cor Mass. ave and East.

Smith Mrs. Mary, (wid. O. II. Smith,) res 49 n Tenn.

Smith Nathaniel, tanner and currier, res e Market, out corporation.

Smith Philip, shoe and bootmaker, 3 n Meridian, res 125 n Noble.

Smith Richard, teamster, res 51 Union.

Smith Richard, butcher, res 26 Mich. road.

Smith Robert, res 224 n Ill.

Smith Robert II., salesman at Mayhew & Co.'s, bds Palmer House.

Smith Samuel F., (Osgood, Smith & Co.,) res 44 s Meridian.

Smith Samuel S., farmer, bds 107 s Alabama.

Smith Mrs. Sarah, 5 Blake building, up stairs.

Smith Mrs. Sophia, dress maker, res 86 Pratt.

Smith Mrs. Sophia, (wid.,) res 55 s Benton.

SMITH STEPHEN, BILL POSTER, res 102 n Miss.

Smith Theodore M., salesman, Bee Hive, bds Macy House.

Smith Thomas, clerk in fruit house, res 21 Ellsworth.

Smith Thomas M., res cor Ala. and Washington.

Smith Thomas W., shoemaker, res n Mo., bet Market and Ohio.

Smith Watt J., Clerk U. S. District Court for Ind., bds 158 w N. York.

Smith William, res s Mo., s of South.

Smith William, wagon maker, res 181 Va. ave.

Smith William, soap factory, Bluff road, Daughertyville.

Smith William II., res 37 n Del.

Smith Wm. A., student at Bryant's Com. Col.

Smith William A., Phœnix saloon, 15 e Wash., res same.

Smith William C., student at Bryant's Com. Col.

Smith William II., clerk, bds 84 n New Jersey.

Smith William P., student N. W. C. University, bds 110 Davidson.

Smith William S., fish dealer, res 192 n Ill.

SMITH & TAYLOR, (Frederick Smith, Isaac Taylor,) TOY STORE, 26 e Wash. See card.

Smither Henry C., clerk, City Grocery, res 49 Ind. ave.

Smither James W., mail agent Cin. R. R., bds 49 and 51 Ind. ave.

Smither J. W., student at Bryant's Com. Col., bds with Jas. Smither, Ind. ave.

Smither Robert G., student 5th Ward Gram. School, bds 49 and 51 Ind. ave.

Smither Theodore, student at Bryant's Com. Col., bds on Ind. ave.

Smithmyer John L. & Co., dealers in statuary, &c., 14 e Market.

Smithson I., cooper, res Stringtown, w Indianapelis.

Smock George, clerk, res 53 s N. Jersey.

Smock George W., book keeper, res 52 s N. Jersey.

Smock Nancy, (wid.) res 17 Huron.

Smock Peter, clerk at arsenal, res n Mo., bet Market and Ohio, on canal.

Smock William C., Deputy Clerk, Court House, res 123 e N. York.

Smyth John, clerk New York Store, bds Spencer House.

Snapp Abigail, (wid.) hair braider, res 55 e Ohio.

Snawp Charles, clerk, J. McLene, under Bates House.

Sneider Cooney, brewer, res Wyoming.

Snell Zacariah, gardner and flower dealer, res 84 Pratt.

Snider Adam, porter, res 95 St. Marys.

Snider Charles W., clerk, A. Clem & Bro., bds 117 n Madison.

Snider Paul, laborer, res 64 Bluff road.

SNYDER DANIEL E., CASHIER BRANCH BANK OF THE STATE OF IND., bds J. B. McChesney.

Snyder Nicholas, white washer, 30 e Buchanan.

Snyder Thomas, machinist, Sinker & Vance, bds 15 w Ohio.

Sock Philip, cooper, bds 82 n Miss.

SOCWELL HENRY M., NEW YORK GROCERY, 17 e Wash., res 18 n New Jersey.

Socwell John C., clerk, New York Groc'y, bds Little's Hotel.

Solomon Charles, cigar maker, bds 30 s Ill.

Solomon II. Solomon, clerk 10 w Wash., bds 24 n Penn.

Solomon Joseph, (J. & M. Solomon,) res 30 s Ill.

Solomon Morris, (J. & M. Solomon,) res 30 s Ill.

Solomon J. & M., dealers in cigars, 30 s Ill.

Souderegger Fidel, res 69 Mad ave.

Souderegger Frank, house and sign painter, res 69 Mad ave.

Sonnerfield Henry, grocery, 115 s Tenn.

Hats of every description, color and price, at Davis'.

Sonnerfield William, teamster, res cor Central and Noble.

Soos George, shoemaker, res 178 e Ohio.

Soule Charles E., printer in Gazette office, 127 s Ill.

Soule Mrs. Margaret, (wid.) res 127 s Ill.

Southard James P., retired, res 68 e Vt.

Southard James M., blacksmith, res 46 s Benton.

Soyer John B., wagon maker, res w Indianapolis.

Spade Jacob, works in rolling mill, res 186 Ind. ave.

Spaeth Christian, assistant butcher, bds 152 w Mich.

Spaldin John W., carriage maker, res 110 n East.

Spann James R., carpenter, res 130 e Ohio.

SPANN JOHN S., REAL ESTATE AND INSURANCE AGENT, s w cor Wash. and Meridian, up stairs, res 73 n Penn.

Speake Eldon L., clerk, Boyd & Palmer, bds 131 n Miss.

Speake James E., clerk, A. G. office, bds 131 n Miss.

Speaker Nancy, res s Ill., near Pogues run.

Spear Frederick, (Schwear & Spear,) res e Wash.

Spean Precilla, (col. wid.) res 65 s Noble.

Speckman Henry, cigar maker, 37 s Ill., res same.

Spech Bermard, porter, Rev. Simon Seigris, res 46 s Del.

Spellans Timothy, brick moulder, res 100 s Noble.

Spencer Charles F., salesman, Bee Hive, bds Macy House.

SPENCER MILTON, GROCER, 202 c Wash. res 132 n e cor. Market and Liberty.

SPENCER HOUSE, M. Harth, proprietor, cor s Ill. and La.

Spencer Stephen, hats and caps, 32 w Wash., res 194 n Ill.

Spiegel Augustus, (Spiegel, Thoms & Co.,) res n e cor Vt. and Liberty.

Spiegel Christian, (Spiegel, Thoms & Co.,) res cor North and East.

SPIEGEL, THOMS & CO., (Christian Spiegel, Augustus Spiegel, Fred. Thoms, Henry Frank,) WHOLESALE AND RETAIL FURNITURE DEALERS AND MANUFACTURERS, 73 w Wash.

Spillers Robert T., printer, H. H. Dodd & Co., bds Lingenfelter, Circle.

Spitznorgel Leo., barber, Odd Fellow's Hall, bds 116 e Market.

Splain Thomas, laborer, res 29 Davidson.

Splan James, laborer, res West, bet Md. and Georgia.

Spoller Charles S., baggage master, Bell. R. R., bds Palmer House.

Sponable Mary J., (wid.) res 101 n Tenn.

Sponlae Henry, clerk, Conrad Sponsel's, 277 s Del.

Sponsel Conrad, grocer and liquor dealer, 277 s Del., res same.

Spott Martha, (wid.) tailoress, res 55 e Ohio.

Spotts William, (Jordan & Spotts,) res 6 cor Noble and South.

Sprandel George, works in armory, res 106 w Vt.

Sprenge Charles, (Ostermeyer & Sprange,) res 228 e Wash.

Spray Joseph, hostler, res 65 s Penn.

Sprow Mrs. Louisa, washer, res 82 e Vt.

Spring Adam, stone cutter, res w South.

Springer David, carpenter, res 5 Chatham.

Springer James E., book keeper, res 238 Va. ave.

Springer Martin B., moulder, res 109 e Georgia.

Springsteen Abram, brick mason, res 111 e Market.

Springsteen Jefferson, painter, res 31 Spring.

Spurgin John M., (Ryan & Spurgin,) res n East.

Spurgin Joseph, painter, res 92 n East.

Staats George D., janitor, Odd Fellows Hall, res 6 e Mich.

Stabler Michael, teamster, res 45 Spring.

Stacy Milton H., dyer and finisher, Ohio Premium Woolen Factory, res 141 n West.

Stackhouse J. F., clerk, J. T. Wingate, bds Macy House.

Stackhouse James S., clerk, Wingate grocery store, 21 w Wash., bds 19 Ky. ave.

Staffard Meridith, (col.,) laborer.

Staffard Henry, (col.,) hostler, Jenkins stable, bds. Joseph Spray.

Stagg Chas. W., attorney, Temperance Hall, bds. 79 w Ohio.

Stagg J. R., meat store, 119 Vir. ave.

Stahlhuth Chas., porter, 20 w Wash., res First, bet Meridian and Ill.

Stahlhuth Fred., carpenter, res 99 Peru Railroad.

Stahr Julius, brick maker, bds 23 s East.

Stakely Benjamin, machinist, res 36 n Noble.

Staker Franklin, moulder, res 276 s Del.

Stallard Mrs. Clara, (wid.,) res 78 n East.

Stalon Joseph A., (Kirlin & Stalon,) res cor Ill., and First.

Stalon Mary Anne, (wid.,) res 23 e McCarthy.

Stanfer Henry, machinist, Sinker & Vance, bds Cal. House.

STAPP JAMES H., REAL ESTATE OFFICE, 72 w Wash.

Stark Gustave, carpenter. res 81 Fort Wayne ave.

Stark Herman, private, 76th Reg. Ind. Vol., res 184 e Wash.

Needle more readily adjusted in the Florence than any other.

Starling Mrs. S. S., teacher in oil painting and water colors, Indianapolis Female Institute.

STARLING SAMUEL, (S. & Co.,) 3 n Ill., res 165 n Ill.

STARLING & CO., (Sam'l Starling, R. Beebe, G. W. Hawes,) grocers, 3 n Ill.

Starr John, millwright, res cor Merrill and Bluff Road.

Station House, Fred. Scheer, prop., s Ill., opp. Union Depot.

Staub Joseph, merchant tailor, 2 Odd Fellows Hall, res 110 n Noble.

Stauper Henry, machinist, 136 s Ill., bds California House.

Stauh John, laborer, res Winston, bet Ohio and New York.

Stauss Gustave, finisher, car shop, e Market near Cady.

Steadly Andrew, shoemaker, bds 155 Mass. ave.

Steadman Dr. E. P., physician, res 40 Mass. ave.

Stebens John, finisher, Wash. Foundry, res 141 s Ala.

Stedman Percival, clerk, in I. & C. R. R. office, res 117 s Ala.

Steele Chas. M., agent for Cincinnati papers, bds 121 n Ala.

STEELE MRS. MARY, DRESS MAKER, 22 New & Talbots building.

Steele Thos. J., printer, bds 165 n Liberty.

Steele Wm. H., carpenter, res 165 n Liberty.

Steele Thos. J., printer, Sentinel office, bds 165 n Liberty.

Steffens Chas., (Steffins & Co.,)res 169 s Ala.

Steffens Ernest F., (Steffens & Co.,) res Blake, bet N. York and Vermont.

Steffens Ferdinand, res Blake, bet New York and Vermont.

STEFFENS CHAS. & CO., (C. W. Steffens, E. F. Steffens,) MATHEMATICAL, OPTICAL AND PHILOSOPHICAL INSTRUMENT MAKERS, cor Wash. and Meridian.

Stegall Jerry, blacksmith, res cor New York and Miss.

Steiback Chas., carpenter, res 103 s Del.

Stein Fred., justice of the peace, office, Judah's block, res cor Market and Cady.

Stein Henry, school teacher, English and German, 54 e South.

Steiner Jacob, res 156 n East.

Steinhilber Martin, coffee house, res w National Road.

Stellharue Christ., carpenter, res 176 n Noble.

Stellharne Fred., carpenter, res 150 Davidson,

Stelser Jacob, laborer, res 64 St. Joseph.

Stelter W., billiard saloon, Union Hall, res 160 s Ala.

Stelzell John, (Henning & Stelzell,) res 13 w North.

Stephens Mrs. Merinda, (wid.,) res 78 s East.

Stephens Alexander D., printer, II. H. Dodd & Co., res 78 s East.

Stephens A., (Stephens & Son,) bds Bates House.

Stephens Geo. P., sutler, bds 8 Vir. ave.

Stephens Harrie A., (Stephens & Son,) res Cleveland Ohio.

Stephens Levi B., brick maker, res 246 Madison.

Stephens Samuel, boiler maker, res 71 s Benton.

Stephens Samuel R., (Stephens & Son,) salesman, traveling agent.

Stephens Thaddeus, M. D., over Harrison's bank, res cor First and Ill.

STEPHENS A. & SON, (Alvin Stephens, Harvie A. Stephens,) WHOLESALE DEALERS IN TEAS, COFFEE AND SPICES, cor Market and East.

Stephenson Samuel, laborer, res Bluff Road Doughertyville.

Stergen George, brick moulder, res Bluff Road, Doughertyville.

STERM ISRAEL, PEA RIDGE HOUSE. 14 s Penn, res in rear.

Stern Rev. M. G. J., German Reform. res 15 n Ala.

Steubing Philip, laborer, res 119 n Noble

Steubing William, foreman, Ind. Central machine shop, bds 119 n Noble.

Stevens H. C., bds Littles Hotel.

Stevens Miss Lew. res Davidson.

STEVENSON REV. DAVID, STATE LIBRARIAN, bds E. Alvord.

Stevenson Columbus S., Major pay master U. S. A., office, 8½ c Wash.

Stevenson John, cooper, res. Mo., bet Vermont and Wash.

Steward Axiom, (col.) cook Palmer House res 137 n Tenn.

Steward Jacob, well digger, res 334 s Delaware.

Steward John, turner, res 43 e McCarthy.

Steward Mrs. Margaret, (wid.,) res 108 c South.

Stewart Andrew, teamster and farmer. res Elizabeth.

Stewart Austen John, clerk, J. McLaggert & Co.

Stewart Chas G., (Bowen, Stewart & Co.) bds Mrs. Tyler, 8 Vir. ave.

Stewart Miss Lou, teacher in Indianapolis McLean Female Seminary.

Stewart Daniel, (Stewart & Morgan,) bds 163 n Ill.

Stewart Geo. H. W., professor of music, bds Pyle House.

Stewart Harriet B., Wm. Stewart, bds 49 n Tenn.

Stewart Jackson, laborer, J. Drum, bds J. Drum.

Call at No. 15 Pennsylvania Street.

Stewart James, carpenter, res 232 Indiana ave.

Stewart John A., brakeman, T. & R. R. R. bds 221 n Tenn.

Stewart John Austen, bds Spencer House.

Stewart Joseph W., (col.,) barber, bds near col., Methodiist Church.

Stewart Robt., photographer, 26 and 28 w Wash., bds 195 n Ill.

Stewart Sophia W., (wid., Wm. Stewart,) res 87 n Ill.

Stewart Rev. Thomas II., Baptist, res 110 Davidson.

STEWART & MORGAN, (Daniel Stewart, Stephen W. Morgan,) WHOLESALE DRUGGISTS., 40 e Wash.

Stewart Annie, (wid.,) res Stephen, near Vir. ave.

Stewart Robt., boarding house, 12 w Georgia.

Stecker Fred., painter, res. 169 Railroad.

Stiedel George, file cutter, res 55 n Noble.

Stiegmann Charles, grocer and dry goods merchant, Madison ave, in McCarthy's adddition.

Stien Joseph, shoemaker, res 266 s Del.

Stienman John, tailor and renovater, 25 s Meridian, res same.

Stilding Christian, laborer, res 115 e N. York.

Stiles John, carpenter, res 124 n East.

Still Charles, plasterer, bds 108 s Tenn.

Stillwell George W., res 5 n Noble.

Stilter Wm., billiard saloon, Union Hall, res 160 Ala.

Stilting Charles, laborer, res 106 n Noble.

Stilwell J. D. B., student at Bryant's commercial college, bds 48 Ver.

STILTZ J. GEORGE, SEED AND AGRICULTURAL STORE, 74 e Wash.

Stin Joseph, shoemaker, res 266 s Del.

Stinninter Andy, laborer, res 68 St. Joseph.

Stiver George, teamster, bds 295 w Wash.

Stoak Benjamin, painter, res 108 s Tenn.

Stockinger John, stone cutter, res 171 e Wash.

Stockman George W., bds 83 s Tenn.

Stockwell Daniel, laborer, res Mich. road.

Stoelting Frederick, grocery and provision store, res 163 n West.

Stofal John, switchman, Union Depot, res 54 s Noble.

Stohrer Emil, salesman, bds C. Fridger, e Market.

Stokes Richard M., carpenter, bds 74 n Tenn.

Stolte's brick yard, cor Stephen and Vir. ave.

Stolte Henry, clerk, 281 s Del.

Stolte Wm., brickmaker, res 279 s Del.

Stone Frank, clerk, cigar store, bds at Speckman's.

Stone Timothy S., (V. K. Hendricks & Co.,) Worcester, Mass.

Stone Wm. O., (V. K. Hendricks & Co.,) res 59 e Market.

Stoneman Wm., book-keeper, bds Samuel Beck's.

Stoner John P., printer, Gazette office, res 13 Ky. ave.

Story Riley T., printer, Ind. School Journal, bds e St. Clair.

Stortz Charles, painter, bds Pea Ridge House.

Stout Benj. C., (O. B. Stout & Bro's,) res 100 n Tenn.

Stout Carhart, coal agent, res 101 s Tennessee.

Stout David L., (O. B. Stout & Bro's,) res 100 u Tenn.

Stout John R., (O. B. Stout & Bro's,) res 100 n Tenn.

Stout Oliver B., (O. B. Stout & Bro's,) res e Market.

STOUT OLIVER B. & BRO'S, (Benj. C. Stout, David L. Stout, John R. Stout, Oliver B. Stout and Richard C. Stout,) GROCERS, 42 w Wash.

Stout Richard C., (O. B. Stout & Bro's,) res w Maryland.

STOVER REV. DANIEL, UNITED BRETHREN, res cor Orient and Mich. road.

Stowell Myron A., (Willard & Stowell,) bds Bates House.

Strang Gabrael L., shoemaker, res 268 e Wash.

Strange Wm. R., notary public, court house, res 108 e Ver.

Strassner Frederick, tailor, res 207 n Ala.

Strauss Solomon, clerk, Moritz, Bro. & Co., bds Palmer House.

Strayback Charles, baker, Mt. Jackson.

Streicher Jacob, carpenter, res 121 Ft. Wayne ave.

Streif David, (Streif & Dietz,) res Market bet Noble and Davidson.

STREIF & DEITZ, (David Streif & Ferdinand Deitz,) TANNERS AND CURRIERS, cor Wash. and Davidson.

STREIGHT COL. A. D., 51st IND. REG., PUBLISHER, 4 Yohn's block.

Stretcher Elmira, (wid) res 59 e Md.

Stretcher Howard, res 59 e Md.

Stretcher Jacob, carpenter, res 121 Ft. Wayne ave.

Strickland David H., foreman Sheet's paper mill, bds National Hotel.

STRICKLAND T. C., CITY HOTEL, 77 and 79 s Ill.

Strickler Samuel, works Hinesly's stable, res s Penn., near Pogues run.

Stripp Peter, railroader. res 11 e Ga.

Stringer Mary, (wid. Leonard Stringer,) res 14 w North.

Stringmier Frederick, laborer, res Mass. ave., bet Noble and Railroad.

Stroh John, hostler, bds E. Knight's.

Over 100 Florence Machines in use in the city of Indianapolis.

Strong Wm., shoemaker, A. Lintz, 39 w Wash., bds Knight's.

Strubinger George, laborer, res 269 n Ill.

Struckmann Frederick, laborer, res 57 Union.

Stuart Alexander, student at Bryant's commercial college, bds 31 Ky. ave.

Stuck Mathew, laborer, res 269 s East.

Stuck Peter, teamster, res 184 s N. Jersey.

Stuck Wm., wcod hauler, res 267 s East.

Stucke Charles, cooper, res 27 Spring.

Stump Mrs. Christina, (wid. Henry Stump,) res 228 n Ala.

Stumph George F.. brickmason, res n Noble, bet N. York and Ver.

Stumph Henry, brewer, city brewery, res in rear.

Stumph John, stonemason, res 139 n Ala.

Stumph John B., city assessor, 14 New & Talbot's block, res Cady, bet Wash. and Market.

Stumph John II., laborer, res 148 n East.

Stundon Thomas, laborer, res 43 Lou.

Sturdivant Rev. Charles, principal McLean's seminary, res 27 n Meridian.

Sturdevant Charles N., Jr., student at Bryant's commercial college, bds Female Institute.

Sturm Miss F., teacher, Indianapolis Female Institute.

Sturm Fred C., in ordnance department, res 40 n Miss.

Sturm R. C., ordnance department, 21 w Wash., res 40 n Miss.

STURM COL. H., CHIEF OF ORDNANCE, off. 21 w Wash., res 40 n Miss.

Sudbock Herman, student at Bryant's commercial college.

Sudbrock Frank, wood sawyer, res 120 Davidson.

Suddith, laborer, res 124 Davidson.

Suer Lewis, sawmaker, Wyoming.

Suess Michael, tailor, res 270 s Del.

Suess Charles, tailor, res 270 s Del.

Suess Max, tailor, res 270 s Del.

Suesz Godfrey G., shoemaker, res 147 e Ohio.

Suhr Albert, watchman Madison engine house, res 123 Bluff road.

Suhre Henry, laborer, res Winston, bet N. York and Ver.

Suit James, machinest, bds 107 s Tenn.

SULGROVE BERRY R. EDITOR STATE JOURNAL, res 87 w South.

Sulgrove Eli L., harness maker, 20 w Wash., bds 53 w Md.

Sulgrove James W., (Sulgrove, Reynolds & Co.,) res 59 w Md.

Sulgrove James, (Sulgrove, Reynolds & Co., res 59 w Md.

Sulgrove Jerome, harness maker, res 72 Ky. ave.

Sulgrove John M., harness maker, 20 w Wash., res 59 w Md.

Sulgrove Milton M., harness maker, res 66 n Ill.

SULGROVE, REYNOLDS & CO., (James Sulgrove, James W. Sulgrove, John Reynolds,) SADDLERY AND HARDWARE DEALERS, 20 w Wash.

Sullivan Mrs. Abby, (wid.) res 98 Md.

Sullivan Arthur, runner Little's Hotel.

Sullivan Daniel, shoemaker, res rear 60 North.

Sullivan Daniel, laborer, res 12 East.

Sullivan James, teamster, bds 24 n West.

Sullivan John, railroader, res 218 Ind. ave.

Sullivan John B., carpenter, res 40 Pratt.

Sullivan Timothy, laborer, res 147 e Ohio.

Sullivan William, Justice Peace, off. cor Wash and Penn., res 197 n Meridian.

Sullivan William H., book keeper, 74 w Wash., cor Cal. and Vt.

Summers Albert B., carpenter, res James, bet St Clair and Ind. ave.

Summons Robert, printer, Journal off., bds 119 w Wash.-

Sundker John, brick moulder, res 281 s Del.

Suter James S., clerk, res 104 Mass. ave.

Sutmire William, railroader, res 54 Union.

Sulton Joseph, plasterer, res 136 n Ala.

Swain James, bds Macy House.

Swales John F. S., stone cutter, res 12 Willard.

Swam Thomas C., laborer, res 83 n New Jersey.

Swang William, cooper, res 46 s East.

Swank William B., cooper, 58 s East.

Swatz Peter, works at rolling mill, res 5 Willard.

Swatz Fred, laborer, res 129 Peru R. R.

Swatz Mrs. Mary, (wid.) res 129 Peru R. R.

Sweeney Pat, laborer, res 13 Union.

Sweeney Thomas, machinist, Sinker & Vance, bds s Del.

Sweeny Eugine, laborer, res 127 e New York.

Sweeny John, tobacconist, res 8 first floor Blake's building.

Sweetser Rebecca, (wid.) res 50 n Pennsylvania.

Sweetser George M., box delivery clerk P. O., bds 50 n Penn.

Sweetser James M., attorney at law, res 50 N. Penn.

Sweinhart Peter, plasterer, res 233 Ind. ave.

Sweinhart William, cutter, J. & P. Gramling, res 165 n Ala.

Swicour Charles, laborer, res 87 Union.

Swift Mrs. Mary, res 52 n Liberty.

Swincheart Augustus, shoemaker, bds Edmond Swineheart.

Swineheart Edmond, shoemaker, res out corp., Morrison.

Wool hats at No. 15 Pennsylvania St.

Swinesback William, butcher shop 243 s Del.

Swing Edward, butcher, res 89 w New York.

Swing Peter F., law student, res 91 n Meridian.

Syder John, moulder, res 186 s Ala.

Syerup Henry, grocery and feed store, cor East and Mass. ave., res 139 Massachusetts ave.

Syms James, screw maker, res 22 s Delaware.

Symmes James, machinist, Sinker & Vance, ress 222 s Ala.

T

Taes John, cabinet maker, res 238 Mad. ave.

Taffe George, city policeman, res Oak and corp.

Taggart Sam'l millwright, res 64 n Miss.

Tairbairn Richard, painter, res in rear of 100 s Noble.

Talbott Charles H., clerk, Talbott & Co., res 66 n Tenn.

Talbott John M., (Talbott & Co.,) res 66 n Tenn.

Talbott J. M. & Co., (John M. Talbott, Washington H. Talbott,) wholesale dealers in hats, caps and straw goods, 3 s Meridian.

Talbott Richard L., (Alford, Mills & Co.,) res 64 e North.

Talbott Washington H., (Talbott & Co.,) res cor Meridian and Ohio.

Talbott William P., general trader, bds 20 Va. ave.

TALBOTT W. H. & CO., (Washington H. Talbett, George M. Jenison,) WATCHES, JEWELRY AND SILVERWARE, 24 e Wash.

Tangany Patrick, clerk, Clark's saloon, res 12 s Ill.

Tapking Frederick, (Tapking & Becker,) res Liberty, bet N. York and Vt.

Tapking John, cabinet maker, res 65 N. Jersey.

Tapking & Becker, (Fred. Tapking, Jacob Becker,) merchant tailors, 65 e Wash.

Tarkington John S., (Newcomb & Tarkington,) res 35 e Ohio.

Tarkington William S., book keeper, Stewart & Morgan, bds 163 n Ills.

Tarlton James A., (Tarlton & Keen,) res 152 n Penn.

Tarlton John, (Belles & Tarlton,) Oriental House, res same.

TARLTON & KEEN, (James A. Tarlton, Hiram W. Keen,) WHOLESALE AND RETAIL GROCERS, 8 and 10 s Meridian.

TARR MARTIN M., BOWLING SALOON, 18 w Ga.

Tatum Rev. David, Friends' Society, res cor East and Cherry.

Taylor Abijah, agent for Louck's hair oil, res 195 n N. Jersey.

Taylor Calvin, (Taylor & Taylor,) bds 175 Mass ave.

Taylor David M., book keeper, Branch Bank of the State, bds Macy House.

Taylor George, porter, New York Store, res N. Jersey.

Taylor Isaac J., (Smith & Taylor,) 20 e Wash.

Taylor Isaac H., bds Oriental House, res Cincinnati.

Taylor Israel, book keeper, Coffin & Co., res 57 Mass ave.

Taylor James, carpenter, bds Ray House, e Del.

Taylor Mrs. Jane, res 135 e N. York.

Taylor Napoleon B., (Taylor & Taylor,) res cor Ala. and Mich.

Taylor Oliver, (col.) cook in Buckeye saloon, bds same.

Taylor Robert A., res 175 Mass. ave.

Taylor Robert R., carpenter, res w Market.

Taylor Thomas, painter, res 112 n Miss.

Taylor Wiley, (col.) bds 127 n East.

Taylor William, engineer, res 97 Peru R. R.

Taylor William A., courier, John Fishback, bds 147 Va. ave.

TAYLOR WILLIAM H., COPPERSMITH, 268 e Wash., res same.

Taylor William H., tinner, 182 e Washington.

Taylor & Taylor, attorneys at law, (Calvin Taylor, Napoleon B. Taylor,) 50 e Wash.

Teal Nathaniel, M. D., off. 5 2d floor Blake's building, res n Ill.

Teckenbrock Christopher, blacksmith, res 3 Md.

Teckenbrock Henry W., engineer, res 75 Bluff road.

Tenbrock Charles, sup't of live animal show, bds Oriental House.

Temper James, carpenter, res Grove.

TEMPERANCE HALL, Wash., bet Ill. and Meridian.

Temper Thomas, gas fitter, bds 34 Ky. ave.

Tennis John M., salesman, Bee Hive, bds Macy House.

Tennis Wm. H., salesman, Bee Hive, bds Macy House.

Teits William, cigar maker, res 133 e Wash.

Teneyck & Bro., (Jeremiah A. Teneyck & Richard F. Teneyck) shoe and boot makers, 260 w Wash., res 20 n Cal.

Teneyck J. A., (Teneyck & Bro.,) res 20 n Cal.

Teneyck R. F., (Teneyck & Bro.,) res 20 n Cal.

Teneyck John, shoe and boot maker, res 86 Ind. ave.

Teneyck Nelson, shoemaker, res 192 w Md.

Tenis Peter, laborer, n Winston, bet N. Y. and Vt.

Tepy Harman, laborer, 271 Virg. ave.

Terrell Mrs. Cosiah, (wid. John Terrell,) res rear 52 n Penn.

Terrell W. H. H., military sec'y to Gov. Morton, res Smith's block, w Market.

Terry Mrs. Jane, (wid.,) res 221 s Penn.

Tetaz Henry L., laborer, bds 86 Spring.

Thalman Isaac, laborer, 180 e Ohio.

Thalman Isaac, book keeper Hoosier woolen factory, res 244 w Wash.

Thalman John, baker, 27 n Ala., res same.

Thatcher Amos, laborer, res 15 e Geo.

Thatcher James, pump maker, res e Huron.

Thayer Daniel, (Thayer & Cook,) res 145 & 147 e Market.

Thayer George, clerks 80 w Wash., bds 145 e Market.

THAYER & COOK, (Daniel Thayer and Baldwin Cook,) GROCERS AND PRODUCE DEALERS, 79 e Wash.

Thayer Daniel W., railroader, res 28 s Benton.

Thayer Geo., student at Bryant's Com. Col., bds D. Thayer's.

Thayer George, salesman, bds 145 e Market.

Thayer Selden, (Wilmot & Thayer,) res 145 e Market.

Thedu William, laborer, res Mich. road.

Theick Henry, machinist, res Mich. road.

Theodore Thomas, brick mason, res 125 n East.

Therner Gerhardt, laborer, res Mich. r'd.

Thess John, cabinet maker, 166 Madison ave.

THE STORE SALOON, M. CLARK, PROPRIETOR, 61 s Ill.

Thoms Mrs. Ann, res 14 Willard.

Thoms Frederick, (Spiegel, Thoms & Co.) res s e cor Liberty and Vt.

Thomas Albert, wagon driver, city grocery, bds 61 n Noble.

Thomas Benj., finisher, Hoosier woolen factory, res w National road.

Thomas Charles, clerk, city grocery, bds 61 n Noble.

Thomas Conrad, bar keeper, Youngerman's saloon, res 61 n Noble.

Thomas Mrs. E. Martha, (wid.,) res 257 s Del.

Thomas George, res 61 n Noble.

Thomas James F., carpenter, res cor Tenn. and McCarthy.

Thomas John, discharged sold., w Washington.

Thomas John, manager rolling mill, res s Merid., bet McCarthy and Merrill.

Thomas Lewis, painter, res 67 n East.

Thomas Lewis L., carpenter, res 110 n Miss.

Thomas Kempton, farmer, Mt. Jackson.

Thomas Mary J, milliner, 46 w Wash., res same.

Thompson Daniel J., fish dealer, 7 e Wash., res 124 n Noble.

Thompson Eli, carpenter, res 133 w N.Y.

Thompson Hugh, machinist, res 9 Lord.

Thompson James, moulder, res 184 s Penn.

Thompson J. C., student at Bryant's Com. Col., bds in country.

Thompson John, works at rolling mill, res 61 Madison ave.

Thompson John, blacksmith, res 75 s N. Jersey.

THOMPSON MARY, DRY GOODS AND GROCERIES, cor Del. and South.

Thompson Richard M., machinist, res 66 e Louisiana.

Thompson Wm. A. C., confectionery and fruit, 7 e Wash., bds same place.

Thomson Mrs. Anna, (Thomson & Son) res 65 n Ala.

THOMSON QUINTIN, BAKER, 4 s Meridian, res same.

THOMSON & SON, (Anna Thomson and Wm. Thomson,) BOOKS AND STATIONERY, 7 n Penn.

Thomson Daniel J., stone mason, res 124 n Noble.

Thomson Milton, soldier 63 reg, res alley bet Ohio and N. Y.

Thomson W. Clinton, physician and surgeon, res 62 n Ill.

Thomson William, (Thompson & Son,) res 65 n Ala.

Thonssen Edlepp B., (firm of Thonssen & Lahey,) res 67 w Wash.

Thonssen & Lahey, wholesale notion house, 67 w Wash.

THORNBERRY WM., UNION LAUNDRY, cor Noble and Wash., res 134 n Ala. See card.

Thorne John, butcher, res 103 e Geo.

Thornby Orion, machinist, Forest, s of Lawrenceburg machine shop.

Thorp Caleb, artist, over Bee Hive, res 69 Fort Wayne ave.

Thorp John D., deputy sheriff, res 39 e Market.

Thorpe Thomas D., photographic rooms 2 w Wash., res 69 Fort Wayne ave.

Thurston Wm. B., (firm of Pomroy, Fry & Co.,) res 9 e Mich.

Tierney Martin, blacksmith, res 241 s Penn.

Tilford Benjamin, cabinet maker, bds 169 s Del.

Tilford Elizabeth, (wid. A. L. Tilford,) res 192 n Miss.

Tilford J. M., Pres. Ind. Jour. Co., res 64 n Meridian.

Tilford Samuel, clerk military headquarters, bds 64 n Meridian.

Tilly Harman, (H. & T. Tilly,) res Bluff road.

Tilly H. & T., (Harman Tilly and Theodore Tilly,) soap, candle and oil factory, Bluff road.

Tilly Theodore, (H. & T. Tilly,) res Bluff road, Doughertyville.

Timmermann Herman, street contractor, res Liberty, bet N. Y. and Vt.

Tindall George P., pastor 2d Presbyterian church, res 112 n Del.

Tindall Henry, captain U. S. A., res 110 n Tenn.

Tine Gotlib, drayman, res bet East and Chatham, n of St. Clair.

Tinne Henry, laborer, Peru R. R., near city limits.

Tinner Henry, res 50 n Liberty.

Tiner Henry R., distributing clerk in P. O, bds Macy House.

Tinsley Miss L. H., music teacher Indianapolis Female Institute, res same.

Tippee Herman. boiler maker, (Sinker & Vance,) res 271 Virg. ave.

Tipton Jesse A., traveling agent for J. A. Heidlinger's tobacco and cigar manufactory, bds Palmer House.

Tittman Alex., machinist, res McOuate's building, Ky. ave.

Titcomb Daniel, (Wallace & Titcomb,) egg packer, res 48 e Market.

Todd Chas. N., late principal of McLean Fem. Inst., res 132 n Penn.

Todd Chas. N., student at Bryant's Com. College.

Todd John M., real estate agent, 13 s Ill., res 150 n East.

Todd Martin M., prop'r Buckeye saloon, s East, cor Geo. and Ill., res same.

Todd Samuel A., (Delzell & Todd,) res 124 n Del.

Tomlinson James M., (Tomlinson & Cox) bds cor Meridian and St. Clair.

TOMLINSON & COX, (James M. Tomlinson and Wm. C. Cox,) DRUGGISTS, 18 e Wash.

Torbett Oliver B., attorney at law, office Temp. Hall, res out city.

Tolton Stewart, clerk N. Y. store, bds Macy House.

TOUSEY GEORGE, PRES'T BRANCH BANK STATE IND., res 80 n Meridian.

Tousey Lydia, (wid. Tho. Tousey,) res 31 Ellsworth.

TOUSEY & BYRAM, (Oliver Tousey & Norman Byram,) DRY GOODS AND NOTIONS, 70 e Wash.

Tousey Oliver, (Tousey & Byram,) res cor Meridian and Ver.

Tout Zenus F., milliner store, 22 s Ill.

Townman Jesse D., carpenter, res 55 St. Joseph.

Townsend J. M., auditor, Bellefontaine R. R. line, res 20 n Mer.

Tracy Mathew S., student at Bryant's commercial college, bds n Penn.

TRAEYSER L. F., PIANO FORTE MANUFACTURER, 13 s Ala. See card.

Trask George, sawyer for Peru R. R., res 125 w N. York.

Traub Charles, renovator of furniture, cor N. York and Mass. ave., res cor Plum and Cherry.

Traub Conrad, laborer, res 117 Ft. Wayne ave.

Traub Israel, painter, res 214 n Ala.

Traub Jacob, gardner, res w Indi'apolis.

Trauer Rudolph, turner, bds s e cor Liberty and Ver.

Traver Charles H., operator in railroad stock, bds 30 n Penn.

Traver George M., at bee hive dry goods store, res 30 n Penn.

Travies Albert, teamster, res 130 e North.

Trendlemahn, Henry, laborer, res 28 Forest.

Tressler Sidney P., salesman, Jones, Hess & Davis, bds 17 Ind. ave.

Trester John, hackman, res 146 Blake.

Treter John, stonemason, res n N. Jersey. n of St. Clair.

Trimmer John, printer, res 103 Ind. ave.

Tripse Sylvanus L., book-keeper, Hudnut's mills, bds cor Md. and Penn.

Triselm Frederick, laborer, e Dougherty.

Trotter John, laborer, res 160 e Ohio.

Troup Mrs. Mary, (wid) seamstress, res 152 e Market.

Trowbridge Joseph, carpenter, res, 3 Water.

Trueblood James, res 139 n Del.

Trueblood Newton A., book-keeper, bds Beck's, s Del.

Truman Wm., messenger, Adams express, bds Bates House.

Trump Jacob, bricklayer, res 163 n Miss.

Trumbull James L., U. S. Q. M. department, bds Kinder House.

Truxell K., last maker, bds 159 Vir. ave.

Tucker Wm. S., salesman, 3 Bates House, bds Oriental House.

Tuel Martin, laborer, res 177 s East.

Tuley Wm., bds Ray House.

Tully House, s Ill., near Lou.

Tull Mrs. Amanda, (wid) res 119 s N. Jersey.

Tuohey James, clerk, McKernan & Pierce, bds Pyle House.

Tuohey Michael A., works in State Library, bds Pyle House.

Turk John, laborer, bds California House, 136 s Ill.

Turksess John, blacksmith, res 62 Ky. ave.

Turner J., carpenter, bds 232 w Wash.

Turner Augustus, (col) barber, 17 w Wash., res cor Tenn. and Ga.

Turner Burton, (col) carpenter, res 82 on alley, bet Mich. and Ver.

Turner Chauncey L., clerk, U. S. disbursing office, bds 122 n Ill.
TURNER JAMES, TOWNSHIP TRUSTEE, Court House, res 121 s Ala.
Turner M. C., clerk, 84 w Wash., res n Tenn.
Turner Theodore F., student at Bryant's commercial college, bds James Turner.
Turner Wm., brickmason, res 65 Merrill.
Turner Wm. H., general commission merchant, 84 w Wash., res 270 n Ill.
Turquin Martin, res 138 e N. York.
Tursey Mrs. Pamelia, (wid) res w Indianapolis.
Tutewiler C. W., student at Bryant's commercial college, bds Mass. ave.
Tutewiler Charles, tinner, bds 65 Mass. ave.
Tutewiler Henry, Sen., plasterer, res 65 Mass. ave.
Tutewiler Henry, Jr., clerk for Col. Wilder, 17th Ind. reg.
Tutewiler John W., clerk, bds 75 Mass. ave.
Tutting Joseph, shoemaker, bds 51 s Ill.
Tuttle B. F., dealer in flour, grain, &c., 27 w Wash., res 83 n Mer.
Tuttle Dennis, bds 83 n Mer.
Tuttle Gaylord P., res 79 n Meridian.
Tyer Geo. W., boss in Hill's planing mill, res 89 s East.
Tyler Alonzo P., boarding house, 8 Vir. ave.
TYLER LEWIS H., DRY GOODS AND CLOAKS, 2 w Wash., res same.

U

Uhlendorff George, clerk, Exchange Saloon, bds Spencer House.
Umversaw John, city marshal, res 147 Ala.
Umversaw Lewis, (Umversaw & Co.,) res 24 Vir. ave.
UMVERSAW & CO., (Lewis Umversaw & Jacob Krauss,) LIVERY STABLE, 11 and 13 w Pearl.
Underhill Robert F., flour mill, Bluff road, res same.
Union Hall, 107, 109, 111 and 113 e Wash.
Union House, Geo. Ilg, proprietor, cor Ill. and South.
Union Railway office, Union Depot.
Union Steam Bakery, 11 s Penn.
United States Arsenal Depot, w Market.
United States Arsenal, 1½ miles e National road.
UNITED STATES EXPRESS CO., JAS. BUTTERFIELD, AGENT, cor Wash. and Meridian.
United States Quarter Master's Office, cor Wash. and N. Jersey, Capt J. A. Ekin, A. Q. M.
United States Ware House, cor Mer. and Louisiana.

Upfold Rt. Rev. George, Bishop of Indiana, Protestant Episcopal Church, res 51 n Tenn.
Upham Alfred, res 113 n Mer.
Uphaus Henry, Jr., student at Bryant's commercial college, bds 188 s Del.
Unich Miss, millinery and dressmaking, 6 Yohn's block.

V

Vail Sidney J., teacher, deaf and dumb asylum, e Indianapolis.
Vajen J. H., wholesale and retail hardware, 21 w Wash., res cor N. York and Penn.
Van Antwerp, blacksmith, 8 n East, res 22 n Liberty.
Vanbergen Wm., carpenter, res 45 w Mich.
Vanblaricum Ben., laborer, res w Indianapolis.
Vanblaricum Jesse, capt. of night watch, res 177 w Wash.
Vanblaricum Michael, laborer, res w Indianapolis.
Vanblaricum Wm., res 49 w South.
Vanbrocklin Bela F., in the army, res 117 n West.
Vance Mrs. Mary J., (wid. Lawaence M. Vance,) e Wash., e of Pogues run.
Vance Samuel C., (Sinker & Vance,) bds e Wash., e of Pogues Run.
Vance Thomas, cabinet maker, res Ver., bet Noble and Liberty.
Vance Thomas P., clerk, res 94 n East.
Vancamp Gilbert C., (Williams & Vancamp,) res 116 Ohio.
Vandegrift Benton C., Post Office clerk, bds 33 Kentucky ave.
Vandegrift Henry, res 33 Ky. ave.
Vendegrift Wm. H., telegraph operator, Cincinnati depot, bds 33 Ky. ave.
Vandegrift Benj., printer, res 98 n Miss.
Vangrift Wm., plasterer, bds 64 Mass. ave.
Van Houten C. W., (Van Houten & Graham,) 34 n Ill.
Van Houten Isaac H., clerk, 34 n Ill., bds 145 Vir. ave.
Van Houten & Graham, (Cornelius W. Van Houten & John J. Graham,) grocery, 34 n Ill.
Vanlaningham Minervia, res 198 n N. Jersey.
Vanlaningham Lemuel, secretary gas co., res cor North and Del.
Vannida Philip, salesman, J. Kahn, bds 197 n Noble.
Vanslack Ellen, (wid. Nathan Vanslack,) res 68w Mich.
Van Tine H. C., book keeper, Daily State Sentinel, bds Bates House.
Vantoot David, farmer, Mt. Jackson.
Vantoot Harvey, laborer, Mt. Jackson.

Printed instructions accompany every Florence Sewing Machine.

CITY GROCERY.

C. L. HOLMES,

WHOLESALE AND RETAIL

GROCER,

Produce & Commission Merchant,

AND DEALER IN

FOREIGN FRUITS, &C.,

No. 31 West Washington Street,

INDIANAPOLIS, INDIANA.

☞Agent for Longworth's Still Catawba Wine.☜

BENNETT F. WITT,

ATTORNEY FOR SOLDIERS,

And Authorized United States Claim Agent,

Office S. W. corner Washington and Meridian Streets,

INDIANAPOLIS, IND.

D. S. McKERNAN,

ATTORNEY AT LAW,

And Agent for the Collection of Soldier's Claims,

Will give prompt attention to the collection of Officers and Soldiers' Pensions, Bounty, Back Pay, Pay for Extra Duty, and all other debts arising on account of services rendered the Government; also, Horses or other Property lost while in service.

Office No. 8 W. Washington St., Indianapolis, Ind.

P. O. BOX 1004. ENCLOSE A STAMP.

REFERENCES.---Gov. Morton, Adjt. Gen. Noble, Judge Reid, of Connersville, Judge Perkins, of the Supreme Court.

Vanney Miss Rachel, bds s Tenn., near Pouges run.
Vater Elanor, (wid., Thos. Vater,) res 41 w Walnut.
Vater Thos. J., res 45 w Walnut.
Vater S., Western Union Telegraph Office, res 41 w Walnut.
Vaughan Jacob W., carpenter, res 152 n Miss.
Vawter John A., engineer, res 39 e McCarthy.
Vawter Marion, engineer, res 18 Union.
Veach Joseph, teamster, res 144 e Wood.
Veach Nelson, carpenter, res 132 e St. Clair.
Veach Pat., soldier, 71st Reg. Ind. Vol., res 184 n Del.
Veas Louis, carpenter, res 190 n East,
Veaux Hall, cor South and Penn.
Venacle James, gardener, res w Indianapolis.
Venerable Willis, (col.) hod carrier, res cor East and St. Clair.
Verbergrell John, carpenter, res Winston.
Vernickle Joseph, City Bakery, 201 e Wash., res same,
Vetter A. & J., furniture, 97 e Wash.
Vetter John, cabinet maker shop, 185 s Penn., res same.
VICKERS WM. B., DRUGGIST, Odd Fellows cor., res 69 Alabama.
Vicksler David, butcher, res 39 s Ill.
Victor Louis, laborer, res 36 Spring.
Vieweg Augustus, (Becker & Vieweg,) res 103 e Wash.
Vincent Felix A., manager Metropolitan Theatre.
Vincent Geo. D., carpenter, res. 97 Davidson.
Vincent John A., salesman, Stephens & Son, bds Bates House.
Vincent Mrs. Nancy, (wid.) res 182 s Penn.
Vincent Samuel, plasterer, bds 50 s East.
Vincent Wm. II., carpenter, res 91 Davidson.
Vinnedge John A., (Maguire, Jones & Co.,) res 85 s Tenn.
Vinnedge Joseph D., (James Vinnedge & Co.,) res 41 e Michagan.
Vinton Almus E., (Hasselman & Vinton,) res 23 n Meridian.
Viblland Ugene L., clerk, (Maj. McClure,) bds Mrs. Strecher.
Viquesney Gustave, marble cutter, res 144 c East.
Virt Daniel, laborer, res 97 Mass. ave.
Virt John W., harness maker 34 w Wash. bds s Ala.
Virt T. W., laborer, res 28 s Ala.
Vixler David, butcher, res 39 s Ill.
Voegtle Jacob, stoves and tinware, 177 e Wash., res 125 e Market.
Voigt David, harness maker, res 111 s Tenn.

Voigt Bernard, musician, res 108 n Noble.
Voigt Louis, Centrel House, 44 s Mer.
Voigt Henry, salesman, (W. J. Holiday & Co.,) res 113 w Mich.
Voliquette Ben., U. S. service, res 142 McCarthy.
Volley John, blacksmith, res 29 s Liberty.
Vahmer Otto P., res 159 e St. Clair.
Volmer Chas., wholesale wines, liquors, 65 w Wash., res 141 n Noble.
Volz Mrs. Eliza, (wid.) res 190 e Wash., up stairs, 3d story.
Volz John, works rolling mill, bds 190 e Wash., up stairs.
Vondersaar John, laborer, res Blake.
Vonnegut Clemens, dealer in foreign and domestic hardware, leather, &c., 142 e Wash., res same.
Voorhees Mary J., (wid., Abraham Vorhees,) res 97 n Ill.
Vorhees Jacob, plasterer, res 91½ Fort Wayne ave.
Voorhees Wm. II., soldier, Co. F. 63d Reg., res Ash and Corporation.
Vordermarke R., chair maker, res 89 McCarthy.

W

WACHTSTETTER JOHN, SALOON, 14 Louisiana, res s near Madison Depot.
Wachtstetter Jacob, Meridian Saloon and boarding house, 25 s Mer., res in rear.
Wachtstetter Gottlieb, prop'r Morris House Saloon, res 14 Williard.
Wachtel Moses, (Kalzenstern & Wachtel,) res 101 s East.
Wachter Lawrence, shoemaker, Galt House s Ill., res Bluff Rroad.
Waddle John, dry goods merchant, res 11 e North.
Wadkin John H., (col.) barber, Yohn's Block, bds 126 w Ohio.
Waggoner Conrad, laborer, Bluff Road.
Waggoner Henry, brick moulder, res Bluff Road, Doughertyville.
Wagoner John, grocer, res Bluff Road.
Wagner John, laborer, res w Indp'ls.
Wagner Anthony, teamster, res 164 n Noble.
Wainright Samuel, tinware and job shop, 11 s Ill., res cor New York and Meridian.
Wald Jerry, works at rolling mill, bds 81 w South.
Walden Wm., white washer, res 131 n West.
Walden Wm., shoemaker, bds Jefferson House.
Walden Mrs. Mary T., res 63 w Lou.
Walk Anthony, shoemaker, 150 e Market, res same.
Walk Lewis, boarding house, 14 and 16 w Georgia.

Walker Isaiah D., attorney at law, Maj. 2d cavalry, bds Palmer House.

Walker Jacob S., lumber merchant, w Market, bet Miss. and Canal, res 7 Ill.

Walker Lindsey, hostler, Hinesley's stable, bds Farmers Hotel.

Walker Mary J., (wid., Wiley F. Walker,) res 188 Ind. ave.

Walker Samuel, Jr., U. S. Quartemasters department, bds 122 n Ill.

Walker Thos. R., salesman, Center Shoe Store, bds Macy House

Walker Wm. W., track layer, bds 107 s Tenn.

Walkup Andrew, conductor, Jefferson R. R., bds Palmer House.

Wall James, carpenter, res 119 w Georgia.

Wall Thos., laborer, res cor East and Lawrenceburgh R. R.

Wallace Andrew, wholesale grocer and commission merchant, 38 Vir. ave., res. 34 n Delaware.

Wallace Alexander G., res e Market.

Wallace Mrs. Beuleh, dressmaker, res 79 Massachusetts.

Wallace James, copyist, res 176 n New Jersey.

Wallace Mrs. Kate A., bds 115 w Maryland.

Wallace Oliver J., driver, Tarlton & Keene, bds 167 n N. Jersey.

Wallace Samuel, livery stable, res 176 n New Jersey.

Wallace Samuel, brickmason, bds 176 n New Jersey.

Wallace W. John, res 161 c Market.

WALLACE WILLIAM, COUNTY CLERK, court house, res 121 n Del.

Wallace William, laborer, res cor Wash. and Orient.

Wallace William W., grave stone and monumental manufactory, 92 s Ill., res 94 s Ill.

Wallace William P. & Co., produce dealers 37 cor Md. and Va. ave.

Wallace Mrs. Zerelda, (wid.) res 139 n New Jersey.

Wallace & Titcomb, (—— —— Wallace, Daniel Titcomb,) egg packers.

Waller Benj., boot and shoe maker, res 131 Ind. ave.

WALLICK JOHN F., MANAGER WESTERN UNION TELEGRAPH OFFICE, bds 87 n Ill.

Wallingford Mrs. Catharine, res Vt., bet Liberty and Noble.

Wally John, blacksmith, res 29 s Liberty.

Walmsley John, tailor, res 58 e Mich.

Walpole Bryan C., notary public, bds 156 s Ill.

Walpole Robert L., (Walpole T. D. & R. L.,) res 4 e Vt.

Walpole Thomas D., (Walpole T. D. & R. L.,) res 156 n Ill.

WALPOLE T. D. & R. L., (Robert L. Walpole, Thomas D. Walpole,) ATTORNEYS AT LAW, 16½ e Wash.

Walsh Andrew, shoemaker, bds Ky. ave.

Walsh Mrs. Hanora, (wid.) res 308 s Del.

Walsh James, works Washington foundry, bds Washington House.

Walsh John, cooper, 312 s Del.

Walsh Maurice, clerk Palmer House saloon, res 303 s Del.

Walsh Thomas, boiler maker, Wash. foundry, res 216 s Ala.

Walsh William, laborer, res 71 Mad. ave.

Walsman Frederick, cook, 7 n Ill., res 14 s Ill.

Walton Elias H., family groceries, cor Del. and N. York, res 59 n Penn.

Walton William, works rolling mill, res w Merrill.

Wand Alexander, boot and shoe manufacturer, 39 s Meridian, res 131 n Penn.

Wand John, car inspector, I. C. R. R., res cor McCarthy & Green.

Wand John, boot and shoe maker, 38 w Wash., res 11 Huron.

Wands Hannah, washer woman, res 204 s Del.

Wands William, medical student, bds McCarthy.

Ward John, laborer, res Elizabeth.

Ward Homer, conductor, Bellf. R. R.

Ward Lucinda, (wid.) res 262 Ind. ave.

Ward Merrit, Gov. teamster, bds 176 Mass. ave.

WARE DR. C. J., off. Market, opp. P. O.

Ware Robert, conductor, Peru R. R., bds 75 South.

Wanger William, res 217 n N. Jersey.

Waring Frank T., book keeper, Chase & Dawes, bds n Del.

Warman Enoch, farmer, res w Indianapolis.

Warnell George, painter, bds 23 Ind. ave.

Warren Charles, retailer of liquors, res 66 n Miss.

Warner Charles G., printer, res 69 n Del.

Warner George, works foundry, res 109 e McCarthy.

Warner John, brakesman, on T. & R. R. R., bds Union House.

Warner Thomas, pressman, Journal office, res n Del.

Warner Wallace, brickmason, res 182 e N. York.

Warren George S., salesman, Fancy Bazaar, bds Macy House.

Warriner Marcus, bds Little's Hotel.

Warnburg Wellington, laborer, res 243 n N. Jersey.

Warter William, butcher, res e Market, near Cady.

Washington Miss Alice, res 53 n East.

Washington Charles, carpenter, res 86 Huron.

In buying the Florence you get the worth of your money.

Washington Foundry, (Lewis W. Hasselman, Almus E. Vinton,) opposite e end Union depot.

Washington Hall, 78 w Wash.

Washington House, 83 s Md.

Wasment Louis, tailor, res Keely's block, bet New York and Ohio.

Wasper Marks, machinist, res 142 McCarthy.

Waters John G., res 16 w Mich.

Waters Samuel D., laborer, res Bluff road, Doughertyville.

Watkins George A., clerk, Palmer House saloon, res same.

Watson Elmer, photographer, 26 and 28 w Wash.

Watson James, tailor, 86 e Wash., bds Farmers' Hotel.

Watson James, engineer, bds 5 Forest ave.

Watson J. M., machinist, res National road, e Pogue's run.

Watson Joseph S., printer, Sheets', res 127 w Md.

Watson Robert H., railroader, res 99 Meek.

Watson Samuel W., book keeper, Harrison's bank, res 73 w Wash.

Watson William, tin, sheet iron and coppersmith, bds Edward Hotel.

Watters John, res 16 w Mich.

Waugh Harrison, teamster, bds 105 n Tenn.

Wawich Henry, laborer, res 25 Harrison.

Way Truman, road master, Peru R. R., res 115 McCarthy.

Weakley Joseph, soldier, 73 n N. Jersey.

Weakly Mrs. Mary, (wid.) res 73 n New Jersey.

Weakly Jerry A., salesman, A. D. Wood, res 97 w N. York.

Wenner John, (Matthew & Weaner,) U. S. saloon, bds Mikle's brewery.

Weathers Michael, laborer, 137 e New York.

Weaver Charles C., (Weaver & Maguire,) res 79 n Ill.

Weaver Edwin, saddler, res 172 s Ala.

Weaver Frederick, laborer, res 173 R. R.

Weaver Henry, moulder, res 350 s Del.

Weaver William W.,(Weaver & Williams,) res 147 n Ill.

Weaver William, fruit dealer, cor West and Md., res 40 w La.

WEAVER & MAGUIRE, (Charles C. Weaver, Henry P.Maguire,) GROCERY AND PROVISION STORE, 1 Ind. ave.

WEAVER & WILLIAMS, (William H. Weaver, Charles Williams,) UNDERTAKERS, 72 w Wash.

Webb Calvin F., student at Bryant's Com. Col., bds n Penn.

Webb John, student at Bryant's Com. Col., bds Little's Hotel.

Webb Mary, (wid.) res 69 s Penn.

Webb William, blacksmith and wagon factory, Mt. Jackson.

Webur Frederick, laborer, res 173 R. R.

Webster George C., clerk, China tea store, res cor Penn. and Md.

Webster Harvey, fireman Marion engine house, res 43 Mass. eve.

Weekly Jeremiah, tinner, res 97 w New York.

Weeks Richard, works for Munson & Johnston, res Wabash, bet N. Jersey and East.

Weeks William H., wholesale and retail grocer and commission house, 31 s Meridian, bds Palmer House.

Wefrink William, tailor, bds station house.

Weghorst Henry, gardner, s e part city.

Weglin James, clerk, Simon & Dernham, 1 w Wash., bds e Wash., near Blind Asylum.

Wehle Lukas, shoe store 197 e Wash., res same.

Wehling Chas., wagon maker, res 19 s Alabama.

Wehn Christ., currier, res 234 Madison ave.

Weibbel John E., barber, 12 n Ill., res 188 n Ill.

Weigand Louis, paper angent, res 12 s Ala.

Wrig'e Gotleib, currier, 65 n Noble.

Weiglein Henry F., Franklin House, 46 and 48 s Meridian..

Weinkert John, clerk, J. H. Vagan, bds Pyle House.

Weiland Christ., switchman, Central depot, res 20 Union.

Weinbarger Herman, clerk, John C. Weinbarger, res 59 s Meridian.

WEINBARGER JOHN C.,CONFECTIONER AND RESTAURANT KEEPER, 10 w Lou., res 15 w Georgia.

WEINBARGER & MATLER, (John C. Weinbarger, Louis P. Matler,) ¦NEWS, PERIODICAL AND FANCY DEALERS, in Union R. R. Depot.

Weis Peter, boot and shoemaker shop, 61 Madison ave., res same.

Weisner Christopher, brewer, Yoming

Weivel Edward, barber, res 188 n Ill.

Welch John, conductor, Jeffersouville R. R., bds Ray House, s Del.

Welch John, laborer, Peru R. R., res bet Ohio and New York.

Welch Judson, forage master, Nashville, Tenn., res 111 n Meridian.

Welch Pat., bar tender, Exchange Restaurant, bds Macy House.

Welking Henry, shoemaker, res 37 n Noble.

Wells Dr. M., dentist, res 4 Yohns Block, bds 68 e Vermont.

Wells Dr. G. A., dentist, over Harrisons' bank, bds Bates House.

The Takeup for thread the best in use, because it is perfectly uniform.

Wells Wm. F., saw mill, 1es 85 e N. York.

Wells Wm. M., works Sentinel office, bds Palmer House.

Welsh James, boiler maker, Sinker & Vance, bds Washington House.

Weltz Chas., confectioner, 43 n Ill., res n Liberty.

Wender Philip, U. S. service, res 58 Hosbrook.

Wenger Frank, bds 20 n Noble.

Wenger Geo. M., saloon, n Noble, res same.

Wenner Geo., stone cutter, bds Union House.

Wenner Jacob J., city expressman, res 172 e Ohio.

Wentze W. W., conductor, I. & C. R. R., res 119 s Ala.

Werbe Christopher G., notary public, Market, bet Railroad and Davidson.

Werbe Louis F., grocery and provision store 185 w Wash.

Werden Elias, (Werden & Co.,) res Pittsfield Mass.

Werden & Co., (Elias Werden, Daniel G. Williams,) wholesale booksellers, stationers and wall paper, 26 e Wash.

Werker Jacob, machinist, Sinker & Vance, res s Del.

Wert Franklin, tinner, bds 63 n Ala.

Wert Joseph, boot and shoemaker, 6 s Meridian, res 63 n Ala.

Wesling Conrad, drayman, res Mich., bet Noble and Railroad.

West Frank, artist, 33 w Wash., bds Bates House.

West Geo. H., clerk, Gov. office, res 49 w Michigan.

Westover Johathan M., moulder, Roots foundry, res 64 Merrill.

Wetsoll Geo., bds Littles Hotel.

WESTERN MACHINE SHOP, SINKER & VANCE, s Penn.

WERSTERN UNION TELEGRAPH CO., n w cor Wash. and Meridian, John F. Wallick, manager,.

WESTERN SCHOOL BOOK HOUSE, Odd Fellows Hall.

Weymouth Amos, blacksmith, res 160 McCarthy.

Whaland Mrs., bds 17 e Market.

Wheatley John, book keeper, bds 108 e Ohio.

Wheatley Wm. M., (McCord & W.,) res 108 e Ohio.

Wheeler Ephriam, (col.) barber, res 143 e New York.

Wheeler James H., teacher of singing, music room, Temperance Hall, w Wash.

Wheeler W. R., bds Littles Hotel.

WHEELER & WILSON, SEWING MACHINES, Wm. Summer & Co., agents, office, 17½ w Wash.

Whilan Thomas, carpenter, bds Lingertfelters.

Whipple Chas. W., machinist, res 44 e Louisiana.

Whitesell Wm. H., student, at Bryant's Commercial College.

White Alonzo M., school teacher, res 159 n East.

White Chas., laborer, res 47 w Georgia.

White Jacob, laborer, res 135 Bluff Road.

White James, works Rolling Mill, bds Willard,

White James, (col.) teamster, res 11 n Harris.

White Joseph, resident farmer, res 120 n Noble.

White Richard, laborer, res Michigan Road.

White Sarah, (wid., Samuel E. White,) res 67 n Miss.

White Susan A., (wid.) res 135 McCarthy.

White Thomas, works at Rolling Mill, bds on Williard.

White Washington, (col.) porter, res 57 w Georgia.

Whitehead Halsey, carriage maker, bds 74 n Tenn.

Whitehead Thos., miller, res w National Road.

Whitehead Thos., carpenter, res 188 cor s Ala., and Merrill.

Whitehouse Wm. C., carpenter, res 141 w Market.

Whiteman Peter, wood chopper, res 155 Railroad.

Whiting John, switchman, res cor Meek and Noble.

Whitley Pat., laborer, bds on Williard.

Whitney Chas. C., telegraph operator, res cor New York and Del.

Whitney Theopolis, carpenter, res 98 s Maryland.

WHITCOMB JEROME G., FREIGHT AGENT, Jeffersonville and Indianap'ls R. R., res 60 e Market.

Whitridge Samuel, painter, bds 181 n N. Jersey.

Whitridge Wm., house and sign painter and stencil cutter, 82 e Wash., res 181 n N. Jersey.

Whitset Courtland, Capt. U. S. A., res 244 Vir. ave.

Whitset Isaac, bricklayer, res 244 Vir. ave.

Whitset John A., U. S. service, res 244 Vir. ave.

Whitsitt John B., engineer, on I & C. R. R., res 16 n N. Jersey.

Whitsit Peter B., bricklayer, bds 244 Vir. ave.

Whittenberg Chas., (K. & W.,) res 111 e Ohio.

Whittemore John B., engineer, Central R. R., res 53 Davidson.

Wick Wm. W., attorney at law, res 33 Ind. ave.

The demand for the Florence is much greater than can be supplied.

Indianapolis and Madison

1863. **1863.**

RAIL ROAD.

New arrangement to commence Monday, Feb. 2d, 1863·

TWO PASSENGER TRAINS DAILY,

(SUNDAYS EXCEPTED,) BETWEEN

INDIANAPOLIS AND MADISON.

Leave the Union Depot, Indianapolis, at 6.30 A. M., and 3.00 P. M., arriving at Madison at 11.35 A. M. and 7.50 P. M.

Leave the Depot at Madison at 6.00 A. M. and 3.00 P. M., arriving at Indianapolis at 11.00 A. M. and 7.50 P. M.

The train leaving Indianapolis at 6.30 A. M., connects with that leaving Columbus at 8.45 A. M. for Shelbyville and Rushville, arriving at Shelbyville at 10.35 A. M., and Rushville at 12.30 P. M.

Leaving Rushville at 1.30 P. M., Shelbyville at 2.55 P. M., connects at Columbus with the I. & M. train, arriving at either Indianapolis or Madison, the same evening.

This Road forms a line with the Packets at Madison, for the

TRANSPORTATION OF FREIGHT

Between Cincinnati, Indianapolis and points West.

TARIFF OF FREIGHTS AS LOW AS BY ANY OTHER ROUTE.

Shippers and Merchants West, will find it to their interest to ship by this line.

D. C. BRANHAM, Superintendent.

INDIANAPOLIS AND CINCINNATI

SHORT — **LINE**

RAIL ROAD.

Shortest Route by 30 Miles.

The Only Route Without Change of Cars.

Three Trains leave Indianapolis daily, on the arrival of Trains from Peru Lafayette and Terre Haute.

Through to Cincinnati in Advance of all other Routes.

Connecting at Cincinnati with all the Great Eastern and Southern Railroad Lines, and with Steamers on the Ohio River.

The Line of the Indianapolis and Cincinnati Railroad commences at Indianapolis, the Capital of Indiana, and passing through the towns of

SHELBYVILLE, GREENSBURG, LAWRENCEBURG AND NORTH BEND,

(In view of the Residence and Tomb of the late General Harrison,) terminates at Cincinnati, the Queen City of the West.

This road was projected with a view to accommodate the travel and trafic, which, coming from the North-West, seeks, throughthe Railroad City, (Indianapolis,) a direct avenue to the great Commercial Metropolis of the West.

For this purpose the two cities have been connected by a direct line of Railroad of uniform guage, 110 miles in length, built in a style second to no other road in the Union, being first class in all its equipments for the transportation of passengers and freight in the shortest time and at low rates.

With favorable and reliable arrangements with all connecting Roads, throughout the entire West, this Line guarantees unusual care and the amplest accommodations to its patrons.

SLEEPING CARS ATTACHED TO ALL NIGHT TRAINS.

☞The Company's exclusive Telegraph Line is used, when necessary, to govern the movement of Trains, and Loughridge's celebrated Patent Car Brakes are attached to all Passenger trains, by which they can be perfectly controlled; besides all the other modern improvements necessary for the comfort and safety of Passengers, the managers of this road have liberally provided.

☞FARE THE SAME AS BY ANY OTHER ROUTE.☜

BAGGAGE CHECKED THROUGH.

H. C. LORD, President.

W. H. L. NOBLE, Gen'l Ticket Agent.

PERU & INDIANAPOLIS

1863.

Rail Road.

This Road is seventy-five miles in length, runs through the center of Marion, Hamilton, Howard and Miami Counties, and extends from Indianapolis to Peru, passing through the flourishing towns of Noblesville, Cicero, Tipton, Sharpesville and Kokomo, connecting at Peru with the Toledo & Wabash Rail Way, for Wabash, Huntington, Ft. Wayne, Toledo and Detroit, forming the most direct route to those points. Also, makes close connections at Kokomo with trains on the C. & C. Air Line R. R., for Logansport, Valparaiso and Chicago. This route is shorter by 32 miles, and two hours quicker than any other route to Chicago, and all points in the North-west.

Splendid State-room Sleeping Cars have been recently put on, and are being run through to Chicago. The trains on this Road make close connections at Indianapolis with Trains on

JEFFERSONVILLE AND INDIANAPOLIS,

TERRE HAUTE & RICHMOND,

Indiana Central.

And the other numerous Railroads diverging from Indianapolis, for all points East, South and West.

Freight and Passengers carried as low as by any other Route.

This route is 62 miles shorter to the Lakes from Indianapolis, than by any other road. The Company have added largely to to their rolling stock during the past year, and now have excellent facilities for transporting Freight and Passengers. The road is in excellent running condition, and is a safe and reliable route.

DISTANCES.

INDIANAPOLIS to	Miles.		Miles.
James' Switch	6	Sharpsville	46
Phipp's	9	Fairfield	49
Castleton	11	Kokomo	54
New Britton	17	Cassville	59
Noblesville	22	Miamitown	63
Cicero	28	Leonda	69
Arcadia	31	Peru	75
Buena Vista	34	Ft. Wayne	131
Tipton	39	Toledo	225
Jackson's Mill	42	Chicago	184

OFFICERS.

DAVID MACY, General Agent and Superintendent,
C. B. ROBINSON, Assistant Superintendent.
V. T. MALOTT, Secretary, Treasurer and General Ticket Agent.
L. N. ANDREWS, General Freight Agent.
F. GILMAN, Master Machinest.

TERRE HAUTE AND RICHMOND

RAIL ROAD

Trains leave Terre Haute for Indianapolis, daily, (Sundays excepted,) as follows:

First Express Train,

Leaves Terre Haute at 1.50 A. M., and arrives at Indianapolis at 4.45 A. M.

Second Express Train,

Leaves Terre Haute at 3.50 P. M., and arrives at Indianapolis at 6.45 P. M.

These Trains make close connections at Indianapolis with Trains for

NEW YORK, BOSTON, PHILADELPHIA, BALTIMORE,

Washington City, Cincinnati, Louisville, &c.

Mail Train,

Leaves Terre Haute at 7.20 A. M., and arrives at Indianapolis at 10.32 A. M.; stops at all way stations, connects at Indianapolis with Trains for

CINCINNATI, CLEVELAND, COLUMBUS AND MADISON.

☞ Passengers will please procure tickets before entering the cars. Through Tickets for all the Eastern Cities, &c., to be had at the Ticket Office. Four Freight Trains leave daily, except Sunday.

FREIGHT ARRANGEMENTT.

Quick time is made by Express Freight Trains, from St. Louis to the East. Only one change between St. Louis and Pittsburg, Buffalo and Cleveland. Stock Shippers will find this the most Superior Route to the East. Any arrangements can be made with James Beebe, corner of Second and Poplar Streets, St. Louis, Missouri, in Valentine & Co's Freight House.

R. E. RICKER, Superintendent.

CHAS. WOOD, Secretary.

THE GREAT
CENTRAL ROUTE.

1863. 1863.

Indianapolis and Columbus
SHORT LINE.

Two Daily Trains to Columbus, Ohio.

Indiana Central Railway.

This line is the Great Central Short Line from St. Louis to Dayton, Columbus, Pittsburg, Cleveland, New York, Boston, and all intermediate points, and is the most desirable route in its facilities and accommodations to passengers and shippers.

Passengers having tickets via this route, can take choice of the four Great Eastern Lines.

Only One Change of Cars between Indianapolis,

PITTSBURG, WHEELING AND CLEVELAND,

Being of Uniform guage with all Railroads East of Indianapolis, this route offers unparalleled inducements to Shippers of Live Stock and Freight.

Passengers desiring to take advantage of the Short line, must be particular to call for tickets via

INDIANAPOLIS AND COLUMBUS,

The only direct route to Zanesville, Newark, Steubenville, Pittsburg, Wheeling, &c.

CINCINNATI,

The only route through Richmond, Hamilton, &c. Two daily trains connect at Cincinnati with Kentucky Central Railroad for Cynthiana, Lexington and Paris. Also, with River Packets for Parkersburg, Marietta, &c.

SECURE YOUR TICKETS VIA INDIANA CENTRAL.

J. A. PERKINS, Gen'l Ticket Agent.

H. G. CAREY, Superintendent.

MUSIC STORE.

Indiana Piano-Forte Wareroom,

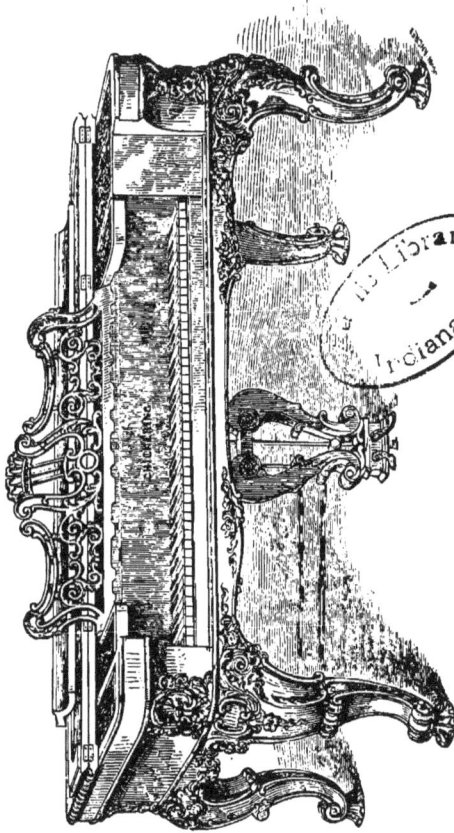

WILLARD & STOWELL.

No. 4 Bates House,

INDIANAPOLIS, INDIANA.

Jeffersonville
RAIL ROAD.

The Great Southern United States Mail and Express Route

FROM INDIANAPOLIS
TO THE
South and South-West,
VIA LOUISVILLE, KENTUCKY,

Connecting with Trains on the

Louisville and Nashville Rail Road,
AND WITH
Louisville and Memphis, and Louisville and New Orleans

LINE PACKETS,

For Nashville, Chattanooga, Memphis, Vicksburg, Jackson, Hunts-
ville, New Orleans, and all the Principal Southern Cities.

TWO TRAINS LEAVE INDIANAPOLIS DAILY,
(SUNDAYS EXCEPTED.)

Passengers from the North, East and West, will find the route by the way of In-
dianapolis & Jeffersonville Railroad, the most expeditious route to the Principal
Cities in the West and South-west.
THROUGH TICKETS sold in all the principal Railroad and Ticket Offices in the
Eastern and Northern States. Remember the route, via Indianapolis and Louis-
ville, via Jeffersonville Railroad.

D. RICKETTS, President.

A. S. GROTHERS, Superintendent.

H. H. REYNOLDS, Gen'l Ticket Agent.

J. G. WHITCOMB, Agent, Indianapolis.

Wideman Joseph M., carpenter, bds Ind. ave.

Wielker Henry, drayman, res 153 old Bellefontaine R. R.

Wiedenhorn Rosa, hair braider, res 46 e Market.

Wieland Chas., laborer, res 32 Union Depot.

Wiener John, saloon keeper, bds 135 w Maryland.

Wien Chas., carpenter, res 145 e Ohio.

Wiggin Chas. P., (Wiggins & Chandler,) bds Bates House.

Wiggins Henry D., works in foundry, res 122 Ohio.

Wiggins & Chandler, (Chas. P. Wiggins, Thomas E. Chandler,) founders and machinists, 262 Wash.

Wightman Theodore, Lieut. U. S. A., res 38 n East.

Wilcox Wm. B., cabinet maker, res 169 s Delaware.

Wilcox Wm. H., res 217 n Ill.

Wilcox Chas. D., machinist, res 71 Spring.

WILDE & HENNINGER, (Otto J. Wilde & Edward Henninger,) FANCY BAZAAR STORE, 71 s Ill. See card.

Wiles Thomas, stoneware dealer, bds 35 n Liberty.

Wiley Delaney, physician and surgeon, 3 e Market, res 26 e Market.

Wiley Wm. Y., (Wiley & Martin,) res 32 e N. York.

WILEY & MARTIN, (Wm. Y. Wiley & L. R. Martin,) REAL ESTATE AGENTS, DEALERS IN LAND WARRANTS, STOCKS, &c., 10½ e Wash. See card, inside back cover.

Wilhelm August, works in Mansur's pork house, res 127 w Ver.

Wilhelm Carle, cabinet maker, res 9 n Liberty.

Wilkes Thomas A., grocery, n East, near Ver., res 155 Mass. ave.

Wilking Henry, shoemaker, res 37 n Noble.

Wilkins Albert, laborer, res 205 n Noble.

Wilkins John, bible depository, res 34 e Market.

Wilkins Peter, city policeman, res 219 n N. Jersey.

Wilkinson Meredith M., carpenter, res Cal., bet Market and Wash.

Wilkinson Wm., livery and sale stable, res 31 n Del.

Wilkinson & Sullivan, livery stable, 10 e Pearl.

Willard Albert B, dealer in satinett and jeans, warps and machine cards, 4 Bates House, res 66 e N. York.

Willard Albert G., (Willard & Stowell,) res 92 Mass. ave.

Willard Wm., teacher, deaf and dumb asylum, e Indianapolis.

WILLARD & STOWELL, (Albert G. Willard & Myron A. Stowell,) WHOLESALE AND RETAIL DEALERS IN MUSIC AND MUSICAL INSTRUMENTS, 4 Bates House.

Willhum Christ., laborer, Peru depot, res 165 Ala.

Williams Charles, carpenter, res 9 n Liberty.

Williams Charles, (Weaver & Williams,) res 20 w Mich.

Williams David, works at rolling mill, res 13 Union.

Williams David, boiler maker, Sinker & Vance, bds n Miss. -

Williams Daniel G., (Werden & Co.,) res 138 n East.

Williams David J., blacksmith, res 136 n Miss.

Williams Edwin M., student at Purdy's commercial college, res 20 n Pennsylvania.

Williams Evan K., works at rolling mill, res Willard, near rolling mill.

Williams Freeman, works in Madison depot, res 38 w Market.

Williams Rev. Gibbon, res 133 n East.

Williams George, (col) teamster, res cor East and St. Clair.

Williams Hubbard, painter, res cor Huron and Noble.

Williams Jacob T., book binder, res 46 n California.

Williams John, works at rolling mill, res s Mich., s of South.

Williams Lafayette, salesman, Werden & Co., bds 204 Mass. ave.

Williams Nellie H., dressmaker, 22 s Ill., res same.

Williams Owen, general agent, res 134 n Ill.

Williams Miss Sue, res 51 and 53 n Liberty.

Williams Thomas, teamster, res 53 Huron.

Williams Wm., (col) barber, McCoy's, bds 145 w Wash.

Williams Wm., tailor, 204 Mass. ave.

Williams Wm. D., salesman, 26 and 28 w Wash., bds 20 s Miss. :

Williamson Frank, porter in Oriental House.

Williamson Hiram, farmer, res w Indianapolis.

Williamson James S., hostler, bds 20 n Penn.

Williamson Levi B., (Williamson & Haugh,) res out corporation.

Williamson Marshall D., furniture and lumber dealer, res 114 n East.

WILLIAMSON & HAUGH, (Levi B. Williamson & Emanuel Haugh,) IRON RAILING AND BANK VAULTS, 2 n Del.

Willard Wm., clerk, res 180 Vir. ave.

Willits Josiah, cooper, res w Wash.

Never mind what others' say about the Florence, come and see it.

Wilmington Edward M., deputy auditor, court house, res 113 n N. Jersey.

Willson Charles G., carriage painter, res 174 s Miss.

Willson Mrs. L. A., (wid) res 45 Lou.

Willson Obediah H., student at Bryant's commercial college, bds D. Yandes.

Wilmot Caroline, (wid) res 175 e South.

Wilmot Samuel, (Wilmot & Thayer,) res 115 n Penn.

WILMOT & THAYER, (Samuel Wilmot & Selden Thayer,) DEALERS IN HATS, CAPS AND FURS, 8 w Wash.

Wilson Abner A., pressman, Journal office, res 134 e Market.

Wilson Alfred J., marble mantle manufacturer, 10 n Del., res same.

Wilson Coleman, telegraph operator, T. H. & R. R. R., res n Ill.

Wilson Charles, in Wood & Foudry's livery stable, res Elizabeth.

Wilson David H., Deputy Treasurer of State, bds 23 Ind. ave.

Wilson Edward, wood chopper, res w Market.

Wilson Mrs. E. G., res 15 s Ill.

Wilson Geo. S., clerk, 72 w Wash., bds Pyle House.

Wilson Israel, (Beard, Binkley & Wilson,) res 191 n Ill.

Wilson James, carpenter, res Michigan road.

Wilson James, marble polisher, bds 10 n Del.

Wilson James, brakesman, C. & I. R. R., res 59 w Lou.

Wilson Jeremiah, laborer, res Bluff road, Doughertyville.

Wilson John, laborer, res 128 w Ga.

Wilson John B., hardware and house furnishing goods, 59 w Wash., res 266 n Ill.

Wilson John, saw maker, Sheffield works, res 174 s Miss.

Wilson John, (col.) hostler, bds Browns.

Wilson John S., carpenter, res n East, bet Market and Ohio.

Wilson Joseph C., clerk, shoe store, bds n Penn., outside corporation.

Wilson James A., painter, res 58 Ind. ave.

Wilson Pat., switchman, Bellefontain R. R., res 196 s Del.

Wilson Lazarus B., res 63 w Maryland.

Wilson Stephen, plasterer, res 254 Madison ave.

Wilson Thos. W., U. S. service, res 114 s N. Jersey.

Wilson Thos. H., clerk, 59 w Wash., bds 266 n Ill.

Wilson Wm., watchman, Madison depot, res 172 s Del.

Winchel Elizabeth A., (wid, Peter Winchel,) res 99 n Meridian.

Wingate E. H., clerk, J. T. Wingate, 27 w Wash., res 141 Vir. ave.

WINGATE J. T., WHOLESALE AND RETAIL GROCER, 27 w Wash., res country.

Wingate Wm., Plaining Mill, res 91 Vir. ave.

Winkle Fred., flour and feed, 157 e Wash., res 70 St Joseph.

Winser John A., student at Bryant's Commercial College, bds in Gazette building.

Winsor John, upholsterer, res cor Bates and Cady.

Winter David E., painter, res 122 e Market.

Wirth John R., works 84 w Wash.

Wirtz Jacob, horse doctor, res 72 e South.

Wise Wm., agent Dayton ale, 74 w Wash., res 94 n Ill.

Wiseman Mrs. Margaret, res 243 w Wash.

Wiseman Simeon S., teamster, res 245 w Wash.

Wiseman Wm., laborer, res 82 e Meek.

Wishard Milton M., druggist, City Hospital, res same.

Wishmire Anthony, laborer, res 148 e Ohio.

Wishmier Christ. F., resident farmer.

Wissert John, city expressman, res 118 e Market.

Withoff Henry, cabinet maker, res 30 s East.

Witcner Daniel, laborer, res 163 s Tenn.

Witmer John K., stone cutter, res 28 w North.

WITT BENNETT F., ATTORNEY FOR SOLDIERS, AND UNITED STATES CLAIM AGENT, s w cor Wash. and Meridian, bds Pyle House. See card.

Witte Lewis S., teller Branch Bank, bds S. Beck's, s Del.

Wittenberg Charles(Kause & Wittenberg,) res 111 e Ohio.

Witzman John, teamster, res 183 e Vt.

Woebz Charles A., confectioner, res Mich., bet Liberty and Noble.

Woerner Philip, groceries, liquors and wines, 78 w Wash., res same.

Woerner Philip F., clerk 73 w Wash., bds same.

Woley Joseph, fireman on I. & C. R. R., bds Ray House, s Del.

Wolf Charles, dyeing, &c., e Wash., res alley, n State House.

Wolf Moses, res 100 n Ill.

Wolfe Adam, bar keeper, Jefferson House, bds same.

Wolfe Charles, secondhand clothing store, 93 e Wash., res Tenn.

WOLFE GEORGE W., PROPRIETOR CINCINNATI HOUSE, 124 s Del. See card.

Wolfe Robert, gun smith, bds 30 Ky. ave.

Wolfenston Girard, bar keeper, bds Ft. Donaldson saloon.

The Florence Sewing Machine never refuses to work.

Wolfram A. T., printer, bds 101 n New Jersey.

Wolfram C. A., printer, bds 101 n N. Jersey.

Wolfrom Christian, tinner, res 101 n N. Jersey.

Wolfram Earnest, assistant book keeper, Indianapolis Branch Banking Co., res 151 n New Jersey.

Wolfram Sarah, res 101 n New Jersey.

Walls Henry, res 96 North.

Woltze William E., watch maker and jewelrer, 164 e Wash., res same.

Worland W., grocery and feed store, cor Va. ave and Del.

Woocher Ferdinand, (Egner & Woocher,) bds Union Hall.

Wood ——, carpenter, res St. Joseph, bet Penn. and Meridian.

Wood Alexander, grocery and provisions, 129 n Ill., res 127 n Ill.

Wood Augustus D., wholesale and retail hardware, 64 e Wash., res 79 n Del.

Wood Rev. D., res 240 s Ala.

Wood Ely, (Wood & Davis,) res n East.

Wood Jacob S., cooper, w Vt.

Wood James, paper maker, Sheets' mills, res s Penn.

Wood John B., res 172 Blake.

Wood John E., (Wood & Foudry,) res 53 n Penn.

Wood John F., clerk, res 36 n East.

Wood John M., livery and sale stable, res 53 Mass. ave.

Wood Levi, M. D., Eclectic, res 99 n New Jersey.

Wood Sarah, (wid.) res 57 n Pennsylvania.

Wood William, inspector of stock U. S. A., res 140 n Penn.

Wood William D., saddler, 20 w Wash., res cor Ill. and Vt.

Wood & Davis, (Ely Wood, Levi Davis,) butchers, 59 e Wash.

Wood & Foudry, (John M. Wood, John E. Foudry,) livery and sale stable, 10 n Penn.

Woods F., laborer, res 188 East.

Woods James, city engineer, off. 4 2d floor Glens' block, res 109 n Ill.

Woods William, brick mason, res w Indiannapolis.

WOODBRIDGE CHARLES A., QUEENS-WARE, CHINA AND GLASSWARE, 16 w Wash., res 87 n Tennessee. See card.

Woodbridge John, clerk, 16 w Wash., bds 87 n Tenn.

Woodruff John, carpenter, res 47 w Georgia.

Wool Mrs. Sophia., (wid.) res w Indianapolis.

Woolen T. W., (Ray & Woolen,) attorneys at law, New & Talbott's building, bds Bates House.

Woolen Mrs. Thomas, res 93 New Jersey.

Woolen William J., cabinet maker, bds 169 n Miss.

Woolen William M., grocery and provision store, res 82 w Vt.

Woolen William W., attorney at law, 43½ e Wash., res 110 n Meridian.

Woolen Milton, constable, res 149 n West.

Worland Simon B , student, Purdy's Com· Col., bds 44 s Penn.

Worland William, groceries, hay, feed, &c., 37 Va. ave., res same.

Wormesly John, tailor, res 58 e Vt.

Worth Alexander, Sec'y I. & C. R. R., res 246 s Ala.

Wort August, brewer, C. F. Schmidt's brewery.

Wortman Gernand, laborer, res 340 s Del.

Wren Edward, wagon maker, res 51 s N. Jersey.

Wrenn John, carpenter, res 192 s Delaware.

Wright Arthur L., Dep. Co. Treas., res 92 n Ala.

Wright Asa, trader, bds 33 n Ala.

Wright Benjamin, clerk, Lynch & Kean, bds 14 e Ohio.

Wright Charles, boarding house, 14 e Ohio.

Wright C. M., (Wright & Bro.,) res 136 s Noble.

Wright Charles, saloon keeper, 91 e Wash., res same.

Wright Charles A., real estate agent, note and stock broker, 30½ w Wash., bds Palmer House.

Wright Edward B.,clerk, New York Store, res 14 e Ohio.

Wright Frank, brewer of ale and porter, ag't for oysters, off. 20 s Meridian, res 112 n Miss.

Wright Herman, farmer, res w Indianapolis.

Wright Jacob T., Co. Auditor, court house' res 117 n Del.

Wright John C., grocer, res 30 n Meridian.

Wright Jesse, farmer, w Indianapolis.

Wright Mansur H.,physician and surgeon, res cor Meridian and Ohio, 12 e Market.

Wright Matilda, dressmaker, 33 n Alabama.

Wright Mary E.,dressmaker, 38½ w Wash., up stairs.

Wright Richard, foreman shoe shop Deaf and Dumb Asylum, res Orient.

Wright Silas, general ward master city hospital.

Wright Thomas, clerk, New York Store res e Ohio.

The Florence Machine is the perfection of mechanism.

WRIGHT THOS. C., GYMNASIUM, cor Maryland and Meridian, bds Palmer House.

Wright William G., pump maker, (Wright & Bro.,) res cor Huron and Pine.

Wright William H., express messenger Adams express,

Wright William M., book keeper, court house, bds 14 e Ohio.

Wright Wesly, (Wright & Writtenhouse,) res 33 n Ala.

Wright William H., messenger Adams Express Co., res n Ala.

WRIGHT & BRO., MANUFACTURERS OF WOODEN SUCTION PUMPS, Md., near Va. ave. See card.

WRIGHT & RITTENHOUSE, (Wesley Wright, Wm. Rittenhouse,) Charter Oak saloon, 15 n Ill.

Wrigley James, machinist, bds Farmers' Hotel.

Writtenhouse William, (Wright & Writtenhouse,) bds Oriental House.

Wualter William, shoemaker, bds Jefferson House.

Wundram William, tailor, res 63 e Wash., up stairs.

Wust John, wood turner, res 97 Ft. Wayne ave.

Wyck Felix A., carpenter, bds 119 n East.

Wycop George, engineer on Jeff. R. R., bds Ray House, s Del.

Wyland William, works pork house, res 69 Bluff road.

Wyse John, brickmason, res 152 n New Jersey.

Wysong Christopher, bricklayer, res s Ill.

Y

Yaeger Charles, City Brewery, res 189 s Penn.

Yaeger John, meat market, 200 e Wash., bds 48 n Liberty.

Yaeger Knott, butcher, 200 e Wash., res 48 n Liberty.

Yandes George B., (Yandes & Co.,) res 64 n Penn.

Yandes Daniel, (Yandes & Co.,) res 80 c Market. .

Yandes & Co., (Daniel Yandes, George B. Yandes,) wholesale hide and leather dealers, 38 e Wash.

Yarbrough Peter, railroader, res 27 Meek.

Yarver Francis, carpenter, res e Vermont.

Yasper Hermon, laborer, Wyoming.

Yeager Christ, grocer, liquor and produce dealer, 215 c Wash., res same.

Yeager William, cooper, res 166 n Noble.

Yeaman Mrs. Eliza, (wid.) res 27 Delaware.

Yewell Solomon, clerk, Mansur & Furgason's pork house, res 195 s Pennsylvania.

Yohn's Block, n e cor Wash and Meridian.

Yohn James C., Paymaster, res 74 n Delaware.

Yolkaneng Charles, laborer, 119 South.

York Henry, agent Fairbank's scales, 74 w Wash., bds Bates House.

Yost Thomas, stone mason, bds 69 w South.

Young Charles, bar tender, 15 n Ill., bds s Miss.

Young Christian, pattern maker, res 7 Ellsworth.

Young D. D., last maker, bds 159 Va. ave.

Young George D., machinist, res 68 s New Jersey.

Young Henry H., publisher Ind. School Journal, Journal office, res 120 n East.

Young Mrs. Hetty N., res 11 s Miss.

Young Nelson R., book keeper, Model Mills, bds 122 n Ill.

Youngerman Charles, blacksmith, res 16 n Del.

Youngerman Charles F., stone cutter, res 168 s Del.

Youngerman George, Youngerman's saloon, cor Wash and Del., res 209 e Wash.

Youngerman Mrs. Mary, (wid.) res Mass. ave.

Youtsey Thomas, turner, res. 229 s East.

Z

Zehringer Landilien, cabinet maker, res 81 Davidson.

Zeigler Alexander, carpenter, res 69 n Noble.

Zeigler Nelson, salesman, Boston Store, bds 71 n Penn.

Zeigler William, proprietor Boston Store, 10 e Wash., res 71 n Penn.

Zellers Henry, mattrass maker, Mo., bet. Market and Ohio.

Zimmer Ferdinand, saloon, 128 e Wash., res same.

Zimmerman Christian, gravel roofing, res 130 e Market.

Zimmerman Christopher, slate and gravel roofer, res 130 e Market.

Zimmerman George, patent roofing, bet Ala. and New Jersey, near Little's Hotel.

Zoble Charles, carpenter, bds 122 Davidson.

Zoble Henry, chair maker, bds 122 Davidson.

Zorger George, clerk in Head-quarters, cor Md. and Del., bds 113 Massachusetts ave.

Zumbush Theodore, watch maker, res 128 s Del., up stairs.

There is no wire rigging to get out of order about the Florence.

STREET DIRECTORY.

The leading Streets are named East, West, North and South, taking Meridian Street for one basis, and Washington for the other. The Streets printed in Capitals are the most important ones in the City.

Agnes, N. and S., N. W. of city.

ALABAMA, N. and S., three blocks E. of Circle.

Ann, from Rolling Mill to McCarty.

Arch, from Jackson to Noble, N.E. of city.

Arizonia, S. of Utah.

Ash, N. of Car Works, N. E of city.

Athon, from Rhode Island to Ind. ave.

Burnhill, from North to Davis.

Bates, from Noble to eastern limits, S. of city.

Benton, from Harrison to Central Track, E. of Noble.

Bicking, from Delaware to East, S. of city.

Blackford, from New York to North, three blocks W. of Canal.

Blake, N. and S., from Washington to Ind. ave., near W. limits.

Bright, from New York to North, N. W. of city.

Broadway, N. of Car Works, N. E. of city.

Buchanan, S. E. of city, three blocks N. of Morris.

Cady, from Harrison to Central Track, E of Benton.

California, from New York to North, two blocks W. of Canal.

Catharine, from West to Canal, S of Merrill.

Cedar, Fletcher's Addition, S. E. of city.

Center, from Dunlop to Ellen, N. W. of city.

Charles, from St. Clair to Peru track.

Chatham, from Mass. ave. to St. Clair, E. of East.

Cherry, from Fort Wayne ave. to Ash, near Northern boundary.

Christian ave., 1 block N. of city limits.

Coburn, S. E. of city, 1 block N. of Morris.

Coe, from Fall Creek to Hiawatha, N. E.

Cottrell, from Georgia to Louisiana, W. of Canal, S. W.

Cross, from Peru Track to city line, N. E.

Curve, from Bellefontaine Car Works, N. E. to city limits.

Decota, from White River to Morris, W. of West.

Davidson, N. and S., E. of Railroad.

Davis, from N. W. city line to Fall Creek.

DELAWARE, N. and S., two blocks E of Circle.

Douglass, from New York to Michigan, N. W. of city.

Dougherty, S. E. of city, two blocks N. of Morris.

Duncan, from Delaware to New Jersey, continuation of Garden.

Dunlop, from Madison ave, 3 blocks S. of Morris.

East, N. and S., 5 blocks E. of Circle.

East Second, W. of city line.

Elizabeth, from Indiana ave. to Blake, N. W. of city.

Elk, Fletcher's Addition, S. E. of City.

Ellen, from North to Indiana ave.

Ellis, from Maryland to S. W. of West.

Elm, from Noble S. E. of Fletcher's Addition.

First, Northern city boundary.

Fifth, 5 blocks N. of city limits.

Fletcher's ave., Fletcher's Addidion, S. E of city.

Forest ave., Fletcher's Addition, S. E. of city.

Forest Home ave., S. of N. W. C. University.

FORT WAYNE AVENUE, from North running N. E. to city limits.

Fourth, 4 blocks N. of city limits.

Franklin, from Morris S. two blocks E. of Madison ave.

Garden, from Canal to Delaware, 6 blocks S. of Circle.

George, from Merrill to Garden, W. of Ill.

GEORGIA, E. and W., three blocks S. of Circle.

Greer, bet. McCarty and Virginia ave.

Grove, from Virginia ave. to city line.

Harris, N. and S., N. W. of city.

Harrison, from Noble to Eastern limits, S. of Ind. & C. R. R.

Henry, from Canal to Miss., S. of South.

High, from McCarty S., E. of Delaware.

Hosbrook, Fletcher's Add., S. E. of city.

Howard North, from First to Seventh, W. of Lafayette Railroad.

Howard South, from Morris S. E. of Madison ave.

The Florence sews rapidly.

Huron, Fletcher's Addition, S. E. of city.

ILLINOIS, N. and S., one block W. of Circle.

INDIANA AVENUE, N. W. Diagonal.

Jackson, N. of Car Works, N. E. of city.

James, N. W. of city.

Japan, from Morris S., three blocks E. of Madison ave.

John, from Peru track to city limits.

Kansas, from Bluff Road to West, S. of city line.

KENTUCKY AVENUE, S. W. Diagonal.

Liberty, N. and S, 6 blocks E. of Circle.

Lord, from Noble to Eastern limits, S. of I. & C. R. R.

LOUISIANA, E. and W., four blocks S. of Circle.

Loukabee, from East to liberty, bet. Vermont and New York.

McCarty, from River to Virginia ave., S. of city.

McGill, from Louisiana to South, W. of Mississippi.

McKernan, from Buchanan to Morris, 3 blocks E. of East.

Madison ave., from South to city line, S. E. Diagonal.

Margaret, S. side City Hospital.

Maria, from Smith to Locke.

MARKET, E. and W., through Circle.

MARYLAND, E. and W., two blocks S. of Circle.

MASSACHUSETTS AVENUE, N. E. Diagonal.

Maxwell, from North to Davis.

Meek, from Noble to Eastern limits, S. of Indiana Central R. R.

MERIDIAN, N. and S., through Circle.

Merrill, from Kentucky ave. to Vir. ave., seven blocks S. of Circle.

MICHIGAN, E. and W., four blocks N. of Circle.

MICHIGAN ROAD, N. E. and S. W., through the city.

Mill, from Fifth to Seventh, W. of Howard.

Minerva, N. and S., N. W. of city.

Minnesota, W. of Canal from Morris, S.

MISSISSIPPI, N. and S., three blocks W. of Circle.•

MISSOURI, N. and S., along Canal.

Morris, Southern boundary line.

Nebraska, from Madison ave. four blocks S. of Morris.

NEW JERSEY, N. and S., four blocks E. of Circle.

NEW YORK, E. and W., two blocks N. of Circle.

Noble, N. and S., seven blocks E. of Circle.

North ave., N. of N. W. C. University.

NORTH, E. and W., five blocks N. of Circle.

Oak, N. of Car Works, N. E. of city.

OHIO, E. and W., one block N. of Circle.

Orient, from Pennsylvania to Ft. Wayne ave., S. of St. Joseph.

Oxford, from Peru Track to city line.

Patterson, N. and S., N. W. of city.

PENNSYLVANIA, N. and S., one block E. of Circle.

Pine, Fletcher's Addition, S E. of city.

Pittsfield, continuation of Mill to Lafayette Railroad Track.

Plum, N. of Car Works, N. E of city.

Powell, from Michigan to North.

Pratt, from Illinois to Fort Wayne ave., N. of Blind Asylum.

Railroad Avenue, N. and S., between Pensylvania and S. Delaware.

Railroad Street, N. and S., along Bellefontaine R. R. track.

Ray, from Canal to Railroad, S. of city.

Rhode Island, from Blake to Western limits, N. of city.

St. Clair, from Indiana ave. to Massachusetts ave, N. of Blind Asylum.

St. Joseph, from Illinois to Fort Wayne ave., N. of Blind Asylum.

St. Mary, E. from Meridian, Northern city boundary.

School, from South to Virginia ave., W. of Noble.

Second, two blocks N. of city limits.

Seventh, seven blocks N. of city limits.

Short, from Morris to Dougherty, W. of Virginia ave.

Sinker, from Alabama to New Jersey.

Sixth, six blocks N. of city limits.

Smith, from Rhode Island to Indiana ave.

SOUTH, E. and W., five blocks S. of Circle.

TENNESSEE, N. and S., two blocks W. of Circle.

Texas, from Madison ave., W. six blocks S. of Morris.

Third, three blocks N. of city limits.

VERMONT, E. and W., three blocks N. of Circle.

Vine, from Jackson to Ash, N. E. of city.

VIRGINIA AVENUE, S. E. Diagonal.

Union, from McCarty to Morris, E. of Bluff Road.

University ave., E. of N. W. C. University.

Utah, S. of Wisconsin.

Walnut, from Canal to Massachusetts ave., N. of Blind Asylum.

WASHINGTON, E. and W., one block S. of Circle.

Watters, from McCarty to Virginia ave.

WEST, N. and S, one block W. of Canal.

Western ave., continuation of Fort Wayne ave.

Wilkins, from Canal to Railroad, S. of city.

Willard, from Garden to Merrill, W. of Tennessee.

Williams, between McCarty and Virginia ave.

Wilson, from Davis to North.

Beauty and utility are combined in the Florence.

BUSINESS MIRROR.

Containing the Name and Location of principal Business
Men in the City, under the Particular Trade or
Profession in which they are engaged.

Academy for Boys.

HAY'S ACADEMY, LAWRENCE G.
HAY, PRINCIPAL, 130 n Tenn.

Agricultural Implements.

Brinkley & Wilson, 85 w Wash.
CASE & MARSH, 86 w Wash.
STILTZ J. GEORGE, 74 e Wash.

Ale Agency.

Wise Wm., (Dayton Agency,) 74 w Wash.

Ambrotype Stock Dealer.

Crapo R. P., 17 w Wash.

Architects.

(*See also Builders.*)

Albon James, Journal building.
Bohlen David A., Ætna building.
Costigan Francis, Oriental House.
Curzon Joseph, Journal building.
Hodgson Isaac, 4 Yohn's block.
May Edwin, 75 n Penn.

Artists.

Bright C. E., 33 w Wash.
Cox Jacob, 42 s Meridian.

Attorneys at Law.

Barbour & Howland, 1½ w Wash.
Beal John A., 82 n East.
Brown A., 151 e South.
Brown Ignatius, 19½ e Wash.
Brown Philip A., 130 n N. Jersey.
Brown Robert D., office State House.
Bufkin John C., 43 e Wash.
CAMPBELL & HEWITT, 34 e Wash.
COLERICK & JORDAN, 18 e Wash.
Colley Sims A., 161 n N. Jersey.
Coulon Charles, 97 e Wash.
DAVIS & BOWLES, 3 New & Talbott's block.
Duncan Robert B., 50 e Wash.
DYE JOHN T., Blackford's building, cor Wash. and Merid.
Elliott Byron K., 24½ e Wash.
Ellsworth Henry, 88 n Meridian.

FERGUSON KILBY, 4 n Penn.
GORDON GEO. E., Odd Fellows' Hall.
HAMLIN & PROTZMAN, 16½ e Wash.
Hannah John, (U. S. Dist. Att'y,) P. O. building.
Harrison & Fishback, 62 e Wash.
HENDERSON WM., Ætna building.
HENDRICKS & HORD, Ætna building.
Hewitt Charles, 84 e Wash.
HOEFGEN SAM'L B., 15½ e Wash.
Holladay Elias G., Little's Hotel.
Johnson Isaac E., 4 Blake's row.
Ketcham Lewis, Blackford's building.
Kiger Harrison F., 15 P. O., 2d floor.
Leathers & Carter, 86 e Wash.
Lewis Joseph A., s w cor Wash & Merid.
McDONALD & PORTER, Yohn's block, cor. Merid. and Wash.
McDONALD & ROACHE, Ætna building, n Penn.
McKERNAN DAVID S., 8 w Wash.
Major Samuel, w Indianapolis.
Major Stephen, 19½ w Wash.
MAJOR & BROWN, Blackford's building
MARTINDALE & GRUBBS, 4 New & Talbott's block.
Milner John, 84 e Wash.
Morrison James, 24½ e Wash.
NEWCOMB & TARKINGTON, 24½ e Wash.
Patterson Wm., 152 e Ohio.
Perrin & Manlove, 45 e Wash.
Quimby Carlos W., 37 e Wash.
RAND & HALL, 24½ e Wash.
RAY & WOLLEN, New & Talbott's buildings, Penn.
Roberts Joseph T., National Hotel.
Smith John M., cor Ill. and Md.
Stagg Charles W., Temperance Hall.
Sweetser James N., 15½ e Wash.
Taylor & Taylor, 50 e Wash.
Torbett Oliver B., Temperance Hall.
Walker Isaiah D., Palmer House.
WALPOLE T. D. & R. L., 16½ e Wash.
Wick Wm. W., 33 Ind. ave.
WITT BENNETT F., s w cor Wash. and Merid. See card.
Woolen W. W., 43½ e Wash.

The Florence will substantiate all that is claimed for it.

Auction and Commission.

CHAPMAN SAMUEL, 10 Bates. See card.
Featherstone Wm. E., 78 e Wash.
Hunt Aaron L., cor East and St. Clair.
Mossler L. J., 10 w Wash.

Auction Sale Stable.

Burrows Geo. W., 14 n Penn.

Bakers.

(*See also Confectioners.*)
Altland Hiram, 165 n Noble.
Ball Anthony, 128 s Ill.
Bollman Frederick, 87 e Wash.
Bossert John, 54 Bluff road.
Brot Leopold, 46 Fort Wayne ave.
Brown John W., jr., 150 n N. Jersey.
Burbidge Thomas, 11 n Penn.
Conway Isaac, 11 n Penn.
Doyle Geo. H., 11 n Penn.
Finter Frederick, 77 Fort Wayne ave.
Grader Herman, 39 n East.
Gray Wm., 64 e South.
Guanter C., 181 e Wash.
Moesch Thaddeus, 73 e Wash.
Mottery Frederick, 11 n Penn.
NICKUM & PARROTT, Union Steam Bakery, 11 n Penn.
Selking Wm., 58 s Meridian.
THOMSON QUINTIN, 4 s Meridian.
Vernickle Joseph, 201 e Wash.

Banks and Bankers.

BANK OF THE STATE OF INDIANA, cor Ky. ave and s Ill.
BRANCH OF THE BANK OF THE STATE, Yohn's block.
FERGUSON KILBY, 2 n Penn.
Fletcher S. A., (Fletcher's Bank,) 30 e Wash.
FLETCHER & SHARPE, (INDIANAPOLIS BRANCH BANKING CO.,) s w cor Penn. and Wash.
HARRISON A. & J. C. S., (Harrison's Bank,) 15 e Wash.

Bank Vaults, Iron Railing, &c.

WILLIAMSON & HAUGH, 2 n Del.

Barbers.

Braboy David E., (col.) Yohn's block.
Brewer Edward, (col.) 53 s Ill.
Curry James H., 50 e Wash.
Close Wm. H., (col.) 49 Mass. ave.
Dickson James H., (col.) under Palmer House.
Fisher Benedict, cor Ill. and La.
Ford Wm., Oriental House.
Frankenstein Frank, under Mason House.
Franklin Wm., (col.) Yohn's block.
Gibbs Henry, (col.) 1 n Ill.
Gibbs Reuben, 1 n Ill.
Glenn Wm., (col.) 17 w Wash.
Gulliver Wm., (col.) cor Wash. and Ky. ave.

Gutig Henry, under Odd Fellows' Hall.
HENNING & STELZELL, (Bates House) 12 n Ill.
Jones Frank, (col.) 53 s Del.
Leininger & Ferling, cor Wash. & Merid.
McPowell James, (col.) Yohn's block.
Meflin, Knox & Mitcham, (col.) under Palmer House.
Mitchel Bussel, (col.) 49 Mass. ave.
Petteford John, (col.) Yohn's block.
Rinkle David, 62 e South.
Rinson Gash, (col.) Spencer House.
Roderus A., 62 e South.
Shoecraft Silas, (col.) 8 & 9 New & Talbott's block.

Barrel Manufacturers.

Breman John, shop near Carlisle Mill.
McNeely Elisha, above Lafayette depot.

Basket Maker.

Bast John, 178 e Market.

Bee Hive Manufacturer.

Barnes Wm., 72 s Ill.

Bible Depository.

Wilkins John, 34 e Market.

Bible Society.

American Bible Society, Wm. Armstrong, Agent, 4 New & Talbott's block.

Billiard Rooms.

Balke Cohas, 175 e Wash.
McDevitt John, Exchange buildings, Ill.
Moninger C., 121 e Wash.

Bill Poster.

SMITH STEPHEN. Leave orders Dodd & Co.'s counting room.

Blacksmiths.

(*See also Wagon Makers.*)
Affantranger Josiah, 139 Ind. ave.
Barton Charles W., cor Miss. & Ind. ave.
GATES, LEMON & SMITH, 14 s New Jersey.
Mayer Xevier, 306 Virginia ave.
Markham Thos., cor. Penn. and Md.
Reymond Samuel, 6 e Maryland.
Seibert Samuel, 252 e Wash.
Smith John G., 36 Ky. ave.
Webb Wm., Mount Jackson.
WILLIAMSON & HAUGH, 2 n Del.

Blank Books and Stationery.

BRADEN WM., 24 w Wash.
Dodd H. H. & Co., 16 e Wash.

Blinds, Doors, &c.

(*See Sash, Doors and Blinds.*)

Boarding Houses.

Bright Mrs. Eliza, 45 n Pennsylvania.
Coen John, 107 s Tenn.
Conner Mrs. Eliza L., 159 Virg. ave.

The Florence Sewing Machine is the handsomest in the world.

SIX STEAM PRESSES

IN CONSTANT OPERATION, AT

H. H. DODD & CO.'S

MAMMOTH

STEAM PRINTING OFFICE.

CALL AND SEE THEM.

Edwards Edward, 53 s Ill.
Fry Miss Rebecca, 122 n Ill.
Happe George, near Union Depot.
Hurd Daniel B., 117 n Missouri.
Hutton Thomas, 48 n Tennessee.
Jack Matthew, 44 n Pennsylvania.
KNIGHT ELIJAH, Georgia, bet Illinois and Meridian.
Kolb William, 30 Kentucky avenue.
LINGENFELTER, WM. H., 19 Circle.
Looker Fidelia, 140 n Mississippi.
McCoy Mrs. Elizabeth, 73 s Noble.
Mann James, 75 s East.
Mathias David, 187 s Tennessee.
Ohio House, Mrs. Neeman proprietress, Market, bet Illinois and Tennessee.
Pedicord Mrs. Lydia, 179 e Market.
Pentecost Mrs. Emma, 20 s Miss.
Reed Mrs. Sarah A., 20 n Pennsylvania.
Scudder Caleb, 46 w Market.
Sell Mrs. Barbara, 103 w South.
Shelly Theresa, 52 s Del.
Smith Mrs. M. C., 44 s Pennsylvania.
Stewart Robert, 12 w Georgia.
Tyler Alonzo P., 8 Virginia avenue.
Walk Lewis, 14 and 16 w Georgia.
Wright Charles, 14 e Ohio.

Book Binders and Blank Book Manufacturers.

Braden Wm., 24 w Washington.
DODD H. H. & CO., old Sentinel building, 18 e Wash.
Douglas James G., Journal Building.
Sheets Wm., 79 w Washington.

Book Publishers.

(*See Publishers.*)

Books and Stationery.

BOWEN, STEWART & CO, 18 w Washington. See card.
Merrill & Co., Glenns' block, e Washington.
THOMSON & SON, 7 n Pennsylvania.
Werden & Co., 26 e Washington.

Books and Stationery, Wholesale.

BOWEN, STEWART & CO., 18 e Washington. See card.

Boots and Shoes.

Aldag August, 137 e Washington.
Aldag Charles, 137 e Washington.
Bruner Charles, 38 w Washington.
Dahl Henry, 39 w Washington.
Davis E. J., 187 e Washington.
Grout Joseph B., 5 w Wash.
HUNTER M. & CO., 19 e Washington.
Jones, Vinnedge, & Co., 17 w Wash.
King James, 37 Indiana avenue.
Kistner John G., 51 s Delaware.
Klein Nicholas, Massachusetts avenue, bet Liberty and Noble.
KNODLE ADAM, 32 e Washington.
LINTZ ANTHONY, 39 w Washington.

Manning E. C., 27 s Illinois.
Maulding, Adams & Co., 53 w Washington.
NEW YORK BOOT AND SHOE STORE, CHASE & DAWES, Propr's, Glenn's Block.
Paul Geo. H., 53 e South.
Reinhardt L., 48 Massachusetts avenue.
Rehling Charles, 176 e Washington.
Rehling William, 186 s Delaware.
Richter T. A., 161 e Washington.
Teneyck & Bro., 260 w Washington.
Walk Anthony, 150 e Market.
Wand Alexander, 39 s Meridian.
Wand John, 38 w Washington.
Wehle Lukas, 197 e Washington.
Weis Peter, 61 Madison avenue.
Wert Joseph, 6 s Meridian.

Boots and Shoes, Wholesale.

Hendricks V. K. & Co., 76 w Washington.
Mayhew E. C. & Co., 3 Roberts' Block, opp. Union depot.
Drum William H., 148 e Washington.

Bowling Saloons.

Drum Wm. H., 248 e Washington.
TARR MARTIN M., 18 w Georgia.
WRIGHT THOMAS C., cor Maryland and Meridian.

Brass Founders.

Davis & Co., s Delaware, near R. R.
Garrett Joseph, (Phœnix,) Union R. R. track, e Union depot.

Brewer.

(*See, also Ale Agency.*)
BUSCHER HENRY, 14 s Alaba.
City Brewery, Charles Faiger, proprietor, 187 s Pennsylvania.
Deitz Peter, Blake, n of North.
Harting & Harting, bet Illinois and Bluff road.
Meikel John P., w Maryland.
SCHMIDT C. F., cor High & Wyoming.
Stumph Henry, City Brewery.
Wright Frank, 20 s Meridian.

Brokers.

Klinginsmith & Bro., 6 Blake Block, 2d floor.
Wright Charles A., 30½ w Washington.

Builders.

(*See, also, Architects.*)
Bunte John, 118 n Mississippi.
Byrket & Beam, 60 s Tennessee.
Carico John, 22 Kentucky avenue.
Carico & Gilkey, 22 Kentucky avenue.
Ebert John, 32 Kentucky avenue.
EDEN & COPELAND, 27 e Market.
EMERSON BOSWELL B., 141 w Market.
Enos Benj. V., 82 n Delaware.

(7)   No difficulty in learning to use the Florence.

Fatout J. L. & M. K., 109 Indiana avenue.
Greer William H., 68 s Delaware.
Rickard Thomas, 81 s Delaware.

Butchers and Meat Market.

BATTY JOHN H., 8 n Pennsylvania.
BOLLIER PAUL, 241 n Illinois.
Bichtel John S., 8 n Pennsylvania.
Blanc, Borst & Lake, 16 n Illinois, Bates House.
Essike A. & R., 112 s Illinois.
Fedrick, Hide & Co., 73 e Washington.
Gardner & Harbert, 5 n Illinois.
Gass Andy, 21 n Noble.
Hahn Louis, w Washington.
Powell David, cor Vt. and Massachusetts avenue
Reeder Edward, 32 n Illinois.
Riggs & Davids, 6 s Meridian.
SCHWEINSBURG WILLIAM, 243 s Delaware. See card.
Seifert Lewis, 75 e Washington.
Stagg J. R., 119 Virginia avenue.
Swinestack William, 243 s Delaware.
Wood & Davis, 59 e Washington.
Yaeger John, 200 e Washington.
Yaeger Knott, 200 e Washington.

Cabinet Makers.

(See, also, Furniture.)

GIMBEL MARTIN, 147 e Washington.
Veter John, 185 s Pennsylvania.

Cancer Doctors.

Howard & Son, 62 s Illinois.

Candy Manufacturers.

(See, also, Confectionery, Wholesale.)

Daggett William, 22 s Meridian.

Carriage Hardware and Trimmings.

Share George K. & Co., 72 w Washington.

Carriage Manufacturers.

DREW SAMUEL E., e Market square.
Grobe & Hider, Doughertyville Bluff road.
Lowe George, 99 e Washington.

Carpets.

(See, also, Drg Goods.)

Roll & Smith, 16 s Illinois.

Carpenters.

See Builders.

China, Glass and Queensware.

HAWTHORN CHARLES E., 88 e Washington. See card.
WOODBRIDGE CHARLES A.,16 w Washington. See card.

Cigars and Tobacco.

HEIDLINGER JOHN A., 3 Palmer House, and 10 Bates House. See card.
Henninger & Co., 87 s Illinois.

Hunt Charles C., 613 e Washington.
Kaufman Solomon, 81 e Washington.
KLOTZ EMIL, 37 e Wash. See card.
Kretsch Peter, 93 s Illinois.
MEYER GEORGE F., 35 w Washington. See card.
Otten Detrick, 159 e Washington.
RASCHIG CHARLES M., 11 e Washington. See card.
Sharp A. W., 12 n Pennsylvania.
Solomon J. & M., 30 s Illinois.

Cigars and Tobacco, Wholesale.

HEIDLINGER JOHN A., 3 Palmer House and 10 Bates House.
MEYER GEORGE F., 35 w Washington.

Cistern Maker.

Brandt George I., 25 Bluff road.

City Sexton.

Alred Garrison, 137 w South.

Cloaks and Mantillas.

IVENS & CO., old P. O. building, s Meridian.
Lane Miss Arabella, 28 w Washington.
TYLER LEWIS H., 2 w. Washington.

Clock Dealers.

(See, also, Jewelers.)

Daumont H. & Co., 17 n Pennsylvania.

Clothiers.

(See, also, Merchant Tailors.)

Becker & Vieweg, 103 e Washington.
Dessar & Bro., 4 e Washington.
Enggoss H., 183 e Washington.
Gerstner Aug. J., 158 Washington.
Glaser Brothers, 2 Bates House.
GOEPPER FREDERICK., 15 e Washington. See card.
GRAMLING J. & P., 41 e Washington. See card.
Hays, Kahn & Co., 9 Bates House.
Kahn A. & Co., 2 Palmer House.
Katzenstein & Wachtel, 3 Bates House.
McGinness Owen, 39 e Washington.
Manheimer David, 55 w Washington.
MORITZ BRO. & CO., 3 e Washington. See card.
Myer Moses, 4 w Washington.
Rice & Bamberger, 6 Bates House.
Rupp F. W., 105 e Washington.
Simon & Dernham, 1 w Washington.

Clothing, Wholesale.

Simon & Dernham, 1 w Washington.

Coal Dealers.

Burk John, 148 n Tennessee.
BUTSCH & DICKSON, e South, opposite Madison Depot. See card.
PERINE PETER R.,12 w Maryland. See card.
ROSS JOHNSON H., 16 e Washington. See card.

The Florence has the greatest range of application.

Coal Oil and Lamps.

ROCKEY HENRY L., 13 s Meridian. See card.

Commercial Colleges.

BRYANT'S COMMERCIAL COLLEGE, cor Washington and Delaware. See adv't.

Purdy's Commercial College, Wm. Purdy principal, Ætna Building.

Commission Merchants.

Coffin B. & Co., 14 s Meridian.
Gallup W. P. & E. P., 74 w Washington.
Goodheart Benj. F., 92 New Jersey.
Jorden & Spotts, cor Peru and Union R. R. track.
LESH L. & A. B., 29 s Meridian.
MYERS JESSE D., 12 s Penn. See card.
POMEROY, FRY & CO., 117 w Washington. See card.
Turner Wm. H., 84 w Washington.
Wallace Andrew, 38 Virginia ave.
Weeks Wm. H., 31 s Meridian.

Confectioners.

(See also Bakers.)

Baldwick Frederick, 30 w Louisiana.
Bartlett Joseph, 38 w Louisiana.
Cunningham F. P., cor Illinois and Market.
Daggett Wm., 22 s Meridian.
Hahn H. & Co., Talbott and New's Building, n Pennsylvania.
Haynes Henry M., 40 w Washington.
Kliber Louis J., 115 e Washington.
WEINBERGER JOHN C.,10 w Louisiana
Thompson Wm. A. C., 7 e Washington.

Confectionery, Wholesale.

Daggett Wm., 22 s Meridian.
Haynes Henry M., 40 w Washington.

Constables.

Gott Thos., 147 s Tennessee.
Ramsay Thomas A., 41 St. Clair.
Scudder Michael B., 131 Mass. ave.
Woolen Milton, 149 n West.

Copper Lightning Rods.

Fiscus Wm. W., 155 e New York.
LOCKE & MUNSON, Blackford's Building.

Coppersmiths.

Cottrell & Knight, 94 s Delaware.
Munson & Johnston, 62 e Washington.
Taylor William H., 268 e Washington.

Dairy.

REILLY JOHN,SUGAR GROVE DAIRY, n of city. See card.

Dancing, Prof. of.

Gresh B. F., 16 cor alley and e Pearl.
Hines Edward, 71 Indiana ave.

Dentists.

Burgess C. C., Odd Follows' Hall.
Frink E. O., 4 Yohn's Block.
Frink S. C., 4 Yohn's Block.
Hunt P. G. C., 32 e Market.
Johnston John F., 11 w Maryland.
Nichols Thomas M., 18 s Meridian.
Wells G. A., over Harrison's Bank.
Wells Dr. M., Yohn's Block.

Directory Publishers.

Campbell & Richardson, old Sentinel Building.
Hawes & Redfield, 13 old Sentinel Building.

Doors and Blinds.

(See Sash, Doors and Blinds.)

Dress Makers.

(See also Milliners.)

Bydon Mrs. Ellen, 139 e Washington.
Carson Miss America, 26 and 28 w Washington.
Churchman Mrs. Lou., 8 e Washington.
Hand Mary A., 11 n Meridian.
Healy Mrs. Ann, 13 n Alabama.
Lake Mrs. Martha, 38 n Pennsylvania.
Lindley Mary, 8 e Washington.
Marshall Mrs. C. M., 12 s Illinois.
Moon Miss Sally, 26 and 28 w Washington.
Patterson Miss Lucy, 26 and 28 w Washington.
Shipley Mrs. Mary, res Ohio, bet Meridian and Illinois.
Shompine Mrs. Clemens, 46 w Maryland.
Smith Mrs. Sophia, 86 Pratt.
STEELE MRS. MARY, 22 New and Talbott's Block.
Unich Miss, 6 Yohn's Block.
Wallace Mrs. Beulah, 79 Massachusetts ave.
Williams Nellie H., 22 s Illinois.
Wright Matilda, 33 n Alabama.
Wright Mary C., 38½ w Washington.

Druggists.

BOYD & PALMER, 14 w Washington.
BROWNING & SLOAN, 22 w Washington. See card.
BRYAN JAMES W., Spencer House Block. See card.
EGNER & WOOCHER, 85 w Washington. See card.
Frauer Emanuel, (German Drug Store,) 185 e Washingtsn.
Lee Henry H., 14 Bates House.
Lowry Wiley M., 49 Massachusetts ave.
Rosengarten Henry, 172 e Washington.
SENOUR JAMES F., 5 Bates House.
STEWART & MORGAN, 40 e Washington.
TOMLINSON & COX, 18 e Washington.
VICKERS WM. B., Odd Fellows' Hall.

The Florence makes the only reliable stithces.

Druggists, Wholesale.

BROWNING & SLOAN, 22 w Washington.

STEWART & MORGAN, 40 e Washington

Dry Goods.

CALLINAN DANIEL J., 28 e Washington. See card.
COOK & CO., 189 e Washington. See card.
GOOD MICHAEL H., 5 e Washington.
HAERLE WM., 36 w Washington.
Houpt Robert, 5 Chatham.
Hume, Lord & Co., 28 w Washington.
JONES, HESS & DAVIS, 3 Odd Fellows' Hall. See card.
Kirlin & Statton, 27 n Illinios.
KRAUSE & WITTENBERG, 43 and 45 e Washington.
Lynch & Keane, 33 w Washington.
NEW YORK STORE, W. & H. Glenn, proprietors, e Washington. See card.
Ostermeyer & Prange, 25 e Washington.
Piel W. F., 240 e Washington.
Rosskey Fred, cor McCarthy and Madison ave.
THOMPSON MARY, cor Delaware and South. See card.
TOUSEY & BYRAN, 70 e Washington.
TYLER LEWIS, 2 w Washington.
Ziegler Wm., (Boston Store,) 10 e Washington.

Dry Goods, Wholesale.

Crossland Jacob A., 75 and 77 w Washington.
MURPHY, KENNEDY & CO., 42 and 44 e Washington.
NEW YORK STORE, W. & H. GLENN, proprietors, e Washington. See card.

Dyers and Renovators.

Dickman Francis, 19 s Meridian.
Harris Joseph, 38 s Illinois.
Wolf Charles, e Washington.

Eating Saloons.

Kissell Jacob, 11 n Illinois.
McKelvey Robert, 32 w Louisiana.
Mason Madison, (col.) near Union Depot.

Egg Packers.

Benson Henry C., 11 Virginia ave.
Meek Edwin S., 11 Virginia aye.
Neall Jonathan R., 88 e Washington.

Embroidery and Stamping.

Lement Frederick T., 16½ s Illinois.

Engraver.

Chandler H. C. & Co., 8 e Washington.

Express Companies and Agents.

ADAMS RXPRESS CO., John H. Ohr, agent, 12 e Washington.

AMERICAN ERPRESS CO., J. Butterfield, agent, cor Meridian and Wash.
UNITED STATES EXPRESS CO., Jas. Butterfield, agent, cor Washington and Meridian.

Fancy Goods.

KLOTZ EMIL, 37 e Wash. See card. ⫯⫯
Langdien Joseph, 160 e Washington.
Mayer Chas., 29 w Washington.
SMITH & TAYLOR, 20 e Washington. See card.
WILDE & HENNINGER, 71 s Illinois. See card.

Female Institutes.

INDIANAPOLIS BAPTIST FEMALE INSTITUTE, cor Pennsylvania and North, Rev. C. W. Hewes, principal.
INDIANAPOLIS McLEAN FEMALE INSTITUTE, cor Meridian and New York, Rev. C. Sturdevant, principal.
ST. MARY'S INSTITUTE, n Meridian, near Ohio, Geo. Herbert, President.

File Works.

MAISCHOSS & McEWEN, Capital City File Words.

Fishing Tackle.

KLOTZ EMIL, 37 e Washington.

Flour and Feed Stores.

BRADSHAW WM. A. & SON, 5 s Delaware. Seed card.
Elliott Jonathan, s East.
Elliott Thomas B., cor Alabama and R. R. track.
ELLIOTT & LUCKEY, 19 s East.
Fowler James P., s East.
Glazier Charles, 16 s Meridian.
Heckman Christopher, 266 e Washington.
MYER JESSE B., 12 Penn.
Neff Wm. & Co., 157 e Washington.
Rusch Fred. P., 83 w Washington.
Winkle Fred., 157 e Washington.

Flouring Mills.

Ætna Mills, Robert G. & James Skillen, proprietors, 250 w Washington.
Bates City Mills, cor Washington and Noble.
Evans & Co., (Capital Mills,) cor Market and Missouri.
HECKMAN & McARTHER, (Bates City Mills,) e Washington.
Model Mills, J. Carlisle, proprietor, w Washington.

Flour Peddler.

Dunn T. J., 92 n Alabama.

Foundries and Machine Shops.

COX, LORD & PECK, Delaware, bet Cincinnati and Central depots. See card.
Hasselman & Vinton, (Washington Foundry,) s Meridian, near Union Depot.

The stitches of the Florence are the worder of all.

Redstone Bros. & Co., s Delaware, opp Cincinnati freight depot.
SINKER & VANCE, s Pennsylvania, near Union track.
Wiggins & Chandler, 262 w Washington.

Fruit Stands.
(*See also Confectionery.*)

Baldwick Frederick, 30 w Louisiana.
Bass Lovel, (col.) cor Bates and Benton.
GROFF, DANIEL B., 51 s Ill.
Weaver Wm., cor West and Md.

Fruit Can Dealers.

Munson & Johnson, e Wash.
Pentecost Mahlon B., 188 e Wash.
Wainwright S. B., s Ill.

Furniture.
(*See also Cabinet Makers.*)

DOHN PHILLIP, 24 s Del.
Meyer J. C., 171 e Wash.
Ramsay John F., 21 s Ill.
Sloan & Burke, 197 s Penn.
SPEIGEL, THOMS & CO., 73 w Wash. See card.

Furniture, Wholesale.

ADAMS GEORGE F., 56 e Wash.
SPEIGEL, THOMS & CO., 73 w Wash.

Gas Company.

INDIANAPOLIS GAS LIGHT AND COKE CO., office Ray's building.

Gas Fitters and Plumbers.

Cottrell & Knight, 94 s Del.
Dunn John C., 24 Ky. ave.
Ramsey & Hanning, rear Glenn's Block.

Grocers.

Barker Thomas D., 190 e Wash.
Barnard J., 18 s Meridian.
Barnitt Thomas, 170 e Wash.
Boyden Myron J., 134 w Wash.
Brado Thomas, cor East and South.
Brandt Christ., National road, e of Pogue's run.
Brat Leopold, 46 Fort Wayne ave.
Bretz Adam, cor Ill. and La.
Breuninger August, w Wash.
Brinker August, 94 w New York.
Butsch Geo., 173 Delaware.
Bywater Edward, 226 e Wash.
Carleton James M., 101 w Wash.
Casselbaum James, 153 Mass. ave.
Christy Albert, 24 w Louisiana.
CITY GROCERY, w Wash.
Clem A. & Bro., cor Mass. ave and n Ala.
COOK & CO., 189 e Wash. See card.
Cusick John, 43 Wash.
Danforth & Simpson, Odd Fellows' Hall.
Darby John, cor Merid. and Md.
Dill Ezekiel B., cor Ala. and North.
Diver James, 42 Mass. ave.
Domon Emil P., 138 s Ill.

Draper Granville W., 32 n Ill.
Emmerich & Reese, 91 & 93 w Wash.
Feil John, 50 Bluff road.
Gath Peter, 237 n New Jersey.
George James, 143 w Wash.
Gold Adam, w National road.
Goodheart Benj. F., 92 New Jersey.
Harmenning Christian, 205 s Del.
Harrington Patrick, 58 e South.
HAUG MICHAEL, 60 e South.
Heiss Levi, 37 Ind. ave.
Helm John, 104 Davidson.
Hind Ed., 155 e Wash.
Hofmeister & Hofmeister, 82 n Noble.
HOGSHIRE W. R. & Co., 25 w Wash.
Hohl Christ. C., 77 e Wash.
Jasper Frederick, 281 s Del.
Jenkins A. W., 120 n Penn.
Johnson James A., 88 Bluff road.
JOHNSON JOHN B., 144 w Wash.
Johnson Wm., 167 s Tenn.
Keane Daniel, 12 Mich. road.
Keely Wm. H., cor Market and Noble.
Keesee Wm. N., 144 Blake.
Kemker Charles, cor Meridian and Mc-Carthy.
Koch Henry H., 198 Mass. ave.
Kirlin & Staton, 27 n Ill.
Keltenbach Henry sr., Mass. ave, bet Liberty and Noble.
Kolb Catherine, 69 s Ill.
Kolb Frederick, 166 e Wash.
KRUG GEORGE, cor Geo. and Liberty.
Kuhlmann Ernest H. L., 137 w Wash.
Langdien Joseph, 160 e Wash.
Lawless Michael, 86 s Noble.
Logan Bernard, 129 w South.
LOHMAN CHARLES, 317 cor Cedar and Virg. ave.
Lonergan John, cor Pine and Noble.
Longenecker Samuel, res w Indianapolis.
McGinness John, 230 e Wash.
McManmon Andy, 153 e Wash.
Mains S., 88 Virginia ave.
Middlemas David C., 200 w Wash.
Moras Joseph, cor Wilkinson and Ill.
Morgan Thomas W., 162 e Ohio.
Morganvick Valentine, 9 Chatham.
Morrow Francis jr., 142 w Wash.
Muller Henry, 142 n Noble.
Munson Wm. L., 21 n Ala.
Neimeyer Wm., cor Geo. and Noble.
Ostermeyer & Prange, 25 e Wash.
Perrott Samuel, 193 Ind. ave.
Pfaffin Theodore, n w cor North and Indiana ave.
Piel W. F., 240 e Wash.
Prasse Henry, 322 Virg. ave.
Reick August, 118 n New Jersey.
Rentz Edward, 126 s Ill.
Richter Wm., 34 Virg. ave.
Riemenscheider Herman, 47 s N. Jersey.
Ries Christopher, cor N. York and Noble.
Rittenhouse Geo. L., 88 e Wash.
Roberts Dwight, 48 w Wash.

The Florence combines all the good qualities of all other machines.

Robinson Alonzo C., 180 n Ill.
Rosebrock Fred., 283 s Del.
Rosebrock Herman H., 168 Virg. ave.
Rosskey Fred., 35 cor McCarthy and
Madison ave.
Sawyer John S., 9 w Wash.
Schoppenhorst Wm., 101 e Wash.
Schott Joseph, 117 e Wash.
Schwear & Spier, e Wash.
Severin Henry, 247 n N. Jersey.
Shmidt Mrs. Christian, National road, e
of Pogue's run.
Simmons Henry, 36 Ind. ave.
SIMPSON M. & R., s w cor Del. & South.
Smith Frederick, 126 n Miss.
SOCWELL HENRY M., (New York
grocery,) 17 e Wash. See card.
Somerfield Henry, 115 s Tenn.
SPENCER MILTON, 202 e Wash. See
card.
STARLING & CO., 3 n Ill.
Stiegmann Charles, Maryland ave.
Stoelting Frederick, 163 n East.
STOUT OLIVER B. & BROS., 42 w
Washington.
Sponsel Conrad, 277 s Delaware.
Syerup Henry, cor East and Massachu-
setts avenue.
TARLTON & KEEN, 8 and 10 s Meri-
dian.
THAYER & COOK, 79 e Washington.
THOMPSON MARY, cor Delaware and
South. See card.
Tuttle B. F., 27 w Washington.
Van Houten & Graham, 34 n Illinois.
Wagner John, Bluff road.
Walton Elias H., cor Delaware and New
York.
WEAVER & MAGUIRE, 1 Indiana av-
enue.
Weeks William H., 31 s Meridian.
Werbe Louis F., 185 w Washington.
Wielles Thomas A., n East, near Vermont.
WINGATE J. T., 27 w Washington.
Woerner Philip, 78 w Washington.
Wood Alexander, 129 n Illinois.
Woollen William M., 82 w Vermont.
Worland William, 37 Virginia avenue.
Wright John C., 30 n Meridian.
Yeager Christ, 215 e Washington.

Groceries, Wholesale.

ALFORD, MILLS & CO., 36 e Washing-
ton.
ALVORD, CALDWELL & ALVORD, 68
e Washington.
HOGSHIRE, W. R. & CO., 25 w Wash-
ington.
HOLLAND & SON, 72 e Washington.
HOLMES C. L., CITY GROCERY, w
Washington. See card.
MAGUIRE, JONES & CO., 7 and 8 Bates
House.
Ryan Thomas F., 73 s Meridian.
Schnull A. & H., 81 e Washington.

STEPHENS A. & SON, cor Market and
East.
TARLTON & KEEN, 8 and 10 s Meri-
dian.
Wallace Andrew, 38 Virginia avenue.
Wieks William H., 31 s Meridian.
WINGATE J. F., 27 w Washington.

Guns and Pistols.

Balleweg & Kindler, 17 Kentucky av-
enue.
Beck Christian, 15 s Meridian.
Beck Jacob, 15 s Meridian.
Beck Samuel, 80 e Washington.
KLOTS EMIL, 37 e Washington.
Parker Edgar, 25 s Illinois.

Gymnasium.

WRIGHT THOMAS C., Georgia, bet Maryland and Meridian.

Halls.

COLLEGE HALL, s w cor Washington
and Pennsylvania.
MASONIC HALL, s e cor Washington
and Tennessee.
TEMPERANCE HALL, Washington, bet
Illinois and Meridian.
METROPOLITAN HALL, cor Tennessee
and Washington.
MILITARY HALL, 24½ e Washington.
ODD FELLOW'S HALL, n e cor Washing-
ton and Pennsylvania.
UNION HALL, s side Washington, bet
Delaware and Alabama.
WASHINGTON HALL, w Washington.

Hardware.

FREESE & KROFF, 11 w Washington.
See card.
KLOTZ EMIL, 37 e Washington. See
card.
LOYD THOMAS A. & CO., 12 w Wash-
ington. See card.
Portage Benjamin, 76 w Washington.
Vajen J. H., 21 w Washington.
Vonnequet Clemens, 142 e Washington.
Wilson John B., 59 w Washington.
Wood Augustus D., 64 e Washington.

Hardware, Wholesale.

Vajen J. H., 21 w Washington.
Wilson John B., 59 w Washington.
Wood Augustus D., 64 e Washington.

Hats, Caps and Furs.

BAMBERGER HERMAN, 16 e Washing-
ton. See card opp. front cover.
Baker & McIver, 22 e Washington.
BROWN WILLIAM P., 20 Kentucky av-
enue. See card.
DAVIS ISAAC, 15 n Pennsylvania.
DONALDSON & CARR, 71 w Washing-
ton. See card.
WILMOT & THAYER, 8 w Washington.
Spencer Stephen, 32 w Washington.

The feed can be reversed without stopping the machine.

Hats and Caps, Wholesale.

BAMBERGER HERMAN, 16 e Washington. See card, opp. front cover.
DONALDSON & CARR, 71 w Washington. See card.
Talbott J. M. & Co., 3 s Meridian.

Hides and Leather.

FISHBACK JOHN, 30 cor Meridian and Maryland.
MOONEYS & CO., s Meridian, near Union depot.
Sharpe Joseph K., 90 e Washington.
Vonnegut Clemens, 142 e Washington.
Yandes & Co., 38 e Washington.

Hominy Mill.

Hudnut Theodore, Pennsylvania, bet Md. and South.

Hoop Skirt Manufacturer.

Goldstone Max, 95 e Washington.

Hosiery, Shirts, &c.

Parker Reginald R., 30 w Washington.

Hotels.

BATES HOUSE, J. L. Holton, prop'r, cor Washington and Illinois.
California House, Adam Kistner, prop'r, 136 s Illinois.
Central House, Louis Voigt, prop'r, 44 s Meridian.
CHICAGO HOUSE, H. Kollman, prop'r, 73 and 75 s Illinois.
CINCINNATI HOUSE, Geo. W. Woolfe, prop'r, 124 s Delaware. See card.
CITY HOTEL, T. C. Strickland, prop'r, 77 and 79 s Illinois.
East Street House, H. Hahn, prop'r s East.
FARMERS' HOTEL, Henry E. Buehrig, prop'r, cor Illinois and Georgia.
Franklin House, Henry F. Weiglein, prop'r, 46 and 48 s Meridian.
Jefferson House, J. Diesler, prop'r, 31 c South.
LITTLE'S HOTEL, A. R. Hyde, prop'r, cor New Jersey and Washington.
MACY HOUSE, William H. Campbell, prop'r, cor Delaware and Market.
MASON HOUSE, Mason & Co., prop'rs, Lousianno, pp. Union depot.
National Hotel, David Bender, prop'r, w Washington.
ORIENTAL HOUSE, Belles & Tarleton, prop'rs, s Illinois. See card.
PALMER HOUSE, Minnie & Harriman, prop'rs, cor Washington and Illinois.
PATTERSON HOUSE, John D. Hamilton, prop'r, n Alabama, bet Market and Ohio. See card.
PEA RIDGE HOUSE, J. Sterm, prop'r 14 s Pennsylvania.
Pyle House, John Pyle, prop'r, cor Maryland and Illinois.

RAY HOUSE, Ray & Lambert, prop'rs, 65 South. See card.
SPENCER HOUSE, M. Harth, prop'r, cor. Illinois and Louisiana. See card.
STATION HOUSE, Frederick Scheer, prop'r, s w cor Union depot. See card.
UNION HOUSE, George Ilg, prop'r, cor Illinois and South. See card.
Washington House, Annie M. Matler, prop'r, 83 s Meridian.

Ice Dealers.

Buckhart Andrew J., 146 n Mississippi.
Butsch Joseph, 84 w South.
PITTS GEO. W., 78 Indiana avenue. See card.

Insurance Companys.

Charter Oak Fire, Columbia Fire, Manhattan Fire, Niagara Fire, Phœnix Fire, Rising Sun Fire, Manhattan Life; C. B. Davis, agent.
Ætna, (Hartford,) Wm. Henderson, ag't.
Arctic, N. Y. Home; Martindale & Grubbs, agents.
Continental Fire, Security Fire, Market Fire, Lorillard Fire, Springfield Fire, New England Fire, N. Y. Mutual Life; John S. Dunlop, agent.
Liverpool & London Fire, Metropolitan Fire; John S. Spann, agent.
Phœnix (Hartford) Fire, Hartford Fire, City (Hartford) Fire, Ætna Life, New England Mutual Life, Home (N. Y.) Life; J. J. Hayden, agent.
Indianapolis Fire Insurance Co., home office Odd Fellows' Hall.

Insurance Agents.

DAVIS CHARLES B., Odd Fellow's Hall.
DUNLOP JOHN S., 7 n Meridian.
Hayden John J., cor Meridian and Washington.
HENDERSON WM., Ætna building.
SPANN JOHN S., s w cor Washington and Meridian.

Intelligence office.

Mann Mrs. Margaret, 37 n Pennsylvania.

Iron Railing.

WILLIAMSON & HAUGH, 2 n Delaware.
SINKER & VANCE, s Pennsylvania.

Iron, Steel, Nails, &c., Wholesale.

ROOT, DELOSS, & CO., 66 e Wash.
Holliday W. J. & Co., 34 e Washington.
POMEROY, FRY & CO., 117 w Washington. See card.

Jewelers.

Bell A. C., 37 w Washington.
BINGHAM W. P. & CO., 50 e Washington. See card.

The Florence Sewing Machines are manufactured at Florence, Mass

BURDICK WILLIAM P., 8 Yohn's block. See card.
Cooper Charles A., 9 e Washington.
CRAFT WILLIAM H., Odd Fellow's Hall.
Daumont Peter A., 9 s Meridian.
Feller Geo., 84 e Washington.
FERGUSON CHAS. A., 7 w Washington.
French C. J., 37 w Washington.
McLENE J., under Bates House.
OEHLER ANDREW, 2 s Delaware. See card.
Rech Mathias, 80 w Washington.
TALBOTT W. H. & CO., 24 e Washington.
Woltze William E., 164 e Washington.

Justices of Peace.

Fisher Charles, 4 Yohn's block.
Kendrick Oscar H., res 128 Davidson.
Stein Fred, Judah's block.
Sullivan William, cor Washington and Pennsylvania, College Hall building.

Law Books.

DODD H. H. & CO., 16½ e Washington.
Merrill & Co., Glenns' block, e Washington.

Lasts, Hubs and Spokes.

Osgood, Smith & Co., s Illinois.

Laundry.

THORNBERRY WM., Union Laundry, cor Noble and Washington. See card.

Leather.

(*See Hide and Leather Dealers.*)

Leather, Wholesale.

MOONEY & CO., cor Meridian and Louisiana.
FISHBACK JOHN, 30 s Meridan.

Lime, Cement, &c., Wholesale.

BUTSCH & DICKSON, e South, opp. Madison depot. See card.

Liquors, Wholesale.

ALVORD, CALDWELL & ALVORD, 68 e Washington.
Brinkmeyer Geo., 82 w Washington.
Brinkmeyer & Co., 82 w Washington.
CONKLIN & COOK, 140 w Wash.
Duncan & Co., 28 s Illinois.
ELLIOTT CALVIN A., 32 s Meridian.
Muller John, 256 e Washington.
Rosenthral Adolph, 38 Louisiana.
Ruschahupt & Buls 82 e Washington.
Volner Charles, 65 w Washington.

Livery and Sale Stables.

Burrows Geo. W., 14 n Pennsylvania.
BRINKMAN & RUSCHHAUPT, 17 s Delaware. See card.
DELZELL & TODD, Maryland, bet Pennsylvania and Meridian.

HINESLEY WM., Pearl, rear of Palmer House. See card.
Landis & Mills, 18 e Maryland.
Patterson James M., 34 e Maryland.
UMVERSAW & CO., 11 and 13 w Pearl. See card.
Wilkinson & Sullivan, 10 e Pearl.
Wood & Foudry, 10 n Pennsylvania.

Locksmiths and Bell Hangers.

Ballweg & Kindler, 17 Kentucky avenue.
Reinhardt Joseph, 49 s Illinois.

Lumber Yards.

Blake, Helwig & Co., cor New York and Canal.
Coburn & Jones, cor Delaware and Massachusets avenue
King Cornelius, cor St. Clair and Alabama.
McCORD & WHEATLEY, 119 s Delaware.
Walker Jacob S., w Market.

Mathematical, Optical and Phylosophical Instrument Makers.

STEFFENS CHAS. & CO., cor Washington and Meridian.

Machine Cards.

Willard Albert J., 4 Bates House.

Mantle Manufacturer.

Wilson Alfred J., 10 n Delaware.

Marble Works.

Dame Jason, 67 e Washington.
Downey M., 127 e Washington.
Goddard & Jennings, cor Tennessee and Market.
JAMES W. W. & CO., 58 s Meridian, near Union depot. See card.
SEYBOLD & RITTER, 40 e Market.
Smith, Ittenbach & Co., 170 s Delaware.
Wallace Wm. W., 92 s Illinois.

Merchant Tailors.

(*See, also, Clothiers.*)

Becker Vieweg, 103 e Washington.
Dessar & Bros., 4 e Washington.
Engoss H., 183 e Washington.
Gerstner Aug. J., 158 e Washington.
Glaser Bro's, 2 Bates House.
GŒPPER FREDERICK, 15 e Washington. See card.
Gramling J. & P., 41 e Washington.
Hatz & Co., 69 s Illinois.
HEITKAM G. H., 17 n Illinois.
Katzenstein & Wachtel, 3 Bates House.
McGinnis Owen, 39 e Washington.
MORITZ BRO. & CO., 3 e Washington.
Richter & Roggs, 144 e Washington.
Ruckle N. D., 36 n Penn.
Rupp F. W., 105 e Wash.
Shoultz Louis, 19 n Penn.
Staub Joseph, 2 Odd Fellows' Hall.
Tapking & Becker, 65 e Wash.

Every Florence has the reversible feed.

Merchant's Dispatch.
CLARK WM. T., AGENT, office cor Va. ave and Ala.

Millinery.
Baker Mrs. S., 24 s Ill.
Dietrichs Margaret, 63 e Wash.
Dunn Mrs. Wm. A. & Co., 5 n Merid.
Kirk Mrs. Elizabeth, 39 n Penn.
Quimby Harriet N., 20 s Ill.
Reed John F., s Ill.
Thomas Mrs. M. J., 216 w Wash.
Tout Zenus F., 22 s Ill.
Unich Miss, 6 Yohn's block.

Mineral Water.
CLARK PHILO, 109 e Wash.

Monthly Publication.
INDIANA SCHOOL JOURNAL, office Journal building.

Museum.
Lewis & Darlin, 68 s Ill.

Music Dealers.
BENHAM A. M. & CO., cor. Ill. and Wash., under Bates House. See card.
WILLARD & STOWELL, 4 Bates House. See card.

Music Teachers.
Allen Mrs. E., 38 e New York.
Brummer Carl, 12 e Mich.
BUTTERFIELD JAMES A., P. O. Box 1222.
Dyer Miss Augusta, at Blind Asylum.
Hines Edward, 71 Ind. ave.
Pearsall Peter R., 26 s Tenn.
Schonaker H. J., 95 n Tenn.
Stewart Geo. H. W., bds Pyle House.
Wheeler James H., Temperance Hall.

News Stands.
COSTELLO JOHN, near Post Office.
THOMSON MRS. A. & SON, 7 n Penn. See card.
WEINBURGER & MATLER, in Union Depot. See card.

Notions.
(See also Fancy Goods.)
Baldwin J. H., 6 e Wash.
Haeree Wm., 36 w Wash.
KLOTZ EMIL, 37 e Wash. See card.
Mayer Charles, 29 w Wash.
Thonssen & Lahey, 67 w Wash.

Newspapers.
INDIANA FREE PRESS, R. Henenger, Prop., (German weekly,) 83 e Wash.
INDIANA STATE SENTINEL, (daily and weekly,) Elder, Harkness & Bingham, Props., 2 s Meridian.
INDIANAPOLIS GAZETTE, (daily and weekly,) Jordan & Burnett, Props., s Meridian.

INDIANA STATE JOURNAL, (daily and weekly,) Journal Co., Props., cor Circle and Meridian.
INDIANA VOLKSBLATT, (German weekly,) Julius Boetticher, Prop., 132 e Wash.
THE WITNESS, M. G. Clarke, Prop., Odd Fellows' Hall.

Nurseries.
Hill John F., 38 n Ala.
Loomis Wm. H., 14 e Market.

Oculist and Aurist.
Gustin Levi, 101 s Tenn.

Oil Painting and Water Colors.
Starling Mrs. S. S., teacher Indianapolis Female Institute.

Opticians.
MOSES L. W., 50 e Wash.
Simmons John H., 25 s Ill.

Paint and White Lead.
Drake & Merryman, 47 e South.

Painter, Historical.
Guezet Alex., 159 s Del.

Painters, House and Sign.
Cook Moses R., cor Merid. and Md.
Greuzard L. S., 136 e Wash.
Helli Lewis, 36 w Louisiana.
Knotts Nim K., old capitol house.
Osgood John B., 16 e Market.
Ryan & Spurgin, 48 w Wash., up stairs.
Sonderegger Frank, 69 Mad. ave.
Whitridge Wm., 82 e Wash.

Paper Mills.
McLENE & CO., s Wash., bank river.
Sheets Wm., 79 w Wash.

Paper Warehouse.
Bowen, Stewart & Co., 18 w Wash. See card.
BRADEN WM., 24 w Wash.
McLene & Co., Bates House.
Sheets Wm., 79 w Wash.

Patent Honey Manufacturer.
Butterfield Merano, 183 n East.

Patent Medicines.
Buell C. H., 105 Virginia ave.
Fish James H., 18 s Ill.
FROST JAMES M., 95 e Wash.

Paper Hangings, &c.
Werden & Co., 26 e Wash.
BOWEN, STEWART & CO., 18 w Wash.
Roll & Smith, 16 s Ill.

Photographers.
Axe Theodore, 8 e Wash.
Bell Chas. G., cor Ill. and Wash., up stairs

The Florence makes four distinct stitches.

Brothers Wm. H., P. O. Gallery.
BRUENING E. & J., 6½ e Wash.
Cox & Clark, (Metropolitan Gallery,) 43½ e Wash.
CRANE & SONS, 19 w Wash.
Johnson C. A., (Star Gallery,) 33 w Washington.
McCoy & Andrews, 25 & 26 New & Talbott's block.
MORRIS JOS. C., 35 e Wash.
HOWARD & DAVIES, 26 & 28 w Wash. See card.
RUNNION WM., 32½ e Wash. See card.
Sargent & Fish, 86 e Wash.
Thorpe Thomas D., 2 w Wash.

Physicians and Surgeons.

ABBETT LAWSON & SON, 20 Virginia ave.
Barbour Samuel, 126 n West.
Barnes Henry F., office Blake's building.
Barnitz Jacob W., 148 n Ill.
Beuts Robert, 47 n Del.
Bodman Elam, 144 n Ill.
Boyd James T., 112 n N. Jersey.
Brubaker Henry W., 18 s Merid.
Bullard Talbot, 23 s Merid.
Bullard Wm R., 23 s Merid.
BURNHAM NORMAN G., 10 w Market.
BUTTERFIELD SEYMOUR A., 162 n East.
Carter David E., 18½ n Ill.
CLARK F. D., 24½ e Wash.
Corliss Corydon T., 283 e Market.
Dickinson James L., last house s East.
Dixon I. C., bds Palmer House.
Dorsey Nicholas J., 48 n Penn.
Dottson J. H., w Indianapolis.
Dougherty Zadock, Cal., bet Market and Wash.
Dunlap John W., bds Oriental House.
Duzan Wm. N., 250 n Tenn.
EWING J. & D., 18 Virg. ave.
Fahnestock Samuel, 115 n Ala.
Gaston John M., 28 e Market.
Gatling Richard J., 44 s Md.
Harriman Joseph H., 134 w Wash.
Homburg K., 26½ w Wash.
Howard & Son, (cancer doctors,) 62 s Ill.
Jameson & Funkhouser, 5 s Merid.
Keely Isaac I., 62 e Mich.
Kendrick Wm. H., 33 n East.
KITCHEN JOHN M., s w cor Wash. & Meridian.
Lee Edward S., 17 Ind. ave.
McCann Sam'l D., 29 n East.
Mears Geo. W., 47 n Merid.
Merrill John F., 156 w Wash.
Miller G. W., 158 n Ill.
Moore Henry B., 164 e Ohio.
Newcomer Frisby S., 6 Blake's building.
Otto Carle, n Noble, bet Wash. and Market.
Parkman Charles, 30 s Tenn.
Parvin Theopolis, 67 n Ala.

Revels Willis R., (col.) 119 n West.
Rhodes John W., 145 n West.
Schindler Robert, 158 e Wash., up stairs.
Smelser Samuel W., 36 St. Clair.
Steadman E. P., 40 Mass. ave.
Stephens Thaddeus, over Harrison's B'k.
Teal Nathaniel, 5 2d floor Blake's build.
Thomson W. Clinton, 62 n Ill.
WARE C. S., e Market, opp P. O.
Wiley Delaney, e Market.
Wood Levi, 99 N. Jersey.
Wright Mansur H., 12 e Market.

Piano Forte Makers.

Ames James, 2 and 3 Blake's Building up stairs.
FREYSER L. F., 13 s Ala. See card. ☒

Piano Fort Dealers.

BENHAM & CO., under Bates House See card.
TRAEVSER L. F., 13 s Ala. See card.
WILLARD & STOWELL, 4 Bates House. See card.

Pictures and Picture Frames.

Leiber Heram, Ætna, Building n Penn.

Plaining Mills.

Byrket & Beam, 60 s Tenn.
Blake, Helwig & Co., cor New York and Canal.

Plants and Flowers.

(See also Nurseries.)

Snell Zacharia, 84 Pratt.

Plasterer.

Glover Joseph W., 84 n Penn.

Plow Manufacturer.

Rapp Fred. J., 154 e Wash.

Plumbers.

(See Gass Fitters and Plumbers.)

Pork Packers.

Coffin B. & Co., 14 s Meridian.
Ferguson James E., 28 n Meridian.
Patterson & Co., New & Talbotts Building.

Portrait Painters.

Hays B. S., 20 w St. Clair.
Reed Peter F., 93 w South.

Printing Offices.

BRADEN WM., 24 w Wash.
CAMERON WM. S., 8 e Pearl. See card.
Chandler H. C. & Co., 8 e Wash.
DODD H. H. & Co., old Sentinel building 18 e Wash.
ELDER, HARKNESS & BINGHAM, 2 s Meridian.
Paine & Downey, e Pearl.
Heninger R., 83 e Wash.
JOURNAL COMPANY, Journal Building, cor Circle and Meridian.

Calm contentment accompanies the purchase of a Florence.

JORDAN & BURNETT, Gazette office.
VOLKSBLATT, (German,) 130 e Wash.

Produce.

(See also Commission Merchants.)

Wallace Wm. P. & Co., 37 cor Maryland and Vir. ave.

Publishers, Books.

(See also Newspapers.)

ASHER & CO., Odd Fellows Hall up stairs.
Campbell & Richardson, old Sentinel building.
Clarke M. G. & Co., Odd Fellows Hall.
DODD H. H. & Co., old Sentinel building 18 e Wash.
HAWES & REDFIELD, 13 e Washington, rooms 12 and 13 up stairs.
Merrill & Co., Glenn's Block.
Morrell Wm. S., old post-office, s Mer.
PARSONS, ADAMS & CO., Odd Eellows Hall.
Perrine C. O., Odd Fellows Hall.

Pump Makers.

Hasket Elijah, 26 Kentucky ave.
Childers John P., 68 s Delaware.
WRIGHT & BRO., Maryland, near Vir ave. See card.

Pyrotechnist.

Raskop Geo., 76 n Ill.

Rag Dealer.

Fogle Samuel, 174 e Wash.

Railroads.

(See Appendix.)

Real Estate Agents.

Delzell & Jones, 37 e Wash., up stairs.
Eldridge Jacob, over City Grocery.
HAMLIN L. A., 16½ e Wash.
Holladay & Neff, 157 e Wash.
Love & Cullom, 1 New & Talbotts Building.
McCARTY NICHOLAS, s w cor Meridian and Wash.
McKERNAN & PIERCE, 39½ w Wash.
McMellin Samuel, 19 w Wash., up stairs.
Phipps Isaac N., 36 e Wash.
SEIDENSTICKER & KAPPES, 150 e Wash.
SMITH FRANK, 50 e Wash., up stairs.
SPANN JOHN S., s w cor Wash., and Meridian up stairs.
STAPP JAMES H., 72 w Wash.
Todd John M., 13 s Ill
WILEY & MARTIN, 10½ e Wash. See card, inside back cover,
Wright Chas, A., 30½ w Wash.

Restaurants.

(See Eating Houses, also Saloons.)

Rolling Mill.

INDIANAPOLIS ROLLING MILL CO., Tenn., 3 squares s of T. H. Depot.

Saddlery and Harness.

ANDRA JOHN, 169 e Wash.
Burgess L. A., 20 w Wash.
HERETH JOHN C., 89 e Wash.
Hincsly A. J. & Co., 34 w Wash.
Nicolai Chas., 268 e Wash.
SULGROVE, BEYNOLDS & CO., 20 w Wash.

Saloons and Restaurants.

(See also Eating Houses)

Astor, Hugh Reix, proprietor, 9 n Penn.
Blaes Nicholas, 48 s Delaware.
Brown A., under Littles Hotel.
Brunner Fred., 126 s Ill.
Burk Geo., 3 Wash.
Buscher Andrew, 51 e South.
Casanover Balthaser, 214 w Wash.
Caylor Sanford, 220 e Wash.
Central, Henry Shaut, w Wash.
Central House Saloon, L. Voigt, prop'r, 44 s Meridian.
CHARLES SALOON, H. Kollman, prop'r 73 s Ill. See card.
CHARTER OAK, Wright & Rittenhouse, prop's, 15 n Ill.
Cobweb, A. S. Burt, prop'r, 16 n Penn.
CRYSTAL PALACE, Edward Beck, pro., 44 w Wash.
Desdler Joseph, 168 e Wash.
State House Saloon, Doty & Lee, prop's, 95 w Wash.
EMPIRE, R. Beebe, prop'r, 22 w Wash. See card.
Exchange, Daniel Bacon, prop'r, Ill., bet. Wash. and Market.
Farmers Hotel Saloon, H. Buehrig, pro.
Feald Goodheart, e Wash.
FEY R., Excelsior, 86 e Wash. See card.
Frenzel John P., 85 s Ill.
Hattendorf ———, 186 e Wash.
HAUG MICHAEL, 60 e South.
Hohl Christ. C., 77 e Wash.
Hugg Martin, Capital Saloon, 14 e Wash.
LANG LOUIS, 13 e Wash. See card.
Lauer Chas., 162 e Wash.
Ledley John, Exchange, 24 w La.
McBAKER THOS., Pearl, 16 cor alley and e Pearl. See card.
Mahan Francis N., Oriental House.
Marble Hall, Nelson R. Church, prop'r, 32 s Ill.
Mattler Stephen, 2 s Delaware.
Meridian Saloon, Jacob Wachstetter, pro. 25 s Meridian.
Miller Chas. O., cor Wash. and East.
Monnenger Daniel, cor Kentucky ave. and Wash.
Morris House Saloon, G. Wachstetter pro.
National, Geo. Rhodius, pro., 27 s Mer.

All purchasers of the Florence use the hemmer practically.

NEEL GEO., cor Wash. and Benton.
Nye & Oton, 65 w Wash.
O'Leary & Renchan, Palmer House Basement.
Petrie John, 222 e Wash.
Phœnix, Wm. A. Smith, 15 e Wash.
Renard Eugene, 278 e Wash.
Richter Florence, 13 n Ill.
Rossman Chas., 119 e Wash.
'Rule & Mahan, 55 s Ill.
ST. NICHOLAS SALOON Eurich & Schaffer, prop's, 7 n.Ill.
Schaub Henry & Co., 6 w Wash.
Seeling Anton, 3 s Del.
THE STORE, Mike Clark, proprietor, 67 S Ill.
Todd Martin M., s e cor Ga. and Ill.
Union Hall, M. Emmenegger, proprietor, 111 to 117 e Wash.
VERANDAH, John Bussey, proprietor, 36 w Lou. See card.
WACHTSTETTER JOHN, 14 Lou. See card.
WASHINGTON HALL, Fahrback & Co., propr's, 78 and 80 w Wash. See card.
WEINBARGER JOHN C., 10 w Lou.
Wenger Geo. M., n Noble.
Wright Charles, 91 e Wash.
Zimmer Ferdinand, 128 e Wash.

Sash, Doors and Blinds.

Behymer Daniel, opp. Court House.
Byrkit & Beam, 60 s Tenn.
EDEN & COPELAND, 27 e Wash.

Saw Works.

SHEFFIELD SAW WORKS, E. C. Atkins, proprietor, 155 s Ill. See card.

Saw Filer.

Heizman Matthias, 33 s Penn.

Saw Mills.

MARSEE & SON, s N. Jersey, near Wash.

Scales.

Haynes Lewis, 74 w Wash.
York Henry, 74 w Wash.

School Book Publishers.

PARSONS, ADAMS & Co., Odd Fellow's Hall.

Scals and Seal Presses.

Ballard Austin, 5 Circle.

Seed Stores.

(See Agricultural Implements.)

Sewing Machine Agents.

CLAFLIN C. C., (Wheeler & Wilson agency,) 19 w Wash.
ELLIOTT JOHN F., (Singer's agency,) 48 e Wash.
SHARP & BELLIS, (general agents for the Florence sewing machine,) 17 n Penn.

Shippers Guide and Gazetteer, N. W. States.

Hawes & Redfield, 18 e Wash.

Silver Smiths.

(See Jewelers.)

Silver Plater.

Wiggins Wm. B., 8 w Wash.

Soap Factory.

Smith Wm., Bluff road, Doughertyville.

Spectacles.

MOSES L. W., 50 e Wash.
SIMMONS & CO., 23 s Ill.

Stair Builders.

Simon Louis & Bro., Ga., bet Penn. and Meridian.

Statuary.

Smithmeyer John L. & Co., 14 e Market

Stencil and Tin Shop.

Rexford Eugene M., 12 Pearl.

Stereotypers.

DODD H. H. & Co., old Sentinel building, 18 e Wash.

Stock Brokers.

(See Brokers.)

Stone Yards.

(See Marble Works.

Stove Manufacturers.

COX, LORD & PECK, Del., bet Cincinnat[i] and Central depots.

Stoves and Tinware.

FRANKEM JONATHAN, cor Vir. ave and Wash. See card.
Goldsberry & Bro., 182 e Wash.
MUNSON & JOHNSTON, 62 e Wash. See card.
McOuat R. L. & A. W., 69 w Wash.
ROOT & CO., 66 e Wash.
Voegtle Jacob, 177 e Wash.
WAINWRIGHT SAMUEL, 11 s Ill.

Straw Goods.

(See Milliners, also, Hats, Caps and Straw Goods.)

Sugar Mills.

(See Agricultural Implememts.)

Tailors.

(See Clothiers and Merchant Tailors.)

Bippus John, 16 n Penn.
Goodman Anthony, 16 n Penn.
N. D. Ruckle, e Market, opp. P. O.

The needles for the Florence Sewing Machines are all numbered.

Tanners and Curriers.

(*See also, Hide and Leather Dealers.*)
SCHMIDT ROBERT, 47 s N. Jersey. See card.
STREIF & DEITZ, cor Wash. and Davidson.

Taxidermist.

Barnitz Jacob W., 148 n Ill.

Tea Stores.

DAGGET WM., 22 s Meridian.
Lee Henry H., 14 Bates House.
Muir James, 33 w Wash.
STEPHENS A. & SON, cor Market and East.

Tea, Coffee and Spices, Wholesale.

STEPHENS A. & SON, cor Market and East.

Teas, Tobaccos, &c., Wholesale.

(*See also, Grocers, wholesale.*)
Muir James, 33 w Market.

Telegraph Office.

Western Union Telegraph Co., J. F. Wallack, manager, n w cor Wash. and Meridian.

Tinners.

(*See Stoves and Tinware.*)

Tin Plate and Tinners Tools.

(*See Hardware, also Coppersmiths.*)

Toys and Notions.

(*See Fancy Goods.*)

Trunks, Valises, &c.

Burton & Shilling, 13 s Ill. See card.
Becker H., 30 w Wash.
Sulgrove & Reynolds, 20 w Wash.

Umbrella and Parasol Manufacturers.

Mayer John F., 65 e Wash.
Myers Martin, 11 s Ala.

Undertakers.

Baily Julius, 8 Bates.
Long Matthew, 28 s Meridian.
WEAVER & WILLIAMS, 72 w Wash.

Veterinary Surgeon.

Ellerby James, office at Wood & Foudry's livery stable.
Wirtz Jacob, 72 e South.

Vinegar Manufacturers.

Bormann Andrew, res Elizabeth.
Denk Andrew, 135 Ind. ave.
Schofield Thomas B. & Co., 49 e South.

Wagon Makers.

(*See also, Blacksmiths.*)
Bristor Samuel, 68 Kentucky ave.
GATES, LEMON & SMITH, 14 s N. Jersey. See card.
Montague Wm. 12 n Ala.
Neiger Fred., cor Mass. ave., and Noble.
RICHMANN CHARLES, 211 e Wash.

Wall Paper.

(*See Paper Hangings, &c.*)

War Claim Agents.

(*See also, Attorneys at Law.*)
HAMLIN & PROTZMAN, 16½ e Wash.
Holladay & Neff, 157 e Wash.
RANSTEAD & MARSHALL, 24 Talbot's block.
WITT BENNETT F. s w cor Wash. and Meridian. See card.

Watch Materials.

(*See Jewelers.*)

Watches.

(*See Jewelers.*)

Willow Ware.

KLOTZ EMIL, 87 e Wash.
MAYER CHARLES, 29 w Wash.

Wines and Liquors.

(*See Liquors, wholesale.*)

Woolen Manufacturers.

Hoosier Woolen factory, G. W. Geisendorf & Co., proprietors, 268 w Wash.
Merritt & Coughlin, Ohio Premium Woolen Factory, s of Wash., bank of river.

Persons using the Florence prefer it to all others.

MARTIN HUG,

CAPITAL SALOON!

NO. 14 EAST WASHINGTON STREET,

INDIANAPOLIS, IND.

CHOICE WINES, LIQUORS AND CIGARS,

Oysters and Game in their Season.

APPENDIX.

GOVERNMENT OF THE UNITED STATES.

The Nineteenth Presidential Term commenced the 4th day of March, A. D. 1861, and will expire the 4th day of March, A. D. 1865.

THE EXECUTIVE.

President—Abraham Lincoln, of Illinois. Salary $25,000.

Vice President—Hannibal Hamlin, of Maine. Salary $6,000.

THE CABINET.

Secretary of State—Wm. H. Seward, of New York. Salary $8,000.

Secretary of Treasury—Salmon P. Chase, of Ohio. Salary $8,000.

Secretary of Interior—John P. Usher, of Indiana. Salary $8,000.

Secretary of Navy—Gideon Welles, of Connecticut. Salary $8,000.

Secretary of War—Edwin P. Stanton, of Ohio. Salary $8,000.

Attorney General—Montgomery Blair, of Maryland. Salary $8,000.

Postmaster General—Edward Bates, of Missouri. Salary $8,000.

SUPREME COURT OF THE UNITED STATES

Is held in the City of Washington, D. C., once in each year, commencing on the first Monday of December.

Chief Justice.

Roger B. Taney, of Maryland.

Associate Justices.

James M. Wayne, of Georgia.
John Catron, of Tennessee.
Samuel Nelson, of New York.
Robert C. Grier, of Pennsylvania.
Nathan Clifford, of Maine.
Noah H. Swayne. of Ohio.
Samuel H. Miller, of Iowa.
David Davis, of Illinois.

Clerk.

William T. Carroll.

Reporter.

J. S. Black.

CIRCUIT COURT OF THE U. STATES,

For the Seventh Judicial District, is held the 3d Monday of May and November, in the Court Rooms over the Post Office.

Noah H. Swayne, Justice.

UNITED STATES DISTRICT COURT,

For the District of Indiana, is held the 3d Mondays of May and November, in the Court Rooms over the Post Office.

Caleb B. Smith, Judge.
John Hanna, Attorney.
D. G. Rose, Marshal.
John H. Rea, Clerk.

UNITED STATES SENATORS FROM INDIANA.

Henry S. Lane—term expires 1867.　|　Thos. A. Hendricks—term expires 1869.

REPRESENTATIVES FROM INDIANA.

1st District, John Law.
2d District, James A. Cravens.
3d District, H. W. Harrington.
4th District, W. S. Holman.
5th District, Geo. W. Julian.
6th District, Ebenezer Dumont.

7th District, Dan. W. Voorhees.
8th District, Godlove S. Orth.
9th District, Schuyler Colfax.
10th District, Joseph K. Edgerton.
11th District, James F. McDowell.

The Florence Hemmer is the most practical in use.

UNITED STATES ASSESSORS AND COLLECTORS FOR INDIANA.

Assessors.	*Collectors.*
1st District, Jas. G. Hutchinson.	1st District, H. B. Shepherd.
2d District, Thos. C. Slaughter.	2d District, Henry Crawford.
3d District, Wm. F. Browning.	3d District, John S. S. Hunter.
4th District, W. V. Kyger.	4th District, James L. Yater.
5th District, John Yaryan.	5th District, Samuel W. Harlan.
6th District, W. A. Bradshaw.	6th District, Theo. P. Haughey.
7th District, Jas. Farrington.	7th District, John G. Crain.
8th District, Joseph Potter.	8th District, John L. Smith.
9th District, David Turner.	9th District, John F. Dodds.
10th District, James S. Frazier.	10th District, Warren H. Withers.
11th District, Winburn R. Pierce.	11th District, DeWitt C. Chipman.

MILITARY.

District of Indiana and Michigan, Military Head Quarters, corner Dealaware and Maryland streets.

Brigadier General Wilcox, commanding district.

Staff of the Brigadier General commanding the district:

Captain Robert A. Hutchins, U. S. V., Assistant Adjutant General.

Major G. C. Lyon, 17th Michigan Volunteers, Chief Provost Marshal.

1st Lieutenant L. C. Bracket, 28th Mass. Volunteers, Aide-de-Camp.

1st Lieutenant Wm. V. Richards, 17th Michigan Volunteers, Aide-de-Camp.

1st Lieutenant Charles A. McKnight, 7th Michigan Volunteers, Acting Aide-de-Camp.

1st Lieutenant L. C. Bracket, Post Adjutant.

Colonel John S. Simonson, Commandent of Post.

Captain Farquier, 19th U. S. Infantry, Assistant.

Captain Henry Tindal, Commandent of Battalion.

Capt. Frank Wilcox, Provost Marshal.

Captain John B. Miller, 13th U. S. Inf., Acting Superintendent, Mustering and Disbursing Officer, for District of Indiana.

1st Lieutenant W. H. Jordan, 9th U. S. Inf., Disbursing Officer.

Captain Orris Blake, 39th Ind. Vol., Adjutant.

Walter K. Scott, Chief Clerk.

Charles T. Flowers, Book-keeper.

D. B. Hunt, in charge of Transportation and Subsistence Department.

Chancey L. Turner, Clerk.

George Zorger, Clerk to Disbursing Officer.

G. Whitelaw Sheilds, Enlistment Department.

Samuel E. Tilford, Copyist.

Captain Jas. A. Ekin, U. S. Assistant Quarter Master.

Wm. H. Hay. Chief Clerk.

Adjutant General's Office, Indiana Militia, North-east corner room State House.

Laz. Noble, Adjutant General.

George W. Dunn, Chief Clerk.

James E. Speake, Clerk.

Dist. Provost Marshal office Blackford's building, D. Braden, Provost Marshal.

THE SOLDIERS' HOME.

In June Capt. Ekin contracted for the Hall now used as the sleeping apartment, and other necessary structures, and all were completed and ready for the reception of soldiers on the 25th of July following. Subsequently it was found necessary to have much more room, a dining hall and other buildings, and the authority was obtained from Washington to go on with the good work. A dining hall was accordingly erected—250 feet long, 24 feet wide and one story high, running parallel with the hall erected before. Also, other buildings and wings to the main one, for commissary and other departments.

The Home is situated in a beautiful grove—a beautiful site selected by Gov. Morton and Capt. Ekin. It is within two hundred yards of White River, two squares south of Washington Street, and a few rods north of the Terre Haute Rail Road. Properly it is divided into two departments, the Soldiers' Home and City Barracks—the latter being the quarters of the 2d battalion of the 63d Regiment, doing duty as Provost Guard. The chief officer, Capt. Frank Wilcox, is commandant and Provost Marshal of the city; Capt. H. Tindall being in command of the

Jencks' Patent Hemmer used only by the Florence.

Battalion or City Barracks. In addition to the Home and Barracks, there is a large guard house used for the confinement of deserters, awaiting trial, and for the punishment of sundry misdemeanors.

The long building which constitutes the sleeping apartment is furnished with 150 beds, which can accommodate 300 men. The roon or hall is well ventilated, and under the direction and care of Mr. Geo. Deaver, steward, is kept scrupulously neat and clean.

The following is a list of the Home and Battalion of the 63d:

Capt. Frank Wilcox, Commandant and Provost Marshal.

Capt. H. Tindall, commanding Battalion.
Lieut. Conner, Acting Adjutant.
Dr. P. H. Jameson, Surgeon in charge.
Dr. J. L. F. Garrison, Acting Assistant Surgeon.
Geo. W. Deaver, Steward.
Oscar Prather, Ward Master.
G. W. Ross, Assistant Ward Master.
Co. E—Lieut. Birch, commanding.
Co. F—Lieut. Plasnick, commanding.
(Capt. Raschig being Post Adjutant at military commanders office, and Lieut. Conner Assistant Adjutant of the Battalion.)
Co. I—Lieut. Hunt, commanding.
Co. G—Capt. Holloway.

STATE GOVERNMENT.

Governor—Oliver P. Morton.
Lieutenant Governor, ———.
President of the Senate—Paris C. Dunning.
Secretary of State—Jas S. Athon.
Auditor of State—Joseph Ristine.
Treasurer of State—Mathew L Brett.
Attorney General—Oscar B. Hord.
Sup't of Public Instruction—Samuel L. Rugg.

LEGISLATURE.

The Senate is composed of 50 members, and the House of Representatives 100. Election biennial.

SUPREME COURT OF INDIANA.

Meets the 4th Monday of May and Nov. of each year.
Judges—James L. Worden, James M. Hanna, Samuel E. Perkins, Andrew Davison.
Clerk—John P. Jones.
Sheriff—Henry H. Nelson.
Reporter—M. C. Kerr.

STATE LIBRARY.

Is in the State House. Office hours from 9 A. M. to 4 P. M. No. of volumes, 21,000. David Stevenson, Librarian.

BANK OF THE STATE OF INDIANA.
Location, Indianapolis, cor Ky. ave. and Ill.
Geo. W. Rathbone, President, Jas. M. Ray, Cashier. Capital $8,162,000. No. of branches 20. The banking business is done altogether through the various branches in different parts of the State.

BRANCHES.

Lima—Jas. B. Howe, Cashier.
Laporte—H. L. Weaver, Cashier.
Plymoth—Theo. Crestner, Cashier.
South Bend—A. B. Judson, Cashier.
Fort Wayne—Chas. D. Bond, Cashier.
Lafayette—John C. Brockenbough Cash.
Logansport—Jas. Cheaney, Cashier.
Richmond—Chas. F. Coffin, Cashier.
Indianapolis—David E. Snyder, Cash.
Connersville—Edw. F. Claypool, Cash.
Rushville—M. C. McReynolds, Cash.
Madison—Geo. B. Fitzhugh, Cash.
Jeffersonville—W. H. Fogg, Cashier.
New Albany—Walter Mann, Cash.
Bedford—Geo. A. Thornton, Cash.
Evansville—Samuel Bayard, Cash.
Vincennes—Wm. J. Williams, Cash.
Terre Haute—Preston Hussey, Cash.
Muncie—John W. Burson, Cash.
Lawrenceburg—John G. Kennedy, Cash.

MARION COUNTY OFFICERS.

Clerk—Wm. Wallace.
Recorder—Wm. J. Elliott.
Treasurer—Geo. F. Meyer.
Sheriff—Wm. J. H. Robinson.
Auditor—Jacob T. Wright.
Coroner—Garrison W. Alred.
Surveyor—Oliver W. Voorhis.

MARION CIRCUIT COURT.
Judge—Hon. Fabius M. Finch.
Clerk—Wm. Wallace.
Prosecuting Attorney—Wm. W. Leathers
Sheriff—W. J. H. Robinson.
Meets on 4th Mondays of March and September.

(8)   Dressmakers recommend the Florence.

MARION COURT OF COMMON PLEAS
Judge—Hon. Chas. A. Ray.
Clerk—Wm. Wallace.
Prosecuting Attorney—Jno. C. Buffkin.
Sheriff—Wm. J. H. Robinson.
Meets on the first Mondays in February, June and October.

COUNTY COMMISSIONERS.

Levi A. Hardesty, Lawrence Township·
Samuel Moore, Perry Township.
Geo. Bruce, Centre Township.

Board meets first Mondays in March
June, September and December.

MARION COUNTY LIBRARY.

Under the charge of nine Trustees·
This Institution was organized under the
special law of 1848. No. of volumes 1900.
Office in court house. Terms per year,
seventy-five cents for two volumes, fifty
cents for one book. Open Saturday, from
9 A. M. to 3 P. M. John W. Hamilton,
Librarian.

CENTER TOWNSHIP OFFICERS.

Justices of the Peace.

Wm. Sullivan, Charles Fisher, Frederick Stein, Oscar H. Kendrick.

Constables.

M. R. Scudder, Thos. Gott, Milton Woollen, Thos. A. Ramsey.

Coroner.

Garrison W. Alred.

Trustee.

James Turner.

TOWNSHIP LIBRARY.

In Court House. No. of Vols., 1000.
Open Saturdays, from 2 to 5 P. M. Free
to all.
John W. Hamilton, Librarian.

CITY GOVERNMENT.

Charter Election 2d Tuesday in May.
Regular Council Meetings 2d and 4th
Mondays of every month.

. CITY OFFICERS, MAY, 1863.

Mayor, John Caven.
Treasurer, Joseph K. English.
Clerk, Cyrus S. Butterfield.
Marshal, John Unversaw.
Deputy Marshal, John S. Russell.
City Engineer, James Wood.
Street Commissioner, John M. Kemper.
Market Master, John Jacob Winner.
Assessor, John B. Stumph.
City Attorney, Richard J. Ryan.

COUNCILMEN.

1st Ward—Sims A. Colley, 2 years; P.
H. Jameson, 4 years.
2d Ward—Theodore P. Haughey, 2
years; Henry Coburn, 4 years.
3d Ward—W. C. Thompson, 2 years;
H. A. Fletcher, 4 years.
4th Ward—John Blake, 2 years; R. B.
Emerson, 4 years.
5th Ward—Stephen McNabb, 2 years;
Samuel Lefevre, 4 years.
6th Ward—Austin H. Brown, 2 years;
William Boaz, 4 years.
7th Ward—S. A. Fletcher, jr., 2 years;
Charles Glazier, 4 years.

8th Ward — William Cook, 2 years;
William Allen, 4 years.
9th Ward—Wm. J. Wallace, 2 years
Joseph Staub, 4 years.

STANDING COMMITTEES.

Judiciary, Colley, Brown, S. A. Fletcher.
Finance, Haughey, Coburn, H. A.
Fletcher.
Accounts, S. A. Fletcher, McNabb,
Thompson.
Fire Department, Allen, Blake,Haughey.
Police, H. A. Fletcher, Brown, Colley.
Streets and Alleys, Brown, Coburn, Cook.
Education, H. A. Fletcher, Jameson,
Staub.
Bridges, Emerson, Boaz, Staub.
Markets, Wallace, Allen, Cook.
Public Buildings, Blake, Boaz, Emerson.
Cisterns, McNabb, Glazier, Lefevre.
Gas Light, Thompson, Lefevre,Wallace.
Revision of Ordinances, Jameson, Colley, Glazier.

POLICE BOARD.

Boaz, Blake, Coburn.

POLICE DEPARTMENT.

Captain of Police, David Powell.
Lieut. of Police, Wm. S. Johnson.

The Florence turns out most work with least noise.

Day Policemen—Jacob B. Powers, Jos. B. Duval, Charles E. Carter, Wm. Britney, M. W. E. Durand, Robert B. Barbee.
Chain Gang, James Stewart.
1st Ward—John Bray, George Taff.
2d—Thomas Amos, Wm. Loucks.
3d—Hannibal Taff, D, B. Charles.
4th—T. J. Foos, Robert Redman.
5th—Samuel Boozer, Fred. Lang.
6th—Henry Powell, S. Wilson.
7th—Andrew Umversaw, Hub. Adams.
8th—Jephthah Bradley, A. Catterson.
9th—J. R. Cotton, J. T. Murphy.

Sealer of Weights and Measures, James Loucks.

Sexton, G. W. Alred.

City Printers, Ellis Barnes, Richard Heninger.

Town Clock Keeper, P. Hand.

BOARD OF SCHOOL TRUSTEES.

1st Ward, John A. Beale, President.
2d Ward, David V. Cully, Secretary.
3d Ward, Isaac H. Roll.
4th Ward, T. B. Elliott.
5th Ward, James Sulgrove.
6th Ward, Alexander Metzger.
7th Ward, Charles Coulon.
8th Ward, Andrew May.
9th Ward, Hermann Lieber.

STEAM FIRE DEPARTMENT.

Chief Fire Engineer, Charles Richmann.
Company No. 1.—Engineer, Frank Glazier; Driver, James A. Isgrigg; Fireman, John Riggs; Hose Driver, John Hamil-

ton; Hosemen, Leonard Gay, Aaron Rosier, Philip Socks, David Hafferd.
Company No. 2.—Engineer, Charles E. Curtis; Fireman, E. H. Webster; Driver, Wm. Dawson; Hose Driver, Wm. Curtis; Hosemen, Charles Youngerman, Frederick Weaser, George Thomas, Wm. F. Schomberg.
Company No. 3.— Engineer, Daniel Glazier; Fireman, Frank Engersoll; Driver, Oren Tutle; Hose Driver, Samuel Blythe; Hosemen, Henry Buscher, Jessy Brown, Casper Threschauer, John Scheidler.
Hook and Ladder Company. — George Kineel, Driver.
Watchmen on Tower—Charles Roads, Milton Huhey.

BOARD OF HEALTH.

Dr. George W. Means.
Dr. Mansur H. Wright.
Dr. John M. Gaston.

INDIANAPOLIS POST OFFICE.

Corner n. Penn. and Market. Alex' H. Connor, P. M. Office open daily from 7 A. M. to 7 P. M. Sundays open 9 to 10 A. M. 3000 boxes and drawers.
Chief Clerk, E. A. Elder.
Clerks—David W. Barnett, John A. Buchanan, Henry Tyner, Henry McWorkman, Geo. G. McChesney, Wm. Deitrich, John F. Owings, Benton C. Vandegrift, John J. Duncan, Samuel E. Frazee, Joseph F. Dougherty, Geoge M. Sweetser, James M. Russell, John Farrell, Nathaniel J. Owings, John F. Wood. Oliver I. Conner, Geo. W. Joseph, Morris Healy, Wm. C. Lynn, Jas. B. Hill, Henry C. McKinnie, Jacob Reimacher.

LOCAL BANKS AND BANKING OFFICERS.

Branch of the Bank of the State, cor Wash and Meridian, Yohn's Block; open from 9 A. M. to 3 P. M. Discount daily. Capital $233,000.
President—Geo. Tousey.
Cashier—David E. Snyder.
Teller—Louis Witte.
Book-keeper—D. M. Taylor.

HARRISONS' BANK.

Location 15 e Wash. Bank open from 8 A. M. to 4 P. M. Discount daily. A. & J. S. C. Harrison, bankers; Samuel W. Watson, book keeper.

NATIONAL BANK.

Capital $1,000,000. Location ———.
President—Wm. H. English.
Vice President—G. W. Riggs.
Cashier—W. R. Nofsinger.
Teller—Lewis Jordon.

INDIANAPOLIS BRANCH BANKING COMPANY.

Location cor Wash. and Penn; open from 8 A. M. to 5 P. M. Discount daily.
Presedent—Calvin Fletcher.
Cashier—Thos. H. Sharpe.
Teller—F. A. W. Davis.
Asst. Teller—Ingraham Fletcher.
Asst. Teller—E. B. Sharpe.
Book-keeper—J. A. Moore.
Asst. Book-keeper—G. Burgner.
Clerk—E. Wolfram.

MERCHANTS BANK.

Location 2 n Penn.; open from 7 A. M. to 6 P. M. Discount daily.
Proprietor—Kilby Furgeson.
Teller—G. R. Gosney.

FLETCHERS BANK.

Location 30 e Wash.; open from 8 A. M. to 4 P. M. Discount daily. Stoughton A. Fletcher, Banker.

Tailors recommend the Florence.

ASYLUMS.

INDIANA INSTITUTE FOR THE EDU-
CATION OF THE DEAF AND DUMB.

Location—East National road, 1½ miles
east of the City.

Board of Trustees—Andrew Wallace,
Esq., President; John M. Kitchen, M. D.;
James C. Burt, M. D.

Superintendent—Thomas Mac Intire,
A. M.

Instructors—Horace S. Gillet, A. M.; W.
H. Latham, A. M., M. D.; W. H. Demotte,
A. M.; William Willard, Sidney J. Vail,
William M. French.

Physician—P. H. Jameson, M. D.

Matron—Miss Julia A. Taylor.

Assistant Matron—Miss L. B. Paige.

Steward—William R. Foster.

Master of Cabinet Shop—Samuel F.
Kahle.

Master of Shoe Shop—Richard M.
Wright.

Gardener—Christian Ramsaier.

Rules for Visitors.

1. The Institution will be opened for
the reception of visitors from 10 to 12
o'clock in the forenoon, and from 2 to 4
o'clock in the afternoon, of Mondays,
Wednesdays and Fridays, during the ses-
sions of school.

2. On these days, and during the hours
specified, an attendant will be in readi-
ness to wait upon vistiors, and to con-
duct them through all parts of the establishment, open to the public.

3. Persons who wish to visit the institution on other days, or at other hours,
than those specified, can only do so by
procuring permits from the President of
the Board, or from one of the Trustees.

4. The vacation extends from the 1st
of July to the 15th of September.

INDIANA INSTITUTE FOR EDUCAT-
ING THE BLIND.

Trustees—A. Wallace, President; John
Beard, Wm. M. Smith.

Secretary—T. A. Lewis.

Physician—J. M. Kitchen, M. D.

Superintendent—W. H. Churchman, A. M.

Assistant Officees—G. M. Ballard, A. M.,
Literary Teacher; L. S. Newell, Music
Teacher; S. McGiffen, Handicraft Teach-
er; Mrs. E. J. Price, Matron; Miss S. J.
Larned, Literary Teacher; Mrs. H. H.
Moore, Literary Teacher; Miss A. A.
Dyer, Music Teacher; Miss E. A. Daw-
son, Handicraft Teacher.

INDIANA INSANE HOSPITAL.

Location—1½ miles west of City.

Commissioners—Andrew Wallace, President; P. H. Jameson, J. W. Moody.

Secretary—T. A. Lewis.

Superintendent—J. H. Woodburn, M. D.

Assistant Physicians—John M. Dunlap,
M. D., J. F. Cravens, M. D.

Steward—W. M. French.

Matron—Mrs. Ellen Bigger.

CHURCH DIRECTORY.

Methodist.

WESLEY CHAPEL.

South-west cor Meridian and Circle
streets.

Pastor, Rev. S. T. Gillet. Services 10½
A. M., and 7 P. M.

ROBERTS CHAPEL.

Cor. Pennsylvania and Market streets·

Pastor, Rev. J. N. R. Miller. Services
usual hours.

ASBURY CHAPEL.

New Jersey street, between South and
Louisiana streets.

Pastor, Rev. J. W. Mellender. Services
usual hours.

STRANGE CHAPEL.

Tennessee street, between New York
and Vermont streets.

Pastor, Rev. Joseph C. Reed. Services
usual hours.

NORTH STREET.

Cor. Alabama and North streets.

Pastor, Rev. Geo. C. Betts Service 10½
A. M., Sabbath School 2 P. M.

German Methodist.

Ohio street, between East and New Jersey streets.

Services usual hours.

Episcopal.

CHRIST CHURCH.

North-east cor Meridian and Circle
streets.

Rector, Rev. T. R. Holcomb. Services
10½ A. M., and 7½ P. M.

Mantua-makers recommend the Florence.

Congregational.

North-west cor Meridian and Circle streets.
Pastor, Rev. N. A. Hyde. Service 10½ A. M.

Presbyterian.

FIRST.

North-east cor Market and Circle streets. Pastor, Rev. Mr. Nixon. Services usual hours.

SECOND.

North-west cor Market and Circle streets. Pastor, Rev. Mr. Tindall. Services usual hours.

THIRD.

North-east cor Ohio and Illinois streets. Pastor, Rev. Mr. Heckman. Services usual hours.

FOURTH.

Cor Market and Delaware streets. Pastor, C. H. Marshal. Services usual hours.

FIFTH, (GERMAN.)

South New Jersey street, near Washington.
Pastor, Rev. C. E. Kuester. Services at the usual hours.

United Presbyterian.

North-west corner Ohio and Delaware streets.
Pastor, Rev. Gilbert Small. Services 10½ A. M. and 7 P. M.

Baptist.

FIRST.

Church building, cor New York and Pensylvania streets.
Pastor, Rev. Mr. Day. Services in Masonic Hall, usual hours.

Universalist.

College Hall, south-west cor Washington and Pennsylvania streets.
Pastor, Rev. B. F. Foster. Services usual hours.

Soldiers' Home.

Service by Rev. A. Eddy Chaplain, at 3 P. M.

Christian.

Cor er Ohio and Delaware streets.
Pastor, O. A. Burgess. Services usual hours.

United Brethren.

Corner Ohio and New Jersey streets.
Pastor, L. S. Chittenden. Service at the usual hours.

Friends Church.

Cor of Delaware and St. Clair streets. Worship at 10½ o'clock on Sabbath, and at the same hour on fourth day, (Wednesday.) Approved ministers, David Tatum, Hannah B. Tatum and Jane Trueblood.

English Lutheran.

FIRST.

Cor New York and Alabama streets.
Pastor, Rev. J. A. Kunkleman. Services usual hours, morning and evening.
Sabbath Schools held at 2 P. M.

Catholic.

ST. JOHN'S.

Georgia street, between Illinois and Tennessee streets.
Pastor, Rev. Augustus Bessonics. Assistant, G. M. Villars. Services at 8 A. M., 10½ A. M., and 3 P. M. (vespers.)

ST. MARYS.

Maryland street, between Pennsylvania and Delaware streets.
Pastor, S. Siecrist. Services as above.

ODD FELLOWS.

GRAND ENCAMPMENT.

David Ferguson, M. W. G. P., Winchester.
T. G. Beharrell, M. E. G. H. P., Jeffersonville.
F. J. Blair, R. W. G., Senior Warden, Peru.
S. Frazier, R. W. G., Junior Warden, Greenwood.
E. H. Barry, R. W. G. Scribe, Indianapolis.
T. P. Haughey, R. W. G. Treasurer, Indianapolis.

Christopher Toler, W. G. Sentinel. Madison.
Jacob T. Williams, Dep. G. Sentinel, Madison.
T. B. McCarty, G. Rep., G. L. U. S., Wabash.
J. T. Sanders, G. Rep., G. L. U. S., Jeffersonville.
Meets semi-annually at Indianapolis, on the third Tuesdays in May and November.

GRAND LODGE OF INDIANA.

J. S. Harvey, M. W., Grand Master, Indianapolis.

Housekeepers recommend the Florence.

Dennis Gregg, R. W. D. Grand Master, Indianapolis.
E. H. Barry, R. W. Grand Secretary, Indianapolis.
T. P. Haughey, R. W. Grand Treasurer. Indianapolis.
G. A. Milnes, R. W. Grand Warden, Tremont.
James E. Blythe, G. Rep., G. L. U. S., Evansville.
Wm. H. Dixon, G. Rep., G. L. U. S., Jeffersonville.
J. Y. Allison, Alt. G. Rep , G. L. U. S., Madison.
Joseph McGranahan, Ait. G. Rep., G. L. U. S. Lawrenceburg.
Rev. B. F. Foster, W. Grand Chap., Indianapolis.
Moses Drake, W. G. Marsh, Ft. Wayne.
Charles Lehman, W. G. Cond., Laporte.
G. W. Jordan, W. G. Herald, Attica.
A. McCain, W. G. Guardian, St. Paul.
Meets semi-annually at Indianapolis, on the third Tuesdays in May and November.

METROPOLITAN ENCAMPMENT No.5.
Henry Allen, C. P.
Thomas Kelly, H. P.
D. A. Kirk, S. W.
James A. Isgregg, J. W.
Stephen Spencer, Scribe.
H. A. Fletcher, Treasurer,
Meets 1st and 3d Mondays of each month.

MARION ENCAMPMENT, No. 35.
Paul Sherman, C. P.
W. P. Noble, H. P.
R. M. Wright, S. W.
James S. Brown, J. W.
James Condell, Scribe.
J. B. Root, Treasurer.
Meets 2d and 4th Mondays of each month.

TEUTONIA ENCAMPMENT No. 57.
Christ. C. Hold, C. P.
Joseph Staub, H. P.
John Schneider, S. W.
Wm. Teckeuheck, J. W.
Frederick Simon, Scribe.
Christ. Heckman, Treasurer.

CAPITAL LODGE No. 124.
J. B. Root, N. G.
Thomas Peck, V. G.
Paul Sherman, Secretary.
A. J. Hinesley, Treasurer.
John F. Wallack, Per. Secretary.
Meets on Friday evenings of each week.

GERMANIA LODGE, No. 129.
John Kistner, N. G.
Wm. Banse, V. G.
John Schneider, Secretary.
J. C. Brinkmeyer, Treasurer.
Tobias Bender, Per. Secretary.
Meets on Thursday evenings of each week.

CENTER LODGE No. 18.
Thomas Farley, N. G.
Thomas Kelly, V. G.
James A. Isgregg, Secretary.
H. A. Fletcher, Treasurer.
Geo. P. Allison, Per. Secretary.
Meets on Tuesday evenings of each week.

PHILOXENIAN LODGE No. 44.
David Anderson, N. G.
Levi Marshall, V. G.
Joseph Kingham, Secretary.
N. S. Byram, Treasuser.
Joseph S. Watson, Per. Secretary.
Meets on Wednesday evenings of each week.

MASONIC.

GRAND COMMANDERY OF KNIGHTS TEMPLAR OF INDIANA.
Grand Officers.
Sir Solomon D. Bayless, Fort Wayne, G. Commander.
Sir William Hacker, Shelbyville, V. E. Dep. G. C.
Sir Harvey G. Hazlerigg, Thorntown, E. Grand Generalissimo.
Sir Austin B. Claypool, Connersville, E. Grand Capt. Gen'l.
Sir Charles Fisher, Indianapolis, Grand Treasurer.
Sir Francis King, Indianapolis, Grand Recorder.
Sir G. C. Beeks, Fort Wayne, Rev. Grand Prelate.
Sir Geo. W. Porter, New Albany, Grand Sen. Warden.
Sir George Vorhis, Fort Wayne, Grand Jun. Warden.
Sir L. B. Stockton, Lafayette, Grand Sword Bearer.
Sir Wm. W. Clinedenst, Centerville, Grand Warden.
Sir Henry Colestock, Indianapolis, G. Capt. Guard.

Examine the Florence before buying.

Next annual conclave of the Grand Commandery to be held at Indianapolis on the 1st Tuesday of April, 1864.

GRAND COUNCIL OF HIGH PRIESTS.

William Hacker, of Shelbyville, M. E. P.

G. W. Porter, of New Albany, V. P.
Caleb Schmidlapp, of Madison, Chaplain.
H. G. Hazelrigg, of Lebanon, Recorder.
H. Hanna, of Wabash, Treas.
E. H. Davis, of Shelbyville, M. of C.
H. L. Beale, of Shelbyville, C.
R. Peden, of. Knightstown, H.
II. Colestock, of Indianapolis, S. & T.

GRAND CHAPTER.

E. W. H. Ellis, Goshen, G. H. P.
Eden H. Davis, Shelbyville, D. G. H. P.
Hugh Hanna, Wabash, G. K.
Thomas Newby, Cambridge City, G. S.
Charles Fisher, Indianapolis, G. T.
Francis King, Indianapolis, G. S.
John Leach, Rolling Prairie, G. C.
Caleb Schmidlapp, Madison, G. C of H.
Wm. Worthington, Attica, G. R. A. C.
Henry Colestock, Indianapolis, G. G.

GRAND LODGE.

Wm. Hacker, Shelbyville, G. M.
Harvey G. Hazelrigg, Lebanon, D.G. M.
Wm. J. Millard, jr., Millersville, S.G.W.
Geo. W. Porter, New Albany, J. G. W.
Charles Fisher, Indianapolis, G. Tr.
Francis King, Indianapolis, G. Sec.
Rev. John Leach, Rolling Prairie, G. Chap.
E. H. M. Berry, Milroy, G. L.
Joseph A. Woodhull, Angola, G. M.
Casper Fogel, Mt. Carmel, G. S. D.
Lyndon A. Smith, Terre Haute, G. J. D.
Henry Colestock, Indianapolis, G. T.

INDIANAPOLIS COUNCIL, NO. 2.

[Meets first Monday of each month.]

John M. Bramwell, T. I. G. M.
Henry Colestock, Dep. do.
Israel Conklin, P. C. W.
Roger Parry, C. G.
Sam'l Campbell, Treas.
Chas. Fisher, Recorder.
Henry Colestock, Sentinel.

RAPER COMMANDERY, NO. 1.

[Chartered 1850. Stated meetings 4th Wednesday of each month.]

Sir Ephraim Colestock, E. C.
Sir John M. Bramwell, G.
Sir Levi Gustin, C. G.
Sir Francis King, P.
Sir Wm. H. Loomis, S. W.

Sir S. A. Fletcher, jr., J. W.
Sir Samuel Campbell, Treas.
Chas. Fisher, Recorder.
Wm. J. Wallace, St. Bearer.
Wm. Sullivan, Sword Bearer.
P. G. C. Hunt, Warden.
Henry Colestock, Sentinel

INDIANAPOLIS CHAPTER, NO. 5.

[Meets the first Friday of each month.]

Charles Fisher, H. P.
Ephraim Colestock, K.
Samuel Campbell, S.
Roger Parry, C. H.
Geo. H. Fleming, P. S.
Winston P. Noble, R. A. C.
W. P. Bingham, G. M. 3d V.
James H. Seybold, G. M. 2d V.
Peter Ritter, G. M. 1st V.
James Sulgrove, Tr.
John M. Bramwell, Sec.
Henry Colestock, Guard.

CENTER LODGE, NO. 23.

[Chartered 1846. Meets at Masonic Hall first Wednesday of each month.]

Wm. T. Clark, W. M.
Winston P. Noble, S. W.
John C. Conner, J. W.
Isaac H. Roll, Tr.
Chas. Fisher, Sec.
J. Solomon, S. D.
Joseph Garrett, J. D.
Chas. A. Judson, John McGrath, Stewards.
H. Colestock, T.

MARION LODGE, NO. 35.

[Chartered 1853. Meets at Masonic Hall third Wednesday of each month.]

J. M. Bramwell, W. M.
Roger Parry, S. W.
Joseph R. Haugh, J. W.
James Sulgrove, Tr.
F. King, Sec.
——————, S. D.
Samuel Campbell, J. D.
Henry Colestock, T.

CONCORDIA LODGE, NO. 178.

[Chartered May, 1855. Meets at Masonic Hall 2d Wednesday in each month.]

Geo. F. Meyer, W. M.
Francis Damme, S. W.
Henry Wellburg, J. W.
L. F. Werbe, Tr.
——————, Sec.
Robert Wolf, S. D.
Ferdinand Nottery, J. D.
H. Colestock, T.

No one asks to return the Florence.

RAILROADS.

BELLEFONTAINE RAILROAD LINE.

Office n w cor Meridian and Louisiana.

OFFICERS.

Gen'l Superintendent—John Brough.
Auditor and Gen'l Ticket Agent—J. M. Townsend.
Cashier—Edward King.
Gen'l Freight Agent—Lucian Hills.
Clerks—E. J. Hinckley, D. M. Boyd, Jr.
Telegraph Operator—W. H. Britney.

INDIANA AND ILLINOIS CENTRAL RAILWAY COMPANY.

Office 24½ East Washington.

OFFICERS

Pres't and Treasurer—Edmund Clarke.
Secretary—B. K. Elliott.

INDIANAPOLIS AND CINCINNATI RAILROAD.

Offices on South Delaware, South of the Railroad track.

OFFICERS.

President and Superintendent—Henry C. Lord.
Assistant Superintendent—J. W. Mills.
Treasurer—W. O. Rockwood.
Secretary—A. Worth.
Gen'l Ticket Agent—W. H. L. Noble.
Gen'l Freight Agent—G. L. Barringer.

INDIANA CENTRAL RAILWAY.

Offices cor Delaware and Vir. ave.

OFFICERS.

President—John S. Newman,
Superintendent—H. C. Carey.
Treasurer—Samuel Hanna.
Gen'l Ticket Agent—J. A. Perkins.
Gen'l Freight Agent—W. A. Bradshaw.
Road Master—.C F. Cunnings.

JEFFERSONVILLE RAILROAD.

Office 43 South Street.

OFFICERS.

President—D. Ricketts.
Superintendent—A. S. Crothers.

Gen'l Ticket Agent—Thos. Carse.
Gen'l Freight Agent—James Ferrier.
Freight Agent, Indianapolis—J. G. Whitcomb.

LAFAYETTE AND INDIANAPOLIS RAILROAD.

OFFICERS.

President—W. F. Reynolds.
Superintendent ———.
Gen'l Agent, Indianapolis—W. H. Parmelee.

MADISON AND INDIANAPOLIS RAILROAD.

Office 43 South Street.

OFFICERS.

President—F. H. Smith.
Superintendent—D. C. Branham.
Treasurer—Thos. Pollock.
Gen'l Ticket Agent—T. P. Mathews.
Gen'l Agent, Indianapolis—R. E. Rockwell.

TERRE HAUTE AND RICHMOND RAILROAD.

Offices Louisiana, West of Union Depot.

OFFICERS.

President—E. J. Peck.
Superintendent—R. E. Ricker.
Secretary—Chas. Wood.
Gen'l Freight Agent, Indianapolis—M. M. Landis.

PERU AND INDIANAPOLIS RAILROAD.

Offices cor Delaware and Washington.

OFFICERS

Superintendent and General Agent—David Macy.
Assistant Sup't—C B. Robinson.
Treasurer and Gen'l Ticket Agent—V. T. Malott.
Gen'l Freight Agent—L. N. Andrews.
Freight Agent, Indianapolis—W. B. Pratt.

SUMMARY,

EMBODYING THE MOST IMPORTANT FEATURES OF THE

NATIONAL TAX LAW,

AS AMENDED.

CAREFULLY COMPILED FROM OFFICIAL SOURCES, AND ARRANGED
EXPRESSLY FOR THE USE OF THE MERCANTILE PUBLIC,

BY CAMPBELL & RICHARDSON.

ARRANGEMENT.

STAMP DUTIES.

Sec 94. *And be it further enacted*, That on and after the first
day of October, eighteen hundred and sixty-two, there shall be
levied, collected, and paid, for and in respect of the several instruments, matters, and things mentioned, and described in the schedule
hereunto annexed, or for or in respect of the vellum, parchment, or
paper upon which such instruments, matters, or things, or any of
them, shall be written or printed, by any person or persons, or party
who shall make, sign, or issue the same, or for whose use or benefit
the same shall be made, signed, or issued, the several duties or sums
of money set down in figures against the same, respectively, or otherwise specified or set forth in the said schedule.

Schedule (B) of Stamp Duties on Documents.

	Duty. Dolls. cts.
Acknowledgment—(vide Conveyance.)	Exempt.
Administration—(vide Probate of Will).	
Adoption of Children, certificate of	5
Agreement or Contract (other than those hereinafter speci- fied) for each sheet or piece thereof.......................	5
Amicable Action, (Am. Sci. fa.) with Confession of Judgment	50
" " without " " "......	50
Appraisement, general; each sheet..............................	5
Approbation of Overseers in insane and spendthrift cases...	5

	Duty. Dolls. cts.
Articles of Copartnership, each sheet......................................	5
" " Shipping, " "	5

Assignment of Mortgage, Lease, or Policy of Insurance is subject to the same stamp duty as that imposed on the original instrument.

" Bond with covenant or guarantee of the amount due thereon, or of collection thereof.........................	5
" Letters Patent..	5
" Judgment.	5
" Bill of Lading...	5

Attestation—(vide General Certificate).

Bank Checks. (See Checks.)

Bills of Exchange (inland) Drafts, Checks or orders drawn upon places other than the place of issue, at sight or on demand, pay the same rates of duty as Bank Checks — **2**

Bills of exchange (inland,) Drafts, etc., exceeding $20,00, otherwise than at sight or on demand; and all promissory notes (except circulating Bank notes), for every sum of $200, or fractional part thereof, if payable on demand, or not exceeding thirty-three days including the grace from the date or sight...................... — **1**

Exceeding	33,	and not exceeding	63......................	2
"	63,	" "	93......................	3
"	93,	" "	4 months............	4
"	4 months "	"	6 "................	6
"	6 "..			10

[N. B.—Premium, Deposit and Stock Notes issued and used by Mutual Insurance Companies which have been held to be within the meaning of this clause, are exempt from stamp duty under the act of March 3d.]

Bills of Exchange (foreign) or letters of credit, drawn *out of* but payable *in* the U. S.; and all such bills drawn *in* but payable out of the U. S. drawn singly or in duplicate, pay the same rates of duty as Inland Bills.

[N. B.—The acceptor is required to affix and cancel the stamp on Bills drawn out of the U. S. before the bill can be discounted, negotiated or paid.]

Bills of exchange when drawn *in* but payable *out of* the U. S., if drawn in a set of three or more, for every bill of each set not exceeding $150 or its equivalent............ — **3**

Exceeding	$150 and not exceeding	$250....................	5
"	250 " "	500....................	10
"	500 " "	1,000..................	15
"	1,000 " "	1,500..................	20
"	1,500 " "	2,250..................	30
"	2,250 " "	3,500..................	50
"	3,500 " "	5,000..................	70
"	5,000 " "	7,500..................	1 00

and for every additional $2,500, or part thereof......... — **30**

Bill of Lading or receipt, (other than Charter Party,) for foreign ports, excepts ports in Br. No. America......... — **10**

" for U. S. ports...Exempt.

Duty.
Dolls. cts.

Bill of Sale of vessels where the consideration shall not exceed $500.. 52

Exceeding $500, and not exceeding $1,000............... 50

For every $1,000 or fractional part of $1,000, in excess of $1,000.. 50

" " Given as security for the payment of money. (See Mortgage.)

Bond given as security for the payment of money. (See Mortgage.)

" Indemnity... 50

" Official, "for the due execution or performance of the duties of any office, etc.," such as Trustee's Executor's, Administrators', and Guardian's Bonds............ 50

" County, City and Town Bonds; Railroad and other Corporation Bonds and Scrip require to be stamped as Promissory Notes under head "Inland Bills Exchange;" (See Decision No. 80.)

" Custom House, such as Warehouse, Enrollment and License Bonds, and such other penal Bonds of a similar character as are used in the business of the Custom House.. 25

" require l in legal proceedings, such as Replevin, Injunction, and to dissolve attachment ....Exempt.

Certificate of Stock in any incorporated Co. (See Decision No 70.)... 25

The power to transfer or sell the Stock usually given at the foot or on the back of the Certificate, requires 25c. stamp.

Where the transfer is made directly by the holder of the Stock without any order being given, no stamp is required.

Certificate of Profits, or any Certificate or memorandum showing an interest in the property, or accumulations of any incorporated Company for a sum not less than $10, and not exceeding $50.................................... 10

Exceeding $50.. 25

Certificate of damage or otherwise, and all certificate or documents issued by any Port Warden, Marine Surveyor, or other person acting as such...................................... 25

[N. B.—When the Collector or Inspector of the Port signs and issues Certificates or papers in the capacity of Port Warden or Surveyor, they must attach this stamp.]

" Of deposit in any bank, or Trust Company, or with any banker or person acting as such, not exceeding $100 2

Exceeding $100.. 5

" Of any other description than those specified. (See Decision No. 75.)... 5

[N. B.—This clause covers the official certificates of Judges and Clerks of Courts, Justice of Peace and other Magistrates, in fact all certificates which *have or may have* any value, either at Law or in

Equity, including Certificates of Record* and of Search; Certificates of Marriage; Certified copies of Records, etc. etc.]

Chattel Mortgage. (See Mortgage.)

Charter Party.—The registered tonage of the vessel, not exceeding 150 tons... $1 00
Exceeding 150 tons, and not exceeding 300 tons......... 3 00
Exceeding 300 tons, and not exceeding 600 tons........ 5 00
Exceeding 600 tons... 10 00

Check, draft, or order, for the payment of money, at sight or on demand, exceeding $20... 2

Any memorandum, check, receipt, or other written or printed evidence of an amount of money to be paid on demand, or at a time designated, (other than as above,) shall be considered a promissory note within the meaning of the law, and shall be stamped accordingly.

Clearance. (See Manifest.)

Contract.—Broker's note or memorandum of sale, of any goods or merchandise, stocks, bonds, exchange, notes of hand, real estate, or property of any kind or description, issued by brokers or persons acting as such   10
[N. B.—The copy which is issued to the party for whom the sale is made requires a stamp as well as that given to the purchaser. No stamp required on the Broker's sales book, or on his final account sales.]

Contract for purchase or sale, or loan of money on security (see sec. 4 of Amended Law,) for every $100...........   50

Conveyance, deed, instrument, or writing, whereby any lands, tenements, or other realty sold, shall be granted, assigned, transferred, or otherwise conveyed to or vested in the purchaser or purchasers, or any other person or persons by his, her, or their direction, when the consideration *or value* exceeds $100, and does not exceed $500...   50
Exceeding $500 and not exceeding $1000................. 1 00
"   1,000 "   "   "   2,500................ 2 00
"   2,500 "   "   "   5,000................ 5 00
"   5,000 "   "   "   10,000................ 10 00
"   10,000 "   "   "   20 000................ 20 00
Every additional $10 000, or part thereof, over $20 000 20 00†
[N. B.—Conveyance of lands *in trust*, which shall be intended only as security, and redeemable before the sale or other disposal thereof, either by express stipulation or otherwise, requires to be stamped as mortgage.]

* The stamp duty on Certificates of Record has been abolished by act of Congress, March 3d, 1863.
† The stamp duty in no case to exceed $1,000.
In all cases of conveyance of real estate by deed, the stamps used must answer to the *value* of the estate conveyed.. When the consideration is nominal, the *value* of the property conveyed is the measure of the stamp duty.

Duty.
Dolls. cts.

When property is sold subject to a mortgage, the
stamp upon the deed must be proportioned to the
value of the equity conveyed.
Deed.—(See Conveyance).
"   of Assignment. (See Assignment).
"   Partition. (See Conveyance).
"   Quit Claim releasing a mortgage.........................Exempt.
"   "   conveying title to property. (See Con-
       veyance).
"   Ground Rent. (See Conveyance. See Decison 84).
    N. B.—The acknowledgment of a deed or other in-
    strument before a Justice of the Peace or other
    qualified officer, forms part of the deed, and does
    not require separate stamp. The certificate of
    record is also exempt from stamp.
Despatch, Telegraphic.—Any despatch or message, the
    charge for which for the first ten words does not ex-
    ceed twenty cents..   1
    When the charge for the first ten words exceeds
    twenty cents (see Decision No. 44)......................   3
Entry of any goods, wares, or merchandise at any custom-
    house, either for consumption or warehousing, not ex-
    ceeding one hundred dollars in value......................   25
    This is construed to refer to the owner's entry.
    The entry by the captain, as in the case of goods
    landed from Canada under the Reciprocity Treaty,
    is the manifest of the cargo, and is therefore ex-
    empt under the last clause of the schedule.
    Exceeding one hundred dollars, and not exceeding five
    hundred dollars in value...................................   50
    Exceeding five hundred dollars in value.................   1 00
Entry for the withdrawal of any goods or merchandise from
    bonded warehouse...   50
Guaranty, covenant of,
      When given with assignment of mortgage, as of
      amount due thereon, or of payment thereof, sub-
      jects the assignment to stamp duty as "agree-
      ment." Guaranty by a third party for the pay-
      ment of money, etc., on a lease, etc., requires
      separate agreement stamp.
Guardian of Minor. Bond..................................., ...   50
               Appraisement...............................   5
Insurance (Life).—Policy of insurance, or other instrument
    by whatever name the same shall be called, whereby
    any insurance shall be made, or renewed, upon any
    life or lives—
    When the amount insured shall not exceed one thou-
    sand dollars...   25
    Exceeding one thousand, and not exceeding five thou-
    sand dollars...   50
    Exceeding five thousand dollars..........................   1 00
    Receipts for payments of premium on life policies

	Duty. Dolls. cts.

are not subject to tax. (See Regulation in regard to Insurance Companies, No. 33.)

Insurance (*marine, inland and fire*).—Each policy of insurance or other instrument, by whatever name the same shall be called, by which insurance shall be made or *renewed** upon property of any description, whether against perils by the sea or by fire, or other peril of any kind, made by any insurance company, or its agents, or by any other company or person, on which the premium or assessment shall not exceed $10 (see Decision No. 29)............   10

[N. B.—If the payment of the annual interest due, or to accrue upon deposit and premium notes used by many companies, forms the basis of a contract or agreement between the company and the policy holder, to continue or "renew" the policy, then the receipt therefor becomes an actual renewal of such policy, and is liable to stamp duty as such.]

Deposit notes are exempt from stamp duty.

Live Stock, Insurance on (vide Marine, Inland, etc.)

Judgment Notes (vide Promissory Notes.)

"   Bond (vide Bond.)

"   Transcript of (certified) vide " Certificate."

Lease, agreement, memorandum, or contract for the hire, use, or rent of any land, tenement or portion thereof—

If for a period of time not exceeding three years......   50

If for a period exceeding three years....................   1 00

Both landlord's and tenant's lease must be stamped.

The surety to pay rent in case of default requires stamp..   5

License, ordinary forms of, such as billiard, dog, show, street, and other licenses issued by State, county, and city officers...Exempt.

"   To manufacture under patent right (vide Agreement)   5

Letters of Administration (vide Probate of Will).

"   Testamentary...Exempt.

Lottery Tickets, not exceeding one dollar............................   50

Exceeding one dollar for every dollar or fractional part thereof (see sec 2 New Law).....................   50

Manifest for custom-house entry, or clearance of the cargo of any ship, vessel, or steamer, from or for a foreign port —except ports in British North America—

If the registered tonnage of such ship, vessel, or steamer does not exceed three hundred tons,.........   1 00

Exceeding three hundred tons, and not exceeding six hundred tons...   3 00

Exceeding six hundred tons........ ....   5 00

[N. B.—The *Master's* inward manifest for entry,

---

* Renewal receipts and certificates, or indorsements of renewal, require the same stamp as the original policy.

Duty.
Dolls. cts.

and outward manifest for clearance, are alone subject to stamp.]

Mortgage of lands, estate, or property, real or personal, her-
itable or movable whatsoever, where the same shall be
made as a security for the payment of any definite
and certain sum of money, lent at the time or pre-
viously due and owing, or forborne to be paid, being
payable, for every $200 or part thereof....................   10

Trust Deed—also any conveyance of any lands, estate, or
property whatsoever, in trust to be sold or otherwise
converted into money, which shall be intended *only as
security*, and shall be redeemable before the sale or
other disposal thereof, either by express stipulation or
otherwise, for every $200 or part thereof..................   10

Personal Bond.—Any *personal bond* given as security for the
payment of money, or of any definite or certain sum
of money, for every $200 or fractional part thereof....   10

    The stamp duty in no case to exceed $1,000.

When an estate that is encumbered by mortgage
or deed of trust is conveyed, subject to the encum-
brance, the stamp must answer to the *value* of the
equity, unless the payment of the mortgage debt
is assumed by the grantor.

Passage Ticket, by any vessel from a port in the United States
to a foreign port, except ports in British North America, thirty dollars or less........   50
    Exceeding thirty dollars.....................................   1 00

Patent Letters, assignment of..   5
  "   License,..   5

Pension Papers...Exempt.

Petition, for judgment on promissory note, or account; (vide
Writ.)

    Suits are commenced in many States in this way,
also by warrant; in such case these documents, as
the original process, require stamp.

Power of Attorney for the sale or transfer of any stock,
bonds, or scrip, or for the collection of any dividends
or interest thereon, (see Decision No. 63)...............   25

Power of Attorney for the sale or transfer of any scrip or
certificate of profits or memorandum, showing an interest in the profits or accumulation of any corporation or association, not exceeding $50....................   10

Power of Attorney or Proxy for voting at any election for
officers of any incorporated company or society, except religious, charitable, or literary societies, or public cemeteries *...   10

Power of Attorney to receive or collect rent...................   25

Power of Attorney to sell and convey real estate, or to rent
or lease the same, or to perform any and all other acts
not hereinbefore specified...................................   1 00

* Power of attorney to sell or transfer stock, etc., and to vote at elections executed in
foreign countries, must be stamped, and the stamps cancelled by the party using them
in the U. S.

	Duty. Dolls. cts.

Insurance Agents' Commissions to take surveys, accept service, etc., requires $1 stamp.

Probate of Will, or letters of administration: Where the estate and effects* for or in respect of which such probate or letters of administration applied for shall be sworn or declared not to exceed the value of two thousand five hundred dollars.. **50**

Exceeding two thousand five hundred dollars, and not exceeding five thousand dollars........................... **1 00**

Exceeding five thousand dollars, and not exceeding twenty thousand dollars................................... **2 00**

Exceeding twenty thousand dollars, and not exceeding fifty thousand dollars.................................... **5 00**

Exceeding fifty thousand dollars, and not exceeding one hundred thousand dollars............................. **10 00**

Exceeding one hundred thousand dollars, and not exceeding one hundred and fifty thousand dollars...... **20 00**

And for every additional fifty thousand dollars, or fractional part thereof...................................... **10 00**

Bonds of executor, administrator, trustee or guardian **50**

Administrator's inventory, with appraisement............ **5**

Guardian of minor—certificate of choice by Justice Peace... **5**

Guardian's inventory with appraisement................... **5**

Promissory Notes (vide Inland Bills Exchange,) Promissory notes payable in bank are nor subject to stamp duty as bank checks.

Protest.—Upon the protest of every note, bill of exchange, acceptance, check or draft, or any marine protest, whether protested by a notary public or by any other officer who may be authorized by the law of any State or States to make such protest....................................... **25**

N.B —The cost of stamp may be added to the note, etc.

Quit Claim (vide Deed.)

Receipts.—Ordinary receipts for money. and all receipts except warehouse receipts, and such as are not otherwise charged in this schedule............................**Exempt**

Summons (vide Writ.)

Telegraph (vide Despatch.)

Trust Deed (vide Mortgage.)

Warehouse Receipt for any goods, merchandise, or property of any kind held on storage in any public or private warehouse or yard.. **25**

Weigh Tickets..**Exempt.**

Writ or other original process by which any suit is commenced in any court of record, either law or equity... **50†**

---

* This is construed to cover the whole estate and effects, both real and personal, of which the testator dies possessed.
The stamp must be affixed to the probate which covers the original letters, whether testamentary or of administration with will annexed.
Letters *de bonis non*, whether with or without will annexed, require the stamp.
† Amicable actions for the institution of suit are liable to stamp as original process
When a stamped writ is returned without "service" being had on it, no stamp is required on the *alias* writ which issues.

Duty.
Dolls. cts.

N. B.—Writ, summons, or other process issued by a justice of the peace, or issued in any criminal or other suits commenced by the United States or any State..Exempt.

As a general rule each copy or part of an Agreement, Bill of Lading, Charter Party, Contract or Lease, relied on as evidence either at law or in equity, must be stamped in order to render it valid.

How to obtain Stamps.

Stamps may be ordered from the office of Internal Revenue, in quantities to suit purchasers. Orders should be accompanied by remittances of Treasury notes, or an original certificate of a U. S. Assistant Treasurer, or designated depository of a deposit made for the purchase of stamps.

The following commission will be allowed on all purchases of—

$ 50 or more, 2 per cent.
  100   "   3   "
  500   "   4   "   } payable in stamps.
 1000   "   5   "

N.B. The name of the state as well as town and county, should be given. If not otherwise ordered, stamps will be sent by mail.

Penalty for Non-use.

The execution or issue of an unstamped paper will render the party executing or issuing it liable to a penalty of fifty dollars. The validity of the paper or instrument itself is also destroyed.

Prosecution.

Collectors are directed to commence proceedings under the Law, against all persons east of the Rocky mountains, who shall wilfully neglect to use stamps.

The Denomination of Stamps.—The rule.

The use of the several *kinds* of stamps is no longer required—a five cent revenue stamp is good for any instrument subject to a duty of five cents.

When stamps of a large denomination are required, those of a smaller value may be used in numbers sufficient to amount to the sum of the stamp required.

Affixing and Cancelling Stamps.*

All papers subject to stamp duty (excepting Bills of Exchange,

---

When defendants in a suit reside in different counties, and a writ is required to be served on each defendant, each writ must have its appropriate stamp.

If certified copies of the original writ are used, each copy is liable to stamp duty of five cents, as certificate.

* See Section 7 of the Act of March 31, 1863.

Powers of Attorney and other instruments executed abroad), must be stamped and the stamp cancelled by the party signing or issuing the paper.

The cancellation may be effected by *printing* as well as by writing the initials, date, etc., across the face of the stamp.

When two or more persons join in the execution of an instrument, the stamp to which the instrument is liable under the law may be affixed and cancelled by any one of the parties.

Bills of Exchange.

To sign or issue, accept or pay any bill, draft or order, or promissory note, without proper stamp, subjects the party to two hundred dollars penalty. Foreign Bills of Exchange must be stamped before acceptance or payment by the drawee. Penalty for payment or negotiation without stamp, one hundred dollars.

Special Exemptions.

Express receipts and applications for pension, bounty, or backpay, are exempt under the last act of Congress. It is the duty of the Commissioner to examine all papers submitted for his decision in regard to their liability to stamp duty, and to report thereon. See Section 103.

Forging and Counterfeiting Stamps.

Any person or persons who shall forge or counterfeit stamps, or make fraudulent use of stamps, dies, etc., is guilty of felony, and on conviction therefor shall forfeit the dies, stamp and articles on which they are placed, pay a fine of $1,000, and be liable to imprisonment at hard labor for five years.

Schedule (C) *of Stamp Duties on Proprietary Articles.*

Duty.
Dolls. Cts.

MEDICINES, etc.—For and upon every packet, box, bottle, pot, phial, or other enclosure, containing any pills, powders, tinctures, troches or lozenges, syrups, cordials, bitters, anodynes, tonics, plasters, liniments, salves, ointments, pastes, drops, waters, essences, spirits, oils, or other preparations or compositions whatsoever, made and sold, or removed for consumption and sale, by any person or persons whatever, wherein the person making or preparing the same has, or claims to have, any private formula or occult secret or art for the making or preparing the same, or has, or claims to have, any exclusive right or title to the making or preparing the same, or which are prepared, uttered, vended, or exposed for sale under any letters patent, or held out or recommended to the public by the makers, venders, or proprietors thereof as proprietary medicines, or as remedies or specifics for any disease, diseases or affections whatever affecting the human or animal body, as follows: where such packet, box, bottle, pot, phial, or

other enclosure, with its contents. shall not exceed, at
the retail price or value, the sum of twenty-five cents,   1
Exceeding 25 cents, and not exceeding 50 cents.......... 2
  "   50 cents,   "   75 cents.......... 3
  '   75 cents,   " $1 00 cents.......... 4
  " $1 00, for every 50 cents, or fractional part
thereof, over $1 00, an additional....................... 2

PERFUMERY AND COSMETICS.—For and upon every packet, box,
bottle, pot, phial, or other enclosure, containing any
essence, extract, toilet, water, cosmetic, hair oil, pomade,
hairdressing, hair restorative, hair dye, tooth-wash,
dentrifice, tooth paste, aromatic cachous, or any similar
articles, by whatsoever name the same heretofore have
been, now are, or may hereafter be called, known, or
distinguished, used or applied, or to be used or applied
as perfumes, or applications to the hair, mouth, or skin,
made, prepared, and sold or removed for consumption
and sale in the United States, where such packet, box,
bottle, pot, phial, or other enclosure, with its contents,
shall not exceed at the retail price or value the sum of
twenty-five cents.. 1
Exceeding twenty-five cents, and not exceeding fifty
cents... 2
Exceeding fifty cents, and not exceeding seventy-five
cents.......... 3
Exceeding seventy-five cents, and not exceeding one
dollar... 4
Exceeding one dollar, for every fifty cents or fractional
part thereof over one dollar, an additional.................. 2

PLAYING CARDS.—For and upon every pack of whatever number, when the price per pack does not exceed eighteen
cents. 1
Over eighteen cents, and not exceeding twenty-five cents
per pack.. 2
Over twenty-five, and not exceeding thirty cents per
pack... 3
Over thirty, and not exceeding thirty-six cents per pack.. 4
Over thirty-six cents per pack............................... 5

Monthly Statement required.

Section 110 enacts, That the maker of any patent medicine, or
other article enumerated in the foregoing schedule, shall make
monthly declaration in writing, that all articles removed, carried or
sent away during the past month, have been duly stamped.

Penalties.

For neglect to affix stamps, ten dollars.
For reissuing stamped wrapper or cover on article, fifty dollars;
and forfeiture of the article.
For evasion of the law by concealing or fraudulently removing un-
stamped goods, one hundred dollars, and forfeiture.
For refusal or neglect to make statement. one hundred dollars.
For making false statement, five hundred dollars.

DUTIES ON MANUFACTURES, ARTICLES, AND PRODUCTS.

Specific and ad valorem Duty.

SEC. 68. *And be it further enacted,* That on and after the first day of September, eighteen hundred and sixty-two, every individual, partnership, firm, association, or corporation (and any word or words in this act indicating or referring to person or persons shall be taken to mean and include partnerships, firms, associations, or corporations, when not otherwise designated or manifestly incompatible with the intent thereof), shall comply with the following requirements, that is to say:

1. Shall furnish statement within thirty days, to assistant assessor.

2. Shall make monthly return to the Commissioner of Internal Revenue.

3. Shall pay duties monthly to the Collector of the District.

4. Under a penalty, for violating these provisions, of seizure and forfeiture of the goods and a fine of five hundred dollars.

5. Proceedings, for neglect or refusal to pay duties, to be taken by the collector.

Manufactures for consumption not exceeding six hundred dollars are exempt.

SEC. 75. *And be it further enacted,* That from and after the said first day of September, eighteen hunpred and sixty-two, upon the articles, goods, wares, and merchandise, hereinafter mentioned, which shall thereafter be produced and sold, or be manufactured or made and sold, or removed for consumption, or for delivery to others than agents of the manufacturer or producer within the United States or Territories thereof, there shall be levied, collected, and paid the following duties, to be paid by the producer or manufacturer thereof, that is to say:

Articles upon which an ad-valorem duty is levied, and the rate thereof.

[The value and quantity of the goods, etc. required to be stated, shall in all cases be estimated by the amount of actual sales.]

Auction sales, on gross amount of sales, one-tenth per cent. (See Decision No 27.)	
sales by judicial or executive officer, by virtue of a judgment or decree of any court, and public sales by executors or administrators......................	Exempt.
Advertisements, on gross receipts for......................	3 per cent.
all receipts for, to the amount of $1,000 in all newspapers whose circulation does not exceed 2,000 copies.........	Exempt.
Banks, on dividends and sums added to surplus or contingent funds, (see Decisions Nos. 13, 14.)......	3 per cent.
Binder's board........	3 per cent.
Bone, manufactures of, not otherwise provided for......	3 per cent.
Brass, manufactures of, not otherwise provided for....	3 per cent.
" rolled in rods or sheets............................	1 per cent.
Bristles, manufactures of, not otherwise provided for..	3 per cent.

Bridges, on gross receipts for tolls.......................... 3 per cent.
Calfskins, American patent.. 5 per cent.
Candles, of whatever material made......................... 3 per cent.
Canal and Turnpike Companies, on interest and dividends .... 3 per cent.
Carpets made to order, (see Decision No. 37.)............ Exempt.
Cloth, of materials other than cotton or wool, before it has been dyed, printed, bleached, or prepared in any other manner, (see Sec. 30 New Law)...... 3 per cent.
Cotton, manfactures of, not otherwise provided for..... 3 per cent.
Copper, manufactures of, not otherwise provided for... 3 per cent.
    " in rods or sheets.. 1 per cent.
Cotton cloth, and all textile or knitted or felted fabrics of, before the same has been dyed, printed, bleached, or prepared in any other manner.................. 3 per cent.
Diamonds, (see Decision No. 39.).......................... 3 per cent.
Emeralds, (see Decision No. 39.)..................... ... 3 per cent.
Express Companies, on gross receipts....................... 2 per cent.
Ferry boats, on gross receipts................................ 1½ per cent.
Flax, manufactures of, not otherwise provided for...... 3 per cent.
Furniture, (see Decision No. 55.)
Furs of all description, when made up or manufactured 3 per cent.
Glass, manufactures of, not otherwise provided for.... 3 per cent.
Goat skins, curried, manufactured, or finished.......... 4 per cent.
Gold, manufactures of, not otherwise provided for...... 3 per cent.
Gold leaf, per pack... 15 per cent.
Gutta percha, manufactures of, not otherwise provided for......... .... 3 per cent.
Hemp, manufactures of, not otherwise provided for..... 3 per cent.
Hog skins, tanned and dressed............................... 4 per cent.
Horse skins, tanned and dressed............................. 4 per cent.
Hose, conducting, of all kinds................................ 3 per cent.
Horn, manufactures of, not otherwise provided for..... 3 per cent.
Income, annual, of every person exceeding $600 and not exceeding $10,000, on the excess over $600... 3 per cent.
    exceeding $10,000, on the excess over $600... 5 per cent.
    from property of any kind in the United States, owned by any citizen of the same residing abroad and not in the employment of the government of the United States...... 5 per cent.
    derived from interest upon notes, bonds, or other securities of the United States .... 1½ per cent.
India rubber, manufacturers of, not otherwise provided for... 3 per cent.
Insurance companies, on all dividends and sums added to surplus or contingent funds 3 per cent.
    inland or marine, upon gross receipts for premiums and assessments........ .... 1 per cent.
    foreign, doing business in the United States, upon gross receipts for premiums and assessments (see Decisions Nos. 29, 33, 65.) .... 1 per cent

Iron, manufactures of, not otherwise provided for......   3 per cent.
   in pigs and bars, and iron not advanced beyond
   slabs, blooms, or loops..................................   Exempt.
Ivory, manufactures of, not otherwise provided for......   3 per cent.
Jewelry...   3 per cent.
Jute, manufactures of, not otherwise provided for......   3 per cent.
Kid skins...:............   4 per cent.
Lead, manufactures of, not otherwise provided for......   3 per cent.
Leather, manufactures of, not otherwise provided for,
   (see Decisions, Nos. 2 and 3.)......................   3 per cent.
Legacies (see Section 111.)
Morocco skins..   4 per cent.
Manufacturers of materials not otherwise provided for,
   (see Decision No. 71.).................................   3 per cent.
Marine engines, (see Decision No. 72.)...............   3 per cent.
Paints ....   5 per cent.
Painter's colors...   5 per cent.
Paper of all descriptions...................................   3 per cent.
Parasols of all kinds ....   3 per cent.
Pasteboard ....   3 per cent.
Paper, manufactures of, not otherwise provided for....   3 per cent.
Patented articles, (see Decision No. 77.)
Pickles...   5 per cent.
Pins, solid head or other ....   5 per cent.
Pottery ware, manufactures of, not otherwise provided
   for......... ....   3 per cent.
Preserved fruits, meats, fish and shell fish, in cans or
   air-tight packages ....   5 per cent.
Railroads, on gross receipts for carrying passengers...   3 per cent.
   Do.   motive power of which is not steam, on
      gross receipts for carrying passengers,
      (see Decisions Nos. 26, 66.)...............   1½ per cent.
   Do.   on *bonds*, on the amount of interest on same   ¾ per cent.
      on the amount of dividends to stockholders   3 per cent.
Sails, tents, shades, awnings, and bags...............   3 per cent.
Savings institutions, on all dividends and sums added
   to surplus or contingent funds, (see Decision No.
   14.)..   3 per cent.
Sheepskins..   4 per cent.
Ships and other vessels......................................   2 per cent.
Shooks, (see Decision No. 60.).............................   3 per cent.
Silk, manufactures of, not otherwise provided for......   3 per cent.
Silver, manufactures of, not otherwise provided for....   3 per cent.
Steamboats, except ferry boats, on gross receipts, (see
   Decision No. 73.)..   3 per cent.
Steel, manufactures of, not otherwise provided for......   3 per cent.
Tin, manufactures of, not otherwise provided for........   3 per cent.
Trust companies, on all dividends and sums added to
   surplus or contingent funds, (see Decision No. 14.)   3 per cent.
Umbrellas of every material................................   3 per cent.
Varnish...   5 per cent.
Willow, manufactures of, not otherwise provided for..   3 per cent.
Wood, manufactures of, not otherwise provided for....   3 per cent.
Wool, manufactures of, not otherwise provided for.....   3 per cent.
Worsted, manufacture of, not otherwise provided for..   3 per cent.

Duty.
Dolls. cts.

Wool, cloths, and all textile or knitted or felted fabrics of, before the same have been dyed, printed, or prepared in any other manner........................... 3 per cent.
Yarns, etc., (see Decision No. 53.) .... Exempt.
Zinc, manufactures of, not otherwise provided for...... 3 per cent.

Enumerated articles and the tax levied thereon.

Ale, per barrel of 31 gallons, (fractional parts of a barrel to pay proportionately).. 60 cents.
Beer, per barrel of 31 gallons, (fractional parts of a barrel to pay proportionately)—see Sec. 12 new law............. 60 cents.
Billiard tables kept for use, each, (see Decision No. 21.). $10 00
Barytes, sulphate of, per 100 pounds........................... 10 cents.
Carriages, including harness used therewith, valued at $75 or over, when drawn by one horse........ $1 00
   drawn by two horses or more, and valued at $75 and not above $200, including harness... 2 00
   valued above $200 and not exceeding $600..... 5 00
   valued above $600, (see Decision No. 21.)...... 10 00
Cassia, ground, and all imitations of same, per pound...... 1 cent.
Cattle, horned, exceeding 18 months old, slaughtered for sale, per head.................................... 20 cents.
   under 18 months old, slaughtered for sale, per head, (see Decision No. 74.)............. 5 cents.
Cement, made wholly or in part of glue, to be sold in a liquid state, per gallon.................... 25 cents.
Chocolate, prepared per pound............................. 1 cent.
Cigars, valued at not over $5 per M., (see Decisions Nos. 48, 76)..................................... $1 50
   valued over $5 and not over $10 per M., (see Decisions Nos. 48, 76.)..................... $2 00
   valued over $10 and not over $20 per M., (see Decisions Nos. 48, 76.)..................... 2 50
   valued at over $20 per M., (see Decisions Nos. 48, 76.)....................................... 3 50
Clocks and time pieces, and clock movements uncased.... 3 per cent.
Coal, on all mineral coals (except such as are known in the trade as pea coal and dust coal) per ton............. 3½ cents.
N.B. On all contracts of lease of coal lands made before the first day of July, eighteen hundred and sixty-two, the lessee shall pay the tax.
Cocoa, prepared, per pound..................................... 1 cent.
Coffee, ground, and all substitutes, per pound............... 3 mills.
Cotton, raw, per pound................................ ½ cent.
Confectionery, made wholly or in part of sugar, valued at 14 cents per pound.................... 2 cents.
   "   exceeding 14 cents, and not exceeding 40 cents per pound...... .... 3 cents.
   "   exceeding 40 cents, or when sold otherwise than by the pound.................... 5 cents.
Coal, all mineral, except pea coal and dust coal, per ton. 3½ cents.
Cloves, ground, and all imitations of the same, per pound 1 cent.

	Duty. Dolls. cts.
Deep skins, dressed or smoked, per pound....................	2 cents.
Distilled spirits, first proof, per gallon........................	20 cents.
Gas, when the product shall be not above 500,000 cubic feet per month, per 1,000 cubic feet..................	5 cents.
above 500,000 and not exceeding 5,000,000 cubic feet per month......................................	10 cents.
above 5,000,000 cubic feet per month...................	15 cents.
Gelatine, in solid state, per pound	5 mills.
Ginger, ground, and all imitations of the same, per pound	1 cent.
Glue, in liquid form, per gallon..............................	25 cents.
in solid state, per pound................................	5 mills.
Gunpowder, valued at 18 cents per pound, or less..........	5 mills.
valued above 18 cents, not exceeding 30 cents	1 cent.
valued above 30 cents per pound.................	6 cents.
Hogs, exceeding 100 pounds, slaughtered for sale...........	6 cents.
Iron, railroad per ton..	$1 50
railroad, re-rolled, per ton...........................	75 cents.
band, hoop and sheet, not thinner than No. 18, wire gauge, per ton.......................................	$1 50
all kinds advanced beyond slabs, blooms, or loops, and not advanced beyond bars or rods, per ton....	1 50
plate less than ¼ inch in thickness, per ton...........	2 00
band, hoop, and sheet, thinner than No. 18, wire gauge, per ton..	2 00
cut nails and spikes, per ton.........................	2 00
plate, not less than ⅛ inch in thickness, per ton......	1 50
cast, used for bridges, buildings, or other permanent structures, per ton, (see Decision No. 8.)............	1 00
bars, rods, bands, hoops, sheets, plates, nails, and spikes, manufactured from iron, upon which the duty of $1 50 has been paid, are only subject to an additional duty of, per ton...........................	50 cents.
hollow ware, per ton of 2,000 pounds..................	$1 50
in pigs, or bars, and not advanced beyond slabs, blooms, or loops, (see Sec. 1 new law)...............	Exempt.
castings, exceeding 10 pounds in weight, per ton...	$1 00
Lager Beer, per barrel of 31 gallons, (fractional parts of a barrel to pay proportionately,) per barrel...........	$1 50
Lead, white, per hundred pounds.......................	25 cents.
Leather, bend, per pound......	1 cent.
butt, per pound......................................	1 cent.
harness, per pound...................................	7 mills.
harness made from hides imported east of Cape of Good Hope, per pound.....................	5 mills.
offal, and damaged, per pound....................	5 mills.
oil dressed, per pound...............................	2 cents.
patent or enamelled, per square foot..............	5 mills.
patent, japanned splits, used for dasher leather, per square foot...................	4 mills.
patent or enamalled skirting, per square foot...	1½ cents.
rough and sole, made from hides imported east of the Cape of Good Hope, per pound..........	5 mills.

	Duty. Dolls. cts.
rough, tanned in whole or in part with oak, per pound..	1 cent.
sole, tanned in whole or in part with oak, per pound..	1 cent.
rough and sole, all other, hemlock tanned, per pound..	7 mills.
calf skins, tanned, each....................................	6 cents.
upper, finished or curried, made from leather tanned in the interest of the parties currying such leather, not previously taxed in the rough, (except calf skins,) per pound, (see Decisions Nos. 2, 3.)..	1 cent.
Mineral or Medicinal Waters, per quart or less..............	1 cent.
more than quart..............	2 cents.
Mustard, ground, and all imitations of, per pound.........	1 cent.
Nails and spikes, cut, per ton....................................	2 cents.
Newspapers, (see Decision No. 25.)	
Oil, animal and vegetable, pure or adulterated, per gallon	2 cents.
lard, pure or adulterated, per gallon......................	2 cents.
mustard seed, per gallon...........	2 cents.
linseed, per gallon..	2 cents.
coal, per gallon....................................	10 cents.
refined, and produced by the distillation of coal exclusively, per gallon..	8 cents.
red, (see Sec. 75).....................................	Exempt.
Passports, U. S., each....................................	$3 00
Pepper, ground, and all imitations of, per pound............	1 cent.
Pimento, ground, and all imitations of same, per pound...	1 cent.
Plate, gold kept for use, per oz. troy, (see Decision No. 21.)	50 cents.
silver, kept for use, per oz. troy, (see Decision No. 21.)..	3 cents.
silver, to the extent of 40 oz., (see Decision No. 21.)	Exempt.
Porter, per barrel of 31 gallons, (fractional parts of a barrel to pay proportionately).............................	$1 00
Saleratus and bicarbonate of soda, per pound..............	5 mills.
Salt, per hundred pounds.......................................	4 cents.
Screws, commonly called wood screws, per pound..........	1½ cents.
Sheep and lambs, slaughtered for sale, each..................	3 cents.
Snuff, manufactured of tobacco. or any substitute, per pound (see Decision No. 76.)...............................	20 cents.
Soap, castile, valued not above 3½ cents per pound........	1 mill.
ditto, above 3½ cents, per pound......................	5 mills.
cream, per pound...	2 cents.
erasive, valued not above 3½ cents, per pound.......	1 mill.
ditto, above 3½ cents...	5 mills.
fancy, per pound..	2 cents.
honey, per pound...............................	2 cents.
palm oil, valued not above 3½ cents per pound........	1 mill.
ditto, above 3½ cents..	5 mills.
scented, per pound...	2 cents.
shaving, per pound..	2 cents.
toilet, all kinds, per pound...............................	2 cents.
transparent, per pound.......................................	2 cents.

	Duty. Dolls. cts.
all other descriptions, white or colored, except soft soap and soap otherwise provided for, valued not above 3½ cents, per pound	1 mill.
ditto, valued above 3½ cents, per pound	5 mills.
Starch, made of potatoes, per pound	1 mill.
made of corn and wheat, per pound	1½ mills.
made of rice or other material, per pound	4 mills.
Steel, in ingots, bars, sheets, or wire, not less than ¼ inch in thickness, valued at 7 cents per pound, or less, per ton	$4 00
ditto, valued at 7 cents, and not above 11 cents, per ton	8 00
ditto, valued above 11 cents, per ton	10 00
Stoves, per ton of 2,000 pounds	1 50
Sugar, brown, Muscovado, or clarified, produced directly from the sugar cane, other than that produced by the refiner, (see Decision No. 61.)	1 cent.
Sugar refiners shall pay 1½ per cent. on the gross amount of the sales of all the products of their manufactories, (see Amendment to section 75, new law.)	
Tobacco, cavendish, plug, twist, fine.cut, and manufactured of all descriptions, (not including snuff, cigars, and smoking tobacco, prepared with all the stems in, or made exclusively of stems,) (see Decisions, Nos. 62, 76.)	15 cents.
smoking, prepared with all the stems in, per pound, (see Decisions No. 62, 76.)	5 cents.
ditto, made exclusively of stems, per pound, (see Decisions Nos. 62, 76.)	5 cents.
Wine, made of grapes, per gallon	5 cents.
Yachts, all pleasure or racing vessels, whether by sail or steam, under the value of $500	$5 00
ditto, valued above $600. and not exceeding $1,000	10 00
ditto, each additional $1,000 in value, (see Decision No. 21.)	10 00
Zinc, oxide of, per 100 pounds	25 cents.

Articles exempt from Tax.

Printed books, magazines, pamphlets, newspapers, reviews, and all other similar printed publications; boards, shingles, and all other lumber and timber; staves, hoops, headings, and timber only partially wrought and unfinished for chairs, tubs, pails, snathes, lasts, shovel and fork handles; umbrella stretchers; pig iron, and iron not advanced beyond slabs, blooms, or loops; maps and charts; charcoal; alcohol made or manufactured of spirits or materials upon which the duties imposed by this act shall have been paid; plaster or gypsum; malt; burning fluid; printer's ink; flax prepared for textile or felting purposes, until actually woven or fitted into fabrics for consumption; all flour and meal made from grain; bread and breadstuffs; pearl barley and split peas; butter, cheese; concentrated milk; bullion, in the manufacture of silverware; brick; lime; Roman cement; draining tiles; marble; slate; building stone; copper, in ingots or pigs; and lead, in pigs or bars, are not regarded as manufactures within the meaning of this act. (See Sec. 29, New Law.)

Manufactures not exceeding $600 exempt.

All goods, wares, and merchandise, or articles manufactured or made by any person or persons not for sale, but for his, her, or their own use or consumption, and all goods, wares, and merchandise, or articles manufactured or made and sold, except spirituous and malt liquors, and manufactured tobacco, where the annual product shall not exceed the sum of six hundred dollars, shall be and are exempt from duty; *Provided,* That this shall not apply to any business or transaction where one party furnishes the materials, or any part thereof, and employs another party to manufacture, make, or finish the goods, wares, and merchandise or articles, paying or promising to pay therefor, and receiving the goods, wares, and merchandise or articles.

LICENCES.

Trades and occupations to be licensed.

SEC. 57. *And be it further enacted,* That from and after the first day of September, eighteen hundred and sixty-two, no person, association of persons, or corporation, shall be engaged in, prosecute, or carry on, either of the trades or occupations mentioned in section sixty-four of this act, until he or they shall have obtained a license therefor in the manner hereinafter provided.

Licences and the rate thereof.

Duty.
Dolls. cts.

Apothecaries, when the annual gross receipts or sales exceed $1,000,
(see Decision No. 18.) $10 00
Architects 10 00
Auctioneers, (see Decision No. 27.) 20 00
Bankers, (see Decisions Nos 13–14.) 100 00
Billiard rooms, license for each table (see Decision No. 21.) 5 00
Bowling alleys, license for each alley 5 00
Brewers, ... 50 00
    when manufacturing less than 500 barrels per year, (see
     Decision No. 57.) 25 00
Brokers, (see Decision NO. 13.) 50 00
    commercial, (see Decision No. 59.) 50 00
    land warrant 25 00
Builders 25 00
Butchers, from stall 10 00
    from wagon, etc. 5 00
Cattle brokers, (see Decision No. 47.) 10 00
Civil Engineers 10 00
Circuses. 50 00
Claim agents, (see Decision No. 45.) 10 00
Coal oil distillers, (see Decisions No. 16, 19, 20.) 50 00
Confectioners, when the annual gross receipts exceed $1,000 ...... 10 00
Contractors 25 00
Dentists 10 00
Distillers of spirituous liquor 50 00
    making less than 300 barrels per year. 25 00
    of apples and peaches, making less than 150 barrels per
     year 12 50
    for a greater quantity, same as other distillers, (see Decisions Nos. 16, 17.)

	Duty.
	Dolls. cts

Eating houses, when the annual gross receipts amount to $1,000...   10 00

Exhibitions—The proprietors or agents of all public exhibitions or shows for money, not enumerated in section 64, shall pay for each license 10 00

Horse dealers 10 00

Hotels, first class...   200 00

  second class,..   100 00

  third class,..   75 00

  fourth class,...   50 00

  fifth class,..   25 00

  sixth class..   15 00

  seventh class 10 00

  eighth class..   5 00

  Steamers and vessels upon waters of the United States, on board of which passengers or travellers are provided with food or lodging, are required to take out a license of the fifth class, viz:..   25 00

Insurance Agents, whose receipts are over $600.............................   10 00

Jackass for hire to Jennies, owners of...   10 00

Jugglers...   10 00

Lawyers, (see Decision No. 10)...   10 00

Livery stable keepers...   10 00

Lottery ticket dealers 1000 00

Manufacturers, when the annual gross receipts exceed the sum of $1,000, (see Decisions No. 46, 49, 71, 79.)...............................   10 00

  Any person or, persons, firms, companies, or corporations, who shall manufacture by hand or machinery, and offer for sale any goods, wares, or merchandise, exceeding annually the sum of one thousand dollars, shall be regarded a manufacturer under this act. *Nursery men,* (see Decision No. 32.)

Patent agents...   10 00

Pawnbrokers...   50 00

Peddlers, when travelling with more than two horses, 1st class...   20 00

  when travelling with two horses, 2d class........................   15 00

  when travelling with one horse, 3d class..........................   10 00

  when travelling on foot, 4th class.................................   5 00

  who sell, or offer to sell, dry goods, foreign and domestic, by one or more original packages or pieces at one time to the same person, (see Decision No. 23.)..........   50 00

  who peddle jewelry...   25 00

  who peddle books, (by subscription.)...............................   25 00

Photographers, when the receipts do not exceed $500 per annum..   10 00

  when the receipts are over $500 and under $1,000.   15 00

  when the receipts are over $1,000 per annum, (see Decision No. 23.)

Physicians...   10 00

Produce dealers, (see Decision No. 33.)

Publishers, (see Decision No. 41.)

Rectifiers, for each license to rectify any quantity of spirituous liquors, not exceeding 500 barrels, of not more than 40 gallons each 25 00

  for each additional 500 such barrels, or any fraction thereof, (see Decision Nos. 15, 16.).........................   25 00

Retail dealers, when the annual gross receipts exceed $1,000, and do not exceed $25,000, (see Decision No. 68.)....................   10 00

Retail dealers in liquor..   20 00

	Duty. Dolls. cts.
Soap makers..	10 00
Surgeons	10 00
Stallions, for hire to mares, owners of...............................	10 00
Steam and other passenger packets, (see Decisions No. 24, 73.).......	25 00
Tallow chandlers...	10 00
Theatres, (see Decision No. 52.)......................................	100 00
Tobacconists, when the annual gross receipts exceed $1,000	10 00
Wholesale dealers, whose annual sales do not exceed $50,000......	25 00
Exceeding $50,000 and not 100,000......	50 00
" 100,000 " 250,000......	100 00
" 250,000 " 500,000......	200 00
" 500,000 " 1,000,000......	300 00
" 1,000,000 " 2,000,000	500 00
" 2,000,000, for each million dollars in excess of two millions..........................	250 00

Wholesale dealers in liquor, pay same license as wholesale dealers.

Exemptions from license.

SEC. 65. *And be it further enacted*, That where the annual gross receipts or sales of any apothecaries, confectioners, eating-houses, tobacconists, or retail dealers, shall not exceed the sum of one thousand dollars, such apothecaries, confectioners, eating-houses, and retail dealers shall not be required to take out or pay for license, anything in this act to the contrary notwithstanding; the amount or estimated amount of such annual sales to be ascertained or estimated in such manner as the Commissioner of Internal Revenue shall prescribe, and so of all other annual sales or receipts, where the rate of the license is graduated by the amount of sales or receipts.

SEC. 66. *And be it further enacted*, That nothing contained in the preceding sections of this act, laying duties on licenses, shall be construed to require a license for the sale of goods, wares, and merchandise, made or produced and sold by the manufacturer or producer at the manufactory or place where the same is made or produced; to vintners who sell, at the place where the same is made, wine of their own growth; nor to apothecaries, as to wines or spirituous liquors which they use exclusively in the preparation or making up of medicines for sick, lame, or diseased persons; nor shall the provisions of paragraph number twenty-seven extend to physicians who keep on hand medicines solely for the purpose of making up their own prescriptions for their own patients.

No license against State prohibition, etc.

SEC. 67. *And be it further enacted*, That no license hereinbefore provided for, if granted, shall be construed to authorize the commencement or continuation of any trade, business, occupation, or employment therein mentioned, within any State or Territory of the United States in which it is or shall be specially prohibited by the laws thereof, or in violation of the laws of any State or Territory; *Provided*, Nothing in this act shall be held or construed so as to prevent the several States, within the limits thereof, from placing a duty, tax, or license, for State purposes, on any business matter or thing on which a duty, tax, or license is required to be paid by this act.

How to obtain licenses.

SEC. 58. *And be it further enacted*, That every person, association of persons, partnership or corporation, desiring to obtain a license to engage in any of the trades or occupations named in the sixty-fourth section of this act, shall register with the assistant assessor of the assessment district in which he shall design to carry on such trade or occupation—first, his or their name or style; and in case of an association or partnership, the names of the several persons constituting such association or partnership and their places of residence; second, the trade or occupation for which a license is desired, third, the place where such trade or occupation is to be carried on; fourth, if a rectifier, the number of barrels he designs to rectify; if a peddler, whether he designs to travel on foot, or with one, two, or more horses; If an inn-keeper, the yearly rental of the house and property to be occupied for said purpose; or, if not rented, the assistant assessor shall value the same. All of which facts shall be returned duly certified by such assistant assessor, both to the assessor and collector of the district; and thereupon, upon payment to the collector or deputy collector of the district, the amount as hereinafter provided, such collector or deputy collector shall make out and deliver a license for such trade or occupation, which license shall continue in force for one year, at the place or premises described therein. (See Decision No. 4.)

Penalty for neglect to procure license.

SEC. 59.   *And be it further enacted*, That if any person or persons shall exercise or carry on any trade or business hereinafter mentioned, for the exercising or carrying on of which trade or business a license is required by this act, without taking out such license as in that behalf required, he, she, or they shall, for every such offence, respectively, forfeit a penalty equal to three times the amount of the duty or sum of money imposed for such license, one moiety thereof to the use of the United States, the other moiety to the use of the person who, if a collector, shall first discover, and if other than a collector, shall first give information of the fact whereby said forfeiture was incurred.

Additional penalties for omission to procure license.

SEC. 24.   [Of the amended law.] *And be it further enacted*, That if any person or persons shall knowingly exercise or carry on any trade or business, for the exercising or carrying on of which trade or business a license is required, without taking out such license as is in that behalf required, he, she, or they shall, for every such offence, upon conviction thereof, in lieu of or in addition to other penalties now imposed by law, at the discretion of the court, be subject to imprisonment for a term not exceeding two years.